Contents

Chapter 13
The Renaissance and Reformation (1300–1650)

Chapter 14
The Beginnings of Our Global Age: Europe, Africa, and Asia (1415–1796)

Chapter 15
The Beginnings of Our Global Age: Europe and the Americas (1492–1750)

Chapter 16
The Age of Absolutism (1550–1800)

Chapter 17
The Enlightenment and the American Revolution (1700–1800)

Chapter 18
The French Revolution and Napoleon (1789–1815)

How to Use This Book

The **Reading and Note Taking Study Guide** will help you better understand the content of *Prentice Hall World History.* This book will also develop your reading, vocabulary, and note taking skills.

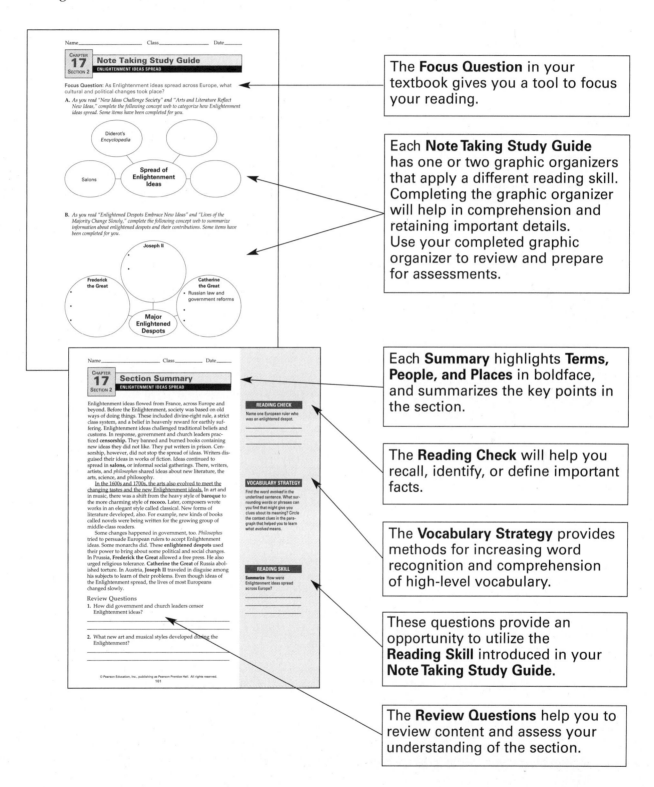

The **Focus Question** in your textbook gives you a tool to focus your reading.

Each **Note Taking Study Guide** has one or two graphic organizers that apply a different reading skill. Completing the graphic organizer will help in comprehension and retaining important details. Use your completed graphic organizer to review and prepare for assessments.

Each **Summary** highlights **Terms, People, and Places** in boldface, and summarizes the key points in the section.

The **Reading Check** will help you recall, identify, or define important facts.

The **Vocabulary Strategy** provides methods for increasing word recognition and comprehension of high-level vocabulary.

These questions provide an opportunity to utilize the **Reading Skill** introduced in your **Note Taking Study Guide.**

The **Review Questions** help you to review content and assess your understanding of the section.

Concept Connector Worksheets support the **Concept Connector** features and the **Concept Connector Cumulative Review** found in each chapter of your text, as well as the **Concept Connector Handbook** found at the end of your textbook. These worksheets will help you to compare key concepts and events and to see patterns and make connections across time. The thematic essay portion of each worksheet will prepare you for social studies exams and assessments.

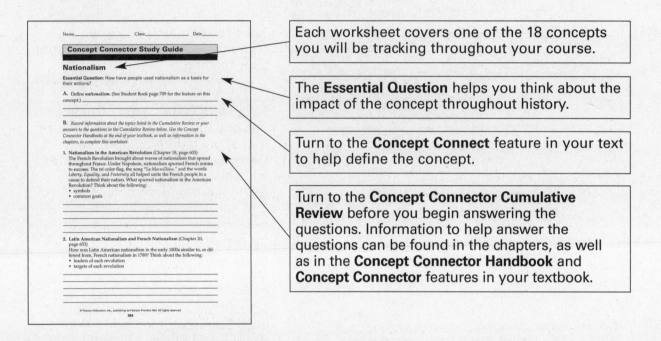

Each worksheet covers one of the 18 concepts you will be tracking throughout your course.

The **Essential Question** helps you think about the impact of the concept throughout history.

Turn to the **Concept Connect** feature in your text to help define the concept.

Turn to the **Concept Connector Cumulative Review** before you begin answering the questions. Information to help answer the questions can be found in the chapters, as well as in the **Concept Connector Handbook** and **Concept Connector** features in your textbook.

Thematic essays are an important part of social studies exams and assessment tests. This portion of the Concept Connector Worksheet provides sample topics for thematic essays.

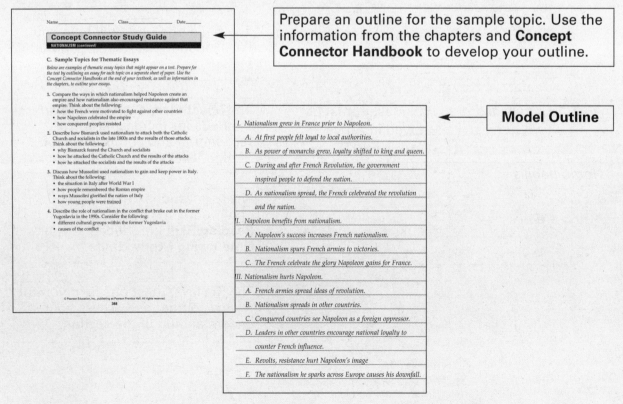

Prepare an outline for the sample topic. Use the information from the chapters and **Concept Connector Handbook** to develop your outline.

Model Outline

Name_____ Class_____ Date_____

Focus Question: What have scholars learned about the ancestors of humans, and how have they done so?

A. *As you read "Studying the Historical Past" and "Investigating Prehistory," complete the following graphic organizer identifying the types of scholars who study the past. Some items have been completed for you.*

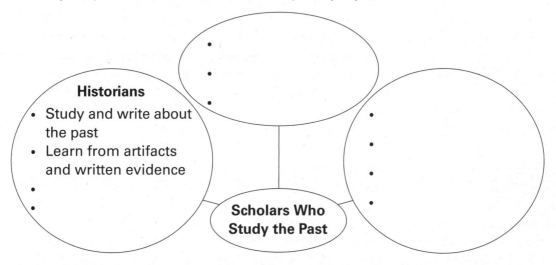

Historians
- Study and write about the past
- Learn from artifacts and written evidence
-
-

Scholars Who Study the Past

B. *As you read "Discoveries in Africa and Beyond," complete this summary table identifying different hominid groups and key details scholars have learned about each group. Some items have been completed for you.*

Hominids	
Group	**Summary**
Australopithecines	• Earliest hominids • Lived in Africa •
Homo habilis	• •
Homo erectus	• • • •
	• Emerged between 100,000 and 250,000 years ago • • •

CHAPTER 1 SECTION 1

Section Summary

UNDERSTANDING OUR PAST

Writing was invented about 5,000 years ago. The period before that is known as **prehistory.** Several kinds of jobs involve studying human history—before and after writing was invented.

Historians learn about the past from **artifacts.** These include clothing, coins, artwork, and tombstones. They also study written materials, such as letters or tax records. Historians try to figure out how reliable this evidence is. They use it to explain why an event, such as a war, happened. What they learn about the past helps us understand events today.

Anthropology is the study of humans and their societies. Some anthropologists study human bones. They want to understand how humans have changed. Others study **cultures,** or people's ways of life. **Archaeology** is part of anthropology. It is the study of past people and cultures through such items as tools, weapons, and pottery. Archaeologists use modern tools such as computers. <u>A method, or technique, for measuring radioactivity helps them figure out the age of objects.</u>

VOCABULARY STRATEGY

Find the word *technique* in the first underlined sentence. Look for the word *technology* in the second underlined sentence. Both words come from a Greek word that means "art" or "skill." Use this word-origins clue to help you figure out what *technique* means.

Before the 1950s, anthropologists knew little about early humans. Anthropologists **Mary** and **Louis Leakey** searched for clues in East Africa at **Olduvai Gorge.** There they found many ancient stone tools. <u>The tools showed that whoever made them had the **technology,** or skills and tools, to survive.</u> Then, in 1959, after more than 20 years of searching, Mary Leakey found the skull of an early hominid. In 1974, anthropologist **Donald Johanson** found many pieces of a hominid skeleton. Called "Lucy," it was at least 3 million years old. Discoveries like these suggest that there were many different hominid groups alive in the past. These included *Homo habilis* and *Homo erectus.* Two groups of *Homo sapiens* arose. One of the groups, called Neanderthals, disappeared 50,000 to 30,000 years ago. The only hominids left on Earth then were early modern humans.

READING SKILL

Summarize In your own words, summarize the important discoveries anthropologists Mary and Louis Leakey made at Olduvai Gorge.

_____

_____

_____

Review Questions

1. List three types of artifacts that historians study.

_____

_____

2. What did Donald Johanson discover?

_____

_____

Note Taking Study Guide

TURNING POINT: THE NEOLITHIC REVOLUTION

Focus Question: How was the introduction of agriculture a turning point in prehistory?

As you read this section in your textbook, complete the following chart to summarize information about the eras of prehistory. Some items have been completed for you.

Eras of Prehistory	
Life Before Farming	**Life After Farming**
• Old Stone Age	• _____ _____ _____
• Nomads; hunted and gathered food	
• Lived in bands of 20 to 30	• Grew own food, no longer nomads
• _____ _____ _____	• Farmers settled the first permanent villages, including Çatalhüyük and Jericho.
• _____ _____ _____ _____	• _____ _____ _____ _____
• _____ _____ _____ _____	• _____ _____ _____
• _____ _____ _____ _____	• _____ _____ _____
• _____ _____ _____	

CHAPTER 1 SECTION 2

Section Summary
TURNING POINT: THE NEOLITHIC REVOLUTION

READING CHECK

What is another name for the New Stone Age?

_____

_____

_____

Prehistory is divided into eras called the **Old Stone Age,** or **Paleolithic Period,** and the **New Stone Age,** or **Neolithic Period.** In both, people made and used stone tools. However, during the New Stone Age, people developed new skills or technologies that changed everyday life.

Early modern humans lived toward the end of the Old Stone Age. They were **nomads,** moving from place to place in small groups to hunt and gather food. These people made simple tools and weapons, built fires for cooking, and wore animal skins. They also developed spoken language. Some people began to bury their dead. Because of this, scholars think our ancestors believed in life after death. Cave paintings around the world show animals and humans. Early humans may have believed the world was full of spirits and forces living in animals, objects, or dreams. These beliefs are known as **animism.**

The New Stone Age began about 12,000 years ago when nomadic people learned to farm. They no longer needed to roam in search of food. As a result, early farmers settled the first villages. <u>This transition from nomadic life to settled farming caused such dramatic changes that it is often called the</u> **Neolithic Revolution.** These early farmers were the first humans to **domesticate** plants and animals.

Archaeologists have unearthed the remains of some of the first Neolithic villages. The site of **Çatalhüyük** is in Turkey, and **Jericho** exists today in the West Bank. In settled farming villages such as these, a council of male elders or warriors made the important decisions. Some settled people began to gain wealth and property. To farm successfully, they developed new technologies, such as calendars to know when to plant and harvest. They used animals to plow the fields. However, not all technologies were invented everywhere at the same time.

VOCABULARY STRATEGY

Find the word *transition* in the underlined sentence. What do you think it means? Think about what it means that people went from being nomads to being farmers. Circle one of the following items to show what you think *transition* means.

1. change

2. lack of change

READING SKILL

Summarize In your own words, summarize how the Neolithic Revolution changed the way people lived.

_____

_____

_____

Review Questions

1. Why did early humans move from place to place?

_____

_____

2. What was the Neolithic Revolution?

_____

_____

Name_____ Class_____ Date_____

Note Taking Study Guide
BEGINNINGS OF CIVILIZATION

Focus Question: How did the world's first civilizations arise and develop?

As you read this section in your textbook, complete the following chart with details from the text to summarize the different phases of the development of civilization. Some items have been completed for you.

The Development of Civilization

Changes Over Time

- Changes in the physical environment have caused civilizations to change.
-
-

Features of Civilizations

- Cities
- Organized governments
-
-
-
-
-
-

Rise of Cities and Civilizations

- Located near major rivers
-
-
-

CHAPTER 1 · SECTION 3

Section Summary
BEGINNINGS OF CIVILIZATION

Early civilizations developed near major rivers. Rivers provided water, transportation, and food. The rich soil around rivers helped farmers grow food **surpluses.** As populations grew, villages grew into cities. However, not everyone lived in them. Away from cities, farmers raised crops in small villages or nomads tended livestock on the **steppes.**

The rise of cities is the main feature of **civilization.** Other features include organized governments, complicated religions, job specialization, social classes, arts and architecture, public works, and writing.

In the new cities, governments were led by chiefs or elders. They handled large projects such as food production, raising armies, and public works. Most people were **polytheistic** and so believed in many gods. Usually the gods represented natural forces, such as the sun. Unlike the **traditional economies** of Stone Age villages, people in cities often worked at non-farming jobs. People's jobs set their social rank. Priests and nobles were usually at the top. Wealthy merchants and **artisans** were next. Most people were peasants and held the lowest rank. Art and architecture developed, too. Artisans decorated palaces and temples with paintings and statues. Many civilizations also developed writing from **pictographs.** Later, as writing grew more complex, only specially trained people called **scribes** could read and write.

Over time, ancient civilizations changed. When groups came into contact, they shared ideas or goods. This **cultural diffusion** was caused by migration, trade, and war. People migrated, or moved, to escape natural disasters. Trade introduced people to new goods or better ways of making them. After a war, the winners forced their ways of life on the losers. Sometimes winners adopted the customs of the losers. Conquered territories expanded the size of cities. This led to the rise of the **city-state** and, later, to the rise of the first **empires.**

Review Questions

1. The earliest civilizations developed near what geographic feature?

_____

_____

2. What types of large projects did governments handle?

_____

_____

CHAPTER
2
SECTION 1

Note Taking Study Guide
CITY-STATES OF ANCIENT SUMER

Focus Question: What were the characteristics of the world's first civilization?

As you read this section in your textbook, complete the concept web below to identify the main ideas about the city-states of Sumer under each heading. Some items have been completed for you.

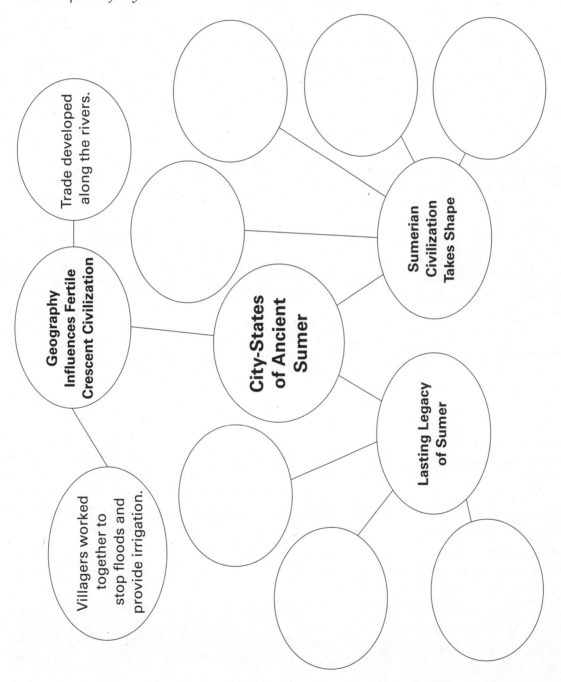

CHAPTER 2 SECTION 1 — Section Summary

CITY-STATES OF ANCIENT SUMER

Around 3300 B.C., **Sumer,** the world's first civilization, arose between the Tigris and Euphrates rivers. This area is called **Mesopotamia.** Mesopotamia is part of an area of the Middle East known as the **Fertile Crescent.** The geography of the Fertile Crescent was very important to the rise of Sumer. Regular floods made Sumerians work together to protect homes and control water to irrigate farms. The region had rich soil, but it lacked timber and stone. Yet, Sumerians built some of the world's first great cities using bricks from common clay and water. Sumerians also became traders along the rivers.

Eventually, Sumer had 12 city-states. They often battled over control of land and water. So people chose war leaders to rule. <u>Over time, war leadership evolved into rule by particular families.</u> Sumerian society was also set up by social rank, in a **hierarchy.** This included an upper class (rulers, priests, officials), a small middle class (lower priests, scribes, merchants), and a large lower class (farmers). Sumerians worshiped many gods at great leveled pyramids called **ziggurats.**

Perhaps the Sumerians' greatest invention was writing. First they used pictographs, or simple pictures that stood for things and ideas. By 3200 B.C. they had developed **cuneiform,** wedge-like shapes that represented words or syllables. Cuneiform let people record complex information. People had access to knowledge beyond just what they could remember. Sumerians also developed early mathematics.

Sumerians left a lasting legacy. Over time, Akkadian, Babylonian, and Assyrian armies swept across the area, spreading Sumerian learning across the Middle East. They also used cuneiform. Babylonians recorded the ancient Sumerian oral poem, *The Epic of Gilgamesh,* in cuneiform. They also used Sumerian learning to develop basic algebra and geometry, create good calendars, and predict eclipses. The Greeks and Romans built on Sumerian learning, too. Their cultures would later influence all of Western civilization.

VOCABULARY STRATEGY

Find the word *evolved* in the underlined sentence. What does *evolved* mean? What context clues can you find in nearby words or phrases? Circle any that help you figure out what *evolved* means.

READING SKILL

Identify Main Ideas What is the main idea of the third paragraph of the Summary? Circle the sentence below that expresses the main idea of that paragraph.

1. Sumerian society ended in 1900 B.C.

2. Sumerians created a writing system.

Review Questions

1. How did geography help Sumer to develop?

_____

_____

2. What was important about the invention of writing?

_____

_____

Note Taking Study Guide

CHAPTER 2 SECTION 2

INVADERS, TRADERS, AND EMPIRE BUILDERS

Focus Question: How did various strong rulers unite the lands of the Fertile Crescent into well-organized empires?

As you read this section in your textbook, complete the table below to identify the main idea about the different empires under each red heading. Some items have been completed for you.

Red Heading	Main Idea
First Empires Arise in Mesopotamia	Powerful leaders create large, well-organized empires. They establish civil and criminal law.
Conquests Bring New Empires and Ideas	Later empires bring new technology, and ideas about laws and culture. One of the world's first libraries is built.

CHAPTER 2 SECTION 2

Section Summary

INVADERS, TRADERS, AND EMPIRE BUILDERS

Many peoples came to power in ancient Mesopotamia and made long-lasting contributions. Some invaders created vast empires. In 2300 B.C., the Akkadian leader, **Sargon,** conquered Sumer and formed the world's first empire. In 1790 B.C., **Hammurabi,** king of Babylon, united Mesopotamia. He was also the first to **codify,** or arrange and set down, the laws. They were then carved on pillars for all to see. Hammurabi's Code included **civil laws,** covering private matters, such as contracts and taxes. It also dealt with **criminal laws,** or crimes against others, such as robbery and murder.

Other conquerors brought new learning. The Hittites knew how to make iron weapons. Their empire ended around 1200 B.C., but ironworking spread to Asia, Africa, and Europe, starting the Iron Age. The Assyrians were feared warriors. However, they also set up one of the world's first libraries.

Later, the Babylonian king **Nebuchadnezzar** controlled the area, rebuilt Babylon, and restored it to greatness. The Babylonian empire stretched from the Persian Gulf to the Mediterranean Sea. However, it fell to Persia in 539 B.C. The Persian empire was huge, stretching from present-day Turkey to India. Emperor Darius I created unity by building roads across the empire and encouraging the use money. People now began moving from a **barter economy** toward a **money economy.** Another uniting force was the belief in a single god and other ideas taught by the Persian prophet **Zoroaster.** Later, both Christianity and Islam emerged, or arose, in the Middle East. They stressed similar beliefs in heaven, hell, and a final judgment day.

Not all achievements were introduced by conquerors. Phoenician sea traders from the eastern Mediterranean formed colonies around the sea. A **colony** is a settlement ruled by people from another land. They spread Middle Eastern culture. This included their greatest achievement—the **alphabet.**

Review Questions

1. Who was Hammurabi?

_____

_____

2. How did Darius I create unity?

_____

_____

CHAPTER 2 SECTION 3
Note Taking Study Guide
KINGDOM ON THE NILE

Focus Question: How did the Nile influence the rise of the powerful civilization of Egypt?

As you read this section in your textbook, complete the outline below to identify the main ideas about the Nile kingdoms under each heading. Some items have been completed for you.

I. Geography was an important factor in shaping Egypt.

    A. Yearly flooding created fertile soil and encouraged cooperation

    B. The Nile helped to unite Upper and Lower Egypt.

II. During the Old Kingdom, Egypt became a strong, centralized state.

    A. _____

    B. _____

III. The Middle Kingdom was a turbulent period.

    A. _____

    B. _____

IV. _____

    A. _____

    B. _____

CHAPTER 2 SECTION 3 — Section Summary

KINGDOM ON THE NILE

Fertile land along the Nile brought early peoples to Egypt, and over time, a powerful civilization arose. Crops grew well in the rich soil created by annual river floods. An early government formed to build dikes, reservoirs, and irrigation ditches.

Egypt was made up of two regions. Upper Egypt went from the Nile's first **cataract,** or waterfall, almost to the coast. Lower Egypt covered the Nile's **delta,** or area at the river's mouth. About 3100 B.C., Menes, the king of Upper Egypt, joined both regions to form one of the first united empires.

Egypt's history is divided into three periods: the Old Kingdom, the Middle Kingdom, and the New Kingdom. Power passed from one **dynasty,** or ruling family, to another, but Egypt generally stayed united for over 2,000 years.

During the Old Kingdom, **pharaohs,** or Egyptian kings, created a strong central government. They set up a **bureaucracy,** with a **vizier**, or chief minister of government. The Great Pyramids were built during the Old Kingdom.

The Middle Kingdom had unpredictable floods and revolts. Yet, leaders increased farmland, sent armies for Nubian gold, and sent traders to exchange goods with Mesopotamian peoples. But by 1700 B.C., the Hyksos had conquered the Nile delta, using a new military tool: war chariots.

After more than 100 years of Hyksos rule, new Egyptian leaders arose and established the New Kingdom. One of these rulers was **Hatshepsut,** the first female pharaoh. She sent trading ships along the Mediterranean and Red Sea. Her stepson, **Thutmose III,** a great military leader, expanded Egypt to its greatest size. Much later, **Ramses II** pushed farther north. During his rule, Egypt fought the Hittites and signed a peace treaty, the oldest surviving document of its kind.

Around 1100 B.C., Egyptian civilization weakened. A series of invaders conquered the rich land. In 332 B.C., the Greeks took over as the last Egyptian dynasty ended. Then, in 30 B.C., the Romans displaced the Greeks.

Review Questions

1. What happened in 3100 B.C.?

_____

_____

2. What are the three main periods of Egypt's history?

_____

_____

Name_____ Class_____ Date_____

Note Taking Study Guide
EGYPTIAN CIVILIZATION

Focus Question: How did religion and learning play important roles in ancient Egyptian civilization?

As you read this section in your textbook, complete the chart below to record the main idea about Egyptian civilization under each heading. Include at least two supporting details for each main idea. Some items have been completed for you.

Egyptian Civilization

Red Heading	Main Idea	Supporting Detail	Supporting Detail		
Religion Shapes Life in Ancient Egypt	Egyptians worship the great lord of the gods, Amon-Re.	The pharaohs receive their right to rule from Amon-Re.	Osiris is important because he is god of the Nile and the underworld.		
How Egyptians Viewed the Afterlife	Belief in the afterlife affects all Egyptians.	Bodies are mummified and people are buried with their possessions.	Tomb of Tutankhamen provides wealth of evidence about Egyptian civilization.		
Egyptians Organize Their Society	Egypt has a class system with the pharaoh at the top.				

CHAPTER 2 SECTION 4

Section Summary
EGYPTIAN CIVILIZATION

READING CHECK

What ancient object did Frenchman Jean Champollion use to figure out the meaning of hieroglyphs?

_____

_____

_____

VOCABULARY STRATEGY

Find the word *radical* in the underlined sentence. What does *radical* mean? What clues can you find in nearby words or phrases? Circle the context clues that helped you figure out what *radical* means.

READING SKILL

Identify Supporting Details
Identify two details from this Summary that support the main idea that Egyptian civilization made lasting contributions.

_____

_____

_____

Ancient Egyptians made lasting contributions to civilization in many fields. Their religion, writing, art, science, and literature have interested people for thousands of years.

During the Middle Kingdom, Egyptians prayed to a supreme god named **Amon-Re.** Around 1380 B.C., pharaoh Amenhotep IV tried to replace Amon-Re with a minor god named Aton. He changed his own name to **Akhenaton,** meaning "he who serves Aton." However, priests, nobles, and peasants turned against Akhenaton's revolutionary changes, and his radical ideas failed. Most Egyptians worshipped the god **Osiris.** He judged souls in the afterlife. His wife, the goddess **Isis,** was also popular. The Egyptians also learned to preserve bodies by **mummification,** or embalming and wrapping in cloth. This was so the soul could return to the body in the afterlife.

Ancient Egyptians made advances in learning. Their first writing, **hieroglyphics,** used symbols and pictures. They later used a script system called demotic. The Egyptians also invented a material to write on, made from **papyrus** plants. After ancient Egypt declined, the meaning of the writing was lost. However, in the early 1800s, Frenchman Jean Champollion **deciphered,** or figured out, the carvings on the **Rosetta Stone.** This stone had three forms of the same passage written in hieroglyphics, demotic, and Greek. By comparing Greek, which he knew, to the other passages, Champollion was able to decode the hieroglyphics.

Egyptians also made advances in science and math. Doctors identified illnesses and performed surgeries. They prescribed medicines—some of which are still used today. Priest-astronomers studied stars and planets and created a 12-month calendar. Egyptian mathematicians developed basic geometry.

Egyptian artwork has lasted thousands of years. These ancient people created monuments, statues, wall paintings, and other objects. Ancient Egyptian literature includes hymns, love poems, and folk tales.

Review Questions

1. Why did Egyptians mummify bodies?

_____

_____

2. Give an example of how Egyptians used mathematics.

_____

_____

Name_____ Class_____ Date_____

Focus Question: How did the worship of only one god shape Judaism?

As you read this section in your textbook, complete the chart below to record the main idea about the roots of Judaism under each red heading. Include at least two supporting details for each main idea. Some items have been completed for you.

Roots of Judaism

Red Heading:	Red Heading:	Red Heading:
The Ancient Israelites Shape a Unique Belief System	The Early History of the Israelites Unfolds	

Main Idea:	Main Idea:	Main Idea:
Israelites are monotheistic.	God makes a covenant with Abraham.	

Supporting Details:	Supporting Details:	Supporting Details:
1. Events reflect God's plan. 2. The Torah records events and God's laws.	1. 2.	1. 2. 3.

Name_____ Class_____ Date_____

READING CHECK

Who is considered the "father of the Israelites"?

_____

_____

_____

VOCABULARY STRATEGY

Find the word *undertook* in the underlined sentence. What does *undertook* mean? Read the underlined sentence aloud, but leave out the word *undertook*. What word could you use in its place so that the sentence still makes sense? Use this strategy to help you figure out what *undertook* means.

READING SKILL

Identify Supporting Details Find two details in the Summary that support the main idea: The law was important to the Israelites.

_____

_____

_____

About 4,000 years ago, ancient Israelites developed Judaism. Unlike neighboring peoples, Israelites were **monotheistic,** believing in only one god. They believed every event reflected God's plan. So, they recorded events and laws in the **Torah,** their holiest text.

According to the Torah, about 2000 B.C., **Abraham** and his people moved to an area called Canaan. Abraham is considered the father of the Israelites. The Israelites believed that God made a **covenant,** or binding agreement, with him. The covenant promised a homeland in Canaan. Later, famine forced the Israelites into Egypt, where they became slaves. Hundreds of years later, **Moses** led the exodus out of Egypt, back to Canaan.

There, they established the kingdom of Israel around 1000 B.C. Under King **David,** the 12 tribes of Israel were united. Then, David's son **Solomon** undertook the task of making Jerusalem a major city. He completed a huge temple and increased Israel's power in the region. However, after his death, the kingdom eventually fell.

Israelite society was **patriarchal,** meaning that men had the greatest authority. Also, the law is a main feature of Judaism. The Torah has laws covering everything from cleanliness to criminal acts. Within the Torah, there are also special laws called the Ten Commandments. These laws stress duties, such as keeping the **Sabbath** holy. Often in Jewish history, **prophets,** or spiritual leaders, arose, who taught **ethics,** or moral standards.

During a 500-year period called the **Diaspora,** the Israelites left or were exiled from Israel. They spread around the world. Still, they kept their identity in close-knit communities. This helped them to survive persecution, or unfair treatment.

Judaism has been an important religion in world history. Both Christianity and Islam emerged from Judaism, creating an ethical legacy we now call the Judeo-Christian tradition.

Review Questions

1. How were the Israelites different from neighboring peoples?

_____

_____

2. What happened to Jews during the Diaspora?

_____

_____

CHAPTER
3
SECTION 1

Note Taking Study Guide

EARLY CIVILIZATIONS OF INDIA AND PAKISTAN

Focus Question: How have scholars learned about India's first two civilizations, the Indus and the Aryan?

As you read this section in your textbook, complete the following chart to sequence important events in the early civilizations of India and Pakistan. Some items have been completed for you.

Event	Earliest civilization in Indus Valley	Cities in Indus Valley abandoned				
Date	2600 B.C.	1900 B.C.				

CHAPTER 3 SECTION 1	Section Summary
	EARLY CIVILIZATIONS OF INDIA AND PAKISTAN

READING CHECK

Who were rajahs?

_____

_____

_____

VOCABULARY STRATEGY

Find the word *embodied* in the underlined sentence. The prefix *em-* means "to put or to cover with." The root word is *body*. Use the meaning of the prefix and root word to help you figure out what *embodied* means.

READING SKILL

Recognize Sequence Sequence the following events:

____ A flood or earthquake hits Indus civilization.

____ People farm in the Indus River valley.

____ Aryans migrate to India.

The Indian **subcontinent** is a large landmass in southern Asia. It has three zones: the Gangetic Plain, with rivers that support farming; the Deccan **plateau,** a raised area of level land too dry for farming; and the coastal plains that receive plenty of rain. Life is greatly affected by **monsoons.** These are winds that bring hot, dry air from the northeast in October and heavy rains from the southwest in mid-June.

Civilization began on the subcontinent around 2600 B.C. on the Indus River. Archaeologists believe organized governments planned cities such as **Harappa** and **Mohenjo-Daro.** They had wide streets, strong building materials, and plumbing systems. Most people farmed, although some traded with Sumer. People probably worshiped many gods and considered certain animals sacred. This may have led to later Indian beliefs, such as the **veneration,** or worship, of cattle. About 1900 B.C., the civilization declined, possibly because of a flood or earthquake.

By 1500 B.C., the Aryans had migrated to India from the north and built a strong civilization. Gradually they changed from nomadic herding to farming. Aryan tribes were led by chiefs called **rajahs.** Their society was divided into four groups. At the top were priests, followed by warriors, farmers and merchants, and workers and servants.

People worshiped gods and goddesses who embodied natural forces, such as the sky and sun. **Indra,** the chief god and god of war, used lightning as a weapon. Priests wrote their sacred teachings called the **Vedas.** Over time, Aryan beliefs began to change, however. The idea of **brahman,** a single spiritual power, influenced later Indian religions. Aryan **mystics** practiced yoga and meditation to connect with the divine.

Although there were many kingdoms, **acculturation** created a common culture by blending traditions and lifeways. Epic poems were part of the common culture. They described early Aryan warfare, important religious beliefs, and values.

Review Questions

1. What were the cities of Harappa and Mohenjo-Daro like?

_____

_____

2. What four groups made up Aryan society? List them from top to bottom.

_____

_____

Name_____ Class_____ Date_____

Focus Question: In what ways were religion and society intertwined in ancient India?

As you read this section in your textbook, complete the following chart to sequence important events in the development of Hinduism and Buddhism. Some items have been completed for you.

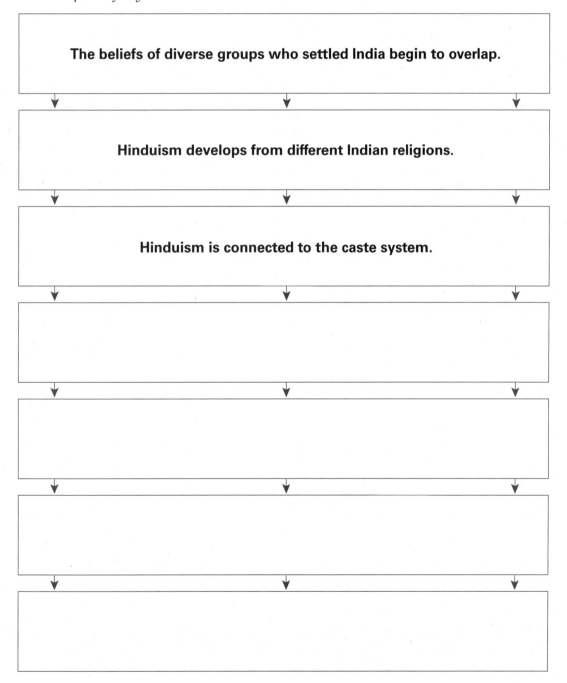

The beliefs of diverse groups who settled India begin to overlap.

Hinduism develops from different Indian religions.

Hinduism is connected to the caste system.

CHAPTER 3 SECTION 2

Section Summary
HINDUISM AND BUDDHISM

READING CHECK

Who is the founder of Buddhism?

_____

_____

_____

VOCABULARY STRATEGY

Find the word *aspirations* in the underlined sentence. Have you ever heard the word before? If you heard someone say that they *aspire* to a career in medicine, does that mean they want or don't want a career in medicine? Use these clues to help you figure out the meaning of *aspirations*.

READING SKILL

Recognize Sequence Which developed first in India: Hinduism or Buddhism? Use the information about Siddhartha Gautama to determine the answer.

_____

_____

_____

Hinduism grew out of many different beliefs. All Hindus share certain beliefs. People have an essential self, or **atman.** Their goal is to achieve **moksha,** or union with the spiritual force called brahman. **Reincarnation,** the rebirth of the soul in another body provides several lifetimes to achieve moksha. **Karma** refers to a person's actions that affect where a person is born in the next life. If they follow their religious and moral duties, or **dharma,** people can achieve moksha. **Ahimsa,** or nonviolence, is an important part of dharma.

Hindu society is based on a system of **castes,** or social groups into which people are born. People of higher castes are considered more spiritually pure; the lowest caste is considered untouchable. Despite inequalities, castes provide social stability and a sense of identity.

Siddhartha Gautama was a Hindu prince born in 563 B.C. He wanted to find out why humans suffered. He began fasting and meditating and eventually believed he understood the cause and cure for suffering. He was called the Buddha, or "the Enlightened One." The Buddha taught the **Four Noble Truths.** They explain life as suffering and give ways to cure it. People should follow the **Eightfold Path,** which includes "right aspirations." The first two steps on the path involve the Four Noble Truths. The path directs people to a moral life and enlightenment. Buddhists strive for **nirvana**, or union with the universe. This releases them from the cycle of rebirth.

Buddhism and Hinduism share many beliefs. However, Buddhism teaches people to seek enlightenment on their own, rather than through priests or gods. It also rejects castes and teaches that everyone can reach nirvana. Buddhism spread throughout Asia but gradually broke into two **sects,** or subgroups, with differing beliefs. Buddhism remained very popular in Asia, but declined in India. Hinduism there absorbed some Buddhist ideas.

Review Questions

1. What is the goal of a Hindu?

_____

_____

2. What is the Eightfold Path?

_____

_____

Focus Question: In what ways did Maurya and Gupta rulers achieve peace and order for ancient India?

As you read this section in your textbook, complete the following timeline to sequence the important events in the Maurya and Gupta periods. Some entries have been completed for you.

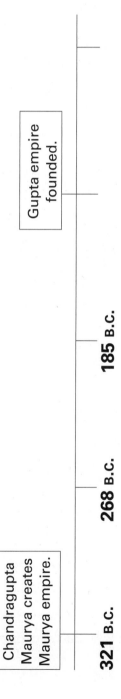

CHAPTER 3 — SECTION 3

Section Summary

POWERFUL EMPIRES OF INDIA

VOCABULARY STRATEGY

Find the word *status* in the underlined sentence. What clues to its meaning can you find in the next two sentences? Compare women's place in society at this time to early Aryan times. What changed? Use these context clues to help you figure out the meaning of *status*.

READING SKILL

Recognize Sequence Which empire ruled first: the Maurya or the Gupta?

_____

_____

_____

Chandragupta Maurya founded the first Indian empire in 321 B.C. The capital of the Maurya empire had schools, libraries, and palaces. The government built roads and harbors, collected taxes, and managed businesses. A secret police force reported on crime and **dissent**, or ideas opposed to those of the government.

Chandragupta's grandson, **Asoka,** continued to expand the empire. Asoka began ruling in 268 B.C. He became a Buddhist and ruled by moral example. He sent **missionaries** to spread Buddhism throughout Asia. To help his people, Asoka built hospitals and roads. However, the empire declined after his death and ended around 185 B.C.

The Gupta dynasty united India from A.D. 320 to about 540. During this time, India enjoyed a period of great cultural achievement called a **golden age.** The arts and learning became very important. Universities attracted students from many parts of Asia. Advances in mathematics include a system of numerals, the concept of zero, and the **decimal system.** We use all of these today. However, in time nomadic people from Central Asia overran the Gupta empire.

For most ancient Indians, everyday life revolved around the rules and duties related to a person's caste, family, and village. Villages grew or made most of what they needed. People met with others from nearby villages while attending weddings, visiting relatives, or going to markets. Parents, children, and grandchildren, known as a **joint family,** lived in the same house. The father served as the head of the household. Children learned their caste duties from their families. Arranging good marriages was important. Some families gave a **dowry,** or payment to the bridegroom. Women now had a lower status than they had had in early Aryan society. For example, they had once been able to serve on councils. Over time, Hindu law limited their position in society.

Review Questions

1. What did Asoka do for his people?

_____

_____

2. What advances made during Gupta rule do we use today?

_____

_____

CHAPTER 3
SECTION 4

Note Taking Study Guide
RISE OF CIVILIZATION IN CHINA

Focus Question: What characteristics defined the civilization that developed in China under its early rulers?

As you read this section in your textbook, complete the following outline to sequence the important events in early China. Some items have been completed for you.

I. **Geography influences China.**

    A. Geographic barriers isolate China.

        1. Brutal deserts and high mountain ranges to west and southwest

        2. Thick rainforests divide China from Southeast Asia.

        3. _____

        4. _____

    B. Civilization begins in the Huang River valley.

        1. Early peoples learn to farm.

        2. Huang River causes frequent flooding and destruction; called "River of Sorrows."

II. **Shang found first dynasty about 1766 B.C.**

    A. _____

    B. Social clases develop

        1. _____

        2. _____

III. **The Zhou overthrow the Shang in 1122 B.C.**

    A. _____

    B. _____

    C. _____

        1. _____

        2. _____

    D. Zhou dynasty ends in 256 B.C.

IV. **Early Religious beliefs**

    A. Chinese pray to many gods and nature spirits

    B. _____

(Outline continues on the next page.)

Name_____ Class_____ Date_____

(Continued from page 31)

V. Two major beliefs emarge.

   A. _____

   B. _____

   C. _____

VI. Chinese Achievements

   A. _____

   B. _____

   C. Develop complex writing system

      1. _____

      2. _____

   D. Create first books

CHAPTER 3
SECTION 4

Section Summary
RISE OF CIVILIZATION IN CHINA

Civilization in China first developed on the Huang River. It carries **loess,** or yellow soil, which raises the water level. People suffered from its frequent floods. The need to control flooding likely led to the rise of government.

The Shang dynasty began about 1766 B.C. Kings ruled with princes. The princes were probably the heads of **clans,** or families claiming a common ancestor. The top level of society included warriors. <u>Scholars think Shang warriors learned about horse-drawn chariots when they interacted with other Asian peoples.</u>

The Zhou overthrew the Shang in 1122 B.C. They promoted the Mandate of Heaven, or divine right to rule. This idea later explained the **dynastic cycle,** or rise and fall of dynasties. If a ruler was corrupt, heaven would let his dynasty fall. The Zhou also established **feudalism.** In this system, nobles had their own land but owed military service and support to a ruler. In the 600s B.C., iron tools were developed, making farming more productive. The population grew. The Zhou dynasty ended due to fighting among feudal lords.

During the Zhou dynasty, two great thinkers emerged. **Confucius** developed a **philosophy,** or system of ideas, that greatly influenced Chinese civilization. He cared about social order and good government. He stressed five key relationships between people. **Filial piety,** or respect for parents, was the most important. **Laozi** founded Daoism. This philosophy emphasized living in harmony with nature. People should look beyond everyday cares and focus on the Dao, or "the way."

The early Chinese discovered how to make silk, which they kept secret for many years. They also invented a system of writing at least 4,000 years ago. Questions were written on **oracle bones.** After heating the bones, priests interpreted the answers. Later, a writing system evolved that included thousands of **characters,** or written symbols. The Chinese turned writing into an art called **calligraphy.**

Review Questions

1. Why did the Zhou dynasty end?

_____

_____

2. Who is Confucius?

_____

_____

READING CHECK

Who founded Daoism?

_____

_____

VOCABULARY STRATEGY

Find the word *interacted* in the underlined sentence. Break the word into parts. The prefix *inter-* means "between," "among," or "with." The word *act* means "to do something." Use these word-part clues to help you figure out the meaning of *interacted.*

READING SKILL

Recognize Sequence Did Confucianism emerge before or after 1122 B.C ? Use the information about the dynasty that ruled during Confucius' life to help you figure out the answer.

_____

_____

_____

CHAPTER

3

SECTION 5

Note Taking Study Guide

STRONG RULERS UNITE CHINA

Focus Question: How did powerful emperors unite much of China and bring about a golden age of cultural achievement?

As you read this section, complete the following chart to sequence the important events in the Qin and Han periods. Some items have been completed for you.

Event				
Qin dynasty begins.				

Date				
221 B.C.	206 B.C.		141 B.C.—87 B.C.	

CHAPTER 3 SECTION 5

Section Summary
STRONG RULERS UNITE CHINA

The Qin Dynasty began in 221 B.C. when the leader of the Qin conquered the Zhou. He called himself **Shi Huangdi,** or First Emperor. He increased his power by following Legalism, a philosophy that said that strength was more important than goodness for a ruler. Shi Huangdi tortured and killed any who opposed his rule. He replaced feudal states with military areas headed by loyal officials. To build unity, he standardized weights, measures, coins, and writing. Thousands of workers joined shorter walls to form the one Great Wall against invaders from the north. Over the centuries, it grew to thousands of miles and became a symbol of Chinese strength.

The Han Dynasty began in 202 B.C. The most famous of the Han emperors, **Wudi,** ruled from 141 B.C. to 87 B.C. Instead of Legalism, Wudi made Confucianism the official belief system of the state. He improved transportation, controlled prices, and created a government **monopoly** on iron and salt. His policy of **expansionism** increased Chinese territory. The trade routes he opened became the Silk Road.

Han rulers chose Confucian scholars as government officials, or **civil servants.** Young men could move up in government through skill, rather than through family influence. They might be tested on their knowledge of the Five Classics. <u>This was a collection of histories, poems, and handbooks, compiled from works by Confucius and others.</u>

The Han dynasty was a golden age for Chinese culture. The Han wrote books on chemistry, zoology, and botany. They invented the suspension bridge, rudder, and paper. Medical treatment included **acupuncture** to relieve pain or treat illness. Artists created beautiful works of jade, ceramic, and bronze. Poets and historians wrote about the greatness of Han cities.

Over time, however, emperors could no longer control **warlords,** or local military rulers. Peasants rebelled. The last Han emperor was overthrown in A.D. 220, ending 400 years of unified rule.

Review Questions

1. How did Shi Huangdi build unity?

_____

_____

2. How did young men move up in the Han government?

_____

_____

READING CHECK

By what philosophy did the Han emperor Wudi rule?

_____

_____

_____

VOCABULARY STRATEGY

Find the word *compiled* in the underlined sentence. In this sentence, the word is used as a verb. It tells how the Five Classics were created. Note that the Five Classics were made up of works by several people. Use these context clues to help you figure out what *compiled* means.

READING SKILL

Recognize Sequence Sequence the following events:

____ Han China enjoys a golden age.

____ Shi Huangdi names himself First Emperor.

____ Work begins on the Great Wall.

CHAPTER 4 SECTION 1

Note Taking Study Guide

EARLY PEOPLE OF THE AEGEAN

Focus Question: How did the Minoans and Mycenaeans shape early Greek civilizations?

As you read the section in your textbook, complete the table below to record the main ideas about the Minoans, Mycenaeans, and Dorians. Some items have been completed for you.

Minoans	Mycenaeans	Dorians
• Successful traders; lived on island of Crete • Rulers lived in large palaces.	• Sea traders; spoke Greek • Dominated the Aegean world from 1400 to 1200 B.C.	• Sea raiders from the north; spoke Greek

CHAPTER
4
SECTION 1

Section Summary
EARLY PEOPLE OF THE AEGEAN

The island of Crete was home to the Minoans. They were a great trading civilization that existed from 1600 B.C. to 1500 B.C. The rulers lived in a large palace at **Knossos.** It housed the royal family and had working areas for artisans. It also included religious **shrines,** areas where gods and goddesses were honored. The walls were covered with colorful **frescoes,** watercolor paintings done on wet plaster. These illustrations revealed much about Minoan daily life.

By 1400 B.C, Minoan civilization disappeared. Although it is not clear why, it is certain that invaders called the Mycenaeans played a key role. The Mycenaeans were also sea traders. Their civilization reached beyond the Aegean to Sicily, Italy, Egypt, and Mesopotamia. They learned many skills from the Minoans. They also absorbed Egyptian and Mesopotamian customs, which they passed on to later Greeks.

The Mycenaeans are best remembered for their part in the **Trojan War,** which took place about 1250 B.C. The conflict may have started because of a rivalry between Mycenae and Troy. Troy was a rich trading city that controlled the vital **straits,** or narrow water passages, connecting the Mediterranean and Black seas. According to legend, the war erupted when the Mycenaeans sailed to Troy to rescue the kidnapped wife of the Greek king.

Much of what we know of the Trojan War and life during this period comes from two epic poems—the *Iliad* and the *Odyssey.* These works are credited to the poet **Homer** who probably lived about 750 B.C. The *Iliad* and the *Odyssey* reveal much about the values of the ancient Greeks. The heroes in the poems display honor, courage, and eloquence.

Invaders from the north, known as the Dorians, defeated the Mycenaeans in about 1100 B.C. After the Dorian invasions, Greece passed several centuries in obscurity. Later, a new Greek civilization would emerge that would dominate the region and soon extend its influence across the Western world.

Review Questions

1. What works of art give clues to Minoan culture?

_____

_____

2. What literary works are credited to the poet Homer?

_____

_____

READING CHECK

According to Greek legend, what caused the Trojan War?

_____

_____

_____

VOCABULARY STRATEGY

Find the word *eloquence* in the underlined sentence. What do you think it means? The word *eloquence* is from the Latin word *eloqui,* meaning "to speak out. Ask yourself: How do you think a hero speaks? Use these word-origin and context clues to help you figure out the meaning of *eloquence.*

READING SKILL

Identify Main Ideas What civilization emerged after the Dorian invasions?

_____

_____

_____

CHAPTER 4 SECTION 2

Note Taking Study Guide
THE RISE OF GREEK CITY-STATES

Focus Question: How did government and culture develop as Greek city-states grew?

As you read this section in your textbook, complete the outline below to record the main ideas and supporting details in this section. Some items have been completed for you.

I. Geography Shapes Greece

   A. Landscape defines political boundaries

      1. Mountains divide the peninsula into isolated valleys; islands lie beyond the rugged coast.

      2. _____

   B. Life by the sea

      1. Seas link the Greeks to the outside world.

      2. _____

      3. _____

II. Governing the City-States

   A. Polis made up of major city or town and surrounding countryside; built on two levels.

      1. _____

      2. _____

      3. Male landowners hold all the power.

   B. Government evolves

      1. First government is a monarchy; the rulers are kings.

      2. _____

      3. Expansion of trade leads to rule by an oligarchy.

   C. Warfare

      1. Changes in military technology

      2. Iron weapons replace bronze.

      3. _____

      4. _____

III. Sparta: A Warrior Society

   A. Daily life ruled by discipline.

      1. Spartan boys prepare for military life.

      2. _____

   B. Women of Sparta

      1. Girls are expected to provide sons for the army.

(Outline continues on the next page.)

Note Taking Study Guide
THE RISE OF GREEK CITY-STATES

(Continued from page 38)

    2. _____

    3. Run households while men are at war

IV. Athens Evolves Into a Democracy

  A. Demands for change

    1. Government goes from monarchy to aristocracy.

    2. Merchants and soldiers resent the power of nobles.

    3. _____

    4. _____

  B. Solon reforms government

    1. Is appointed chief official in 594 B.C.

    2. _____

    3. Economic reforms are introduced.

    4. _____

    5. Tyrants rise to power.

  C. Citizens share power and wealth

    1. _____

    2. Cleisthenes broadens power of ordinary citizens.

  D. A limited democracy

    1. _____

    2. Athens still gives more people a say in government than any other ancient civilization.

  E. Women in Athens

    1. _____

    2. _____

    3. Most poor women work outside the home.

  F. Educating the youth

    1. _____

    2. Boys learn to read, write, study music, rhetoric.

    3. _____

CHAPTER 4 SECTION 2	Section Summary
	THE RISE OF GREEK CITY-STATES

READING CHECK

In Athens, what type of government replaced the monarchy?

_____

_____

_____

For ancient Greek peoples, although they were separated by water, the seas were a link to the outside world. The Greeks became skilled sailors and traders. As they traveled, they gained new ideas. They used these ideas in their own culture.

The Greeks developed their own version of the city-state, called the **polis.** It was made up of a major city and the surrounding countryside. The **acropolis,** or high city, with its many temples, stood on a hill above the city. Because the population of each city-state was small, the **citizens** shared a sense of responsibility for its successes and defeats.

Over time, different forms of government evolved. At first, there was a **monarchy.** Under this system, a hereditary ruler exercises central power. Later, power shifted to an **aristocracy,** or rule by a landholding elite. As trade and wealth grew, government became an **oligarchy**—where a city-state was controlled by a small, wealthy group.

A new method of fighting also developed. The **phalanx** was a large group formation of heavily armed foot soldiers. In the city-state of **Sparta,** Spartans focused on developing strong military skills. They were less interested in trade, wealth, new ideas, or the arts.

VOCABULARY STRATEGY

Find the word *imposing* in the underlined sentence and read the sentence carefully. How is the word *imposing* used? Based on the sentence, do you think powerful Athenians wanted the tyrants' reforms or resisted them? Use context clues to help you figure out the meaning of *imposing.*

In **Athens,** an aristocracy replaced the monarchy. Ordinary citizens were discontented. Slowly Athens moved toward **democracy,** or government by the people. Under the leadership of Solon, government reforms took place. However, unrest still existed. This led to the rise of **tyrants,** or people who gained power by force. They often won support from the merchant class and the poor by imposing reforms to help these groups. In 507 B.C., the reformer Cleisthenes set up a council of citizens and made the assembly a genuine **legislature,** or lawmaking body.

Although rivalries existed between city-states, Greeks had much in common. They spoke the same language, honored the same ancient heroes, and prayed to the same gods.

READING SKILL

Identify Supporting Details
What details support the idea that Greeks benefited by living near the sea?

_____

_____

_____

Review Questions

1. What is an acropolis?

_____

_____

2. What was the focus of Spartan culture?

_____

_____

Name_____ Class_____ Date_____

Focus Question: How did war with invaders and conflict among Greeks affect the city-states?

As you read the section in your textbook, complete the table below to record some supporting details for the main ideas discussed in the section. Some items have been completed for you.

Persian Wars	Athenian Democracy	Peloponnesian War
• Athens is victorious at Marathon.	• Under Pericles, the economy thrives and the government becomes more democratic.	• Greeks outside Athens resent Athenian domination.
• Greek city-states unite against Persia.	•	•
• _____	•	•
	•	•
	•	•
	• Citizens can ostracize public figures considered a threat to the democracy.	•
		• The war ends Athenian domination of the Greek world.

CHAPTER 4 SECTION 3

Section Summary

CONFLICT IN THE GREEK WORLD

In the 500s B.C., the Persians extended their empire to include the Greek city-states in Ionia. Under Persian rule, these city-states were self-governing. However, they resented the Persians. Athens helped the city-states fight against Persia. This led to the Persian Wars, which lasted from 490 B.C. to 479 B.C.

Eventually the Athenians, aided by the Spartans and others, were victorious against the Persians. This victory increased the Greeks' sense of uniqueness. Athens emerged from the war as the most powerful city-state in Greece. To increase its security, it formed an alliance with other Greek city-states, called the Delian League. An **alliance** is a formal agreement between two or more powers to come to one another's defense.

After the Persian Wars, Athens prospered under the leadership of the statesman **Pericles.** The economy thrived and the government became more democratic. At this time, Athens was a **direct democracy,** where citizens took part in the daily affairs of government. Pericles believed that citizens from all classes should participate. Therefore, a **stipend,** or fixed salary, was paid to men who served in the Assembly and its Council.

In addition, Athenians also served on juries. A **jury** is a panel of citizens who make the final judgment in a trial. Athenian citizens could also vote to exile a public figure who seemed to threaten their democracy. This was called **ostracism.**

Pericles helped turn Athens into the cultural center of Greece. The arts were encouraged through public festivals and dramatic competitions. Building projects increased Athens' prosperity by creating jobs for artisans and workers.

Many Greeks outside Athens resented Athenian success, however. Soon, the Greek world was divided. Warfare broke out between Athens and Sparta. This led to the Peloponnesian War, which soon spread throughout Greece. Sparta, helped by the Persians, defeated Athens. Athenian domination of the Greek world ended. However, later the Athenian economy revived and Athens regained its place as the cultural center of Greece.

VOCABULARY STRATEGY

Find the word *uniqueness* in the underlined sentence. What do you think *uniqueness* means? The root word, *unique,* comes from the Latin word *unus* meaning "one." Use this word-root clue and any prior knowledge you might have about the word *unique* to help you figure out the meaning of *uniqueness.*

READING SKILL

Identify Supporting Details How did Athens increase its security after the Persian Wars?

_____

_____

_____

Review Questions

1. What is a direct democracy?

_____

_____

2. Describe Athens under Pericles.

_____

_____

Name_____ Class_____ Date_____

Focus Question: How did Greek thinkers, artists, and writers explore the nature of the universe and people's place in it?

As you read this section in your textbook, complete the concept web below to record the supporting details about Greek achievements discussed in the section. Some items have been completed for you.

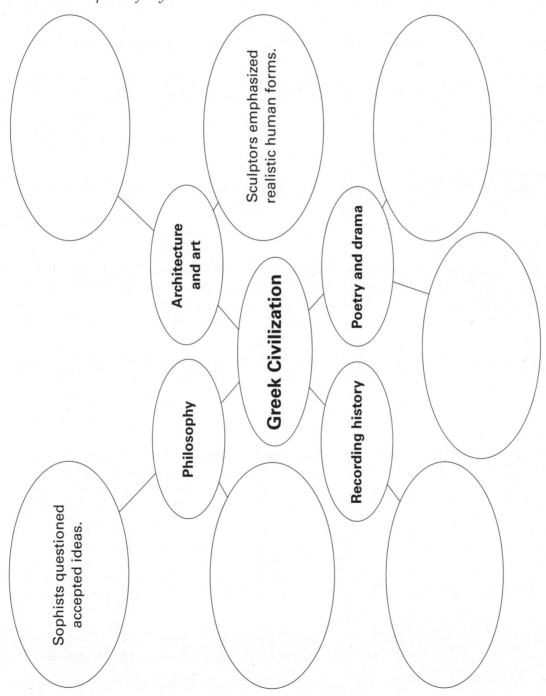

Concept web with central oval labeled **Greek Civilization** connected to:
- **Architecture and art** — Sculptors emphasized realistic human forms.
- **Poetry and drama**
- **Philosophy** — Sophists questioned accepted ideas.
- **Recording history**

CHAPTER 4 SECTION 4

Section Summary

THE GLORY THAT WAS GREECE

READING CHECK

What were the names of the schools started by Plato and by Aristotle?

_____

_____

_____

VOCABULARY STRATEGY

Find the word *rigid* in the underlined sentence. What does it mean? What context clues can you find in the surrounding words or phrases? Circle any context clues in the paragraph that help you figure out what *rigid* means.

READING SKILL

Identify Supporting Details
What did Sophists do to support their belief that success was more important than moral truth?

_____

_____

_____

Ancient Greek thinkers used observation and reason to explain events. These thinkers were called **philosophers,** meaning "lovers of wisdom." Philosophers explored many subjects, from mathematics and music, to **logic,** or rational thinking.

Some philosophers were interested in defining proper behavior. In contrast, the Sophists believed that success was more important than moral truth. They developed skills in **rhetoric,** the art of skillful speaking. They used rhetoric to help in their careers.

The philosopher **Socrates** was a critic of the Sophists. He believed in seeking truth and self-knowledge. Most of what we know about Socrates comes from the writings of his student **Plato.** Plato set up a school called the Academy. Like Socrates, Plato stressed the importance of reason. Plato's most famous student, **Aristotle,** also promoted reason as the main force for learning. He set up a school called the Lyceum, for the study of all branches of knowledge.

Plato argued that every object on Earth has an ideal form. Greek artists and architects showed a similar love of balance, order, and beauty. The most famous example of Greek architecture is the **Parthenon.** The basic plan of the Parthenon is a simple rectangle, with tall columns and a gently sloping roof. Early Greek sculptors carved figures in rigid, formal poses. Later, they created more natural, realistic forms. Sculptors carved their subjects in a way that showed human beings in perfect, graceful forms. In drama, too, the Greeks developed their own style. **Tragedies** are plays about human suffering that usually end sadly. **Comedies** are humorous plays that mock customs or criticize society.

History was also an important study for the Greeks. **Herodotus** is often called the "Father of History." He stressed the importance of research. He visited many lands to chronicle information of actual events. Thucydides wrote a history of the Peloponnesian Wars based on his personal knowledge.

Review Questions

1. What subjects did Greek philosophers explore?

_____

_____

2. What are two types of drama developed by the Greeks?

_____

_____

Focus Question: How did Alexander the Great expand his empire and spread Greek culture throughout the realm?

As you read this section, complete the outline below to record the main ideas and supporting details about the empire of Alexander the Great. Some items have been completed for you.

I. The Empire of Alexander the Great

   A. Philip II conquers Greece

      1. _____

      2. _____

      3. Defeats Athens and Thebes at battle of Chaeronea

      4. Gains control of Greece, but is assassinated shortly thereafter

   B. Alexander takes Persia

      1. _____

      2. _____

      3. _____

   C. Advance into India

      1. Has most of Persian empire under his control; crosses Hindu Kush mountains into Northern India

      2. _____

      3. _____

   D. _____

      1. _____

      2. _____

II. The Legacy of Alexander the Great

   A. Cultures combine

      1. Most lasting accomplishment is spread of Greek culture.

      2. _____

      3. _____

      4. _____

      5. _____

      6. _____

      7. _____

(Outline continues on the next page.)

(Continued from page 45)

B. _____

   1. _____

   2. _____

   3. _____

C. _____

   1. _____

   2. _____

   3. _____

III. Hellenistic Arts and Sciences

  A. New philosophies

    1. Political turmoil contributes to rise of new schools of philosophy.

    2. _____

  B. _____

    1. _____

    2. _____

    3. _____

    4. _____

CHAPTER 4 SECTION 5

Section Summary

ALEXANDER AND THE HELLENISTIC AGE

Macedonian king **Philip II** gained the throne in 359 B.C. He built a powerful army, bringing all of Greece under his control. His goal was to conquer the Persian empire, but he was assassinated before he could try. **Assassination** is the murder of a public figure, usually for political reasons.

After Philip's death, his son, later known as **Alexander the Great,** invaded Persia. After gaining control of much of the Persian empire, he advanced into India. However, in 323 B.C., Alexander died suddenly in Persia from a fever. He was 33. Although his empire soon collapsed, his conquests helped to spread Greek culture across the lands he conquered—from Egypt to India. Local people **assimilated,** or absorbed, Greek ideas, and Greek settlers adopted local customs. Gradually, a new Hellenistic culture emerged. It was a blending of Greek, Persian, Egyptian, and Indian cultures and ideas.

At the heart of the Hellenistic world was **Alexandria,** founded by Alexander in Egypt, with its great library. Like Alexandria, cities of the Hellenistic world hired many architects and artists. Temples, palaces, and other public buildings were much larger and grander than the buildings of classical Greece. The elaborate new style reflected the desire of Hellenistic rulers to show off their wealth and power.

During the Hellenistic age, scholars built on earlier Greek, Babylonian, and Egyptian knowledge. In mathematics, **Pythagoras** created a formula to express the relationship between the sides of a right triangle. The astronomer Aristarchus developed the theory of a **heliocentric,** or sun-centered, solar system. The most famous scientist of the time, **Archimedes,** used physics to make practical inventions. In medicine, the Greek doctor **Hippocrates** studied the causes of illnesses and looked for cures.

Greek works in the arts and sciences set a standard for later Europeans. Greek ideas about law, freedom, justice, and government continue to influence politics today.

Review Questions

1. What cultures contributed to the Hellenistic culture?

_____

_____

2. What was Alexandria?

_____

_____

READING CHECK

Who developed the theory of a heliocentric solar system?

_____

_____

_____

VOCABULARY STRATEGY

What does the word *elaborate* mean in the underlined sentence? Look for context clues that may help you to figure out the word's meaning. Think about what this style must have been like if rulers used it to show off. Circle the words or phrases in the paragraph that could help you figure out what *elaborate* means.

READING SKILL

Identify Supporting Details How did Alexander the Great help to create Hellenistic culture?

_____

_____

_____

Note Taking Study Guide

CHAPTER 5 SECTION 1

THE ROMAN WORLD TAKES SHAPE

Focus Question: What values formed the basis of Roman society and government?

As you read this section in your textbook, complete the flowchart below to identify causes and effects of important events during the Roman republic. Some items have been completed for you.

Cause(s)

- Romans drive out Etruscan rulers.
-
-
-
- Rome defeats enemies.

Event

- The Roman state is founded.
-
-
-
-

Effect(s)

-
- Common people gain access to power without war.
-
-
- Conquered lands remain loyal to Rome, even in troubled times.

CHAPTER 5 SECTION 1

Section Summary
THE ROMAN WORLD TAKES SHAPE

The Romans shared the Italian peninsula with Greek colonists and with the **Etruscans.** The Etruscans ruled most of central Italy for a time. The Romans admired them. They adapted the Etruscan alphabet. They also studied Etruscan engineering.

In 509 B.C., the Romans drove out their Etruscan ruler. This marks the founding of Rome. The Romans then set up a new form of government called a **republic.** In a republic, officials are chosen to represent the people. The most powerful governing body in the republic was the senate. Its 300 members were **patricians,** or upper-class landowners. Each year, the senate nominated two patrician **consuls** to manage the government. In the event of war or other emergency, the senate might choose a temporary **dictator.** During the crisis, he had complete control over the government.

In the early republic, all government officials were patricians. The **plebeians,** or common people, had very little power. Eventually, however, they acquired the right to elect their own officials, called **tribunes.** The tribunes could **veto,** or block, certain laws they felt would not benefit the plebeians. Although the senate still dominated the government, the common people had gained access to power and their rights were protected.

The family was the basic unit of Roman society. Although women were subject to male authority, they did have certain rights. Romans also believed in education for all children, regardless of gender or class. Religion was also a major feature of Roman society during this time.

By 270 B.C., Rome's strong army controlled most of the Italian peninsula. The basic military unit was the **legion.** Each legion included about 5,000 citizen-soldiers. As the Romans took over new territories, they treated their defeated enemies reasonably. Conquered peoples only needed to accept Roman leadership and follow certain laws. Then they were allowed to keep their own customs and local rulers.

Review Questions

1. What was the most powerful governing body of the republic?

_____

_____

2. Who were the consuls?

_____

_____

READING CHECK

What was the basic unit of Roman society during the republic?

_____

_____

_____

VOCABULARY STRATEGY

Find the word *dominated* in the underlined sentence. What does it mean? The word *dominate* originates from the Latin word *dominus,* meaning "master." Use what you know about the word *master* to help figure out the meaning of *dominated.*

READING SKILL

Identify Causes and Effects
Identify one cause and one effect of the changes made to the Roman senate that increased the power of the plebeians.

_____

_____

_____

Name_____ Class_____ Date_____

Note Taking Study Guide

FROM REPUBLIC TO EMPIRE

Focus Question: What factors led to the decline of the Roman republic and the rise of the Roman empire?

As you read this section in your textbook, complete the flowcharts below to record the causes of the decline of the Roman republic and the rise of the Roman empire. Some items have been completed for you.

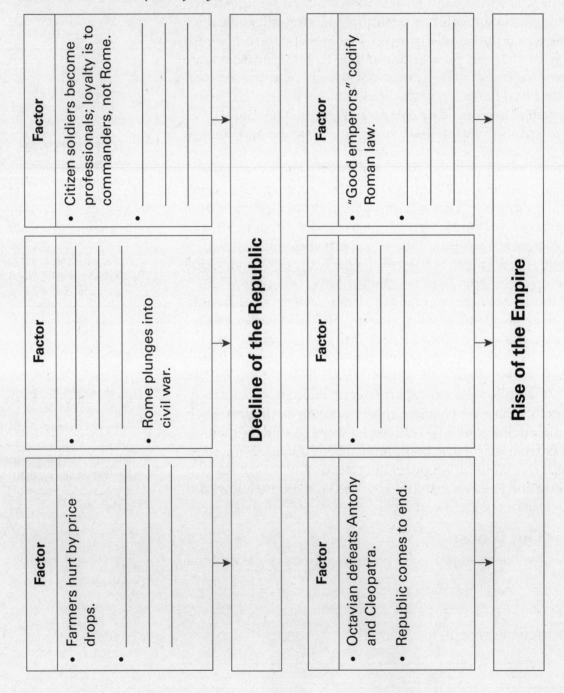

Factor
- Citizen soldiers become professionals; loyalty is to commanders, not Rome.
- _____

Factor
- _____
- Rome plunges into civil war.

Factor
- Farmers hurt by price drops.
- _____

→ **Decline of the Republic**

Factor
- "Good emperors" codify Roman law.
- _____

Factor
- _____

Factor
- Octavian defeats Antony and Cleopatra.
- Republic comes to end.

→ **Rise of the Empire**

CHAPTER 5 SECTION 2

Section Summary

FROM REPUBLIC TO EMPIRE

As the Romans extended their territory around the Mediterranean, they came into conflict with Carthage in North Africa. The two powers battled in three Punic Wars between 264 B.C. and 146 B.C.

Rome was committed to **imperialism,** or establishing control over foreign lands. Rome also controlled trade routes, which brought great wealth. Rich families bought large estates, called **latifundia,** and forced war captives to work as slaves. The gap between the rich and poor grew, leading to corruption and riots.

Rome needed social and political reform. Patrician tribunes **Tiberius** and **Gaius Gracchus** were among the first to try. The senate felt threatened, however, and in a series of riots, the brothers and their followers were killed. This power struggle led to a time of civil war.

Out of the chaos came **Julius Caesar,** successful military commander. With Caesar's fame, a rivalry grew between him and another general, Pompey. Caesar defeated Pompey. Then Caesar's soldiers swept around the Mediterranean, suppressing rebellions. In control, Caesar returned to Rome. He forced the senate to make him dictator for life.

Fearing that Caesar would make himself king, his enemies killed him. His friend Marc Antony and his nephew Octavian joined forces to avenge Caesar. However, they soon battled one another. Octavian defeated Antony and the senate gave him the title of **Augustus,** or "Exalted One." He became the first emperor, marking the beginning of the Roman empire.

Augustus built a stable government. To make the tax system fair, he ordered a **census.** This was a population count. While not all of Augustus' successors were great rulers, some were. **Hadrian** was a great emperor, who codified Roman law, making it the same for all provinces.

During the *Pax Romana,* Roman rule brought peace, prosperity, and order. People all across the empire enjoyed spectacular forms of entertainment.

Review Questions

1. What is imperialism?

_____

_____

2. What did the Roman emperor Hadrian accomplish?

_____

_____

READING CHECK

Who were Tiberius and Gaius Gracchus?

_____

_____

_____

VOCABULARY STRATEGY

Find the word *suppressing* in the underlined sentence. What does it mean? The word *suppress* comes from a Latin word that means "to press under." Use this word-origins clue to help you figure out the meaning of *suppressing.*

READING SKILL

Recognize Multiple Causes
How did Octavian become the first emperor of Rome?

_____

_____

_____

Name_____ Class_____ Date_____

Note Taking Study Guide

THE ROMAN ACHIEVEMENT

Focus Question: How did advances in the arts, learning, and the law show the Romans' high regard for cultural and political achievements?

As you read this section in your textbook, complete the concept web below to list the effects of Rome's cultural and political achievements. Some items have been completed for you.

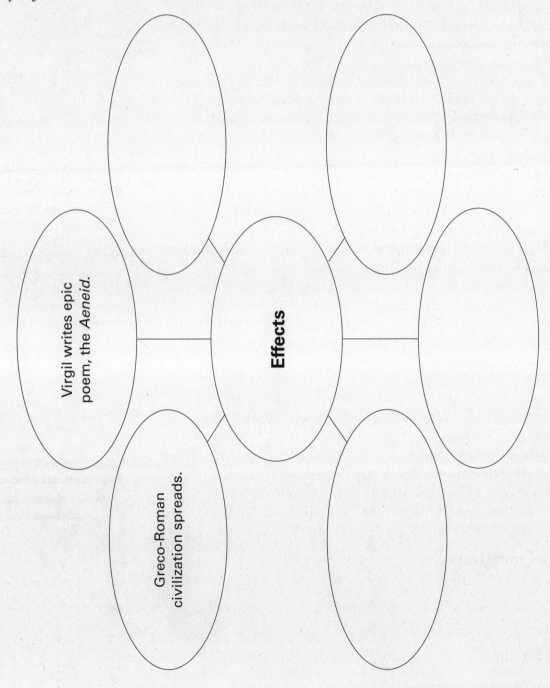

Virgil writes epic poem, the *Aeneid*.

Effects

Greco-Roman civilization spreads.

CHAPTER 5 SECTION 3
Section Summary
THE ROMAN ACHIEVEMENT

Greek art, literature, philosophy, and scientific developments had a huge influence on the Romans. Still, the greatest Roman writers worked in Latin. In his epic poem the *Aeneid*, the poet **Virgil** linked Rome to Greece's heroic past. Others used poetry to **satirize,** or make fun of, Roman society. Roman historians wrote about Rome's glorious past to renew patriotism. In philosophy, Roman thinkers were impressed with the Hellenistic philosophy of Stoicism.

Both Roman and Greek sculptors realistically portrayed their subjects. However, the Romans also focused on individual character. Roman artists portrayed scenes from literature and daily life in frescoes and mosaics. A **mosaic** is a picture made from chips of colored stone or glass.

Another difference between the Romans and the Greeks was their architecture. Unlike the Greeks, the Romans focused on grandeur. They built enormous buildings to symbolize Roman power. The Romans also improved structures such as columns and arches. <u>Utilizing concrete as a building material, they developed the arched dome as a roof for large spaces.</u>

More advances were made in **engineering,** which is the application of science and mathematics to make useful structures and machines. Roman engineers built many **aqueducts,** or bridge-like stone structures that carried water from the hills into Roman cities.

In general, the Romans left scientific research to the Greeks, who were by that time citizens of the empire. **Ptolemy,** the astronomer-mathematician, proposed that Earth was at the center of the universe. This mistaken idea was accepted in the Western world for nearly 1,500 years.

Rome was dedicated to regulating laws and to serving justice. To protect its citizens, Rome developed the civil law. As Rome expanded, the law of nations was established. This applied to both citizens and non-citizens of Rome. When citizenship was extended across the empire, the two systems merged.

Review Questions

1. How did Roman historians try to renew patriotism?

_____

_____

2. What contributions did Romans make to engineering?

_____

_____

READING CHECK

What architectural feature did the Romans develop?

_____

_____

_____

VOCABULARY STRATEGY

Find the word *utilizing* in the underlined sentence. What does *utilizing* mean? The word *utilize* comes from the Latin word *utile* meaning "useful." Use this word-origins clue to help you figure out the meaning of *utilizing*.

READING SKILL

Understand Effects Why did the Romans develop the civil law?

_____

_____

_____

Note Taking Study Guide

CHAPTER 5 SECTION 4

THE RISE OF CHRISTIANITY

Focus question: How did Christianity emerge and then spread to become the official religion of the Roman empire?

As you read this section in your textbook, complete the table below to show the factors that caused the rise of Christianity and its establishment as the official religion of the Roman empire. Some items have been filled in for you.

Causes	Effects
• Growing number of people look for spiritual fulfillment. • Deep divisions exist within the Jewish religion. • _____ _____ • _____ _____ • Jesus teaches Christian beliefs. • Jesus is executed; apostles and disciples spread his message. • _____ _____ • Paul and other missionaries spread the word of Christianity. • _____ _____ • _____ _____ • Constantine issues Edict of Milan, ending persecution of Christians. • _____ _____	• Rise of Christianity • Establishment of Christianity as empire's official religion

CHAPTER 5 SECTION 4

Section Summary
THE RISE OF CHRISTIANITY

Within the Roman empire, there were many religious beliefs. Rome tolerated different religions, as long as citizens worshiped Roman gods, too—including the emperor. Because most people believed in more than one god, this did not cause a problem for a long time.

Later, however, a division arose among the Jews. Many began to follow a Jewish man named Jesus. They believed he was the **messiah,** or anointed king sent by God. Jesus chose 12 **apostles,** meaning "persons sent forth," to help him preach his message. Jesus' teachings led to a new religion—Christianity.

In his teachings, Jesus taught the need for justice, morality, forgiveness, and service to others. **Paul** was a missionary who spread the message of Christianity after Jesus was put to death. Paul said that those who believed in Jesus and complied with his teachings would be saved.

Because Christians refused to worship Roman gods, many were persecuted. They became known as **martyrs,** or people who suffer or die for their beliefs. Still, Christianity continued to spread. In A.D. 313, the Roman persecution of Christians stopped when the emperor **Constantine** issued the Edict of Milan. This granted freedom of worship to all Roman citizens. By the end of the century, Christianity was the Roman empire's official religion.

Under the Church, each Christian community and its **clergy**—those who conduct religious services—were grouped together in a diocese. Every community had its own priest who answered to a **bishop,** a high Church official. Eventually, bishops from five important cities gained more authority. They held the honorary title of **patriarch.** Other bishops, such as **Augustine** of Hippo in North Africa, became important teachers. However, as the Church developed, differences arose. The bishops of Rome came to be called **popes,** and claimed authority over all other bishops. There was also an emergence of **heresies,** or beliefs contrary to official Church teachings.

Review Questions

1. What was the Edict of Milan?

_____

_____

2. What did the bishops of Rome claim?

_____

_____

READING CHECK

Who was Paul?

_____

_____

_____

VOCABULARY STRATEGY

Find the word *complied* in the underlined sentence. What does it mean? Think about what Christians believed would happen if a person did not *comply* with Jesus' teachings. Use this question strategy to figure out the meaning of *complied.*

READING SKILL

Understand Effects Why did some Christians become martyrs?

_____

_____

_____

Name_____ Class_____ Date_____

Focus Question: How did military, political, social, and economic factors combine to cause the fall of the western Roman empire?

As you read this section in your textbook, complete the chart below to list the causes of the fall of the western Roman empire. Some items have been completed for you.

Causes of the Fall of the Western Roman Empire

Military	Social	Political	Economic
• Germanic peoples, fleeing the Huns, invaded the empire.	• Values declined.	• Government became more authoritative and oppressive; loses support of people.	• Population declines due to war and disease.
•	•	•	•
•	•	•	•
•		•	•

CHAPTER 5 SECTION 5

Section Summary
THE LONG DECLINE

In about the A.D. 200s, the Roman empire began to weaken. The golden age of the *Pax Romana* had ended. Rome faced political and economic problems. A decline in traditional values and frequent invasions were threatening the empire.

Corrupt government added to Rome's troubles. Political violence grew. Over and over, emperors were overthrown or assassinated by ambitious generals. Instability was the norm.

In 284, the emperor **Diocletian** set out to restore order. He divided the empire into two parts. He controlled the eastern part. A co-emperor, Maximian, ruled the western part. To help strengthen the weak economy, Diocletian slowed **inflation,** or a rapid rise of prices. He did this by establishing fixed prices on many goods and services.

When the emperor Constantine came into power, he continued Diocletian's reforms. He also granted religious freedom to Christians and founded a new capital, **Constantinople.** This made the eastern empire the center of power.

Although these reforms helped temporarily, they did not stop Rome's long-term decline. In the late 300s, a nomadic people from Asia, called **Huns,** began a savage campaign across much of Europe. This pushed other nomadic tribes into Roman territory. Fierce battles resulted. Soon, Rome itself was under attack. By then, the empire had already lost many of its territories. Roman power in the West was fading.

The main cause for Rome's decline was constant invasion. To fight back, Rome hired **mercenaries,** or foreign soldiers serving for pay, to defend its borders. However, many of these paid soldiers felt no loyalty to Rome. In addition, heavier and heavier taxes were needed to support Rome's military.

As Roman citizens worried about the consequences of a declining empire, patriotism diminished. <u>The upper class, which had once provided leaders, now devoted itself to luxury and to gaining prestige.</u> In 476, Germanic warriors captured Rome and removed the emperor. The Roman empire had ended.

Review Questions

1. What is inflation?

_____

_____

2. Who were the Huns?

_____

_____

READING CHECK

How did Diocletian try to restore order in the Roman empire?

_____

_____

_____

VOCABULARY STRATEGY

Find the word *prestige* in the underlined sentence. What does it mean? Think about how you may have heard the word used. If a job gives a person a lot of *prestige,* what does it give him or her? Use the answer to this question and your prior knowledge to figure out the meaning of the word *prestige.*

READING SKILL

Recognize Multiple Causes
Circle two causes below that contributed to Rome's decline.

1. invasions

2. corruption

3. Christianity

Name_____ Class_____ Date_____

Focus Question: What factors encouraged the rise of powerful civilizations in Mesoamerica?

A. *As you read "People Settle in the Americas," complete the following chart to record the similarities and differences in how early people adapted to climate and geography in different parts of the Americas. Some items have been completed for you.*

Adapting to the Americas	
Climate	**Geography**
• Icy climates to the extreme south and north • _____ _____	• Mountains • _____ • _____ • _____

B. *As you read the rest of this section in your textbook, complete the following Venn diagram in order to recognize the similarities and differences among the cultures of Mesoamerica. Some items have been completed for you.*

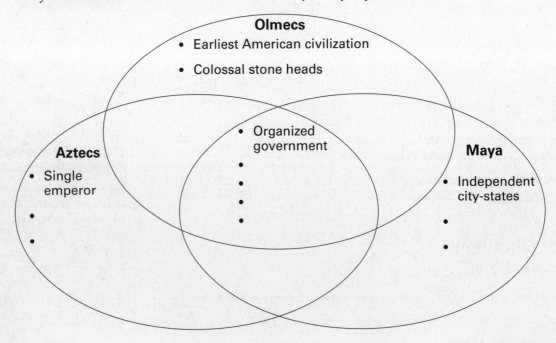

CHAPTER 6 SECTION 1

Section Summary
CIVILIZATIONS OF MESOAMERICA

People first came to the Americas from Asia between 60,000 B.C. and 18,000 B.C. They may have walked across a land bridge or come by boat. By about 1500 B.C., people had settled in **Mesoamerica,** a region made up of Mexico and Central America. There they grew **maize** and other crops, raised animals, and lived in villages. Some of these villages became great cities.

The **Olmecs** formed the first civilization in the Americas. It lasted from about 1500 B.C. to 400 B.C. A class of priests and nobles were its leaders. Later Mesoamerican peoples, including the Maya and Aztecs, adopted features of Olmec culture, such as carved stone, hieroglyphs, and the calendar.

Around 300 B.C., the Maya were building large cities in present-day Guatemala. By the time of the Maya golden age, about A.D. 250, the civilization included large, independent city-states spreading from southern Mexico through Central America. The Maya never formed an empire, however. Instead, cities kept in contact through trade and war. Maya cities included stone temples, palaces, and **stelae**. Stelae were tall stone monuments decorated with carvings. Scribes carved each stela with the names of rulers and dates. They also wrote about astronomy and religion in books of bark paper. Around A.D. 900, the Maya left most of their cities. This may have happened due to frequent warfare or over-farming.

The Aztec civilization began in the **Valley of Mexico.** In A.D. 1325 the Aztecs founded **Tenochtitlán,** their capital. Because it was located on an island in a lake, the Aztecs found ingenious ways to create more farmland; they built **chinampas.** These were human-made islands of mud and reeds.

Unlike the Maya, the Aztecs created an empire. They were at war constantly. As their empire grew, they used **tribute,** or payment from conquered peoples, to beautify Tenochtitlán. They sacrificed war prisoners to the sun god. Some of their gods included the gods of an earlier culture from the city of **Teotihuacán.** Its culture greatly influenced later peoples.

Review Questions
1. Why did the Maya leave their cities?

_____

_____

2. How did the Aztecs use tribute?

_____

_____

READING CHECK

Who were the leaders of Olmec society?

_____

_____

_____

VOCABULARY STRATEGY

Find the word *ingenious* in the underlined sentence. What does *ingenious* mean? It comes from a Latin word that means "natural talent." Think about people who have a natural talent, such as intelligence. Use these clues to help you figure out what *ingenious* means.

READING SKILL

Compare and Contrast How were the Aztecs and Maya cultures alike? How were they different? Think about the Olmec influence on both cultures.

_____

_____

CHAPTER 6 SECTION 2

Note Taking Study Guide

ANDEAN CULTURES OF SOUTH AMERICA

Focus Question: What characterized the cultures and civilizations that developed in the Andes?

As you read this section in your textbook, complete the following chart to contrast the culture of the early peoples of the Andes with the Inca. Use the chart to organize relevant details. Some items have been completed for you.

	Chavín	Moche	Southern Andes	Inca
Location	Northern and central Peru	North coast of Peru	Southern Andes	The Andes from Ecuador to Chile
Unique Achievements	• Large temple complex • •	• • •	• Nazca geoglyphs •	• Huge road network • • • • • • •

Section Summary
ANDEAN CULTURES OF SOUTH AMERICA

The first cultures of South America developed in the Andes. The earliest was the **Chavín** culture. Around 900 B.C., these people built a huge temple complex. Later, between A.D. 100 and 700, the **Moche** people lived along the north coast of Peru. They improved farming techniques, built roads, and used relay runners to carry messages. They made large buildings of **adobe** bricks. Moche artists made ceramic jars in the shape of people and animals.

The **Nazca** people, who lived between 500 B.C. and A.D. 500, are known for the huge pictures of animals they drew in the earth. Other cultures lived in the cities of **Huari** and **Tiahuanaco.** These two cities controlled large territories. They may have been connected through trade or religion because their art is similar.

The people with the most powerful Andean civilization were the Inca. Their culture appeared in the 1100s but grew most powerful after 1438. That is when **Pachacuti Inca Yupanqui** declared himself **Sapa Inca,** or emperor. Eventually, the Inca empire stretched from Ecuador in the north to Chile in the south. The Inca built a network of roads that criss-crossed the empire. The roads covered about 14,000 miles and ran through deserts and over mountains. These roads allowed news and armies to travel quickly to all parts of the empire. All the roads led to the capital city, **Cuzco.**

The Inca worshiped many gods, but the most important was **Inti,** the sun god. Inca rulers had absolute power and ran an efficient government. Nobles ruled provinces, and local officials handled everyday business. Officials kept records on **quipu,** which were colored strings knotted to represent numbers. Everyone had to speak the Inca language and follow the Inca religion. Each village, or **ayllu,** had a leader who assigned jobs and organized work for the government. Farmers built terraces to farm the steep hillsides. They spent part of the year farming for their village and part working land for the emperor.

Review Questions
1. Which peoples lived in South America before the Inca?

_____

_____

2. What was the purpose of the Inca roads?

_____

_____

READING CHECK

Which civilization used adobe for building?

_____

_____

_____

VOCABULARY STRATEGY

Find the word *network* in the underlined sentence. What does *network* mean? You can see that it is a compound word, or a word made from two other words— *net* and *work.* Use what you know about the meanings of the words *net* and *work* to help you figure out the meaning of *network.*

READING SKILL

Contrast How was an Inca farmer's life different from the Inca emperor's life?

_____

_____

_____

CHAPTER
6
SECTION 3

Note Taking Study Guide
PEOPLES OF NORTH AMERICA

Focus Question: What factors contributed to the growth of diverse cultures in North America?

As you read this section in your textbook, complete the following outline to help you compare and contrast the experiences and achievements of various culture areas. Some items have been completed for you.

I. Southwest

   A. Environment—Desert

   B. Settlement Type

      1. Hohokam farmed with irrigation.

      2. Anasazi built cliff dwellings and pueblos.

II. East

   A. Environment—River valleys

   B. Settlement Type

      1. Adena and Hopewell farmed, built earthworks.

      2. _____

      3. Natchez farmed, built earthworks, worshiped sun.

III. Other Areas

   A. Arctic

      1. Inuit hunted and Pshed.

      2. _____

      3. _____

   B. Northwest Coast

      1. _____

      2. _____

      3. _____

   C. _____

      1. _____

      2. _____

      3. _____

CHAPTER 6 SECTION 3

Section Summary

PEOPLES OF NORTH AMERICA

Many Native American culture groups lived in North America before A.D. 1500. Based on environment, scholars have placed the early people of North America into culture areas. This summary covers a few of those culture areas.

Between A.D. 1150 and A.D 1300, the Anasazi of the Southwest culture area built cliff homes on the sides of steep canyon walls. <u>The largest of these housing complexes, at **Mesa Verde,** Colorado, had more than 200 rooms.</u> The cliffs kept them safe from enemies. The Anasazi also built villages on the ground, which were similar to the cliff dwellings. The Spanish called these villages **pueblos. Pueblo Bonito** was the largest. This huge complex was five stories high and had over 800 rooms. In the center was the **kiva,** an underground room used for religious purposes and meetings.

The Adena and Hopewell people of the Northeast farmed in river valleys. They built **earthworks,** which were large piles of earth shaped into burial mounds, animals, and walls. By A.D. 800 these cultures had disappeared. A new people of the Southeast, the Mississippians, began to build large towns. They also built mounds. By about A.D. 1100, their great city of **Cahokia,** in present-day Illinois, had 20,000 people.

The Inuit of the harsh Arctic culture area settled there about 2000 B.C. They adapted by using seals and other animals for food, clothing, tools, and cooking. They built homes from snow and ice. They used dog sleds or kayaks to travel.

The Northwest Coast provided Native Americans with plenty of fish and game for food, and trees for building homes. Wealth gained from trading surplus goods was shared in a **potlatch** ceremony. In this ceremony, a high-ranking person gave gifts to a large number of guests.

Several Native American groups of the Northeast were known as the Iroquois. To prevent constant warfare they formed the **Iroquois League.** This was an alliance of five Iroquois groups, known as the Five Nations.

Review Questions

1. Why did the Anasazi build on cliffs?

_____

_____

2. How did the Inuit adapt to their environment?

_____

_____

READING CHECK

Which Native American culture group built the city of Cahokia?

_____

_____

_____

VOCABULARY STRATEGY

Find the word *complexes* in the underlined sentence. What do you think *complexes* means? Read ahead for context clues. Note that the word *complex* is also used to describe Pueblo Bonito. Use these context clues to help you figure out the meaning of *complexes*.

READING SKILL

Compare and Contrast How were the people of the Northwest Coast culture area different from those in the Arctic culture area?

_____

_____

_____

Name_____ Class_____ Date_____

Focus Question: How did Germanic tribes divide Western Europe into small kingdoms?

A. *As you read this section in your textbook, use the table below to identify main ideas for each red heading. Some items have been entered for you.*

Early Medieval Europe	
Heading	**Main Idea**
Western Europe in Decline	After the collapse of Rome, from about 500 to 1000, Western Europe entered a period of political, social, and economic decline.
The Rise of the Germanic Kingdoms	
The Age of Charlemagne	
Europe After Charlemagne	

B. *As you read "The Age of Charlemagne," use the table below to identify main ideas about Charlemagne's rule. Some items have been entered for you.*

The Age of Charlemagne	
Heading	**Main Idea**
A New Emperor of the Romans	Pope Leo III crowned Charlemagne Emperor of the Romans in 800.
Creating a Unified Christian Empire	
A Revival of Learning	

Name_____ Class_____ Date_____

Section Summary
THE EARLY MIDDLE AGES

After the Roman empire fell, Western Europe was cut off from other cultures, invaded, and divided. The period from 500 to 1000 is sometimes called the Dark Ages. It was actually a time when Greco-Roman, Germanic, and Christian traditions slowly blended. They combined to create a new, **medieval** civilization. This civilization is called the Middle Ages.

In the early Middle Ages, Germanic tribes, such as the **Franks,** divided Western Europe. In 486, **Clovis,** king of the Franks, defeated Gaul, the area that became France. Clovis kept his own customs but also kept Roman customs, and he converted to Christianity. In the 600s, Islam began in Arabia. Muslims, or believers in Islam, created a huge empire. When they crossed into France, **Charles Martel** and his Frankish warriors fought the Muslim armies at the **battle of Tours** in 732. The Franks pushed the Muslims back into Spain.

In 768, Charles Martel's grandson, also named Charles, became king. He built an empire covering what are now France, Germany, and part of Italy. He became known as **Charlemagne,** or Charles the Great. Later, the pope crowned him emperor of the Romans. Charlemagne united Europe by fighting off invaders, conquering peoples, and converting them to Christianity. He also united Europe by blending German, Roman, and Christian traditions. <u>Charlemagne saw education as another way to unify his kingdom.</u> Even though he could not read or write, he felt education was important. He brought back Latin learning. He also set up local schools.

However, the unity did not last. Charlemagne's grandsons split up the empire in 843. About 900, nomads, called **Magyars,** settled in what is now Hungary. They overran Eastern Europe and moved west, but were finally pushed back. In the late 700s, the **Vikings** from Scandinavia began raiding towns along European coasts and rivers. Eventually they settled in England, Ireland, northern France, and parts of Russia.

Review Questions

1. Who stopped the Muslim advance into Europe?

_____

_____

2. What did Charlemagne do to unify his kingdom?

_____

_____

READING CHECK

Where did the Vikings come from?

_____

_____

_____

VOCABULARY STRATEGY

Find the word *unify* in the underlined sentence. What does *unify* mean? The root word *uni-* is Latin for "one." The suffix *-fy* means "make." Use this information about word parts to help you figure out the meaning of *unify.*

READING SKILL

Identify Main Ideas Find the sentences at the beginning of the Summary that represent the main idea of the Summary. Write the sentences on the lines below.

_____

_____

_____

Name_____ Class_____ Date_____

Focus Question: How did feudalism and the manor economy emerge and shape medieval life?

As you read this section in your textbook, use the flowchart below to identify the main ideas for each red heading. One main idea has been entered for you.

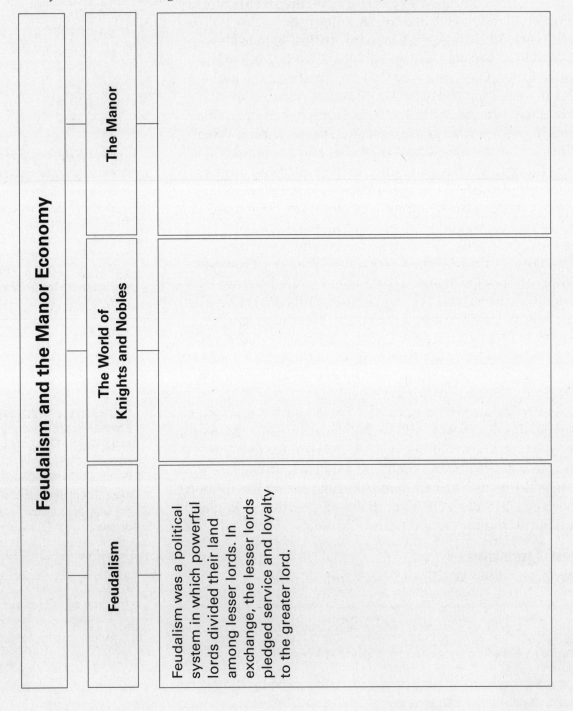

Feudalism and the Manor Economy

The Manor

The World of Knights and Nobles

Feudalism

Feudalism was a political system in which powerful lords divided their land among lesser lords. In exchange, the lesser lords pledged service and loyalty to the greater lord.

CHAPTER 7
SECTION 2

Section Summary
FEUDALISM AND THE MANOR ECONOMY

Medieval society was a web of duties. Even kings and nobles exchanged vows of service and loyalty. These vows were part of a new political and legal system, called **feudalism.** This system was the basis of life during the Middle Ages.

Feudalism was a system of rule made up of lords and lower lords, called **vassals.** They exchanged vows called the **feudal contract.** This contract gave the lords the right to expect military service, payments, and loyalty from their vassals. In return, the lords promised to give their vassals protection and **fiefs,** or estates. Many of these nobles lived in fortress-like homes called castles.

All aristocrats had a place in this structured society. For nobles, war was a way of life. Many trained from boyhood to become **knights.** They learned to ride horseback, fight, and care for weapons. They practiced fighting in pretend battles called **tournaments.** Noblewomen, too, shared in the warrior society. Ladies took over estates while their lords were at war and might even be in charge of defending their lands.

In the Middle Ages, knights had to follow a code of ideal conduct called **chivalry.** It required knights to be brave, loyal, and honest. **Troubadours,** or wandering musicians, often sang about knights and their ladies.

The **manor,** or lord's estate, was the basis of the medieval economy. Everything that people needed was grown or made on the manor. Most peasants on manors were **serfs,** workers tied to the land. Serfs were not slaves, but they could not leave the manor without permission. They had to work the lord's lands several days a week, pay certain fees, and ask permission to marry. In return, they were allowed to farm several acres for themselves and received protection during war. Their work was hard. Hunger and disease were common. Yet, they found times to celebrate, including Christmas and Easter.

Review Questions

1. What was one promise vassals made to their lords in the feudal contract?

_____

_____

2. How was the manor the basis of the medieval economy?

_____

_____

READING CHECK

What was the code of ideal conduct that knights had to follow?

_____

_____

_____

VOCABULARY STRATEGY

Find the word *aristocrats* in the underlined sentence. What does *aristocrats* mean? Reread the paragraph. What group of people is being discussed? Are these people serfs or nobles? Use these clues to help you figure out what *aristocrats* means.

READING SKILL

Identify Main Ideas Write a sentence on the lines below that identifies the main idea of this Summary. Be sure to include the word *feudalism* in your sentence.

_____

_____

_____

Note Taking Study Guide

THE MEDIEVAL CHURCH

Focus Question: How did the Church play a vital role in medieval life?

As you read this section in your textbook, use the concept web below to identify main ideas for all the headings in the section. Some items have been entered for you.

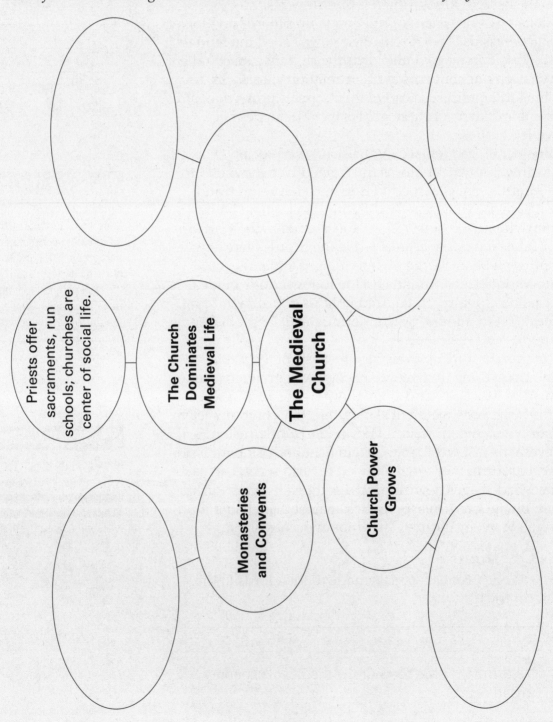

Priests offer sacraments, run schools; churches are center of social life.

The Church Dominates Medieval Life

The Medieval Church

Monasteries and Convents

Church Power Grows

CHAPTER 7 SECTION 3

Section Summary

THE MEDIEVAL CHURCH

During the Middle Ages, the Roman Church grew in power. It became the strongest worldly, or **secular,** and religious force in Western Europe. For most people, churches were the center of village life. The parish priest celebrated mass and administered **sacraments,** or sacred rites. Church doctrine also taught that men and women were equal before God. Yet the Church also taught that women needed men's guidance. Many people went into monasteries or convents to live a religious life. In 530, a monk named Benedict created rules to govern monastery life. These required vows of obedience, poverty, and chastity, or purity. In time, monasteries and convents all across Europe followed this **Benedictine Rule.**

High Church officials, such as bishops or the pope, often stopped warfare among nobles by declaring a Truce of God. Medieval popes developed **papal supremacy,** or authority over rulers. The Church had its own courts and body of laws, known as **canon law,** and gave out punishments. One was **excommunication,** or refusing to give the sacraments and Christian burial. This condemned sinners to hell. Also, rulers could face **interdict,** which kept entire towns, regions, or kingdoms from receiving sacraments and Christian burial.

However, as Church wealth and power grew, so did corruption. Many priests, monks, and nuns ignored their vows. Throughout medieval times, there were calls for reform. In the early 900s, the Benedictine Rule was brought back, and many monasteries and convents began to change. Other reforms came from **friars,** or monks who traveled and preached to the poor. The first order of friars, called the Franciscans, was founded by **St. Francis of Assisi.**

In the Middle Ages, Jewish people settled all across Europe. However, by the late 1000s, prejudice against them had increased in Western Europe. The Church even issued orders to keep Jews from owning land or having certain jobs. Thousands migrated to Eastern Europe.

Review Questions

1. What three vows did the Benedictine Rule require?

_____

_____

2. What caused corruption to grow in the Church?

_____

_____

READING CHECK

What was papal supremacy?

_____

_____

_____

VOCABULARY STRATEGY

Find the word *doctrine* in the underlined sentence. What context clue tells you that it had to do with teaching? Who was doing the teaching? Use these context clues to help you figure out what *doctrine* means.

READING SKILL

Identify Main Ideas Find and underline the sentences that give the main idea of the Summary.

CHAPTER 7 SECTION 4 — Note Taking Study Guide
ECONOMIC RECOVERY SPARKS CHANGE

Focus Question: How did changes in agriculture and trade lead to the growth of towns and commerce?

As you read this section in your textbook, identify the main ideas of each heading using the outline below. Some items have been completed for you.

Economic Recovery Sparks Change

I. **1000s—agricultural revolution changed Europe.**

   A. New technologies allowed farmers to grow more crops.

   B. Food production increased and the population grew.

II. **Warfare and invasions declined.**

   A. Trade expanded into the Middle East and Asia; trade leagues formed.

   B. _____

III. **Growing trade led to a commercial revolution.**

   A. _____

   B. _____

IV. _____

   A. _____

   B. _____

   C. _____

V. _____

   A. _____

CHAPTER 7
SECTION 4

Section Summary
ECONOMIC RECOVERY SPARKS CHANGE

New farming methods started a series of changes in medieval Europe. By the 800s, farmers were using iron plows instead of wooden ones and harnesses fit for horses rather than slower oxen. Also, crop rotation helped soil fertility. With these changes, farmers grew more food, and Europe's population almost tripled between 1000 and 1300.

Trade improved, too, as war declined. Demand for goods grew and trade routes expanded. Trade centers became the first medieval cities. Merchants in these cities would ask the local lord or king for a **charter,** a document establishing rights and privileges for the town in exchange for money.

As trade expanded, new business practices arose. The need for **capital,** or money for investment, stimulated the growth of banks. In addition, merchants sometimes joined together in **partnerships,** pooling their money to finance large-scale ventures. Other business changes included development of insurance and use of credit rather than cash, allowing merchants to travel without having to carry gold. Overall, however, the use of money increased. Peasants began selling their goods to townspeople for cash. Also, by 1300, most peasants were hired laborers, or **tenant farmers,** paying rent for their land.

By 1000, merchants, traders, and artisans had become a new social class between nobles and peasants, called the **middle class.** The members of this class formed **guilds** to control and protect each trade or business. To become guild members, people started in early childhood as **apprentices.** After seven years, an apprentice became a **journeyman,** or salaried worker. Few became guild masters. Unlike in other areas of medieval life, women controlled some trades and even had their own guilds.

Towns and cities expanded rapidly during medieval times. Typical cities were overcrowded, with narrow streets, multi-story houses, and no garbage or sewage systems. They were a fire hazard and breeding ground for disease.

Review Questions

1. How were farmers able to grow more food?

_____

_____

2. What two new business practices arose as trade expanded in the Middle Ages?

_____

_____

READING CHECK

What was a charter?

_____

_____

_____

VOCABULARY STRATEGY

Find the word *stimulated* in the underlined sentence. What does *stimulated* mean? Some synonyms for *stimulated* include *awakened, excited,* and *inspired.* Use what you may know about the meanings of these synonyms to help you figure out the meaning of *stimulated.*

READING SKILL

Identify Main Ideas Write a new title for this Summary. Be sure to include the word *change* in your title.

_____

_____

_____

CHAPTER 8 SECTION 1

Note Taking Study Guide
ROYAL POWER GROWS

Focus Question: How did monarchs in England and France expand royal authority and lay the foundations for united nation-states?

A. *As you read this section in your textbook, use the cause-effect chart to identify the causes for changes in royal power. Some items have been completed for you.*

Royal Power Changes

William the Conqueror	Henry II	John
• Increased power	• Increased power	• Lost power
• Kept land for himself	• Expanded custom into law	• _____
• _____	• _____	• _____
• _____	• _____	• _____

B. *As you read this section in your textbook, use the Venn diagram to compare and contrast the development of royal power in England and France. Some items have been completed for you.*

England   **France**

• Unified kingdom

• Action by nobles limits royal power.

• Conflicts with Church

• _____

• _____

• Patchwork territories

• _____

• _____

CHAPTER 8 SECTION 1

Section Summary
ROYAL POWER GROWS

During the early Middle Ages, European rulers had limited power. By 1300, increases in royal power and control had gradually set the foundations of modern government.

In 1066, **William the Conqueror** took over England. In 1086, William's census, called the *Domesday Book,* was finished. The information in the *Domesday Book* helped William's government set up a tax system. In 1154, Henry II came to power, and he expanded the justice system. Court decisions became the basis of English **common law,** a legal system based on custom and earlier rulings. Henry also set up a **jury** system that led to the modern grand jury.

Henry's son, **King John,** abused his power and was forced to sign the **Magna Carta,** or Great Charter. It required the king to obey the laws. It also established two important principles: **due process of law,** or no arrest without proper legal procedures, and **habeas corpus,** or no imprisonment without a charge. John also agreed not to raise taxes without the consent of his Great Council. This group evolved into **Parliament,** England's legislature. Eventually Parliament controlled the "power of the purse," not approving new taxes unless the monarch met its demands.

Unlike the English, early French rulers did not govern a united kingdom. Then in 987, Hugh Capet became king. He began expanding royal power. The Capets ruled for 300 years. In 1179, Philip II took the throne. He gained control of English lands in Normandy and expanded territories in southern France, adding huge areas to his domain.

Louis IX came to power in France in 1226. Although he persecuted non-Christians, he also outlawed private wars and ended serfdom. By the time of his death in 1270, France had become a centralized monarchy. In 1302, a council, the Estates General, was set up. However, it never gained the "power of the purse" over French royalty.

Review Questions

1. What did the *Domesday Book* help set up?

_____

_____

2. What is the "power of the purse"?

_____

_____

READING CHECK

What important English document required the king to obey the laws?

_____

_____

_____

VOCABULARY STRATEGY

Find the word *domain* in the underlined sentence. What does *domain* mean? What clues can you find in nearby words or phrases? Think about the fact that Philip was a king and that he added lands to something that was his. Circle any words that help you figure out what *domain* means.

READING SKILL

Identify Causes How did the Magna Carta help Parliament gain "the power of the purse"?

_____

_____

_____

CHAPTER 8 SECTION 2

Note Taking Study Guide

THE HOLY ROMAN EMPIRE AND THE CHURCH

Focus Question: How did explosive conflicts between monarchs and popes affect the balance of power in Europe?

As you read this section in your textbook, complete the table below showing the actions of emperors and popes and the effects of their actions. Some items have been completed for you.

Pope or Emperor	Actions	Effects
Otto I	• Cooperated with Church	• Pope crowned Otto emperor.
Gregory VII	• Banned lay investiture, excommunicated Henry IV	• Forgave Henry, then was forced into exile
Henry IV	•	•
Frederick I	•	•
Innocent III	•	•
	•	•

CHAPTER 8
SECTION 2

Section Summary
THE HOLY ROMAN EMPIRE AND THE CHURCH

During the Middle Ages, popes and European rulers grew more powerful. However, they were often in conflict.

By the late 1000s, the rulers of the **Holy Roman Empire** were trying to hold together a vast and varied territory. As part of this, they regularly confronted the pope over naming Church officials. **Pope Gregory VII** wanted the Church to be free from any control by rulers. He banned **lay investiture,** or the process by which rulers rather than the pope appoints a bishop. Holy Roman Emperor **Henry IV** said he had the right to appoint bishops because bishops held lands that were under his control. In 1076, pope Gregory excommunicated Henry and threatened to crown a new emperor. Henry was forced to beg for forgiveness, and Gregory gave it. Later, Henry led an army to Rome, forcing Gregory into exile. Fifty years later a compromise was worked out in the Concordat of Worms. It gave the pope the power to appoint bishops, while rulers had the right to decide what lands the bishops would rule.

Power struggles over land also occurred during the 1100s and 1200s. Holy Roman Emperor Frederick I, called **Frederick Barbarossa,** or "Red Beard," tried to add wealthy northern Italian cities to his empire. Instead, through his son's marriage, he expanded German control in southern Italy. His grandson, Frederick II, also tried, but failed, to control northern Italy. Ultimately, the Holy Roman Empire broke into separate states, while southern Italy went through centuries of chaos.

By the 1200s, the Church reached its peak of power. In 1198, **Pope Innocent III** took office. He claimed that the pope had supremacy, or authority over all other rulers. He excommunicated the English and French kings, and placed their kingdoms under interdict, barring people from religious sacraments. After Innocent's death, French and English rulers grew in power. In the late 1200s, France's Philip IV challenged the pope on the issue of taxes, and then forced the election of a French pope.

Review Questions

1. Why did Henry IV think he had the right to appoint bishops?

_____

_____

2. What were two ways Innocent III controlled monarchs?

_____

_____

READING CHECK

What was the Concordat of Worms?

_____

_____

_____

VOCABULARY STRATEGY

Find the word *confronted* in the underlined sentence. *Confronted* is made from three word parts: the prefix *con-* means "together"; *front* means "the part of something that is facing forward"; *-ed* is a suffix that indicates past tense. Use these word-part clues to help you figure out the meaning of *confronted*.

READING SKILL

Understand Effects Reread the first paragraph of this Summary. What was the effect of the increase in power?

_____

_____

_____

CHAPTER

8

SECTION 3

Note Taking Study Guide

THE CRUSADES AND THE WIDER WORLD

Focus Question: How did the Crusades change life in Europe and beyond?

As you read this section in your textbook, complete the concept web below to identify the causes of the Crusades in the top ovals and the effects of the Crusades in the lower ovals. Some items have been completed for you.

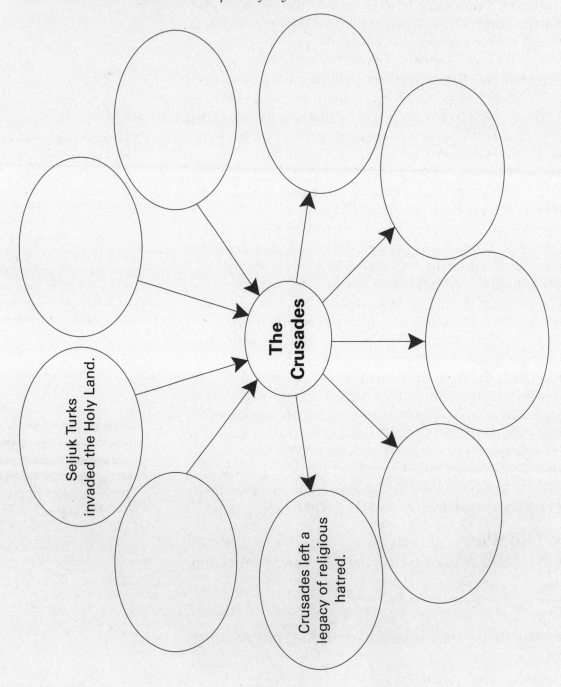

CHAPTER 8 SECTION 3

Section Summary

THE CRUSADES AND THE WIDER WORLD

In 1071, the Seljuk Turks invaded the Byzantine empire, then moved into the **Holy Land.** The Byzantine emperor asked **Pope Urban II** for help. The pope then called for a crusade to free the Holy Land. The **Crusades** were a series of wars Christians fought against Muslims over lands in the Middle East. Only the First Crusade was a success. Christian forces captured Jerusalem in 1099. They then lost the city to Muslims in the Second Crusade and failed to retake it in the Third. By the Fourth Crusade in 1202, Christian knights were fighting other Christians to help Venice against its Byzantine trade rivals.

The Crusades created a great deal of religious hatred. On the other hand, they helped to unify various powers under one leader. The Crusades also produced important changes in the Europe. Trade increased, as Europeans brought back spices and fabrics from the Middle East. Monarchs gained the right to collect taxes to support the Crusades. This made them more powerful. Europeans found out about many new places and people. A few curious Europeans set off for far-off places. In 1271, Marco Polo left Venice for China and wrote about his journey when he returned. Trade and travel brought new knowledge to Europe.

Around 1100, Christian kingdoms in Spain began a struggle called the **Reconquista,** or reconquest. The purpose was to force Muslims from Spain. In 1469, the marriage of **Ferdinand and Isabella** unified Spain. Later in 1492, the Christian monarchs captured the last Muslim center, Granada. Under Muslim rule, Christians, Jews, and Muslims had lived together fairly well. However, Ferdinand and Isabella wanted all their diverse peoples to be Christians. They started a violent campaign against Muslims and Jews. They were helped by the **Inquisition,** a Church court. Those found guilty of non-Christian beliefs were burned at the stake. Thousands of Muslims and Jews fled Spain to escape persecution.

Review Questions

1. Why was the First Crusade a success for Christians?

_____

_____

2. How did the Crusades make monarchs more powerful?

_____

_____

READING CHECK

What were the Crusades?

_____

_____

_____

VOCABULARY STRATEGY

Find the word *diverse* in the underlined sentence. Two antonyms, or words that mean the opposite of *diverse,* are *same* and *alike.* Use your knowledge of these antonyms to help you figure out the meaning of *diverse.*

READING SKILL

Identify Causes and Effects List one cause and one effect of the Inquisition. Think about what Ferdinand and Isabella wanted to achieve.

_____

_____

_____

Name_____ Class_____ Date_____

Focus Question: What achievements in learning, literature, and the arts characterized the High Middle Ages?

As you read this section in your textbook, fill in the flowchart below to record the multiple causes of the cultural and intellectual flowering of the Middle Ages. Some items have been completed for you.

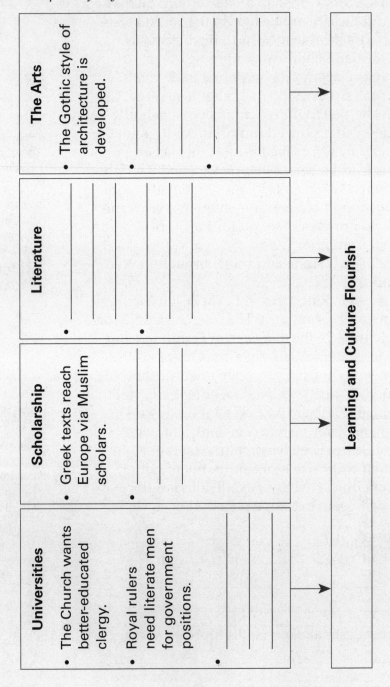

The Arts
- The Gothic style of architecture is developed.

Literature

Scholarship
- Greek texts reach Europe via Muslim scholars.

Universities
- The Church wants better-educated clergy.
- Royal rulers need literate men for government positions.

→ **Learning and Culture Flourish**

CHAPTER
8
SECTION 4

Section Summary
LEARNING AND CULTURE FLOURISH

Europe in the High Middle Ages saw huge growth in education, literature, and the arts. This was caused by wealth from trade, contact with other cultures, and the rediscovery of ancient learning.

By the 1100s, schools were built near cathedrals to train clergy. Some of them became the first universities. Ancient learning had an impact on education, too. Greek texts, which had been translated into Arabic by Muslim scholars, spread to Muslim Spain. There they were translated into Latin. In the 1100s, these new translations initiated a revolution in learning. Greek thinkers, such as Aristotle, had used reason to discover truth. Medieval Europeans had believed that Church teachings and faith were the authority on all questions. Now Christian scholars began to use reason to support their religious faith and beliefs. This method is known as **scholasticism.** The most famous scholastic was **Thomas Aquinas.** He wrote *Summa theologica* to show that faith and reason can work together.

New scientific learning reached Europe at this time, too, including writings on medicine and geometry. Europeans also began using simpler Hindu-Arabic numerals, instead of the harder-to-use Roman numerals.

Latin was the language of Europe's scholars and churchmen. However, new literature appeared in the **vernacular,** or everyday languages of ordinary people. **Dante Alighieri** wrote *Divine Comedy*, an Italian poem about heaven and hell. **Geoffrey Chaucer** wrote the *Canterbury Tales.* That book has been an important source of modern knowledge of English medieval life.

Architecture and the arts also flourished. Dark, low, and heavy Romanesque churches gave way around 1140 to the **Gothic style.** Its key feature was **flying buttresses,** outside stone supports that let walls rise higher with bigger windows, bringing light and height to cathedrals. Other arts of the period include stained glass, religious paintings, and woven wall hangings called tapestries. Artists of the 1300s and 1400s used **illumination,** to decorate prayer books and other texts.

Review Questions

1. What was the goal of scholasticism?

_____

_____

2. How did Gothic style differ from Romanesque ?

_____

READING CHECK

Who wrote *Divine Comedy?*

_____

_____

_____

VOCABULARY STRATEGY

Find the word *initiated* in the underlined sentence. What does it mean? The word *initiated* is a verb and so describes an action. It comes from a Latin word that means "to begin." Use this information about word origins to figure out the meaning of *initiated*.

READING SKILL

Recognize Multiple Causes
Circle the causes below that contributed to the growth of education, literature, and the arts during the High Middle Ages.

1. Greater wealth from trade

2. Contact with other cultures

3. The right of habeas corpus

4. Rediscovery of ancient learning

Name_____ Class_____ Date_____

Focus Question: How did the combination of plague, upheaval in the Church, and war affect Europe in the 1300s and 1400s?

A. *As you read "The Black Death: A Global Epidemic," complete the flowchart to record the causes and effects of Black Death. Some items have been entered for you.*

Causes of Black Death	**The Black Death in Europe**	**Effects of the Black Death**
• Bubonic plague • _____ _____ • _____ _____	• People turn to magic and witchcraft. • _____ • _____ _____ • _____ _____	• One-third of people die. • _____ _____ • _____ _____ • _____ _____

B. *As you read "The Hundred Years' War," complete the flowchart to recognize the causes and the effects of the war. Some items have been entered for you.*

	Hundred Years' War	**Effects**
• English rulers want to retain French lands. • French kings want to extend their power. • _____ _____	• England wins battles due to longbow. • _____ _____ • _____ _____	• French monarchs grow stronger. • English Parliament gains "power of the purse." • _____ • _____ • _____

CHAPTER 8 SECTION 5

Section Summary

A TIME OF CRISIS

Events in Europe during the 1300s and 1400s led to changes that caused the end of the Middle Ages. In the mid-1300s a deadly disease called bubonic plague, or **Black Death,** reached Europe. The **epidemic,** or outbreak, killed one-third of all Europeans. People left cities to avoid close contact with victims. By the late 1300s, fewer workers meant that fewer goods were produced. Survivors wanted higher wages. This led to **inflation,** or rising prices. Villagers were forced off lands as landlords grew crops instead of raising sheep. This led to social unrest, such as peasant revolts.

The Church, too, was in crisis by the late Middle Ages. Death everywhere led to spiritual questions. Many monks and priests had died during the plague. The Church was not able to help people. A pleasure-loving papal court reigned in Avignon in France. Soon, reformers arose within the Church and, in 1378, elected their own pope in Rome. French cardinals elected a rival pope. This Church **schism,** or split, finally ended in 1417.

Another crisis, the Hundred Years' War, began in 1337. England and France fought for control of French lands, the English Channel, and regional trade. England won early victories with their new **longbows,** which were more effective weapons than French crossbows. Yet France made a comeback in 1429, led by 17-year-old Joan of Arc. Joan told Charles VII, the uncrowned French king, that God had sent her to save France. He authorized her to lead an army against the English. Her troops won several battles in just one year, but she was captured and burned at the stake. Yet, her death rallied French forces. Using cannons, powerful new weapons, they drove the English out of most of France. Cannons and longbows led to changes in society as feudal knights gave way to standing armies.

In the end, Europe recovered from the plague, its population grew, and manufacturing and trade increased. This set the stage for the Renaissance, Reformation, and Age of Exploration.

Review Questions

1. How deadly was the bubonic plague?

_____

_____

2. What was the Hundred Years' War fought over?

_____

_____

READING CHECK

Who was Joan of Arc?

_____

_____

_____

VOCABULARY STRATEGY

Find the word *authorized* in the underlined sentence. What does *authorized* mean? The word *authorized* comes from a Latin word that means "power." Think about who normally would be *authorized* to lead armies. Use these clues to figure out what *authorized* means.

READING SKILL

Recognize Causes and Effects
What caused fewer goods to be produced in the 1300s? What was the effect?

_____

_____

_____

CHAPTER 9 SECTION 1

Note Taking Study Guide
THE BYZANTINE EMPIRE

Focus Question: What made the Byzantine empire rich and successful for so long, and why did it finally crumble?

As you read this section in your textbook, complete the table below to keep track of the sequence of events in the Byzantine empire. Some items have been completed for you.

The Byzantine Empire								
Constantinople becomes the capital of the eastern Roman empire.			Byzantine emperor outlaws the worship of icons.		Western Christians help Byzantine empire in the First Crusade.			
330	527–565	532						1453

CHAPTER 9 SECTION 1 — Section Summary
THE BYZANTINE EMPIRE

The Roman emperor Constantine rebuilt Byzantium and named it **Constantinople.** Constantinople got its wealth from trade. In 330, Constantine made Constantinople the capital of the Roman empire. In time, the eastern Roman empire became known as the Byzantine empire.

The Byzantine empire reached its peak under **Justinian.** His armies reconquered lost parts of the old Roman empire. <u>However, these victories were only temporary.</u> Later emperors lost these lands again. After a fire in 532, Justinian made Constantinople even grander, rebuilding the church of Hagia Sophia. Justinian also had the laws of ancient Rome organized into a collection known as **Justinian's Code.** He ruled the empire as an **autocrat,** or sole ruler with complete authority. His wife, **Theodora,** served as his advisor and co-ruler.

The Byzantine emperor controlled Church affairs. He appointed the **patriarch** in Constantinople. The patriarch, not the pope, was the highest Church official in the Byzantine empire. During the Middle Ages, eastern and western Christianity grew apart. This was due in part to a disagreement over **icons,** or holy images. In 1054, other disagreements caused a complete split known as the **Great Schism.** The Byzantine church became known as the Eastern Orthodox Church. The western church became known as the Roman Catholic Church.

By this time, the Byzantine empire was declining. In the 1090s, the Byzantine emperor asked the pope for help against the Muslim Seljuks. This started the First Crusade. In 1204, knights on the Fourth Crusade attacked Constantinople. The Byzantines lost control of trade and much of their wealth. In 1453, Ottoman Turks conquered Constantinople. They renamed it Istanbul, and made it the capital of their empire.

The Byzantines left an important legacy. They combined Christian beliefs with Greek science, philosophy, and arts. Their scholars preserved Greek literature. They also produced their own great books, especially in history.

Review Questions

1. Who controlled the Byzantine church?

_____

_____

2. Who conquered Constantinople in 1453?

_____

_____

READING CHECK

What was the Great Schism?

_____

_____

_____

VOCABULARY STRATEGY

Find the word *temporary* in the underlined sentence. What does it mean? An antonym for this word is *permanent.* Use what you know about the meaning of this antonym to help you figure out what *temporary* means. Which of the phrases below is the correct definition of *temporary*?

1. lasting for a long time

2. lasting for a short time

READING SKILL

Recognize Sequence
Constantinople has also been named Istanbul and Byzantium. List the three names for this city in chronological order.

_____

_____

_____

Name_____ Class_____ Date_____

Focus Question: How did geography and the migrations of different peoples influence the rise of Russia?

As you read this section in your textbook, complete the timeline below to sequence the events in the rise of Russia from the 700s to the 1500s. Some items have been completed for you.

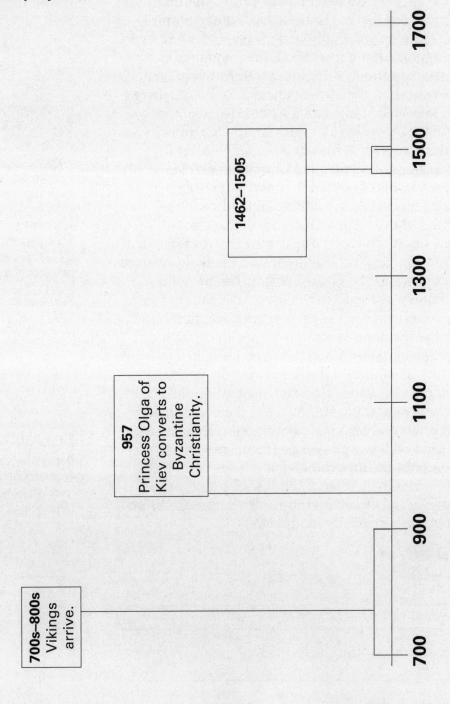

700s–800s
Vikings arrive.

957
Princess Olga of Kiev converts to Byzantine Christianity.

1462–1505

700

900

1100

1300

1500

1700

CHAPTER 9 SECTION 2

Section Summary

THE RISE OF RUSSIA

Russia has three main regions. The northern forests are cold, with poor soil. In the south, fertile land made farming possible. The **steppe** is an open, treeless grassland. It provided pasture for herds and allowed nomads to move from Asia into Europe.

Two peoples came together to form the first Russian state. The Slavs came from Asia to southern Russia. Vikings traveled south along Russia's rivers, and traded with the Slavs and with Constantinople. The city of **Kiev** was at the center of this trade. Russians date the start of their country at 862, when a Viking tribe called the Rus began to rule. Kiev was their capital.

In the 800s, Constantinople sent missionaries to Russia. Two Orthodox monks developed the **Cyrillic** alphabet, which is still used in Russia. During the reign of the Rus king Vladimir, Orthodox Christianity became the religion of the Rus. Russians soon began to follow other aspects of Byzantine culture.

Between 1236 and 1241, Mongols invaded Russia. They were known as the **Golden Horde.** They controlled Russia for the next 240 years. They demanded tribute, but let Russian princes continue to rule. <u>They also tolerated the Russian Orthodox Church.</u> Trade increased under the Mongols. However, Mongol rule cut Russia off from Western Europe, where many advances were being made.

In 1380, the princes of Moscow led other Russians to a victory against the Golden Horde. Moscow then became Russia's political and spiritual center. **Ivan the Great,** who ruled between 1462 and 1505, took control of much of northern Russia. He tried to limit the power of the nobles and sometimes called himself **tsar.** This is the Russian word for Caesar. His grandson, Ivan IV, became the first Russian ruler officially crowned tsar. However, Ivan IV became unstable and violent, earning the name **Ivan the Terrible.**

Review Questions

1. What region of Russia allowed nomads from Asia to move into Europe?

_____

_____

2. When did the Rus adopt Orthodox Christianity?

_____

_____

READING CHECK

What does the word *tsar* mean?

_____

_____

_____

VOCABULARY STRATEGY

Find the word *tolerated* in the underlined sentence. What does it mean? The previous sentence states that the Mongols "<u>let</u> the Russian princes <u>continue</u> to rule." If they "<u>also</u> *tolerated*" the Russian Orthodox Church, do you think they let the Russian people continue to practice their beliefs? Use this context clue to help you understand the meaning of the word *tolerated.*

READING SKILL

Recognize Sequence Three groups are mentioned in the Summary: the Mongols, the Slavs, and the Vikings, or Rus. List these groups in the order in which they came to Russia.

_____

_____

_____

Name_____ Class_____ Date_____

Focus Question: How did geography and ethnic diversity contribute to the turmoil of Eastern European history?

A. *As you read "Geography Shapes Eastern Europe" and "Migrations Contribute to Diversity," complete the concept web to record the conditions and events that led to the diversity of peoples and cultures in Eastern Europe. Some items have been completed for you.*

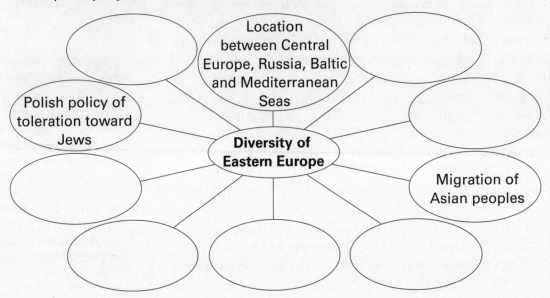

B. *As you read "Three Early Kingdoms Develop," complete the chart below to help you sequence the events in the history of these countries. Some items have been completed for you.*

Important Events in Eastern Europe		
Poland	**Hungary**	**Serbia**
• Missionaries bring Roman Catholicism to West Slavs (900s).	• Magyars settle in Hungary and adopt Roman Catholicism.	• _____
• _____	• _____	• Serbs accept Orthodox Christianity (800s).
• _____	• _____	• _____
• _____	• _____	• _____
• _____	• _____	• _____

CHAPTER 9 SECTION 3	**Section Summary**
	SHAPING EASTERN EUROPE

Eastern Europe borders Central Europe in the west, and Russia in the east. This region includes the **Balkan Peninsula.** Because migration into Eastern Europe was easy, many ethnic groups settled there. An **ethnic group** is a large group of people who share the same culture. West Slavs from Russia settled in Poland and other parts of Eastern Europe. South Slavs settled in the Balkans. Asian peoples, Vikings, and Germanic peoples also migrated to Eastern Europe. <u>At times, different groups tried to dominate the region.</u>

Many cultural and religious influences spread to Eastern Europe. Byzantine missionaries brought Eastern Orthodox Christianity and Byzantine culture to the Balkans. German knights and missionaries brought Roman Catholic Christianity to Poland and other areas. In the 1300s, the Ottomans brought Islam to the Balkans. Jews came to Eastern Europe to escape persecution in Western Europe. Poland, in particular, became a refuge for Jews because their liberties were protected there.

During the Middle Ages, there were many kingdoms and states in Eastern Europe. In 1386, Queen Jadwiga of Poland married Duke Wladyslaw Jagiello of Lithuania. Their union created Poland-Lithuania, the largest state in Europe. However, the nobles gradually became more powerful than the monarch. They met in a **diet,** or assembly, to pass laws. Poland-Lithuania declined and eventually ceased to exist.

The Magyars from Asia settled in Hungary and became Roman Catholics. Nobles forced the Hungarian king to sign the **Golden Bull of 1222.** This limited the king's power. The Mongols overran Hungary in 1241, but soon withdrew. However, the Ottomans ended Hungarian independence in 1526.

Some of the South Slavs in the Balkans became the ancestors of the Serbs. Most Serbs became Orthodox Christians. They set up a state based on a Byzantine model. Serbia reached its height in the 1300s, but it, too, fell to the Ottomans in 1389.

Review Questions

1. Why did so many different groups settle in Eastern Europe?

_____

_____

2. What two countries combined in 1386 to form the largest state in Europe?

_____

_____

READING CHECK

What people brought Islam to the Balkans?

_____

_____

_____

VOCABULARY STRATEGY

Find the word *dominate* in the underlined sentence. What does it mean? The word *dominate* comes from the Latin word *dominus,* which means "master" or "lord." How might a group of people become the "master" of a region? Which of the following words is closest in meaning to *dominate*?

1. control

2. leave

READING SKILL

Recognize Multiple Causes
Many Jewish people migrated from Western Europe to Poland in the 1300s. What was one reason why they sought refuge in Poland?

_____

_____

_____

Note Taking Study Guide
THE RISE OF ISLAM

Focus Question: What messages, or teachings, did Muhammad spread through Islam?

A. *As you read the section "Muhammad Becomes a Prophet" in your textbook, complete the following timeline to help you record the sequence of events. Some items have been completed for you.*

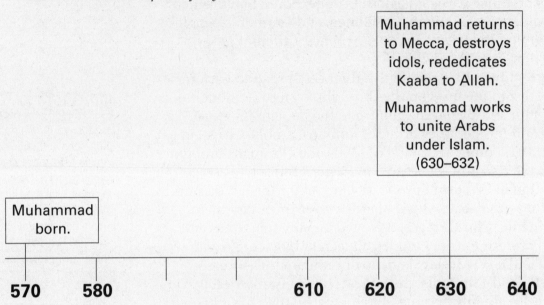

Muhammad returns to Mecca, destroys idols, rededicates Kaaba to Allah.

Muhammad works to unite Arabs under Islam. (630–632)

Muhammad born.

570   580   610   620   630   640

B. *As you read the section "Teachings of Islam" in your textbook, complete the following concept web to keep track of the teachings of Islam. Some items have been completed for you.*

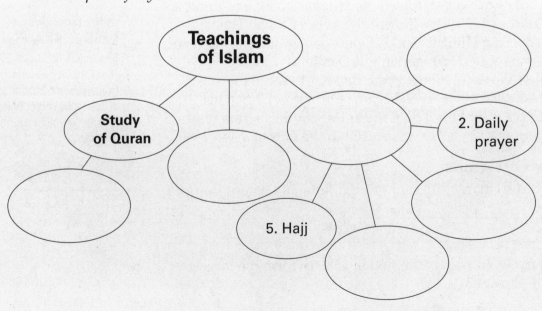

Teachings of Islam

Study of Quran

2. Daily prayer

5. Hajj

CHAPTER 10 SECTION 1

Section Summary
THE RISE OF ISLAM

The religion of Islam, whose followers are called Muslims, began in the Arabian Peninsula. There in A.D. 570, **Muhammad** was born in the oasis town of **Mecca.** As a youth, he was a shepherd. He worked with nomadic herders called **Bedouins.** Later Muhammad became a successful merchant. As an honest man, he was troubled by the greed he saw around him.

According to Muslim tradition, Muhammad became a prophet at age 40 when he was asked by an angel to become God's messenger. Muhammad began teaching, but few listened and some threatened him. In 622, he and some followers fled to **Yathrib,** later called **Medina.** The trip was called the **hijra.** There, Muslim converts agreed to follow his teachings. Meccan leaders, however, grew angry. Battles broke out between them and Muslims. However, Muhammad triumphantly returned to Mecca in 630. He destroyed the idols in the **Kaaba,** and dedicated it to Allah. The Kaaba became Islam's holiest site. Muhammad died in 632.

The **Quran** is the sacred text of Islam. It teaches about God's will and provides a guide to life. All Muslims must perform certain duties, known as the Five Pillars of Islam. These are declaring faith, praying five times daily, giving charity to the poor, fasting during the holy month, and making the **hajj,** or pilgrimage to Mecca. Muslims gather in **mosques** to pray directly to God. <u>Priests do not mediate between the faithful and God.</u> Another duty for Muslims is **jihad.** This is the need to struggle in God's service.

Islam also governs daily life. One way this is done is through the **Sharia,** a body of laws that applies religious principles to all legal situations. According to the Quran, women are spiritually equal to men but have different roles.

Because Jews and Christians worship the same God and study God's earlier teachings, Muslims call them "People of the Book." These groups have had religious freedom in most Muslim societies.

Review Questions

1. How did leaders in Mecca react to Muhammad?

_____

_____

2. What role does the Sharia play in Islamic life?

_____

_____

READING CHECK

According to Islamic belief, how did Muhammad become God's messenger?

_____

_____

_____

VOCABULARY STRATEGY

Find the word *mediate* in the underlined sentence. What do you think it means? Read the previous sentence and this sentence again. Think about the phrase "between the faithful and God." In some religions, what role might priests serve between people and God? Use this clue to help you write a definition of *mediate.*

READING SKILL

Identify Main Ideas What is the main idea of the third paragraph of this Summary?

_____

_____

_____

CHAPTER
10
SECTION 2

Note Taking Study Guide
BUILDING A MUSLIM EMPIRE

Focus Question: How did Muhammad's successors extend Muslim rule and spread Islam?

A. *As you read this section in your textbook, complete the following timeline to record the major events in the spread of Islam and the rise and fall of Muslim empires. Some items have been completed for you.*

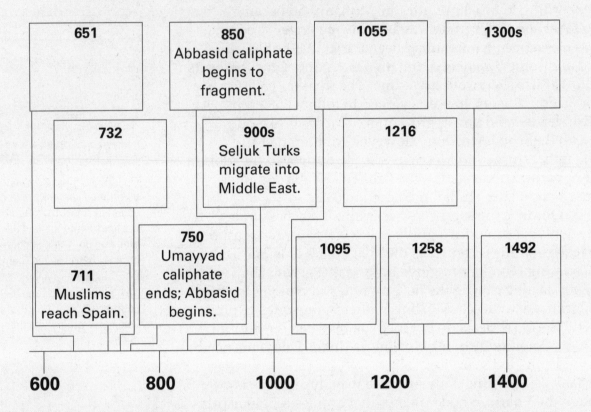

B. *As you read the section "Divisions Emerge Within Islam" in your textbook, complete the following Venn diagram to record points on which Sunni and Shiite Muslims agree and differ. Some items have been completed for you.*

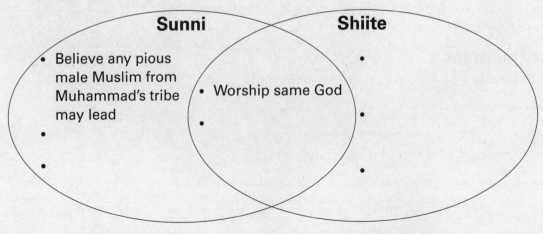

CHAPTER 10 SECTION 2

Section Summary
BUILDING A MUSLIM EMPIRE

In 632, **Abu Bakr** led Muslims as the first **caliph,** or successor to Muhammad. He united all Arab tribes. Under the first four caliphs, Arabs conquered the Persians and part of the Byzantine empire. <u>However, a schism between Sunni and Shiite Muslims occurred after Muhammad's death.</u> It still exists today. **Shiites** believe that Muslim leaders must be descendants of Muhammad's son-in-law, Ali. They also must serve as religious leaders and interpret the Quran. **Sunnis** believe pious male Muslims from Muhammad's tribe can lead without performing religious duties. Today, about 90 percent of Muslims are Sunni. Both groups share basic Muslim beliefs. They differ, however, in religious practices, laws, and rules about daily life. A third group, **Sufis,** meditate and fast to connect with God.

In the 700s, from their capital at Damascus, the Sunni **Umayyads** expanded the Muslim empire from Spain to the Indus River Valley. Many people were under their rule. Non-Muslims were charged a tax, but Jews, Christians, and Zoroastrians could worship freely.

However, under the Umayyads, tension grew between the wealthy and those who had less. In 750, Abu al-Abbas captured Damascus. He defeated the Umayyads and founded the **Abbasid** dynasty. The Abbasids treated all Muslims equally, ended conquests, supported education and learning, and governed efficiently. **Baghdad** became their new capital. Mosques with tall, slender **minarets** were built in the cities. Markets sold goods from far-off lands.

In Spain, a surviving Umayyad established a separate Muslim state. This government tolerated other religions, supported scholars, and constructed grand buildings. Umayyad rule lasted in parts of Spain until 1492.

As the Abbasid empire declined, dynasties such as the Seljuk Turks took power. Their **sultan** controlled Baghdad by 1055. Then, in the 1200s, the Mongols attacked across southwest Asia. They burned and looted Baghdad in 1258.

Review Questions

1. How did the Umayyads treat Jews and Christians?

_____

_____

2. Who was Abu al-Abbas?

_____

_____

READING CHECK

Which group of Muslims is the largest today?

_____

_____

_____

VOCABULARY STRATEGY

Find the word *schism* in the underlined sentence. What do you think it means? A sentence in the paragraph says Abu Bakr *united* all Arab tribes. The underlined sentence begins with the word *however. However* is a word that often signals an opposite action. Use these context clues to write a definition of *schism*

READING SKILL

Recognize Sequence Circle the event that happened first.

• Umayyads take power.

• Damascus becomes the capital.

• Abu Bakr becomes the caliph.

• The Muslim empire expands into Persia and the Byzantine empire.

CHAPTER
10
SECTION 3

Note Taking Study Guide
MUSLIM CIVILIZATION'S GOLDEN AGE

Focus Question: What achievements did Muslims make in economics, art, literature, and science?

As you read this section in your textbook, complete the following chart to categorize the advances made during the golden age of Muslim civilization. Some items have been completed for you.

Muslim Achievements	
Economics	• Built a vast trading network • _____ • Developed a sophisticated accounting system • _____ • _____ • _____
Arts	• Restricted religious art images • _____ • _____
Literature	• _____ • _____ • Best-known literature includes *The Thousand and One Nights.*
Philosophy	• _____ • _____
Sciences	• Al-Khwarizmi pioneered study of algebra and wrote math text. • _____ • Hospitals had facilities similar to today's emergency rooms. • _____ • _____

The Abbasid empire stretched into Asia, the Middle East, Africa, and Europe. As a result, Muslim civilization adopted the traditions of many cultures. Muslim traders crossed the Sahara, traveled the Silk Road, and sailed to India and Asia. They exchanged products and ideas. They introduced Islam to many regions. A common language and religion helped fuel economic growth. Soon Muslims developed partnerships and credit, and introduced banking. Artisans manufactured goods for trade.

Social mobility, or the ability to move up in society, was possible through religious, scholarly, or military achievements. Although slavery was common, Islamic law taught that freeing slaves was a charitable act.

Art and literature were influenced by the many cultures in the empire and by Islam. Early oral poetry focused on nomadic life. Later poets developed complex poems. Great Muslim poets include **Firdawsi,** who wrote the history of Persia, and **Omar Khayyám,** a scholar and astronomer who wrote *The Rubáiyát.* Storytellers used short, colorful anecdotes to entertain people. In architecture, buildings showed Byzantine influences, and mosques included domes and minarets. Artists used **calligraphy**, the art of beautiful handwriting, as decoration.

Education was important. Both boys and girls were taught to read so they could study the Quran. Several cities were great centers of learning, where scholars made advances. The philosopher **Ibn Rushd** influenced many Christian thinkers. **Ibn Khaldun** set standards for studying history. In mathematics, **al-Khwarizmi** was a pioneer in algebra.

Muslim medicine advanced rapidly. **Muhammad al-Razi,** head physician in the hospital at Baghdad, and **Ibn Sina,** a famous Persian doctor, both wrote works that became standard medical textbooks in Europe for 500 years. Other doctors improved ways to save eyesight and mix medicines.

Review Questions

1. In what ways could Muslims move up in society?

_____

_____

2. How did Muslim medical knowledge affect Europe?

_____

_____

READING CHECK

Why were Muslim boys and girls educated?

_____

_____

_____

VOCABULARY STRATEGY

Read the underlined sentence. What does the word *anecdotes* mean? Look for clues in the other words or phrases in the sentence. For example, the word *short* is a context clue that explains the length of *anecdotes.* The word *colorful* is a clue, too. Think about how *anecdotes* were used. Use the context clues to help you write a definition for *anecdotes.*

READING SKILL

Categorize Sort the following Muslim advances into categories:

- Elaborate rules for poetry
- Mixing medicines
- Developing partnerships
- Calligraphy
- A system of credit
- Improvements in eye treatments

Focus Question: How did Muslim rule affect Indian government and society?

As you read this section in your textbook, complete the following outline to record supporting details about Muslim empires in India. Some items have been completed for you.

I. The Delhi Sultanate

   A. The Sultan of Delhi defeats the Hindus

      1. Muslim Turks and Afghans push into India around 1000.

      2. _____

      3. _____

   B. Muslim rule changes Indian government and society.

      1. _____

      2. Trade increases.

      3. _____

II. Muslims and Hindus Clash

   A. Hindu-Muslim differences

      1. Hindus worship many gods and support castes.

      2. _____

   B. _____

      1. _____

      2. Some Hindus convert to Islam.

      3. _____

III. Mughal India

   A. Babur founds the Mughal dynasty

      1. Remaining Delhi sultanate is defeated.

      2. _____

   B. Akbar the Great

      1. _____

      2. _____

      3. _____

   C. _____

      1. Son's wife, Nur Jahan, manages government well and supports culture.

      2. _____

CHAPTER 10 SECTION 4

Section Summary

INDIA'S MUSLIM EMPIRES

Rival princes fought for control of India after about 550. Later, Muslim armies pushed in. By the 1100s, they controlled northern India. A **sultan,** or Muslim ruler, established **Delhi** as the capital of the Delhi sultanate, which ruled from 1206 to 1526. <u>Muslim attacks included onslaughts that killed many Hindus and destroyed Buddhist temples.</u>

Muslim rulers changed Indian government. Sultans welcomed immigrants and scholars, and trade increased. The culture created beautiful art and architecture.

With the Muslim advance, Hindu and Muslim religious beliefs clashed, creating many conflicts. Muslims worshiped a single god, while Hindus prayed to several. Hindus accepted the caste system, while Islam promoted equality.

Gradually, however, the cultures blended. Muslim rulers allowed Hindus to practice their religion. Some **rajahs,** or local Hindu rulers, continued governing. Some Hindus converted to Islam. Muslims adopted some Hindu customs and beliefs. A new language, Urdu, blended several languages. A new religion, **Sikhism,** combined Muslim and Hindu ideas.

The great Muslim leader **Babur** defeated armies of the Delhi sultanate and established the **Mughal** dynasty. It ruled from 1526 until 1857. The Mughal lands included much of the Indian subcontinent. Babur's grandson, **Akbar,** or Akbar the Great, ruled from 1556 to 1605. He organized a strong central government, improved the army, and supported international trade. He allowed Hindus to work in the government and promoted peace through religious tolerance.

After Akbar's death, his son's wife, **Nur Jahan,** managed the government with skill, and supported Indian culture. She was the most powerful woman in Indian history until the 1900s. The height of Mughal literature, art, and architecture came during the reign of Akbar's grandson, **Shah Jahan.** As a tomb for his wife, he built the **Taj Mahal.** It remains a spectacular monument to the Mughal empire.

Review Questions

1. How did Muslim rule change India?

_____

_____

2. How did Akbar demonstrate religious tolerance?

_____

_____

READING CHECK

What is the Taj Mahal?

_____

_____

_____

VOCABULARY STRATEGY

Find the word *onslaughts* in the underlined sentence. What does it mean? Look for context clues in nearby words and phrases. For example, one context clue tells you what happened during the *onslaughts*—people were killed. Use this and other context clues to help you write a definition for *onslaughts.*

READING SKILL

Identify Supporting Details
Circle the detail below that supports this statement: Muslim and Hindu cultures blended.

• Sikhism developed.

• The Taj Majal was built.

• Akbar supported international trade.

Note Taking Study Guide
THE OTTOMAN AND SAFAVID EMPIRES

Focus Question: What were the main characteristics of the Ottoman and Safavid empires?

As you read this section in your textbook, complete the following chart to record characteristics of the Ottoman and Safavid empires. Some items have been completed for you.

Characteristics	Ottomans	Safavids
Capital	Istanbul	
Dates		
Strongest ruler		Shah Abbas
Extent of empire		
Type of Islam		
Relationship with Europe	Respected and feared; Ottomans attacked Europe and controlled parts of it	

CHAPTER 10 SECTION 5
Section Summary
THE OTTOMAN AND SAFAVID EMPIRES

The **Ottomans** were nomads who had expanded into Asia Minor and the Balkan Peninsula by the 1300s. In 1453, they captured Constantinople. They renamed it **Istanbul** and made the city the capital of their empire.

Suleiman ruled over the Ottoman empire at its height, from 1520 to 1566. He expanded it into Asia, Africa, and Europe. It lasted for centuries. Suleiman ruled with a council, but he had absolute power. The Ottoman justice system was based on the Sharia, as well as royal edicts.

Military men made up the highest social class. They were followed by intellectuals, such as scientists and lawyers. Below them were men involved in trade and production, and farmers. Everyone belonged to a religious community, which provided education and other services. A Jewish community developed after Jews were expelled from Spain. They brought important international banking connections with them.

Some young Christian boys were converted to Islam by the government and given training. They were chosen to be **janizaries**, the elite force of the Ottoman army. The brightest students might become government officials.

Ottoman poets, painters, and architects created great works under Suleiman. However, after his death, the empire began to decline. By the 1700s, the Ottomans had lost control of some of their lands in Europe and Africa.

By the early 1500s, the **Safavids** united an empire in Persia (modern Iran.) They were Shiite Muslims. Their greatest king, or **shah**, was **Shah Abbas**. He ruled from 1588 to 1629, built a strong military, and made alliances with European nations. He also lowered taxes, encouraged industry, and tolerated other religions. The capital at **Isfahan** became a center for silk trading. After Abbas' death, religious disputes weakened the empire and it ended in 1722. In the late 1700s, the **Qajars** won control of Iran, made **Tehran** their capital, and ruled until 1925.

Review Questions

1. How did Suleiman rule?

_____

_____

2. What factor ended the Safavid empire?

_____

_____

READING CHECK

What happened in 1453?

_____

_____

_____

VOCABULARY STRATEGY

Find the word *edicts* in the underlined sentence. What do you think it means? Notice that *edicts* were royal and related to the justice system. Use these clues to help you decide which of the following is a definition for *edicts*.

a. Order having the force of law

b. Power, related to a ruler

READING SKILL

Synthesize Information Write two sentences describing Ottoman society.

_____

_____

_____

CHAPTER 11 SECTION 1

Note Taking Study Guide

EARLY CIVILIZATIONS OF AFRICA

Focus Question: How did geography and natural resources affect the development of early societies throughout Africa?

As you read this section in your textbook, complete the following outline to record the important effects caused by Africa's geography and natural resources. Some items have been completed for you.

I. **The influence of geography**

  A. Geographic patterns

    1. Vegetation affects where and how people live.

    2. _____

       _____

    3. Great Rift Valley and Mediterranean and Red seas promote travel and trade.

  B. Resources spur trade

    1. _____

       _____

    2. Camels can cross vast deserts.

II. **People and Ideas Migrate**

  A. The Sahara dries out

    1. Neolithic farmers cultivate the Nile Valley.

    2. Farming spreads, climate change occurs.

    3. _____

       _____

    4. _____

       _____

    5. People are forced to find new areas to live.

  B. The Bantu migrations

    1. _____

       _____

    2. Their language, based on a root language called Bantu, gives this movement its name.

(Outline continues on the next page.)

Note Taking Study Guide
EARLY CIVILIZATIONS OF AFRICA

(Continued from page 98)

III. Nubia Flourishes Along the Nile

   A. Rivals Egypt for control of region

   B. _____

      _____

   C. Nubian capital moves to Meröe

     1. _____

       _____

     2. Meröe rich in resources, such as iron ore and timber; makes it possible to produce iron tools and weaponry.

IV. _____

   A. African Civilizations have strong ties to regions across the Mediterranean and Red seas.

   B. _____

      _____

   C. After Rome defeats Carthage in Third Punic War, uses farmlands to feed armies.

CHAPTER 11 SECTION 1

Section Summary
EARLY CIVILIZATIONS OF AFRICA

READING CHECK

What natural resources helped Nubians manufacture tools and weapons?

_____

_____

_____

VOCABULARY STRATEGY

Find the word *utilized* in the underlined sentence. What do you think it means? Think about how the word is used. You can see that it is a verb, which describes an action. What action is being described? Who is doing what? Use the answers to these questions to help you write a definition of *utilized*.

READING SKILL

Identify Causes and Effects
Identify one effect of each of the following causes:

Rome conquered Carthage.

_____

_____

Muslim Arabs took North Africa.

_____

_____

In Africa there are grassy plains, called **savannas,** and the **Sahara,** the largest desert in the world. These vegetation zones influenced how people lived. Rivers with **cataracts,** or waterfalls, limited travel. On the other hand, an interior valley and the Mediterranean and Red seas provided trade routes. By A.D. 200, camel caravans moved across the Sahara.

Before 2500 B.C., the Sahara supported farming. After a climate change, however, the process of **desertification** slowly changed the land to a vast desert. People had to move to find new farmland. Between 1000 B.C. and A.D. 1000, West African speakers of the **Bantu** languages migrated south and east. These Bantu migrations influenced modern languages. The Bantu people also brought skills and blended with other cultures.

About 2700 B.C. **Nubia,** or Kush, developed on the upper Nile. Egypt controlled Nubia for about 500 years, beginning in 1500 B.C. As a result, Nubians adapted many Egyptian traditions.

Forced to move by Assyrian invaders, Nubians established a new capital at **Meroë** around 500 B.C. From there, the Nubians eventually controlled trade routes. Meroë was rich in iron ore and timber. The Nubians used these resources to make iron tools and weapons, improving their ability to defend themselves. Still, about A.D. 350, invaders from the southern kingdom of Axum conquered Nubia.

On the Mediterranean, the Phoenician settlement of Carthage emerged as a North African power. It dominated trade in the western Mediterranean from 800 B.C. to 146 B.C. At the end of the Third Punic War, however, Rome conquered Carthage. <u>The Romans then utilized North Africa's farmlands to provide grain for their armies.</u> They also built roads, dams, and cities. Later Romans brought Christianity to the region.

Muslim Arabs took control of North Africa in the 690s. Arabic became the dominant language, and Muslim civilization grew. Over time, Islam replaced Christianity, spreading to West Africa through traders.

Review Questions
1. How did the Mediterranean and Red seas affect early Africa?

_____

_____

2. What effects did the Bantu migrations have?

_____

_____

_____

Name_____ Class_____ Date_____

Focus Question: How did the kingdoms of West Africa develop and prosper?

As you read this section in your textbook, complete the following flowchart to record causes and effects related to the development of West African kingdoms. Some items have been completed for you.

Causes
- People become farmers.
- Gold and salt are widely available.

Event
- Food surplus exists.
- One product is traded for another.

Effects
- Trade develops between villages.
- Cities develop along trade routes.

CHAPTER 11 SECTION 2

Section Summary

KINGDOMS OF WEST AFRICA

READING CHECK

What caused Songhai's decline?

_____

_____

_____

VOCABULARY STRATEGY

Find the word *administered* in the underlined sentence. What does the word mean? It is related to the word *administration,* which means, "a group that directs a government or enterprise, like a school." Use this word-family clue to help you write a definition of *administered.*

READING SKILL

Identify Causes and Effects
Identify one effect of Askia Muhammad's rule in Songhai.

_____

_____

_____

When early farmers in West Africa began to produce **surplus,** or extra, food, they traded it for goods from other villages. Eventually, trade routes developed that connected Africa with Asia and Europe. Cities grew near popular routes. Salt was a valuable product, or **commodity,** along with gold. Gold was common in West Africa, and salt was plentiful in the Sahara. People needed salt to stay healthy and preserve food and because of this, a trader might exchange one pound of salt for one pound of gold.

The ancient kingdom of **Ghana** developed in West Africa around 800 A.D. It became a center of trade, and the king controlled the salt and gold trade. <u>The king also administered justice, kept the peace, and ran the government in other ways.</u> Ghana was prosperous, and Muslims moved there from the north. They served as government officials and introduced new ideas. In time, however, Ghana was swallowed up by a new power, the West African kingdom of **Mali.**

About 1235, **Sundiata** defeated his enemies and established the empire of Mali. About 1312, **Mansa Musa,** Mali's greatest ruler, came to power. He improved the justice system and supported religious tolerance. He created ties with Muslim states during his pilgrimage to Mecca. He also brought back Islamic scholars to provide religious teaching.

After Mali weakened, the kingdom of **Songhai** developed in West Africa. After 1492, Emperor Askia Muhammad established a Muslim dynasty there. He expanded the territory and improved the government. Later, internal conflicts weakened Songhai, which was conquered by Morocco in about 1591.

Some smaller societies prospered in West Africa from A.D. 500 to 1500. Benin arose in the rain forests of the Guinea coast in the 1300s. At about the same time, the Hausa built clay-walled cities. Hausa artisans produced goods and traded with Arab merchants. Each Hausa city had a ruler who was often a woman.

Review Questions

1. Which two trade goods were important to early West African kingdoms?

_____

_____

2. What was unique about the Hausa's rulers?

_____

_____

Name_____ Class_____ Date_____

Focus Question: What influence did religion and trade have on the development of East Africa?

As you read this section in your textbook, complete the following flowchart to record the effects of trade on East African societies. Some items have been completed for you.

Effects of Trade on East African Societies

Great Zimbabwe
- Trade network brings wealth.
-
-

Coastal City-States
- Swahili language is developed.
- Local rulers build strong, independent city-states.
-
-

Ethiopia
- Christianity helps establish a distinct culture.

Axum
- Christianity is brought to region.
- Trade brings wealth.
-

READING CHECK

Who was King Lalibela?

_____

_____

_____

VOCABULARY STRATEGY

Find the word *unifying* in the underlined sentence. What does *unifying* mean? Its prefix *uni-* means "one." Use this clue to help you write a definition of *unifying*.

READING SKILL

Understand Effects What effect did the blending of African and Arab cultures have on language and culture in East Africa?

_____

_____

_____

The kingdom of **Axum** conquered Nubia about A.D. 350. By about A.D. 400, Axum controlled a rich trade network. A key part of this was the port of **Adulis** on the Red Sea. The Axum trade routes connected Africa, India, and the Mediterranean. As a result, traders from other regions brought unique cultural influences, along with goods, to Axum.

In the 300s, Christianity became Axum's official religion. At first, Christianity strengthened trade between Axum and other Christian countries. However, as Islam spread across North Africa in the 600s, Axum became isolated and slowly lost power.

Axum's legacy lived on in a portion of present-day **Ethiopia.** There, Christianity and descendants of the Axumites survived for centuries. This was due in part to the unifying influence of Christianity. This gave Ethiopia a single, unique identity among Muslim neighbors. Ethiopia developed a distinct culture. For example, under **King Lalibela** in the 1200s, eleven remarkable churches were carved into the solid rock of mountains.

After Axum declined, Muslim communities arose along the East African coast. They were set up by Arabs and Persians trading with Asia. By the 600s, ships regularly sailed to India and back. Trade goods from Africa, Southeast Asia, and China helped the East African cities grow wealthy. Relations between cities were generally peaceful. By the 1000s, a blending of African, Asian, and Arab influences combined to create a new language and culture, both called **Swahili.**

South and inland from the coastal cities was **Great Zimbabwe,** the capital city of the Zimbabwe empire. The empire reached its height around 1300. There, people mined gold and traded goods across the Indian Ocean. Little is known about Great Zimbabwe's government. Artifacts show that its artisans were skilled jewelry makers and weavers. By the 1500s, Zimbabwe was in decline. Later, Portuguese traders tried, but failed, to find the former empire's source of gold.

Review Questions
1. How did Christianity affect Axum?

_____

_____

2. What happened after Zimbabwe's decline?

_____

_____

Name_____ Class_____ Date_____

Focus Question: What factors influenced the development of societies in Africa?

As you read this section in your textbook, complete the following concept web to record the factors that influenced the development of African societies. Some items have been completed for you.

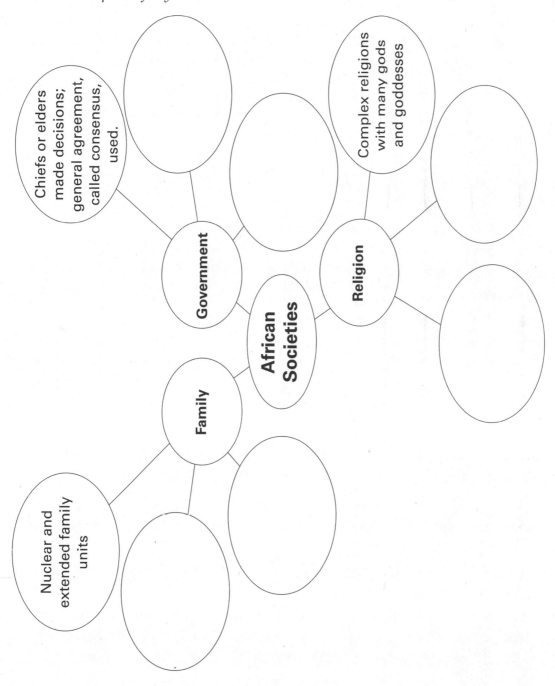

Chiefs or elders made decisions; general agreement, called consensus, used.

Complex religions with many gods and goddesses

Government

African Societies

Religion

Family

Nuclear and extended family units

READING CHECK

H_w did the Kongo kings rule t__ir lands?

_____

_____

_____

VOCABULARY STRATEGY

Find the word *complex* in the underlined sentence. What does it mean? Look for clues to its meaning in the same sentence and in the sentences that follow. For example, the word *varied* and the phrase *involving many gods, goddesses, rituals, and ceremonies* provide clues that can help you figure out the word's meaning. Use these context clues to help you write a definition of *complex*.

READING SKILL

Recognize Multiple Causes
What encouraged a sense of community and common values?

_____

_____

_____

CHAPTER 11 SECTION 4

Section Summary

SOCIETIES IN MEDIEVAL AFRICA

Some people in medieval Africa lived with an extended family of several generations. Others lived within a **nuclear family** of one set of parents and their children. Some families were **patrilineal,** passing inheritances through the father's side. Others passed property down on the mother's side and so were **matrilineal.** A **lineage** was a group of families who shared a common ancestor. A clan was made up of several lineages with one, often legendary, ancestor. Membership in a kin group gave people a sense of belonging.

In small societies, decisions might be made by **consensus,** or general agreement. The decisions followed open discussions where the opinions of elders carried the most weight. Women sometimes took strong roles, acting as peacemakers.

In large empires, villagers had to pay taxes, provide soldiers, and follow orders from the king at a distant court. However, in Kongo, a kingdom in central Africa around A.D. 1500, the king had limited powers. There, areas were governed by appointed officials. However, each village had its own chiefs. Soldiers were only called up in time of need.

Medieval African religions were varied and complex, involving many gods, goddesses, rituals, and ceremonies. Many people believed in one supreme being. Others honored the spirits of ancestors. By A.D. 1000, Christianity and Islam had become popular and absorbed many local practices and beliefs.

The arts in Africa date back 4,000 years to the Egyptian pyramids. Some art had special meaning, such as gold-and-blue kente cloth, a West African textile. Only rulers and wealthy people could wear it. Cloths, jugs, bowls, and jewelry might be decorative or serve religious or ceremonial purposes.

Written histories from Africa describe laws, religion, and society. In Muslim regions, Arabic was a common written language. In West Africa, **griots,** or professional storytellers, recited ancient folktales, stories, and oral histories. These encouraged a sense of community and common values.

Review Questions

1. What are patrilineal and matrilineal families?

_____

_____

2. Who were griots?

_____

_____

Focus Question: Describe the political, economic, and cultural achievements of the Tang and Song dynasties.

As you read this section in your textbook, complete the Venn diagram below to compare and contrast the Tang and Song dynasties. Use the overlapping portion of the circles for information that applies to both dynasties. Some items have been completed for you.

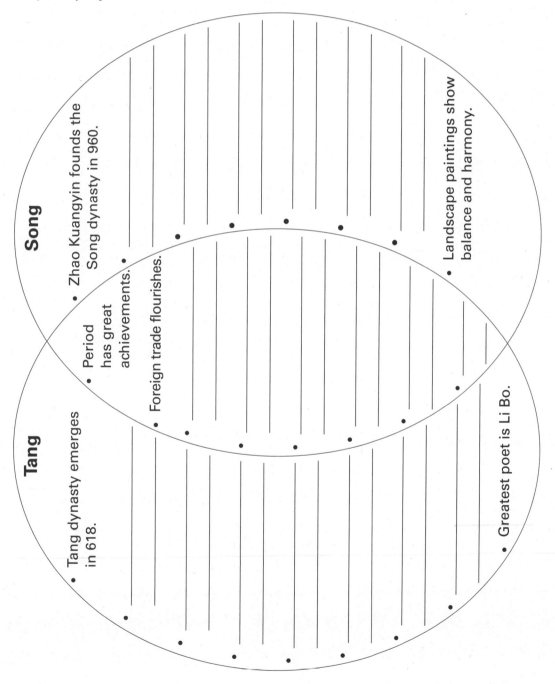

Song

- Zhao Kuangyin founds the Song dynasty in 960.
- Landscape paintings show balance and harmony.

Tang

- Tang dynasty emerges in 618.
- Greatest poet is Li Bo.

- Period has great achievements.
- Foreign trade flourishes.

CHAPTER
12
SECTION 1

Section Summary

TWO GOLDEN AGES OF CHINA

At the end of the Han dynasty, China broke apart. During the Sui dynasty (589–618), Sui Wendi reunited China. In 618, Li Yuan and his son Li Shimin led a revolt and set up the **Tang dynasty.** Eight years later, Li Shimin compelled his father to step down. Li Shimin then took the throne under the name **Tang Taizong.** Later Tang rulers conquered many territories and forced Vietnam, Tibet, and Korea to become **tributary states.** Other Tang rulers restored the Han system of government. Tang emperors also undertook **land reform** in which they gave land to peasants. However, the Tang eventually grew weaker. In 907, the last Tang emperor was overthrown.

In 960, Zhao Kuangyin founded the **Song dynasty.** The Song ruled for 319 years. They were threatened by invaders from the north. Nonetheless, the Song period was a time of great achievement. A new type of rice was imported from Southeast Asia. The new rice made farming more productive and created food surpluses. This freed more people to take part in trade, learning, or the arts.

In Tang and Song China, the emperor was at the head of society. Scholar-officials had the highest social status. Most of them came from the **gentry,** or wealthy landowning class. The majority of Chinese were poor peasant farmers. Merchants had the lowest social status because their riches came from the work of others. Women had higher status at this time than they did later. However, when a woman married, she could not keep her **dowry,** or payment she brought to her marriage, and she could never remarry.

The Tang and Song developed a rich culture. Song landscape painting was influenced by Daoist beliefs. Buddhist themes influenced Chinese sculpture and architecture. The Indian stupa developed into the Chinese **pagoda.** Poetry was the most respected form of literature. Probably the greatest Tang poet was Li Bo.

Review Questions

1. What group benefited from Tang land reform?

_____

_____

2. What threat did the Chinese face during the Song dynasty?

_____

_____

Name_____ Class_____ Date_____

Focus Question: What were the effects of the Mongol invasion and the rise of the Ming dynasty on China?

As you read this section in your textbook, complete the timeline below to record important events during the Mongol and Ming empires. Some items have been completed for you.

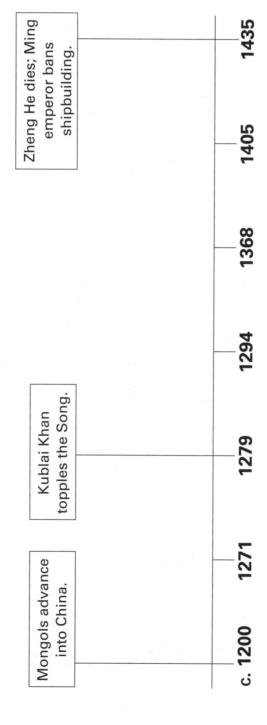

Zheng He dies; Ming emperor bans shipbuilding.	1435
	1405
	1368
	1294
Kublai Khan topples the Song.	1279
	1271
Mongols advance into China.	c. 1200

Section Summary
THE MONGOL AND MING EMPIRES

What does *Genghis Khan* mean?

_____

_____

_____

Find the word *dominate* in the underlined sentence. What does it mean? The word *dominate* comes from the Latin word *dominus*, which means "master." Use this word-origin clue to help you understand the meaning of *dominated*. Which of the following words is closest in meaning to the word *dominated*?

1. served

2. ruled

Recognize Sequence List the following dynasties in correct chronological order: Ming, Song, Yuan

_____

_____

_____

The Mongols were nomads. They grazed their animals on the **steppes** of Central Asia. In the early 1200s, a Mongol leader united the clans. He took the name **Genghis Khan,** meaning "Universal Ruler." Under Genghis Khan, Mongol forces conquered a vast empire. After his death, his sons and grandsons continued to expand the Mongol empire. <u>For the next 150 years, they dominated much of Asia.</u> The Mongols created peace within their empire. They controlled and protected the Silk Road, and trade flourished.

Genghis Khan's grandson, **Kublai Khan,** conquered the Song in China in 1279. He called his dynasty the **Yuan.** Only Mongols could serve in his military and highest government jobs, but he let Chinese officials continue to rule the provinces. He welcomed foreigners, including Ibn Battuta and **Marco Polo.** Polo's writings about China sparked European interest. The pope sent priests to China, and Muslims also set up communities there. Chinese products, such as gunpowder and porcelain, made their way to Europe.

The Yuan dynasty declined after Kublai Khan's death in 1294. After a time, Zhu Yuanzhang formed a rebel army that defeated the Mongols. In 1368, he founded the **Ming** dynasty. Ming China was very productive. Better methods of fertilization improved farming. The Ming repaired the canal system. This made trade easier and allowed cities to grow. Ming artists created beautiful blue-and-white porcelain. Ming writers wrote novels and the world's first detective stories.

Early Ming rulers sent Chinese ships to distant lands. They did this to show the glory of their empire. **Zheng He**'s voyages were the most famous. Between 1405 and 1433, he led seven expeditions to Southeast Asia, India, the Persian Gulf, and East Africa. After Zheng He died in 1435, the Ming emperor no longer allowed large ships to be built. Chinese exploration came to an end.

Review Questions

1. Name two reasons why Ming China was very productive.

_____

_____

2. What happened to Chinese exploration after Zheng He died?

_____

_____

CHAPTER 12 SECTION 3 — Note Taking Study Guide

KOREA AND ITS TRADITIONS

Focus Question: How are Korea's history and culture linked to those of China and Japan?

As you read this section in your textbook, complete the concept web below to record important information about Korea. Some items have been completed for you.

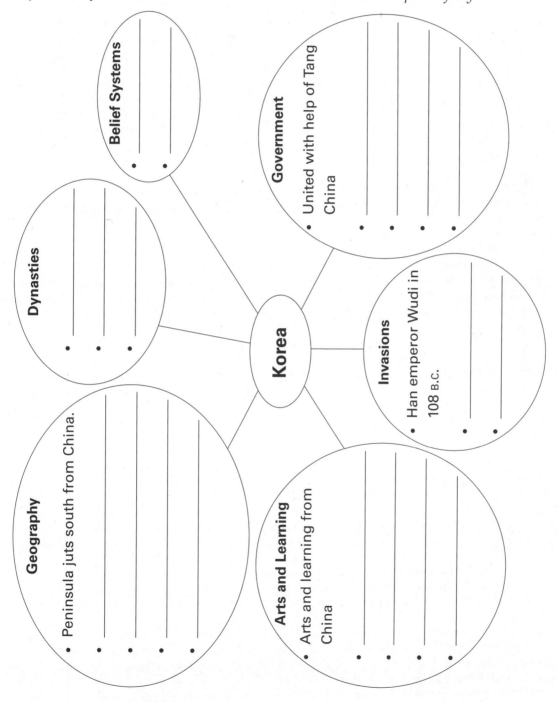

Belief Systems

Government
- United with help of Tang China

Dynasties

Korea

Invasions
- Han emperor Wudi in 108 B.C.

Geography
- Peninsula juts south from China.

Arts and Learning
- Arts and learning from China

Name_____ Class_____ Date_____

READING CHECK

What is the name of the Korean alphabet?

_____

_____

_____

VOCABULARY STRATEGY

Find the word *evolved* in the underlined sentence. What do you think it means? Do you think the Koreans created their ways of life quickly or slowly? Use this context clue to help you understand the meaning of *evolved*.

READING SKILL

Categorize List events and developments that took place during each of Korea's three dynasties: Silla, Koryo, and Choson. Be sure to include how those events and developments were adapted by the Koreans.

_____

_____

_____

_____

_____

Korea is located on a peninsula south of the Chinese mainland. The earliest Koreans probably migrated from Siberia and northern Manchuria. They evolved their own ways of life before they were influenced by China. In 108 B.C., the Han emperor, Wudi, invaded Korea, and Chinese ideas soon spread there.

Between A.D. 300 and 600, local rulers built three kingdoms in Korea. The three kingdoms were often at war with one another or with China. Still, Chinese ideas continued to spread. Missionaries brought Buddhism to Korea. Korean monks then traveled to China and brought back Chinese arts and learning. In 668, the Silla kingdom united the Korean peninsula. Under the **Silla dynasty,** Korea became a tributary state of China. Koreans were influenced by Confucian ideas but adapted them to fit their own traditions.

In 935, the **Koryo dynasty** replaced the Silla. Confucianism and Buddhism were both important during this time. Koreans also learned from the Chinese how to make porcelain. Then they perfected the technique for making **celadon.** This is porcelain with an unusual blue-green glaze.

The Mongols invaded Korea in 1231 and occupied the country until the 1350s. When their rule ended, the Koryo returned to power. In 1392, the Korean general Yi Song-gye overthrew them. He set up the **Choson dynasty.** This was the longest-lasting, but final, Korean dynasty.

In 1443, **King Sejong** decided that the Chinese writing system was too complex. Sejong had experts develop **hangul,** the Korean phonetic alphabet. Hangul spread quickly because it was easier to use than written Chinese. This led to a high **literacy rate.**

In the 1590s, Japanese armies invaded Korea. To stop them at sea, Admiral Yi Sun-shin sailed his ships into the Japanese fleet. After six years, the Japanese armies withdrew from Korea. As they left, they took many Korean artisans with them. They wanted the artisans to introduce their skills to Japan.

Review Questions

1. From where did the earliest Koreans probably come?

_____

_____

2. What was the last Korean dynasty?

_____

_____

CHAPTER 12 SECTION 4 Note Taking Study Guide

THE EMERGENCE OF JAPAN AND THE FEUDAL AGE

Focus Question: What internal and external factors shaped Japan's civilization, and what characterized Japan's feudal age?

As you read this section in your textbook, complete the table below with examples of internal and external factors that shaped Japan's civilization. Some items have been completed for you.

Influences on Japan	
Internal Factors	**External Factors**
• Geography both protected and isolated Japan. • _____ • _____ • _____ • _____ • _____ • _____ • _____	• Korean artisans settled in Japan. • _____ • _____ • _____ • _____ • _____ • _____ • _____ • _____
• Urban culture produced Kabuki and bunraku plays.	• Landscape painting was influenced by Zen reverence for nature and by Chinese paintings.

CHAPTER 12 SECTION 4

Section Summary

THE EMERGENCE OF JAPAN AND THE FEUDAL AGE

READING CHECK

What were the main ideas of bushido?

_____
_____
_____

Japan is located on an **archipelago,** or chain of islands. In early times, the seas around Japan both protected and isolated it. This region also has many volcanoes, earthquakes, and killer tidal waves called **tsunamis.**

Early Japanese society was divided into clans. The clans worshiped kami, or natural powers. The worship of the kami became known as **Shinto.** In the 500s, missionaries from Korea brought Buddhism to Japan. They also brought knowledge of Chinese culture. In the 600s, Prince Shotoku sent nobles to study in China. The nobles brought back Chinese ideas. In 710, the Japanese emperor built a new capital at Nara, modeled after the Chinese capital.

The Japanese kept some Chinese ways but discarded others. This process is known as **selective borrowing.** The Japanese revised the Chinese writing system but added **kana,** symbols that represent syllables. Women, such as Murasaki Shikibu, wrote some of the most important works of Japanese literature.

VOCABULARY STRATEGY

Find the word *stressed* in the underlined sentence. What does it mean? Use what you know about the word *stressed* to figure out which sentence below uses *stressed* the way it is used in the underlined sentence.

1. The student was *stressed* from studying for final exams.

2. The principal *stressed* the importance of being quiet in assembly.

Japan became a feudal society. The emperor was the head of this society, but he was very weak. The shogun had the real power. Minamoto Yoritomo became shogun in 1192. He set up the Kamakura shogunate. The shogun gave land to lords who agreed to support him with their armies. These lords were called daimyo. They gave land to warriors called **samurai.** Samurai developed a code of values called **bushido.** This code emphasized honor, bravery, and loyalty.

Kublai Khan tried to invade Japan in 1274 and 1281. However, typhoons wrecked the Mongol ships each time. Still, after the attempted invasions, the Kamakura shogunate ended. In 1600, Tokugawa Ieyasu defeated his rivals to become master of Japan. The Tokugawa shoguns created an orderly society. Agriculture improved, and trade prospered. During Japan's feudal period, a Buddhist sect called **Zen** became popular. Zen monks were scholars, yet they stressed the importance of reaching a moment of "non-knowing."

READING SKILL

Categorize List the levels in Japanese feudal society.

_____
_____
_____

Review Questions

1. What religion was brought to Japan from Korea?

_____

_____

2. Why did Prince Shotoku send nobles to China?

_____

_____

Note Taking Study Guide

DIVERSE CULTURES OF SOUTHEAST ASIA

Focus Question: How was Southeast Asia affected by the cultures of both China and India?

As you read this section in your textbook, complete the outline below to summarize the diverse features of Southeast Asia. Some items have been completed for you.

I. **Geography of Southeast Asia**

   A. Location

      1. Mainland set apart by mountains and plateaus.

      2. _____

   B. Trade routes in the southern seas

      1. _____

      2. _____

      3. _____

   C. Early traditions

      1. Developed own cultures before outside influences arrived

      2. _____

      3. _____

      4. Women had greater equality than elsewhere in Asia.

         a. _____

         b. _____

II. **Indian Culture Spreads to Southeast Asia**

   A. Indian influence reaches its peak

      1. Indian merchants and Hindu priests spread their culture.

      2. _____

      3. _____

      4. _____

   B. _____

      1. Traders spread Islamic beliefs and culture to Indonesia and other parts of Southeast Asia.

      2. _____

(Outline continues on the next page.)

CHAPTER
12
SECTION 5

Note Taking Study Guide

DIVERSE CULTURES OF SOUTHEAST ASIA

(Continued from page 115)

III. New Kingdoms and Empires Emerge

   A. _____

      1. In Irrawaddy Valley (present-day Myanmar)

      2. _____

      3. _____

      4. _____

   B. The Khmer empire

      1. _____

      2. _____

      3. In 1100s, King Suryavarman II built temple complex at Angkor Wat.

   C. Srivijaya empire flourishes.

      1. _____

      2. _____

      3. _____

IV. _____

   A. Geography

      1. Annam (now northern part of Vietnam)

      2. _____

   B. Chinese domination

      1. Han armies conquered region in 111 B.C.; controlled by China for next 1,000 years.

      2. _____

      3. _____

   C. The Vietnamese preserve their identity.

      1. _____

      2. _____

Name_____ Class_____ Date_____

Southeast Asia is made up of two regions, mainland and island Southeast Asia. The mainland region includes Myanmar, Thailand, Cambodia, Laos, Vietnam, and Malaysia. The island region has more than 20,000 islands, including Indonesia, Singapore, and the Philippines. In early times, sea trade between China and India had to pass through the Malacca or Sunda straits. Southeast Asian islands controlled these straits, which made them very important. Southeast Asian women took part in the spice trade and had greater equality than in other parts of Asia. **Matrilineal** descent, or inheritance through the mother, was common. Indian merchants and Hindu priests spread their religion and culture throughout Southeast Asia. Later, monks brought Theravada Buddhism there. Indian traders eventually carried a third religion, Islam, to the region.

Many kingdoms and empires developed in Southeast Asia. The kingdom of Pagan arose in present-day Myanmar. In 1044, King Anawrahta united the region. He brought Buddhism to the Burman people. His capital was filled with magnificent **stupas.** Indian influences also shaped the Khmer empire. Its greatest rulers controlled much of present-day Cambodia, Thailand, and Malaysia. Khmer rulers became Hindus, but most ordinary people were Buddhists. In Indonesia, the trading empire of Srivijaya prospered from the 600s to the 1200s. It controlled the Strait of Malacca. Both Hinduism and Buddhism reached Srivijaya.

Northern Vietnamese culture grew around the Red River, which irrigated rice **paddies.** In 111 B.C., Han armies conquered Vietnam. China remained in control for 1,000 years. During that time, Confucian ideas influenced the Vietnamese. Mahayana Buddhism from China also had a strong effect on Vietnam. However, Theravada Buddhism had a greater impact in the rest of Southeast Asia. In A.D. 39, two sisters, Trung Trac and Trung Nhi, led an uprising that briefly drove out the Chinese. In 939, Vietnam finally broke free from China.

Review Questions

1. What are the two regions of Southeast Asia?

_____

_____

2. What empire controlled the Strait of Malacca?

_____

_____

READING CHECK

What country controlled Vietnam for 1,000 years?

_____

_____

_____

VOCABULARY STRATEGY

Find the word *impact* in the second underlined sentence. What does it mean? The first underlined sentence contains a synonym for the word *impact.* What is that synonym? Use this context clue to help you understand the meaning of *impact.*

READING SKILL

Summarize Summarize how India influenced Southeast Asia. Include the religious beliefs that came from India.

_____

_____

_____

CHAPTER 13 SECTION 1 — Note Taking Study Guide
THE RENAISSANCE IN ITALY

Focus Question: What were the ideals of the Renaissance, and how did Italian artists and writers reflect these ideals?

As you read this section in your textbook, complete the following outline to identify main ideas and supporting details about the Italian Renaissance. Some items have been completed for you.

I. **What was the Renaissance?**

   A. A changing worldview

      1. Reawakened interest in classical Greece and Rome

      2. New emphasis on human experience and individual achievement

   B. A spirit of adventure

      1. Looked at universe in new ways

      2. _____

   C. The growth of humanism

      1. Study of classical Greece and Rome to understand their own times

      2. _____

II. **Italy: Cradle of the Renaissance**

   A. Italy's history and geography

      1. _____

      2. _____

      3. _____

   B. _____

      1. _____

      2. _____

III. **Renaissance art and artists flower**

   A. _____

      1. _____

      2. _____

   B. _____

      1. _____

      2. _____

(Outline continues on the next page.)

(Continued from page 118)

C. _____
  1. _____
  2. _____
D. _____
  1. _____
  2. _____
E. _____
  1. _____
  2. _____
F. _____
  1. _____
  2. _____
IV. _____
  A. _____
    1. _____
    2. _____
  B. _____
    1. _____
    2. _____

Name_____ Class_____ Date_____

What does *Renaissance* mean?

_____

_____

_____

Find the word *comprehend* in the underlined sentence. What clues to its meaning can you find in the surrounding text? In this case, there is a synonym, or word that means the same as *comprehend,* in the same sentence. Circle the word in the sentence that could help you figure out what *comprehend* means.

Identify Main Ideas What were two main features of the Renaissance?

_____

_____

_____

A new age began in Italy in the 1300s and eventually spread throughout Europe. It was called the Renaissance, meaning "rebirth." It marked the change from medieval times to the early modern world. During medieval times, people focused on religion. In contrast, Renaissance thinkers explored human experience. There was a new emphasis on individual achievement. At the heart of this age was an intellectual movement called **humanism.** Humanists studied the classical culture of Greece and Rome. They used that study to comprehend, or understand, their own times. They emphasized the **humanities**—subjects including rhetoric, poetry, and history. Poet Francesco **Petrarch** was an important Renaissance humanist.

Italy was the birthplace of the Renaissance for many reasons. Italy had been the center of the Roman empire. Rome was also the seat of the Roman Catholic Church. The Church was an important **patron,** or supporter, of the arts. Italy's location encouraged trade. Trade provided the wealth that fueled Italy's Renaissance. In Italy's city-states, many merchant families had become rich through trade. One was the Medici family of **Florence.** They were important patrons of the arts.

Renaissance art reflected the ideas of humanism. Painters returned to the realism of classical times. They developed new techniques for representing humans and landscapes. The discovery of **perspective** allowed artists to create realistic art and paint scenes that looked three-dimensional. The greatest of the Renaissance artists were **Leonardo** da Vinci, **Michelangelo,** and **Raphael.**

Some Italian writers wrote guidebooks to help ambitious men and women rise in the Renaissance world. The most widely read of these was *The Book of the Courtier,* by **Baldassare Castiglione.** His ideal courtier was a well-educated, well-mannered aristocrat who mastered many fields. **Niccoló Machiavelli** wrote a guide for rulers on how to gain and maintain power. It was titled *The Prince.*

Review Questions
1. What intellectual movement was key to the Renaissance?

_____

_____

2. What is one reason why the Renaissance began in Italy?

_____

_____

Name_____ Class_____ Date_____

Focus Question: How did the Renaissance develop in northern Europe?

As you read this section in your textbook, complete the following chart to record the main ideas about the Renaissance in the North. Some items have been completed for you.

Renaissance in the North

Humanists

- Humanists stress education and classical learning to bring religious and moral reform.
- Erasmus spreads humanism to a wider audience and calls for a translation of the Bible into the vernacular.

Artists and Writers

- Flemish painter Jan van Eyck portrays townspeople and religious scenes in realistic detail.
- Flemish painter Pieter Bruegel uses vibrant colors to portray scenes of peasant life.

Printing Revolution

- In 1455, Johann Gutenberg produces the first complete Bible using a printing press.
- Printed books are cheaper and easier to produce.

CHAPTER 13 SECTION 2 — Section Summary
THE RENAISSANCE IN THE NORTH

By the 1400s, northern Europe enjoyed enough economic growth to start its own Renaissance. An astounding invention—the printing press—helped spread Renaissance ideas. In about 1455, **Johann Gutenberg** produced the first complete Bible using a printing press. The printing press caused a printing revolution. Before, books were copied by hand. They were rare and expensive. Printed books were cheaper and easier to produce. Now more books were available, so more people learned to read. Printed books exposed Europeans to new ideas and new places.

The northern Renaissance began in the prosperous region of **Flanders.** It was a rich and thriving trade center. Flemish painters were known for their use of realism. Among the most important Flemish painters were Jan van Eyck, Pieter Bruegel, and Peter Paul Rubens. Painter **Albrecht Dürer** traveled to Italy to study the techniques of the Italian masters. Dürer applied the painting techniques he learned in Italy to **engraving,** a printmaking technique. Many of his engravings and paintings portray the theme of religious upheaval. He brought back Renaissance ideas to northern Europe.

Northern European humanist writers also helped spread Renaissance ideas. The Dutch priest and humanist Desiderius **Erasmus** wanted the Bible translated into the **vernacular,** or everyday language. Then many more people would be able to read it. The English humanist **Sir Thomas More** called for social reform in the shape of a **utopian** society. He pictured a society where people lived together in peace and harmony. The major figure of Renaissance literature, however, was the English poet and playwright William **Shakespeare.** His plays explore universal themes, such as the complexity of the individual. He set his plays in everyday, realistic settings. Shakespeare's love of words also enriched the English language. He alone added 1,700 new words to the language.

Review Questions

1. Identify one major change caused by the invention of the printing press.

_____

_____

2. What theme did Dürer explore in many of his works?

_____

_____

Name_____ Class_____ Date_____

Focus Question: How did revolts against the Roman Catholic Church affect northern European society?

As you read this section in your textbook, complete the following concept web to identify main ideas about the Protestant Reformation. Some items have been completed for you.

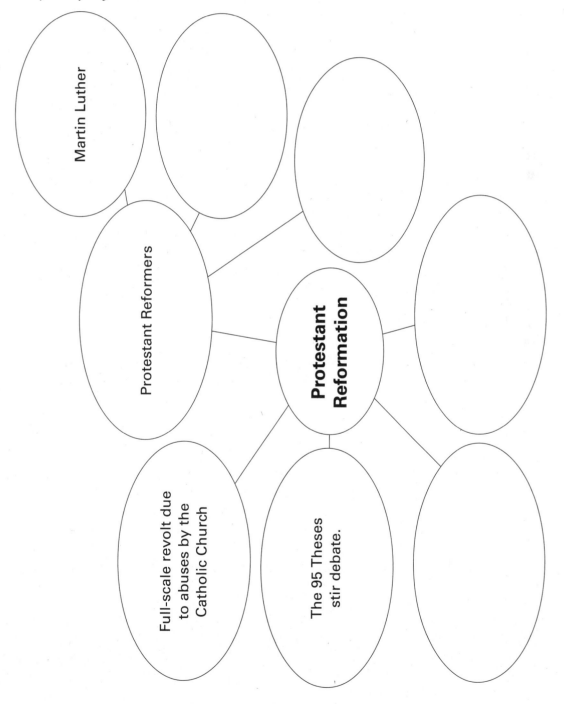

Martin Luther

Protestant Reformers

Protestant Reformation

Full-scale revolt due to abuses by the Catholic Church

The 95 Theses stir debate.

CHAPTER
13
SECTION 3

Section Summary
THE PROTESTANT REFORMATION

In the 1500s, the Renaissance in northern Europe sparked a religious upheaval. It was known as the Protestant Reformation. Many Christians began to protest some practices in the Catholic Church. Popes, for example, led lavish lives. Many Christians also began to question why the Church in distant Rome should have authority over them.

Protests against Church abuses turned into a revolt. A German monk named **Martin Luther** helped start it. He was outraged by the actions of a priest near **Wittenberg** in Germany. The priest offered **indulgences,** or the lessening of time a soul would have to spend in purgatory, to Christians who paid money to the Church. Luther wrote 95 Theses, or arguments, against indulgences. He argued that the pope had no authority to release souls from purgatory. <u>At the heart of Luther's doctrines were several beliefs.</u> One of these was that all Christians have equal access to God through faith and the Bible.

Throughout Europe, Luther's 95 Theses stirred hot debate. The new Holy Roman emperor, **Charles V,** ordered Luther to answer to the **diet,** or assembly of German princes. Luther refused to give up his views. Thousands hailed Luther as a hero and rejected the pope's authority. The printing press helped spread Luther's ideas. Soon, Luther's followers—now called Protestants—were found all over Europe.

In Switzerland, the reformer **John Calvin** also challenged the Catholic Church. Calvin shared many of Luther's beliefs. However, he preached **predestination,** the idea that God had long ago determined who was saved. Protestants in **Geneva** asked Calvin to lead them. He set up a **theocracy,** or government run by church leaders. Reformers from all over Europe visited Geneva to learn about Calvin's ideas and put them into practice. In the 1600s, some English Calvinists sailed to the Americas to escape persecution.

Review Questions

1. What was the Protestant Reformation?

_____

_____

2. What event caused Luther to write the 95 Theses?

_____

_____

CHAPTER
13
SECTION 4

Note Taking Study Guide

REFORMATION IDEAS SPREAD

Focus Question: How did the Reformation bring about two different religious paths in Europe?

As you read this section in your textbook, complete the following flowchart to identify main ideas about the spread of the Protestant Reformation in Europe. Some items have been completed for you.

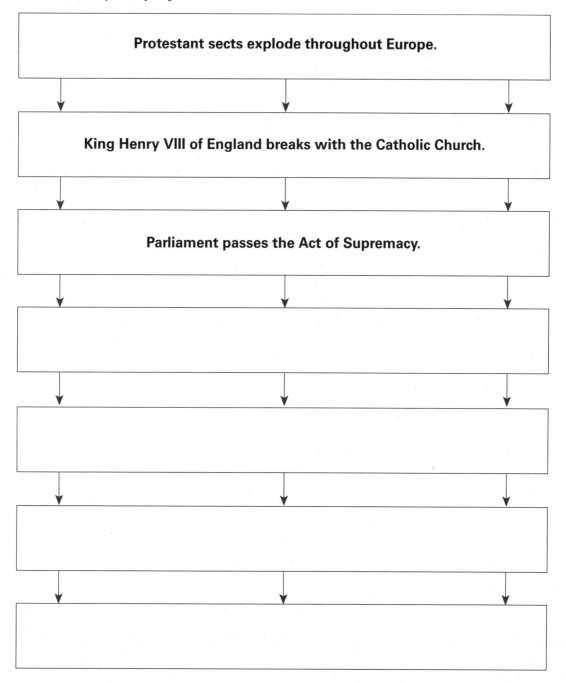

Protestant sects explode throughout Europe.

King Henry VIII of England breaks with the Catholic Church.

Parliament passes the Act of Supremacy.

CHAPTER 13 SECTION 4

Section Summary

REFORMATION IDEAS SPREAD

READING CHECK

What was the reform movement of the Catholic Church?

_____

_____

_____

As the Reformation continued, new Protestant **sects,** or religious groups that had broken away from an established church, sprang up. In England, the break with the Catholic Church came from King **Henry VIII,** who wanted to end his marriage. The pope refused to annul the marriage. Furious, Henry had Parliament pass a series of laws to take the English church from the pope's control. Henry appointed **Thomas Cranmer** archbishop of the new church. Cranmer annulled the king's marriage. In 1534, Parliament passed the Act of Supremacy. It made Henry the head of the Church of England.

Many Catholics, including Sir Thomas More, refused to accept the Act of Supremacy and were executed. The Catholic Church **canonized** More. After Henry's death, his son Edward VI became king. Under Edward, Parliament passed laws bringing Protestant reforms to England. When Edward died, his Catholic half-sister **Mary Tudor** became queen. She wanted England to be Catholic again. Hundreds of English Protestants were burned at the stake. After Mary's death, her half-sister **Elizabeth** ruled. She enforced reforms known as the Elizabethan settlement. This was a **compromise** between Protestant and Catholic practices. Elizabeth restored unity to England. She kept many Catholic traditions, but made England Protestant.

VOCABULARY STRATEGY

Find the word *rigorous* in the underlined sentence. What clues to that word's meaning do nearby words give? Notice the examples in the sentence that describe the Jesuit program. Use context clues and examples in the sentence to help you learn what *rigorous* means.

At about this time, a reform movement took hold within the Catholic Church. It was called the Counter Reformation. The pope's **Council of Trent** reaffirmed Catholic views. A Spanish knight, **Ignatius of Loyola,** founded a new religious order called the Jesuits. Their rigorous program included strict discipline, thorough religious training, and absolute obedience to the Church. **Teresa of Avila** established an order of nuns dedicated to prayer and meditation. Both Catholics and Protestants persecuted radical sects. Innocent people were put to death as witches. In Venice, Jews were pressured to convert, and ordered to live in a quarter of the city called the **ghetto.**

READING SKILL

Identify Main Ideas What was the result of the Elizabethan settlement?

_____

_____

Review Questions

1. Why did Henry VIII break from the Catholic Church?

_____

_____

2. What happened when Thomas More refused to accept the Act of Supremacy?

_____

_____

CHAPTER
13
SECTION 5

Note Taking Study Guide
THE SCIENTIFIC REVOLUTION

Focus Question: How did discoveries in science lead to a new way of thinking for Europeans?

As you read this section in your textbook, complete the following chart to identify main ideas about the Scientific Revolution in Europe.

Thinkers of the Scientific Revolution		
Nicolaus Copernicus	Developed sun-centered universe theory	
Tycho Brahe	Provided evidence to support Copernicus's theory	
Johannes Kepler	Calculated the orbits of planets around the sun	
Galileo Galilei		
Francis Bacon		
René Descartes		
Andreas Vesalius		
Ambroise Paré		

CHAPTER 13 SECTION 5

Section Summary

THE SCIENTIFIC REVOLUTION

In the mid-1500s, the Scientific Revolution occurred. It changed how people thought about the universe. Before the Renaisance, Europeans believed Earth was the center of everything. In 1543, Polish scholar **Nicolaus Copernicus** suggested that the solar system was **heliocentric,** or centered around the sun. The work of Danish astronomer **Tycho Brahe** supported Copernicus's theory. The German astronomer and mathematician **Johannes Kepler** used Brahe's data to calculate the orbits of the planets. His work also supported Copernicus's theory.

Many scientists built on the foundations laid by Copernicus and Kepler. In Italy, **Galileo** built a telescope and observed that Jupiter's four moons move slowly around that planet. They moved in the way Copernicus said that Earth moves around the sun. Galileo's discoveries caused an uproar. Other scholars attacked him because his observations contradicted ancient views about the world. The Catholic Church condemned him. His ideas challenged the Christian teaching that the heavens were fixed in position to Earth, and perfect.

VOCABULARY STRATEGY

Find the word *contradicted* in the underlined sentence. It begins with the prefix *contra-,* which means "against." Use the meaning of the word's prefix and context clues in the paragraph to help you figure out what *contradict* means.

Despite the Church's objection, a new approach to science emerged. It was based on observation and experimentation. To explain their data, scientists used reasoning to propose a logical **hypothesis,** or possible explanation. This process became known as the **scientific method.** Two giants of this new approach were Englishman **Francis Bacon** and Frenchman **René Descartes.** They used different scientific methods to understand how truth is determined. Bacon stressed experimentation and observation. Descartes emphasized reasoning.

Dramatic changes occurred in many branches of science at this time. English chemist **Robert Boyle** explained that matter is composed of particles that behave in knowable ways. **Isaac Newton** used mathematics to show that a force keeps the planets in orbits around the sun. He called this force **gravity.** He also developed a branch of mathematics called **calculus.**

Review Questions

1. Before the Renaissance, what planet did Europeans believe was the center of the universe?

_____

_____

2. Why did the Church condemn Galileo?

_____

_____

Focus Question: How did the search for spices lead to global exploration?

As you read this section in your textbook, complete the following flowchart to identify causes and effects of European exploration. Some items have been completed for you.

Columbus Sails West

-
-
-

Portugal Leads

- Rounds southern tip of Africa
-
-

Reasons to Explore

- Control trade
- Gain direct access to Asia
-

Name_____ Class_____ Date_____

What was the main source of the spices Europeans wanted?

_____

_____

_____

Find the word *authority* in the underlined sentence. Sometimes a word will be defined nearby. Clue words or phrases that signal a definition include *which means, also known as,* and *or.* Notice that *authority* is defined within this sentence. Find the clue word that signals the definition. Circle the word in the sentence that could help you figure out what *authority* means.

Identify Causes and Effects

Identify one cause of European exploration.

_____

_____

_____

Identify one effect of Portugal's explorations along the coast of Africa.

_____

_____

_____

By the 1400s, Europe's demand for trade goods, especially valuable spices, was growing. The chief source of spices was the **Moluccas,** an island chain in present-day Indonesia. Arab and Italian merchants controlled most trade between Asia and Europe. Europeans outside Italy wanted their own access to Asia's trade goods.

Prince Henry encouraged Portuguese sea exploration. He believed that Africa was the source of the riches the Muslim traders controlled. He also hoped to reach Asia by going along the African coast. **Cartographers** prepared maps for the voyages. In 1497, **Vasco da Gama** led four Portuguese ships around the southern tip of Africa. Evenually, they reached the great spice port of Calicut on the west coast of India. Soon, the Portuguese seized ports around the Indian Ocean and created a vast trading empire.

Now others looked for a sea route to Asia. The Italian navigator **Christopher Columbus** persuaded Ferdinand and Isabella of Spain to pay for his voyage. In 1492, Columbus sailed west with three small ships. When the crew finally spotted land, they thought they had reached the Indies, or Southeast Asia. What Columbus had actually found were previously unknown lands.

The Spanish rulers asked Spanish-born Pope Alexander VI to support their authority, or power, to claim the lands of this "new world." The pope set the **Line of Demarcation.** This gave Spain rights to lands west of the line; Portugal had rights to lands east of the line. Both countries agreed to these terms in the **Treaty of Tordesillas.**

Europeans still had not found a quick sea route to Asia, however. In 1519, a Portuguese nobleman named **Ferdinand Magellan** sailed west from Spain to find a way to the Pacific Ocean. In 1520, he found a passageway at the southern tip of South America. Magellan was killed along the way, but the survivors of this voyage were the first to **circumnavigate,** or sail around, the world.

Review Questions

1. Why did European explorers seek a direct sea route to Asia?

_____

_____

2. Who was Vasco da Gama?

_____

_____

Name_____ Class_____ Date_____

Focus Question: What effects did European exploration have on the people of Africa?

As you read this section in your textbook, complete the following chart to identify the effects of European exploration in Africa. Some items have been completed for you.

Effects of European Exploration

New African States

- Asante kingdom emerges in the area of present-day Ghana.
- _____

Slave Trade

- European involvement encourages broader Atlantic slave trade.
- _____
- _____

European Footholds

- Portuguese establish forts and trading posts.
- Portuguese attack coastal cities of East Africa.
- _____

CHAPTER 14 SECTION 2

Section Summary

TURBULENT CENTURIES IN AFRICA

READING CHECK

Which African ruler tried to stop the slave trade?

_____

_____

_____

VOCABULARY STRATEGY

Find the word *unified* in the underlined sentence. What clue can you find in its prefix, *uni-?* Think of other words that have the same word part, such as *unicycle* or *unicorn.* What do a unicycle and a unicorn have in common? Use the information about the word part *uni-* to help you figure out what *unified* means.

READING SKILL

Identify Effects Identify one major effect of the slave trade on African states.

_____

_____

_____

The Portuguese gained footholds on the coast of West Africa by building small forts and trading posts. From there, they sailed around the coast to East Africa. There they continued to build forts and trading posts. They also attacked Arab trading cities in East Africa, such as **Mombasa** and **Malindi.** They eventually took over the East African trade network.

Europeans began to view slaves as the most important part of African trade. By the 1500s, European interest caused the slave trade to grow into a huge moneymaking business. Europeans especially needed workers for their **plantations,** or large estates, in the Americas and elsewhere. Some African leaders tried to slow down or stop the slave trade. The ruler of Kongo, **Affonso I,** was one. He had been taught by Portuguese **missionaries,** and wanted to maintain ties with Europe but stop the slave trade. He was unsuccessful.

The slave trade had major effects on African states. Some small states disappeared forever because of the loss of so many young people. At the same time, new states arose. Their ways of life depended on the slave trade. The **Asante kingdom** emerged in the area of present-day Ghana. In the late 1600s, an able military leader, **Osei Tutu,** won control of the trading city of Kumasi. From there, he conquered neighboring peoples and unified the Asante kingdom. Under Osei Tutu, the Asante kingdom set up a **monopoly,** or sole control, over gold mining and the slave trade. The **Oyo empire** arose as waves of Yoruba people settled in the region of present-day Nigeria. Its leaders used wealth from the slave trade to build a strong army.

By the 1600s, several other European powers had built forts along the west coast of Africa. In 1652, Dutch immigrants arrived at the very tip of the continent. They built **Cape Town,** the first permanent European settlement. Dutch farmers, called **Boers,** settled the lands around the port.

Review Questions

1. How did the Portuguese gain footholds on the coasts of Africa?

_____

_____

2. Who was Osei Tutu?

_____

_____

CHAPTER 14
SECTION 3

Note Taking Study Guide
EUROPEAN FOOTHOLDS IN SOUTH AND SOUTHEAST ASIA

Focus Question: How did European nations build empires in South and Southeast Asia?

As you read this section in your textbook, complete the flowchart below to identify causes and effects of European exploration in South and Southeast Asia. Some items have been entered for you.

Portugal	Netherlands	Spain	Britain
• Builds a rim of trading outposts and controls spice trade between Europe and Asia • _____	• Establishes Cape Town and gains a secure foothold in the region • _____	• _____ • _____	• _____ • _____

CHAPTER 14 SECTION 3 — Section Summary
EUROPEAN FOOTHOLDS IN SOUTH AND SOUTHEAST ASIA

VOCABULARY STRATEGY

Find the word *strategic* in the underlined sentence. The word describes the settlement of Cape Town. What can you learn about Cape Town from the next sentence? Use these context clues to help you decide which word below is a synonym for *strategic*.

1. favorable

2. unfavorable

READING SKILL

Identify Causes and Effects
Identify one cause and one effect of the Mughal emperors' decision to grant trading rights to Europeans.

_____

_____

_____

After Vasco da Gama's successful voyage to India, the Portuguese returned to the Indian Ocean. They were under the command of **Afonso de Albuquerque.** In 1510, the Portuguese seized the island of **Goa** off the coast of India. Then, they took the trading port of **Malacca.** In less than 50 years, the Portuguese built a trade empire with military and merchant **outposts.** For most of the 1500s, they controlled the spice trade between Europe and Asia.

The Dutch challenged the Portuguese control of Asian trade. In 1599, a Dutch fleet returned from Asia with a cargo of spices. Soon after, the Dutch set up colonies and trading posts around the world. <u>This included their strategic settlement at Cape Town.</u> From Cape Town they could repair and re-supply their ships. In 1602, a group of wealthy Dutch merchants formed the **Dutch East India Company,** which had full **sovereign** powers. This meant that the company could build armies, wage war, negotiate peace treaties, and govern overseas territory. Soon, the Dutch East India Company came to control much of southern Asia. Meanwhile, Spain took over the **Philippines,** which became a key link in its huge empire.

Mughal India was at the center of the valuable spice trade. The **Mughal empire** was larger, richer, and more powerful than any kingdom in Europe. Therefore, Mughal emperors saw no threat in granting trading rights to Europeans. Europeans were permitted to build forts and warehouses in coastal towns.

Over time, the Mughal empire weakened, however, and French and British traders fought for power. Like the Dutch, both the British and the French had formed East India companies. The British used their army of **sepoys,** or Indian troops, to drive out the French. By the late 1700s, the British East India Company had used its great wealth to take over most of India.

Review Questions

1. How did the Portuguese build a trade empire?

_____

_____

2. What are sovereign powers?

_____

_____

CHAPTER 14 SECTION 4

Note Taking Study Guide

ENCOUNTERS IN EAST ASIA

Focus Question: How were European encounters in East Asia shaped by the worldviews of both Europeans and Asians?

As you read this section in your textbook, complete the following chart to understand the effects of European contacts in East Asia. Some items have been completed for you.

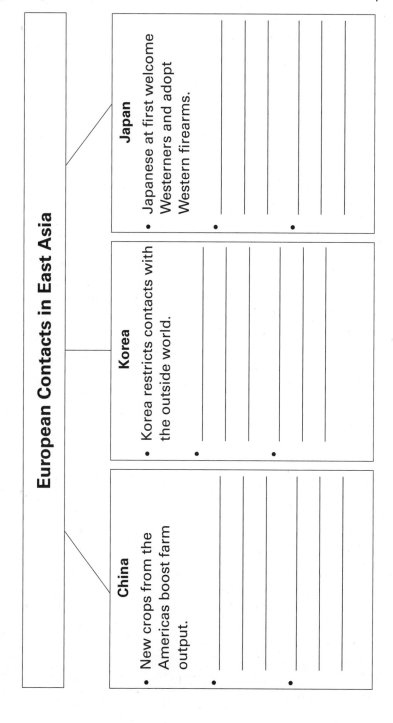

European Contacts in East Asia

Japan
- Japanese at first welcome Westerners and adopt Western firearms.

Korea
- Korea restricts contacts with the outside world.

China
- New crops from the Americas boost farm output.

CHAPTER
14
SECTION 4

Section Summary

ENCOUNTERS IN EAST ASIA

READING CHECK

What did the Manchus name their new dynasty?

_____

_____

_____

VOCABULARY STRATEGY

Find the word *allegiance* in the underlined sentence. Think about your prior knowledge of this word. You may say the Pledge of Allegiance at public events. What does it mean when you pledge your *allegiance* to something? Use prior knowledge to help you figure out what *allegiance* means.

READING SKILL

Identify Effects Explain what caused the shoguns in Japan to grow hostile toward foreigners.

_____

_____

_____

Portuguese traders reached China in 1514. They wanted Chinese silks and porcelains, but the European goods they brought to trade were not as fine as Chinese products. The Chinese, therefore, asked to be paid in gold or silver. The Ming rulers let the Portuguese and other Europeans set up a trading post at **Macao,** in present-day **Guangzhou.** Portuguese missionaries came with the traders. Later, Jesuits arrived, too. The Jesuit priest **Matteo Ricci** made a strong impression on the Chinese, who welcomed learning about Europe.

Eventually, the Ming dynasty weakened. In 1644, the **Manchus,** a people from Manchuria, seized Beijing and made it their capital. They set up a new dynasty called the **Qing.** Two rulers oversaw the most brilliant age of the Qing—Kangxi and his grandson **Qianlong.** Under both emperors, the Chinese economy expanded. Internal trade grew. The Qing kept the Ming policy of restricting foreign traders, however. When **Lord Macartney** led a British diplomatic mission to China, his attempt to negotiate for expanded trade failed.

Like China, Korea restricted contact with the outside world. In the 1590s, a Japanese invasion devastated Korea. Then in 1636, the Manchus conquered Korea. In response, Korea excluded all foreigners except the Chinese and a few Japanese. It became known as the "Hermit Kingdom."

The Japanese at first welcomed Westerners. Traders arrived in Japan at a time when warrior lords were struggling for power. The warrior lords quickly adopted Western firearms. Jesuit priests converted many Japanese to Christianity. The shoguns, or rulers, however, grew hostile toward foreigners. <u>They worried that Japanese Christians owed their allegiance to the pope rather than to them.</u> The shoguns expelled foreign missionaries and barred all European merchants. To learn about world events, however, they let one or two Dutch ships trade each year at a small island in **Nagasaki** harbor. Japan remained isolated for more than 200 years.

Review Questions

1. How did the Ming learn about Europe?

_____

_____

2. Why did Korea become known as the "Hermit Kingdom"?

_____

_____

Name_____ Class_____ Date_____

Focus Question: How did a small number of Spanish conquistadors conquer huge Native American empires?

As you read this section of your textbook, fill in the chart below to help you sequence the events that led to European empires in the Americas. Some items have been completed for you.

Spain Establishes an Empire

Columbus
- Columbus arrives in the West Indies.
- Spanish offended by Taínos.
- _____

Cortés
- Cortés lands on coast of Mexico and begins trek toward Tenochtitlán in 1519.
- _____
- _____
- _____
- _____

Pizarro
- _____
- Captures ruler and kills thousands of Incas
- _____
- _____
- _____

CHAPTER
15
SECTION 1

Section Summary
CONQUEST IN THE AMERICAS

READING CHECK

What was the name of the Aztec capital destroyed by Hernán Cortés?

_____

_____

_____

In 1492, Christopher Columbus reached the Caribbean islands in the present-day West Indies. Columbus' first encounter with Native Americans began a cycle of meeting, conquest, and death, which was repeated across the Western Hemisphere.

Columbus first met the Taíno people and claimed their land for Spain. A wave of Spanish **conquistadors,** or conquerors, soon followed. They brought weapons and horses. Without knowing, they also brought diseases, which wiped out Native Americans, who had no **immunity,** or resistance. Within a few decades, the hundreds of Spanish who came to the Americas were able to conquer millions of Native Americans.

Explorer **Hernán Cortés** reached Mexico in 1519 and moved toward the Aztec capital, **Tenochtitlán.** An Indian woman, **Malinche,** helped him form **alliances** with native peoples who had been conquered by the Aztecs. Cortés reached Tenochtitlán, where he was welcomed by the ruler, **Moctezuma.** Soon, however, relations became strained. <u>Cortés imprisoned Moctezuma and compelled him to sign over lands and treasure to the Spanish.</u> In 1521, Cortés destroyed Tenochtitlán.

Another Spanish adventurer, **Francisco Pizarro,** wanted riches from Peru's Inca empire. Pizarro reached Peru in 1532 after its ruler had won a bloody **civil war,** or war between people of the same nation. Pizarro captured the ruler, Atahualpa, eventually killing him. Spanish forces seized Inca lands. After that they claimed much of South America for Spain. A few years later, Pizarro was killed by another Spanish group.

Spain's impact on the Americas was huge. The Spanish took vast fortunes in gold and silver, making Spain the greatest power of Europe. They opened sea routes for the exchange of goods, people, and ideas. However, they also brought death to Native Americans. Many survivors converted to Christianity, seeking hope. Others, like the Maya, resisted Spanish influence by keeping their own religion, language, and culture. This left a large imprint on Latin America.

VOCABULARY STRATEGY

Find the word *compelled* in the underlined sentence. The word is a verb and so describes an action. Do you think Moctezuma was willing or unwilling to do what Cortés wanted him to do? Use the answer to this question to help you figure out what *compelled* means.

READING SKILL

Recognize Sequence What happened two years before Cortés destroyed Tenochtitlán in 1521?

_____

_____

_____

Review Questions

1. How did the Spanish conquer millions of Native Americans?

_____

_____

2. How were the Maya able to resist Spanish influence?

_____

_____

Focus Question: How did Spain and Portugal build colonies in the Americas?

A. *As you read "Ruling the Spanish Empire," fill in the chart below to record the steps the Spanish took to establish an empire in America. Some items have been completed for you.*

Governing the empire	Catholic Church	Trade	Labor
• Viceroys • _____ _____	• Converted Native Americans to Christianity • _____ _____ • _____ _____	• _____ _____ • Laws passed forbidding colonists from trading with other European nations or even with other Spanish colonies.	• Native Americans forced to work under brutal conditions on plantations and in mines under encomienda system. • _____ • _____

B. *As you read "Colonial Society and Culture" and "Beyond the Spanish Empire," fill in the Venn diagram below to compare and contrast the Spanish and Portuguese empires. Some items have been filled in for you.*

Spanish empire   **Portuguese empire**

• Claimed most of South America

• _____ _____

• Native Americans wiped out by disease.

• _____ _____

• _____ _____

• Claimed Brazil

• _____ _____

CHAPTER 15 SECTION 2	Section Summary
	SPANISH AND PORTUGUESE COLONIES IN THE AMERICAS

READING CHECK

Who ruled the Spanish colonies in the Americas?

_____

_____

_____

VOCABULARY STRATEGY

Find the word *drastic* in the underlined sentence. What does *drastic* mean? What clues can you find in nearby words or phrases? Circle any context clues in the paragraph that could help you figure out what *drastic* means.

READING SKILL

Recognize Sequence Number the following events in the correct order:

____ Slaves are brought to the Americas by the Spanish.

____ Spain passes laws to end abuse of workers.

____ Bartolomé de Las Casas condemns the encomienda system.

Spanish settlers followed conquerors into the Americas. There they built colonies and created a culture that blended European, Native American, and African traditions. By the mid-1500s, Spain's empire ran from modern California to South America.

The monarchy appointed **viceroys** to rule. To make the empire profitable, Spain forbade colonists to trade with any nation but Spain. Conquistadors were granted **encomiendas,** or the right to demand work from Native Americans.

Native Americans were forced to work under terrible conditions. <u>Disease, starvation, and cruelty caused a drastic decline in their population.</u> A priest, **Bartolomé de Las Casas,** begged the king to end the abuse. Such laws were passed in 1542. But Spain was too far away to enforce them. Some landlords forced people to become **peons,** or paid workers who were forced to work to repay huge debts. Also, colonists brought in millions of African slaves.

A blending of cultures resulted. Native Americans contributed building styles, foods, and arts. Settlers contributed Christianity and the use of animals, especially horses. Africans contributed farming methods, crops, and arts.

However, society had a strict structure. At the top were **peninsulares,** or people born in Spain. Next were **creoles,** or native-born descendants of Spanish settlers. Below them were the **mestizos,** people of Native American and European descent, and **mulattoes,** people of African and European descent. At the bottom were Native Americans and African slaves.

Portugal, too, had territory in South America in Brazil. As in Spanish colonies, Native Americans in Brazil were nearly wiped out by disease. Brazil's rulers also used African slaves and Native American labor. There, too, a new blended culture developed.

In the 1500s, wealth from the Americas made Spain the most powerful nation in Europe, followed by Portugal. Pirates often attacked treasure ships from their colonies. Some pirates, called **privateers,** even had the approval of their nations' governments.

Review Questions

1. What were encomiendas?

_____

_____

2. How were the Spanish and Portuguese colonies alike?

_____

_____

CHAPTER 15 SECTION 3

Note Taking Study Guide

STRUGGLE FOR NORTH AMERICA

Focus Question: How did European struggles for power shape the North American continent?

As you read this section of your textbook, complete the following timeline to show the sequence of events in the struggle for North America. Some items have been completed for you.

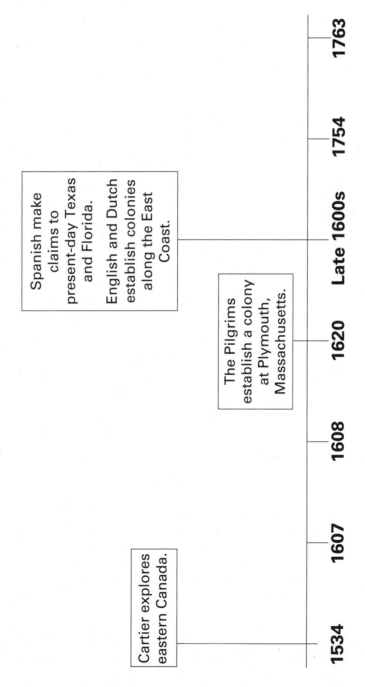

Spanish make claims to present-day Texas and Florida.

English and Dutch establish colonies along the East Coast.

The Pilgrims establish a colony at Plymouth, Massachusetts.

Cartier explores eastern Canada.

1534 — 1607 — 1608 — 1620 — Late 1600s — 1754 — 1763

CHAPTER 15 SECTION 3

Section Summary
STRUGGLE FOR NORTH AMERICA

In the 1600s, the French, Dutch, English, and Spanish competed for lands in North America. By 1700, France and England controlled large parts of North America. Their colonies differed in many ways.

In 1534, Jacques Cartier explored and claimed for the French much of eastern Canada, called **New France.** Eventually, France's empire reached from Quebec to the Great Lakes and down the Mississippi River to Louisiana. The first lasting French settlement was set up in 1608 in Quebec. Hard Canadian winters discouraged settlement, however. Many settlers gave up farming for more profitable fur trapping and fishing. In the late 1600s, French king Louis XIV wanted greater **revenue,** or income from taxes. He named officials to manage his North American colonies. He also sent soldiers and more settlers.

In the early 1700s, New France's population was small. However, English colonies were growing along the Atlantic coast. The first permanent English colony, Jamestown in Virginia, was established in 1607. In 1620, **Pilgrims,** or English Protestants who rejected the Church of England, started a colony called Plymouth in Massachusetts. They wrote a **compact,** or agreement, known as the Mayflower Compact. It set rules for governing their new colony.

In the 1600s and 1700s, the English set up 13 North American colonies in all. English kings kept control over them through royal governors. But English colonists had more self-government than French or Spanish colonists. The English had their own representative assemblies that could advise the governor and decide local issues.

During the 1700s, England and France became rivals. In 1754, the **French and Indian War** broke out in North America. Then in 1756, it spread to Europe, India, and Africa and was called the Seven Years' War. Although the war dragged on, the British ultimately prevailed. In 1763, the **Treaty of Paris** ended this worldwide war. France had to give up Canada to Britain.

Review Questions

1. How did Canadian winters affect French settlement?

_____

_____

2. What could English representative assemblies do?

_____

_____

Focus Question: How did the Atlantic slave trade shape the lives and economies of Africans and Europeans?

As you read this section in your textbook, complete the following flowchart to record the sequence of events that led to millions of Africans being brought to the Americas. Some of the items have been completed for you.

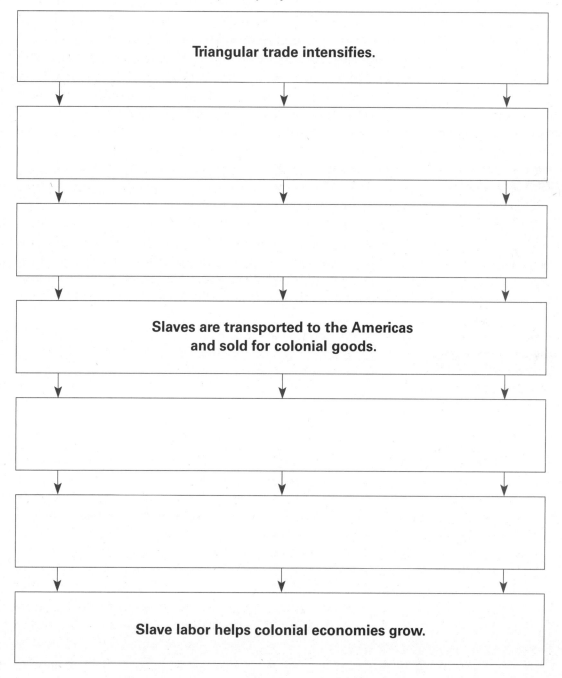

Triangular trade intensifies.

Slaves are transported to the Americas and sold for colonial goods.

Slave labor helps colonial economies grow.

Section Summary
THE ATLANTIC SLAVE TRADE

READING CHECK

Which European nation was the first to bring slaves to the Americas?

_____

_____

_____

VOCABULARY STRATEGY

Find the word *restrained* in the underlined sentence. What does *restrained* mean? People were *restrained* "in holding pens." Use these clues and other context clues to help you figure out what *restrained* means.

READING SKILL

Recognize Sequence Make a diagram of the triangular trade to show the directions of the main flow of goods between Africa, the Americas, and Europe.

Empires grew in the 1500s, and trade increased between the Americas and other parts of the world. Spain was the first major nation to buy slaves for its colonies, but the slave trade grew as other European countries set up colonies. Slave labor became a way to make huge profits, but at the cost of millions of lives.

The trade of slaves became known as **triangular trade,** a series of Atlantic sea routes joining Europe, Africa, and the Americas. On the first leg of the triangle, merchant ships brought European goods to Africa, where they were traded for slaves. On the second leg, known as the **Middle Passage,** slaves like **Olaudah Equiano,** were sent to the Americas, where they were traded for colonial goods. On the final leg, these products were traded for other colonial goods and then shipped to Europe, where they were traded for European goods.

The Middle Passage was a horrible journey for Africans. They were captured and forced to walk as much as one thousand miles. Many died on the way. Those who lived were restrained in holding pens in African port cities until European ships came. Hundreds were packed below deck for the long voyages. Up to half died from disease, cruelty, suicide, and dangers, such as storms, pirate raids, and **mutinies,** or revolts, by slaves trying to return home.

The triangular trade went on because it brought huge profits. It made merchants and traders rich and helped colonial economies grow. However, for Africans it was a disaster. African societies were torn apart, and lives were cut short or ruined. By the mid-1800s, when the slave trade finally ended, an estimated 11 million African slaves had reached the Americas, while another 2 million had died during the Middle Passage.

Review Questions

1. What three main areas of the world were connected by the triangular trade?

_____

_____

2. Why did the triangular trade go on, even though it ruined or ended the lives of millions of people?

_____

_____

CHAPTER 15 SECTION 5

Note Taking Study Guide

EFFECTS OF GLOBAL CONTACT

Focus Question: How did the voyages of European explorers lead to new economic systems in Europe and its colonies?

A. *As you read "The Columbian Exchange," complete the following flowchart to record the sequence of events that led to the Columbian Exchange, as well as the effects. Some of the items have been completed for you.*

Causes	Columbian Exchange	Effects
• Age of exploration begins. • _____ • _____	• _____ • _____ • Named for Columbus, whose voyage began the exchange	• _____ • Native American diets improve; horses and donkeys transport goods and people. • _____ • New crops lead to population growth all over the world. • Millions of people migrate. • Populations wiped out by disease and war.

B. *As you read "A Commercial Revolution," complete the following flowchart to record the sequence of events that led to new global economic systems, as well as the effects. Some of the items have been completed for you.*

Causes	New Economic Systems	Effects
• _____ _____ • Growing demand for goods • Fierce competition for trade and empires	• Capitalism • _____ • Mercantilism	• _____ • Putting-out system led to capitalist-owned factories of the Industrial Revolution. • _____ • Merchants and skilled workers prospered. • Middle-class families enjoyed a comfortable life.

CHAPTER 15 SECTION 5

Section Summary
EFFECTS OF GLOBAL CONTACT

Exploration in the 1500s and 1600s led to European control of the globe. By the 1700s, worldwide contact had caused huge changes to people in Europe, Asia, Africa, and the Americas.

When Columbus returned to Europe in 1493, he brought back American plants and animals. He carried European plants, animals, and settlers back to the Americas. A vast global interchange began. Named for Columbus, it was called the **Columbian Exchange.** Sharing different foods and animals helped people around the world. Later, this dispersal of new crops from the Americas led to worldwide population growth.

Another result of global contact was economic change. In the 1500s, **inflation** increased in Europe, due to all the silver and gold from the Americas. Inflation is a rise in prices because of sharp increases in the money supply. This period of rapid inflation in Europe was known as the **price revolution.** Out of these changes came **capitalism,** an economic system of privately owned business. **Entrepreneurs,** or people who take financial risk for profits, were key to the success of capitalism. Europe's entrepreneurs created businesses and joined investors in overseas ventures. This changed local economies into international trading economies. Fierce competition for trade and empires, in turn, led to a new economic system, called **mercantilism.** Under this system, a nation's wealth was measured in gold and silver, and nations had to export more than they imported. Mercantilists also pushed governments to impose **tariffs,** or taxes on imported goods. This would give an advantage to local products by making imports cost more.

Economic changes, however, took centuries to affect most Europeans. However, by the 1700s, many social changes had happened, too. Nobles, whose wealth was in land, were hurt by the price revolution. Merchants who invested in new businesses grew wealthy. Skilled workers in growing cities also prospered, creating a thriving middle class.

Review Questions

1. Why did mercantilists push governments to impose tariffs?

_____

_____

2. By the 1700s, who was being helped by economic changes?

_____

_____

Name_____ Class_____ Date_____

Focus Questions: How did Philip II extend Spain's power and help establish a golden age?

As you read this section in your textbook, use the outline to identify main ideas and supporting details about Spain's power. Some details have been completed for you.

I. Charles V Inherits Two Crowns

    A. Ruling the Hapsburg empire

        1. Spain

        2. Holy Roman Empire and Netherlands

    B. Charles V abdicates

        1. Charles enters monastery in 1556 and divides empire.

        _____

        3. _____

II. Philip II Solidifies Power

    A. Centralizing power

        1. Philip II reigns as an absolute monarch.

        2. Rules by divine right

    B. Battles in the Mediterranean and the Netherlands

        1. Philip fights wars to advance Spanish Catholic power.

        2. Protestant provinces of the Netherlands declare their independence.

    C. The armada sails against England.

        1. Philip considers Elizabeth I of England his enemy.

        2. Spanish armada is defeated.

    D. An empire declines

        1. _____

        2. _____

        3. _____

        4. _____

        5. _____

(Outline continues on the next page.)

(Continued from page 147)

III. Spain's Golden Age

A. _____

_____

B. _____

_____

C. _____

_____

D. _____

_____

E. _____

_____

CHAPTER 16 SECTION 1

Section Summary

SPANISH POWER GROWS

In 1516, **Charles V** was the king of Spain and ruler of the Spanish colonies in the Americas. In 1519, he inherited the **Hapsburg empire.** This included the Holy Roman Empire and the Netherlands. Ruling two empires involved Charles in constant warfare. In addition, <u>the empire's large territory was too cumbersome for Charles to rule well.</u> The difficult and demanding responsibilities led him to give up his throne in 1556. He divided his kingdom between his brother Ferdinand and son Philip.

Philip II was successful in increasing Spanish power in Europe and strengthening the Catholic Church. Philip also ruled as an **absolute monarch**—a ruler with complete authority over the government and the lives of the people. He also declared that he ruled by **divine right.** This meant he believed that his right to rule came from God. Philip was determined to defend the Catholic Church against the Protestant Reformation in Europe. He fought many battles in the Mediterranean and the Netherlands to extend and preserve Spanish Catholic power.

To expand his kingdom, Philip II needed to eliminate his enemies. Elizabeth I of England was his chief Protestant enemy. Philip prepared a huge **armada,** or fleet, to carry an invasion force to England. However, English ships were faster and lighter than Spanish ships. After several disasters, the Spanish sailed home defeated. The defeat of the armada marked the beginning of the end of Spanish power.

While Spain's strength and wealth decreased, the arts in Spain flourished under Philip's support. The years between 1550 and 1650 are often called Spain's *Siglo de Oro,* or "golden century." Among the famous artists of this time was the painter **El Greco.** His work influenced many other artists. This period also produced several remarkable writers. One of the most important was **Miguel de Cervantes.** His *Don Quixote,* which pokes fun at medieval tales of chivalry, was Europe's first modern novel.

Review Questions

1. What territories were included in the Hapsburg empire?

_____

_____

2. Why did Philip fight many battles?

_____

_____

READING CHECK

What is an absolute monarch?

_____

_____

_____

VOCABULARY STRATEGY

Find the word *cumbersome* in the underlined sentence. What does *cumbersome* mean? What clues to its meaning can you find in the surrounding words, phrases, or sentences? Circle the words in the paragraph that could help you figure out what *cumbersome* means.

READING SKILL

Identify Main Ideas and Supporting Details What details in this Summary support the main idea: Spanish power grew in the early 1500s?

_____

_____

_____

Name_____ Class_____ Date_____

Focus Question: How did France become the leading power of Europe under the absolute rule of Louis XIV?

As you read this section in your textbook, complete the concept web to identify supporting details about the rule of King Louis XIV. Some details have been completed for you.

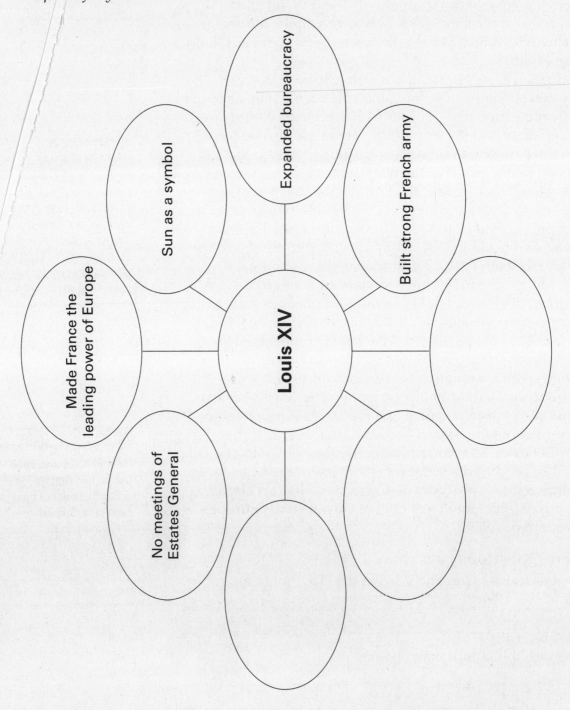

CHAPTER 16 SECTION 2 — Section Summary

FRANCE UNDER LOUIS XIV

In the late 1500s, France was torn by religious conflict between French Protestants, called **Huguenots,** and Catholics. During the St. Bartholomew's Day Massacre, thousands of Huguenots were killed. In 1598, **Henry IV** issued the **Edict of Nantes.** This protected Huguenots by allowing them to follow their religion.

After Henry's assassination in 1610, his nine-year old son, Louis XIII, became king. **Cardinal Richelieu** was his chief minister. For 18 years Richelieu worked to make the central government stronger. Then in 1643, five-year-old **Louis XIV** became king. As he grew older, he chose to control the government himself. Louis XIV called himself the Sun King to symbolize his importance.

Louis XIV appointed **intendants** to the royal government. These were royal officials who collected taxes, recruited soldiers, and carried out the king's policies. To boost the country's economy, Louis's finance minister, **Jean Baptiste Colbert,** started expanding business and trade. Taxes helped to finance the king's extravagant lifestyle.

Outside Paris, Louis XIV transformed a hunting lodge into the palace of **Versailles.** This palace represented the king's power and wealth. Ceremonies were held there to emphasize the king's importance. For example, high-ranking nobles would compete to be part of the king's morning ritual known as the *levée,* or rising. These kinds of ceremonies were meant to keep nobles at Versailles with the king. That way, Louis could gain their support and keep them from battling for power.

Under Louis XIV, France became Europe's most powerful state. However, some of Louis's decisions caused the country's prosperity to erode. His lifestyle and the wars he fought were costly. Rival rulers joined together to keep the **balance of power.** They wanted military and economic power spread evenly among European nations. For example, in 1700, when Louis's grandson inherited the throne of Spain, nearby nations fought to prevent the union of France and Spain.

Review Questions

1. What was the Edict of Nantes?

_____

_____

2. What did Versailles symbolize?

_____

_____

READING CHECK

Why did France's economy decline?

_____

_____

_____

VOCABULARY STRATEGY

Find the word *erode* in the underlined sentence. A related word is *erosion.* Think about what happens when a hillside *erodes.* Use your prior knowledge to help you figure out the meaning of *erode.*

READING SKILL

Identify Supporting Details A main idea in this Summary is that Louis XIV increased his power. What details can you find that support this main idea?

_____

_____

_____

Name_____ Class_____ Date_____

Focus Question: How did the British Parliament assert its rights against royal claims to absolute power in the 1600s?

As you read this section in your textbook, complete the flowchart to identify supporting details about the evolution of Parliament. Some details have been completed for you.

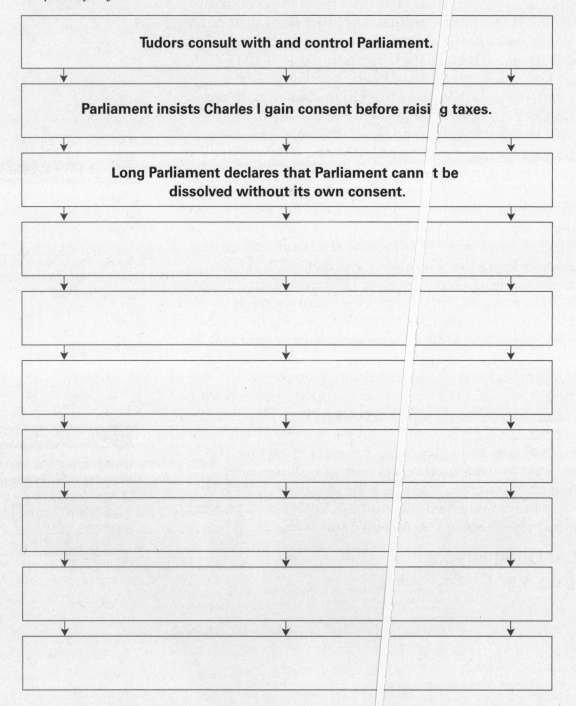

Tudors consult with and control Parliament.

Parliament insists Charles I gain consent before raising taxes.

Long Parliament declares that Parliament cannot be dissolved without its own consent.

CHAPTER 16 SECTION 3

Section Summary
PARLIAMENT TRIUMPHS IN ENGLAND

The first Stuart king, **James I,** inherited the throne in 1603. He claimed absolute power. James clashed with Parliament. He also clashed with **dissenters**—Protestants who disagreed with the Church of England. One such group, the **Puritans,** wanted simpler services and a more democratic church without bishops.

In 1625, James's son **Charles I** inherited the throne. He, too, claimed absolute power. Tensions between Charles and Parliament turned into the English Civil War. It lasted from 1642 to 1651. Supporters of Charles were called Cavaliers. The supporters of Parliament were known as Roundheads. **Oliver Cromwell,** the leader of the Parliament forces, guided them to victory. In January 1649, Parliament had Charles executed.

The House of Commons then abolished the monarchy and declared England a republic, called the Commonwealth. It was ruled by Cromwell. Many new laws were passed, reflecting Puritan beliefs. <u>Cromwell did not tolerate open worship for Catholics.</u> He did respect the beliefs of other Protestants and welcomed Jews back to England. Eventually, people tired of the strict Puritan ways. Cromwell died in 1658. In 1660, Parliament invited Charles II, the son of Charles I, to rule.

Charles II's successor, James II, was forced from the throne in 1688. Protestants feared that he planned to restore the Roman Catholic Church. Parliament offered the crown to James's Protestant daughter, Mary, and her husband, William. This peaceful change of rulers is known as the Glorious Revolution. However, William and Mary first had to accept the **English Bill of Rights.** The Bill of Rights made sure that Parliament had more power than the ruler. This helped establish a **limited monarchy.**

Over time, Britain's government became a **constitutional government**. The law set limits on power. A **cabinet,** or group of parliamentary advisors who set policies, developed. In essence, the British government was an **oligarchy**—a government run by a few powerful people.

Review Questions

1. What was the result of the English Civil War?

_____

_____

2. Who was Oliver Cromwell?

_____

_____

READING CHECK

Why was James II forced from the throne?

_____

_____

_____

VOCABULARY STRATEGY

Find the word *tolerate* in the underlined sentence. What do you think it means? In the next sentence, there is a phrase that means the same thing as *tolerate.* Use that context clue to help you figure out the meaning of *tolerate.*

READING SKILL

Identify Supporting Details The Bill of Rights was a triumph for Parliament. What details in this Summary support that main idea?

_____

_____

_____

Name_____ Class_____ Date_____

Focus Question: How did the two great empires of Austria and Prussia emerge from the Thirty Years' War and subsequent events?

As you read this section in your textbook, use the table to identify supporting details about the emergence of Austria and Prussia as European powers. Some details have been completed for you.

Rise of Prussia	Rise of Austria
• Hohenzollern rulers take over German states. • •	• Austrian ruler keeps title of Holy Roman Emperor. • Ferdinand, Hapsburg king of Bohemia, tries to suppress Protestants and assert power over nobles. • •

Name_____ Class_____ Date_____

CHAPTER 16 SECTION 4

Section Summary
RISE OF AUSTRIA AND PRUSSIA

By the seventeenth century, the Holy Roman Empire had become a mix of many small, separate states. In theory, the Holy Roman emperor, who was chosen by seven leading German princes called **electors,** ruled these states. Yet, the emperor had little power. This lack of power contributed to a series of wars that are together called the Thirty Years' War. It began when **Ferdinand,** the Catholic Hapsburg king of Bohemia, wanted to control Protestants and declare royal power over nobles. This led to a widespread European war.

The Thirty Years' War had a terrible effect on the German states. **Mercenaries,** or soldiers for hire, burned villages, destroyed crops, and killed villagers. There was famine and disease, which caused severe **depopulation,** meaning populations were very low.

It was not until 1648 that a series of treaties known as the **Peace of Westphalia** were set up. <u>These treaties aspired to bring peace to Europe and sought to settle other problems between nations.</u>

While Austria was becoming a strong Catholic state, one of the German states, called **Prussia,** emerged as a new Protestant power. The Prussian ruler **Frederick William I** came to power in 1713. He placed great importance on military values.

In Austria, **Maria Theresa** became empress following her father's death in 1740. That same year, **Frederick II** of Prussia seized the Hapsburg province of Silesia. This led to the **War of the Austrian Succession.** Maria Theresa could not force Frederick out of Silesia. She did, however, preserve her empire and won the support of most of her people. She also strengthened Hapsburg power. She reorganized the government and forced nobles and clergy to pay taxes.

Frederick II continued to use his army to build his country's strength. His acts made Prussia a leading power. By 1750, Austria and Prussia were considered great European powers along with France, Britain, and Russia.

Review Questions
1. Describe the Holy Roman Empire of the seventeenth century.

_____

_____

2. How did Maria Theresa strengthen Austria?

_____

_____

READING CHECK

Who were the great European powers by 1750?

_____

_____

_____

VOCABULARY STRATEGY

Find the word *aspired* in the underlined sentence. The word *strived* is a synonym for *aspired.* Apply what you already know about *strived* to help you learn the meaning of *aspired.*

READING SKILL

Identify Supporting Details
What details support the main idea that the Thirty Years' War had a terrible effect on the German states?

_____

_____

_____

CHAPTER 16 SECTION 5 — Note Taking Study Guide

ABSOLUTE MONARCHY IN RUSSIA

Focus Question: How did Peter the Great and Catherine the Great strengthen Russia and expand its territory?

As you read this section in your textbook, complete the Venn diagram to identify the main ideas about the reigns of Peter the Great and Catherine the Great. Some ideas have been completed for you.

Catherine

- Established warm-water port on Black Sea
- •
- •

Adopted Western Ideas

Peter

- Visited European countries
- Controlled the Church and nobles
- Created a standing army
- •
- •

CHAPTER 16
SECTION 5

Section Summary
ABSOLUTE MONARCHY IN RUSSIA

In the early 1600s, Russia was far behind the more advanced western European nations. By the end of that century, however, a new tsar, **Peter the Great,** turned Russia into a leading power.

To modernize Russia, Peter began a new policy of **westernization**—the adoption of Western ideas, technologies, and culture. Many resisted change. To enforce this new policy, Peter became an **autocratic** monarch. This meant that he ruled with unlimited authority.

All Russian institutions were under Peter the Great's control. He executed anyone who resisted the new order. He forced the **boyars**—landowning nobles—to serve the state in civilian or military positions. <u>Peter also stipulated that they shave their beards and wear Western-style clothing.</u>

Peter built up Russia's military power and extended the borders. To increase Russia's trade with the West, the Russians needed a **warm-water port.** The nearest port was on the Black Sea in the Ottoman empire. Peter, however, could not defeat the Ottomans.

Determined to expand Russia's territory, however, Peter fought a long war against Sweden. On the land he won, he built a beautiful capital city, **St. Petersburg.** It became the symbol of modern Russia. When Peter died in 1725, he had expanded Russian territory, gained ports on the Baltic Sea, and created a strong army.

In 1762, **Catherine the Great** followed Peter's lead in embracing Western ideas and expanding Russia's borders. She, too, ruled as an absolute monarch. She was able to defeat the Ottoman empire and finally won the warm-water port on the Black Sea.

In the 1770s, Russia, Prussia, and Austria each wanted Poland as part of their territory. To avoid war, they agreed to **partition,** or divide up, Poland. In 1772, Russia gained part of eastern Poland, while Prussia and Austria took over the west. Poland ceased to exist.

Review Questions

1. Who transformed Russia into a leading power?

_____

_____

2. What kept Peter the Great from gaining a warm-water port?

_____

_____

READING CHECK

What does *westernization* mean?

_____

_____

_____

VOCABULARY STRATEGY

Find the word *stipulated* in the underlined sentence. It comes from a Latin word that means "to bargain." Think about the bargaining process. Usually people have to agree on specific terms. Use this word-origins clue to help you figure out the meaning of *stipulated.*

READING SKILL

Identify Main Ideas Circle the statement below that identifies the main idea of the Summary.

Catherine the Great freed the serfs.

Peter and Catherine enjoyed Western-style clothing.

Peter and Catherine ruled as absolute monarchs.

Name_____ Class_____ Date_____

Focus Question: What effects did Enlightenment philosophers have on government and society?

As you read this section in your textbook, complete the following table to summarize each thinker's works and ideas. Some items have been completed for you.

Thinkers' Works and Ideas	
Hobbes	• *Leviathan* • _____
Locke	• *Two Treatises of Government* • _____ • _____
Montesquieu	• _____ • _____ • _____
	• _____ • _____ • _____
	• _____ • _____ • _____ • _____
	• _____ • _____
	• _____ • _____ • _____

CHAPTER 17 SECTION 1

Section Summary

PHILOSOPHY IN THE AGE OF REASON

In the 1500s and 1600s, the Scientific Revolution changed the way people looked at the world. They began to use reason and science to learn how things worked. For example, they found that rules govern natural forces such as gravity. Scientists and others began to call these rules the **natural law.** They believed that natural law could be used to solve society's problems, too. In this way the Scientific Revolution sparked another revolution in thinking known as the Enlightenment.

Two important English thinkers of the Enlightenment were **Thomas Hobbes** and **John Locke.** Hobbes argued that people were naturally cruel and selfish. They needed to be controlled by a powerful government, such as an absolute monarchy. According to Hobbes, people made an agreement, or **social contract.** In this contract, people gave up their freedom in exchange for an organized society. In contrast, Locke thought that people were basically good. He believed that people had **natural rights,** or rights that belonged to all humans. These are the right to life, liberty, and property. Locke rejected absolute monarchy. He thought a government of limited power was best.

French Enlightenment thinkers, called *philosophes,* also believed that people could use reason to improve government, law, and society. These thinkers included Baron de **Montesquieu, Voltaire,** Denis **Diderot,** and Jean-Jacques **Rousseau.** Montesquieu, for example, developed the ideas of separation of powers and of checks and balances. These ideas would be used by the Framers of the United States Constitution. In a set of books called the *Encyclopedia,* Diderot explained the new ideas on the topics of government, philosophy, and religion.

Other thinkers, including **Adam Smith,** focused on using natural law to reform the economy. Instead of government control, they urged the policy of **laissez faire.** This allowed the free market to regulate business.

Review Questions

1. What is the natural law?

_____

_____

2. Which of Montesquieu's ideas appear in the U.S. Constitution?

_____

_____

READING CHECK

Who were the *philosophes*?

_____

_____

_____

VOCABULARY STRATEGY

Find the word *philosophy* in the underlined sentence. The word *philosophy* comes from a Greek word that means "love of wisdom." *Philosophe,* which means "philosopher," comes from the same ancient Greek word. Reread the paragraph about the *philosophes.* Use the word-origin clues to help you figure out what *philosophy* means.

READING SKILL

Summarize What did Thomas Hobbes believe about people and the government?

_____

_____

CHAPTER 17 SECTION 2

Note Taking Study Guide

ENLIGHTENMENT IDEAS SPREAD

Focus Question: As Enlightenment ideas spread across Europe, what cultural and political changes took place?

A. As you read "New Ideas Challenge Society" and "Arts and Literature Reflect New Ideas," complete the following concept web to categorize how Enlightenment ideas spread. Some items have been completed for you.

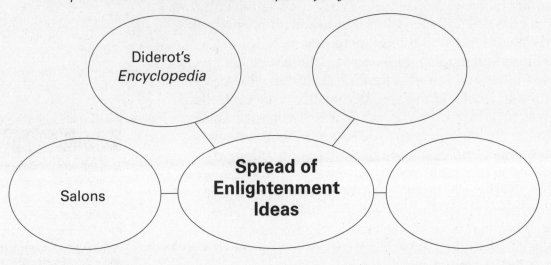

B. As you read "Enlightened Despots Embrace New Ideas" and "Lives of the Majority Change Slowly," complete the following concept web to summarize information about enlightened despots and their contributions. Some items have been completed for you.

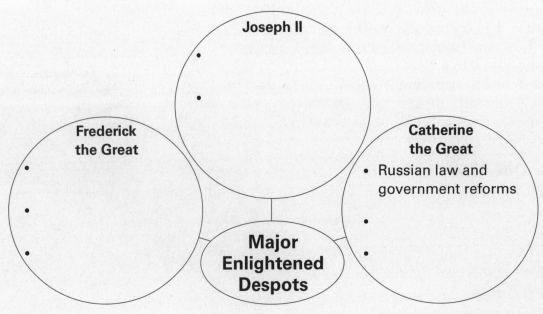

CHAPTER 17 SECTION 2

Section Summary
ENLIGHTENMENT IDEAS SPREAD

Enlightenment ideas flowed from France, across Europe and beyond. Before the Enlightenment, society was based on old ways of doing things. These included divine-right rule, a strict class system, and a belief in heavenly reward for earthly suffering. Enlightenment ideas challenged traditional beliefs and customs. In response, government and church leaders practiced **censorship.** They banned and burned books containing new ideas they did not like. They put writers in prison. Censorship, however, did not stop the spread of ideas. Writers disguised their ideas in works of fiction. Ideas continued to spread in **salons,** or informal social gatherings. There, writers, artists, and *philosophes* shared ideas about new literature, the arts, science, and philosophy.

In the 1600s and 1700s, the arts also evolved to meet the changing tastes and the new Enlightenment ideals. In art and in music, there was a shift from the heavy style of **baroque** to the more charming style of **rococo.** Later, composers wrote works in an elegant style called classical. New forms of literature developed, also. For example, new kinds of books called novels were being written for the growing group of middle-class readers.

Some changes happened in government, too. *Philosophes* tried to persuade European rulers to accept Enlightenment ideas. Some monarchs did. These **enlightened despots** used their power to bring about some political and social changes. In Prussia, **Frederick the Great** allowed a free press. He also urged religious tolerance. **Catherine the Great** of Russia abolished torture. In Austria, **Joseph II** traveled in disguise among his subjects to learn of their problems. Even though ideas of the Enlightenment spread, the lives of most Europeans changed slowly.

Review Questions

1. How did government and church leaders censor Enlightenment ideas?

_____

_____

2. What new art and musical styles developed during the Enlightenment?

_____

_____

READING CHECK

Name one European ruler who was an enlightened despot.

_____

_____

_____

VOCABULARY STRATEGY

Find the word *evolved* in the underlined sentence. What surrounding words or phrases can you find that might give you clues about its meaning? Circle the context clues in the paragraph that helped you to learn what *evolved* means.

READING SKILL

Summarize How were Enlightenment ideas spread across Europe?

_____

_____

_____

Note Taking Study Guide

BIRTH OF THE AMERICAN REPUBLIC

Focus Question: How did ideas of the Enlightenment lead to the independence and founding of the United States of America?

As you read this section in your textbook, complete the following timeline with events that led to the formation of the United States. Some items have been completed for you.

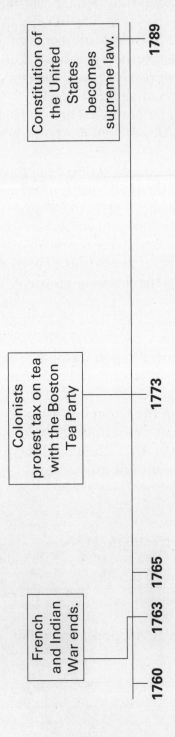

Constitution of the United States becomes supreme law. — 1789

Colonists protest tax on tea with the Boston Tea Party — 1773

1765

1763

French and Indian War ends.

1760

CHAPTER 17 SECTION 3

Section Summary

BIRTH OF THE AMERICAN REPUBLIC

In the mid-1700s, Britain was a global power. <u>The new king, George III, wanted to assert his leadership and expand his rule.</u> Britain's huge territories included 13 colonies in North America. However, society and politics in these colonies developed in their own way. Some colonists began to feel that maybe they would do better if they did not belong to Britain.

Tensions between the colonists and Britain grew. The British Parliament passed laws, such as the **Stamp Act,** that increased colonists' taxes. The colonists felt they should not be taxed because they had no one to speak for them in the British Parliament. A series of violent clashes with British soldiers strengthened the colonists' anger. Leaders from each colony, including **George Washington,** met in a Continental Congress to decide what to do. In April 1775, however, tensions exploded into war. The American Revolution began.

On July 4, 1776, American leaders adopted the Declaration of Independence. Written mostly by **Thomas Jefferson,** it includes John Locke's ideas about the rights to "life, liberty, and property." It outlines the reasons for wanting to be free of British rule and claims **popular sovereignty.** This principle states that all government power comes from the people.

At first, it did not look like the Americans could win. Britain had trained soldiers and a huge fleet. However, later France and other European nations joined the American side, and helped bring about the British surrender at **Yorktown, Virginia.** In 1783, the **Treaty of Paris** ended the war.

Leaders of the new American nation, such as **James Madison** and **Benjamin Franklin,** wrote the Constitution creating a **federal republic.** The new government was based on the separation of powers, an idea borrowed from Montesquieu, an Enlightenment thinker. The Constitution included the Bill of Rights, which listed basic rights that the government must protect.

Review Questions

1. Why did colonists feel they should not be taxed?

_____

_____

2. What ideas of John Locke are in the Declaration of Independence?

_____

_____

READING CHECK

What kind of government did the Constitution create?

_____

_____

_____

VOCABULARY STRATEGY

Find the word *assert* in the underlined sentence. What context clues can you find in the surrounding words, phrases, or sentences that hint at its meaning? Think about what a king would do if he wanted to *assert* his leadership. Circle the word below that has the same meaning as *assert*.

1. declare

2. deny

READING SKILL

Recognize Sequence Place the following events in order:

- Declaration of Independence written

- Continental Congress meets

- Treaty of Paris signed

- Parliament passes Stamp Act.

1._____

2._____

3._____

4._____

Name_____ Class_____ Date_____

Focus Question: What led to the storming of the Bastille, and therefore, to the start of the French Revolution?

As you read this section in your textbook, complete the following chart by identifying the multiple causes of the French Revolution. Some items have been completed for you.

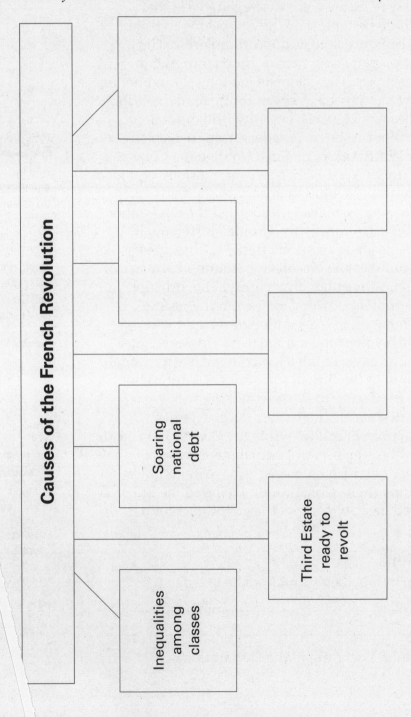

Causes of the French Revolution

- Soaring national debt
- Inequalities among classes
- Third Estate ready to revolt

CHAPTER 18 SECTION 1

Section Summary

ON THE EVE OF REVOLUTION

Under France's **ancien régime**, there were three social classes, or **estates**. The clergy made up the First Estate. The nobles made up the Second Estate. Everyone else, including the **bourgeoisie,** or middle class, belonged to the Third Estate. Most of the Third Estate was made up of rural peasants. <u>Its poorest members were urban workers.</u>

Members of the Third Estate resented the privileges enjoyed by the other classes. The First and Second Estates, for example, paid almost no taxes. Yet peasants paid taxes on many things. People began to question this inequality.

Economic troubles added to France's social problems. France was deeply in debt because of **deficit spending.** Bad harvests sent food prices soaring. **Louis XVI** chose **Jacques Necker** as his financial advisor. Necker proposed taxing the First and Second Estates, but the nobles and high clergy forced the king to dismiss him. As 1788 ended, France was nearly bankrupt. Louis XVI called for the **Estates-General** to meet at Versailles. The Estates-General was the lawmaking body made up of the three classes. Before the meeting, the king had all three estates prepare **cahiers,** or notebooks, listing their complaints. The long lists of problems showed how deeply the Third Estate resented the other two estates.

The Estates-General met in May 1789. Delegates of the Third Estate took a daring step. They claimed to represent the people of France and formed a new National Assembly. Locked out of their meeting place, the delegates took their famous **Tennis Court Oath.** They swore never to separate until they had established a just constitution.

On July 14, 1789, the streets of Paris buzzed with rumors that royal troops were going to occupy the city. A crowd gathered outside the **Bastille,** a grim fortress used as a prison. They demanded weapons that were stored there. When the commander refused, the angry mob stormed the Bastille, sparking the French Revolution.

Review Questions

1. What were the three classes during France's ancien régime?

_____

_____

2. Why was France in debt?

_____

_____

READING CHECK

Which social classes paid the least in taxes?

_____

_____

_____

VOCABULARY STRATEGY

Find the word *urban* in the underlined sentence. Notice that the word *rural* appears in the previous sentence. *Rural* means "country." *Rural* is an antonym of *urban,* so it has the opposite meaning. Use what you know about the word *rural* to help you figure out what *urban* means.

READING SKILL

Recognize Multiple Causes
List two causes of the French Revolution.

_____

_____

_____

CHAPTER
13
SECTION 2

Note Taking Study Guide

THE FRENCH REVOLUTION UNFOLDS

Focus Question: What political and social reforms did the National Assembly institute in the first stage of the French Revolution?

As you read this section in your textbook, complete the following outline by identifying the main ideas and supporting details in this section. Some items have been completed for you.

I. Political crisis leads to revolt

   A. The Great Fear

      1. Inflamed by famine and rumors

      2. _____

   B. Paris Commune comes to power.

      1. _____

      2. _____

II. The National Assembly acts

   A. Special privilege ends.

      1. _____

      2. _____

   B. Declaration of the Rights of Man

      1. _____

      2. _____

   C. _____

      1. _____

      2. _____

III. The National Assembly presses onward

   A. The Church is placed under state control.

      1. _____

      2. _____

   B. _____

      1. _____

      2. _____

   C. _____

      1. _____

      2. _____

(Outline continues on the next page.)

CHAPTER
18
SECTION 2

Note Taking Study Guide
THE FRENCH REVOLUTION UNFOLDS

(Continued from page 166)

IV. _____

    A. _____

        1. _____

        2. _____

    B. _____

        1. _____

        2. _____

    C. _____

        1. _____

        2. _____

    D. _____

        1. _____

        2. _____

Name_____ Class_____ Date_____

CHAPTER

18

SECTION 2

Section Summary

THE FRENCH REVOLUTION UNFOLDS

READING CHECK

What kind of government did the sans-culottes want?

_____
_____
_____

VOCABULARY STRATEGY

Find the word *proclaimed* in the underlined sentence. What do you think it means? The words *proclamation, declaration,* and *announcement* are all synonyms of *proclaimed.* They are words with similar meanings. Use what you know about these synonyms to figure out the meaning of *proclaimed.*

READING SKILL

Identify Supporting Details
Identify two Enlightenment goals that are found in the Constitution of 1791.

_____
_____
_____

In France, the political crisis of 1789 happened at the same time as a famine. Starving peasants took out their anger on the nobles. Many **factions,** or dissenting groups of people, struggled for power. Moderates looked to the **Marquis de Lafayette** for leadership. However, a more radical group, the Paris Commune, took over the city's government.

The storming of the Bastille and the peasant revolts forced the National Assembly to act. Nobles gave up their privileges. In late August, the Assembly issued the Declaration of the Rights of Man and the Citizen. It proclaimed that all male citizens were equal. However, it did not grant equal rights to women. Journalist **Olympe de Gouges** wrote a declaration that did, but the Assembly did not accept it.

In the meantime, the king hesitated to accept reforms. His queen, **Marie Antoinette,** angered many for spending money while people starved. Thousands of women marched to Versailles, where the royal family lived. They demanded the king return to Paris. The National Assembly soon drafted the Constitution of 1791. It reflected Enlightenment goals, stating that all male citizens were equal under the law, and placing the Church under state control.

Events in France caused debate all over Europe. Some praised the reforms. European rulers, however, feared the French Revolution. They worried that the rebellion would spread. The horror stories told by French **émigrés** who fled the revolution added to the fear.

In October 1791, the newly elected Legislative Assembly took power. However, it did little to improve conditions. Working-class men and women called **sans-culottes** pushed for more radical action. Some demanded a **republic.** The **Jacobins,** a revolutionary political club, supported the sans-culottes. The radicals soon controlled the Legislative Assembly. They were eager to spread the revolution and declared war against Austria and other European monarchies.

Review Questions
1. Who was Olympe de Gouges?

_____
_____

2. Why did European rulers fear the French Revolution?

_____
_____

Name_____ Class_____ Date_____

Focus Question: What events occurred during the radical phase of the French Revolution?

As you read this section in your textbook, complete the following timeline to show the sequence of events that took place during the radical phase of the French Revolution. Some dates have been completed for you.

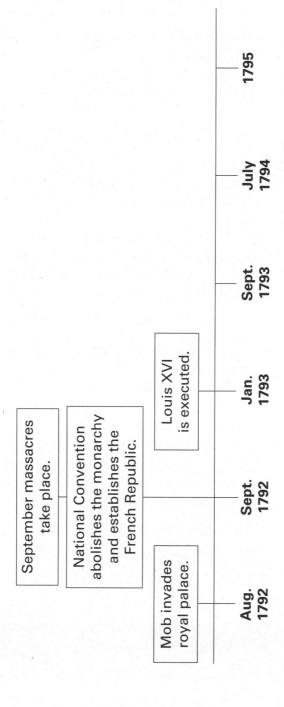

Name_____ Class_____ Date_____

READING CHECK

Who helped to create the Reign of Terror?

_____

_____

_____

VOCABULARY STRATEGY

Find the word *radical* in the underlined sentence. Notice that the word *more* appears before *radical*. Read the sentence aloud, skipping the word *radical*. Then ask yourself, "The Convention was more *what* than earlier assemblies?" Use the word *more* and your prior knowledge to figure out what *radical* means. Check your definition in a dictionary.

READING SKILL

Recognize Sequence What happened before radicals called for the National Convention to be established?

_____

_____

_____

In 1793, the revolution entered a dangerous and bloody phase. Tensions rose between revolutionaries and those hoping to restore the king's power. On August 10, 1792, a mob stormed the royal palace. Radicals called for the election of a new legislature called the National Convention. **Suffrage,** or the right to vote, was given to all male citizens, not just property owners.

The Convention that met in September 1792 was more radical than earlier assemblies. It voted to end the monarchy and establish the French Republic. Louis XVI and most of his family were put on trial and beheaded.

Counter-rebellions inside France worried the Convention. To deal with these, they created the Committee of Public Safety. Maximilien **Robespierre** led the Committee. He helped to create the **Reign of Terror.** The Terror lasted from September 1793 to July 1794. During that time, courts held trials for those who resisted the revolution. Many were falsely accused. About 17,000 people were beheaded by **guillotine,** including Robespierre.

With Robespierre's death, the revolution entered a less-extreme stage. Moderates wrote the Constitution of 1795. It set up a Directory of five men to lead the nation, and a two-house legislature. However, rising prices and corruption remained. To prevent chaos politicians then turned to military hero **Napoleon** Bonaparte.

The French Revolution greatly changed France. The old social order was gone. The monarchy was gone. The Church was under state control. **Nationalism,** or strong feelings of pride and love for one's country, had spread throughout France. From the city of **Marseilles,** troops marched to a new song that later became the French national anthem. Revolutionaries also made social reforms. They set up systems to help the poor. They also ended slavery in some French colonies.

Review Questions

1. What did the New National Convention do in 1792?

_____

_____

2. Identify one major change that the French Revolution brought to France.

_____

_____

Name_____ Class_____ Date_____

Note Taking Study Guide
THE AGE OF NAPOLEON

Focus Question: Explain Napoleon's rise to power in Europe, his subsequent defeat, and how the outcome still affects Europe today.

As you read this section in your textbook, complete the flowchart to list the main ideas about Napoleon's rise to power and his defeat. Some items have been completed for you.

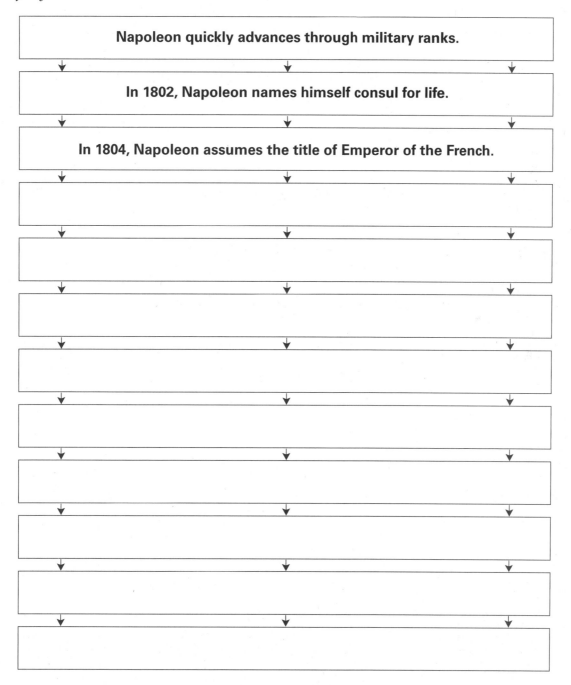

Napoleon quickly advances through military ranks.

In 1802, Napoleon names himself consul for life.

In 1804, Napoleon assumes the title of Emperor of the French.

Name_____ Class_____ Date_____

READING CHECK

What was one of Napoleon's most lasting reforms?

_____

_____

_____

VOCABULARY STRATEGY

Find the word *anticipate* in the underlined sentence. If you were a general, how would changing your battle plans affect your enemies? Use this clue to figure out what *anticipate* means.

READING SKILL

Identify Main Ideas Circle the sentence below that summarizes the main idea of this section Summary.

- The Russian winter defeated Napoleon.

- Napoleon changed Europe.

- Napoleon conquered the British.

The last phase of the revolution is known as the Age of Napoleon. Napoleon Bonaparte started his rise to power as a young officer. By 1804, he had become emperor of France. At each step on his rise, Napoleon held a **plebiscite.** People voted, but Napoleon always kept absolute power.

Napoleon made the central government stronger. All classes of people supported his economic and social reforms. One of his most lasting reforms was the **Napoleonic Code.** This new code of laws embodied Enlightenment principles of equality, religious tolerance, and the end of feudalism.

From 1804 to 1812, Napoleon fought to create a vast French empire. Before each battle, he drafted a completely new plan. <u>Because of this, opposing generals could never anticipate what he would do next.</u> He rarely lost. Napoleon **annexed,** or added to his empire, most European nations except Russia and Britain. He tried to wage economic warfare through the **Continental System.** This system closed European ports to British goods. Many Europeans did not like this blockade. In Spain, patriots waged **guerrilla warfare,** or hit-and-run raids, against the French.

In 1812, Napoleon invaded Russia. The Russians burned crops and villages. This **scorched-earth policy** left the French without food or shelter. The French retreated from Moscow through the Russian winter. Only about 20,000 of 600,000 soldiers made it back to France alive.

The Russian disaster destroyed Napoleon's reputation for success. In 1815, British and Prussian forces crushed the French at the Battle of Waterloo. Napoleon was forced to **abdicate.** After Waterloo, European leaders met at the **Congress of Vienna.** The Congress tried to create a lasting peace through the principle of **legitimacy,** or restoring monarchies that Napoleon had unseated. They also set up the **Concert of Europe** to try to solve conflicts.

Review Questions

1. What reforms won support for Napoleon from all classes?

_____

_____

2. What destroyed Napoleon's reputation for success?

_____

_____

CHAPTER 19
SECTION 1

Note Taking Study Guide
DAWN OF THE INDUSTRIAL AGE

Focus Question: What events helped bring about the Industrial Revolution?

As you read this section in your textbook, complete the following flowchart to list multiple causes of the Industrial Revolution. Some items have been completed for you.

New technologies
- New sources of energy such as steam and coal emerge.
-

Growing labor force
-

Agricultural revolution
- Farming methods improve.
-
-

Industrial Revolution

Section Summary

DAWN OF THE INDUSTRIAL AGE

READING CHECK

Who formed a labor force for the Industrial Revolution?

_____

_____

_____

VOCABULARY STRATEGY

Find the word *statistics* in the underlined sentence. Think about your prior knowledge of this word. For example, you may have seen *statistics* shown in graphs or charts. What was their purpose in those cases? Use your prior knowledge and the context clues in the sentence to help you figure out what the word *statistics* means.

READING SKILL

Recognize Multiple Causes Identify two causes of the agricultural revolution.

_____

_____

_____

The Industrial Revolution started in Britain. In 1750, most people worked on the land using handmade tools. When the Industrial Revolution began, the rural way of life in Britain started to disappear. By the 1850s, many country villages had grown into industrial towns and cities. New inventions and scientific "firsts" appeared each year. For example, an American dentist first used an **anesthetic** during surgery.

A series of related causes helped spark the Industrial Revolution. It was made possible, in part, by another revolution—in agriculture. This agricultural revolution improved the quality and quantity of food. Farmers mixed different kinds of soils or tried new kinds of crop rotation to get higher yields. Meanwhile, rich landowners pushed ahead with **enclosure.** Enclosure is the process of taking over and consolidating land once shared by peasant farmers. As millions of acres were enclosed, farm output and profits rose. The agricultural revolution created a surplus of food, so fewer people died from hunger. Statistics show that the agricultural revolution contributed to a rapid growth in population.

Agricultural progress, however, had a human cost. Many farm laborers lost jobs. They then migrated to towns and cities. There, they became the labor force that operated the new machines of the Industrial Revolution.

Other factors that helped trigger the Industrial Revolution were new technologies and new sources of energy and materials. One vital power source was coal, used to develop the steam engine. In 1764, Scottish engineer **James Watt** improved the steam engine. Watt's engine became a key power source. Coal was also used to produce iron. Iron was needed to make machines and steam engines. In 1709, Adam Darby used coal to **smelt** iron, or separate iron from its ore. Darby's experiments led to the production of less expensive and better-quality iron.

Review Questions

1. How did the Industrial Revolution change rural life in Britain?

_____

_____

2. What other revolution contributed to the start of the Industrial Revolution?

_____

_____

Note Taking Study Guide
BRITAIN LEADS THE WAY

Focus Question: What key factors allowed Britain to lead the way in the Industrial Revolution?

As you read this section in your textbook, complete the following concept webs to identify causes and effects of Britain's early lead in industrialization. Fill in the first concept web with causes. Fill in the second concept web with effects. Some items have been completed for you.

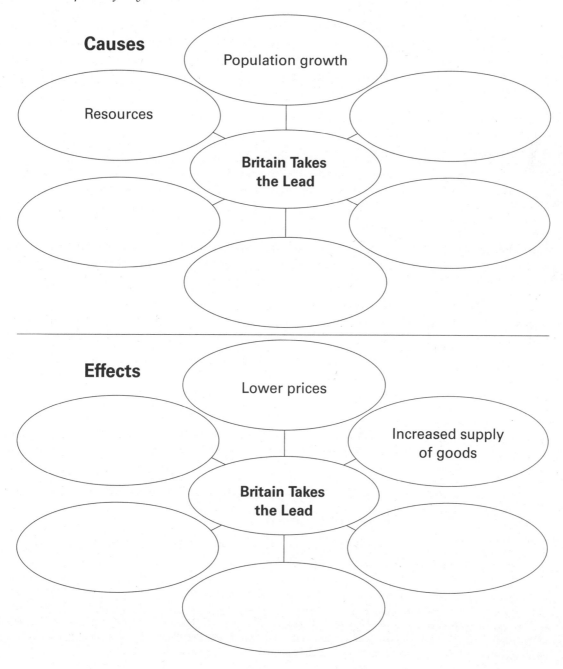

Causes

Population growth

Resources

Britain Takes the Lead

Effects

Lower prices

Increased supply of goods

Britain Takes the Lead

CHAPTER 19 SECTION 2

Section Summary
BRITAIN LEADS THE WAY

The Industrial Revolution began in Britain for several reasons. Population growth was one. Another was Britain's plentiful natural resources, such as rivers, coal, and iron. Also, the growing population and ready workforce increased the demand for goods. To increase production of goods, however, another key ingredient was needed—money. Money was necessary to start businesses. People accumulated **capital,** or money, to invest in an **enterprise,** or business. **Entrepreneurs** managed and assumed the financial risks of starting these new businesses.

The Industrial Revolution developed in Britain's textile industry. British merchants created the **putting-out system.** In this system, raw cotton was given to peasant families. They made it into cloth, in their homes. Production was slow, however. As the demand for cloth grew, inventors came up with new machines, such as the flying shuttle and the spinning jenny. These increased production and revolutionized the British textile industry. Meanwhile, in the United States, people had to figure out how to produce enough cotton to keep up with these faster spinning and weaving machines. The cotton gin, invented by **Eli Whitney,** greatly increased the production of cotton. To house these new machines, manufacturers built the first factories. There, spinners and weavers came each day to work, instead of staying at home.

As production increased, people needed faster and cheaper ways of moving goods, too. Some capitalists invested in **turnpikes.** These toll roads soon linked every part of Britain.

The invention of the steam locomotive spurred the great revolution in transportation. It made the growth of railroads possible. The world's first major rail line ran between the British industrial cities of **Liverpool** and **Manchester.** It started running in 1830. In the following decades, railroad travel became faster and railroad building boomed. As you can see, each change led to another, rapidly affecting the way people lived.

Review Questions

1. How did population growth lead to the Industrial Revolution?

_____
_____

2. How did machines change the textile industry?

_____
_____

CHAPTER 19 SECTION 3
Note Taking Study Guide
SOCIAL IMPACT OF THE INDUSTRIAL REVOLUTION

Focus Question: What were the social effects of the Industrial Revolution?

As you read this section in your textbook, complete the following table to understand the effects of industrialization. Some items have been filled in for you.

Industrialization	
Benefits	**Challenges**
• Created jobs	• Crowded cities
• Wealthy middle class	• Pollution
•	• Struggle for survival in slums
•	•
•	
•	•
•	

CHAPTER 19
SECTION 3

Section Summary

SOCIAL IMPACT OF THE INDUSTRIAL REVOLUTION

READING CHECK

What new social class emerged during the Industrial Revolution?

_____

_____

_____

VOCABULARY STRATEGY

Find the word *contaminated* in the underlined sentence. What clues to the word's meaning can you find in the surrounding words, phrases, or sentences? How do the words *sewage* and *awful stench* help you figure out what *contaminated* means?

READING SKILL

Understand Effects Explain three effects of the Industrial Revolution on the lives of the workers.

_____

_____

The Industrial Revolution brought **urbanization,** or the movement of people to cities. Masses of people moved from farms to cities because of changes in farming, soaring population growth, and demand for workers. Almost overnight, small villages around mines grew into cities. Other cities grew up around the factories that were built in once-quiet market towns.

Those who benefited most from the Industrial Revolution were entrepreneurs. They made up a new middle class created by the Industrial Revolution. The wealthy and the middle class lived in nice neighborhoods. The poor lived in crowded tiny rooms in **tenements,** multistory buildings divided into apartments. These tenements had no running water and no sewage or sanitation system. <u>Sewage rotted in the streets or was dumped into rivers, which contaminated drinking water and created an awful stench.</u> This led to the spread of diseases.

Working in a factory system was very different from working on a farm. In rural villages, people worked hard, but the amount of work varied with each season. The factory system was a harsh new way of life. Working hours were long. Shifts lasted from twelve to sixteen hours, six or even days a week. Tired workers were injured by machines that had no safety devices. Working conditions in mines were even worse than in the factories. Factories and mines also hired many boys and girls. These children often started working at age seven or eight, a few as young as five.

The early industrial age brought terrible hardships. In time, however, reformers pressed for laws to improve working conditions. **Labor unions,** or workers' organizations, won the right to ask for better wages, hours, and working conditions.

Despite the social problems created by the Industrial Revolution, it did have some positive effects. More jobs were created and wages rose. As the cost of railroad travel fell, people could travel farther for less money than ever before.

Review Questions

1. Why did people migrate from farms to cities during the Industrial Revolution?

_____

_____

2. What were working conditions like in factories?

_____

_____

CHAPTER 19 SECTION 4

Note Taking Study Guide

NEW WAYS OF THINKING

Focus Question: What new ideas about economics and society were fostered as a result of the Industrial Revolution?

As you read this section in your textbook, complete the following outline to identify main ideas about the new economic and social theories. Some items have been completed for you.

I. **Laissez-faire economics**

   A. Adam Smith and free enterprise

      1. _____

      2. _____

II. **Malthus on population**

   A. Malthus holds bleak view.

      1. Population will outpace food supply.

      2. _____

      3. _____

   B. Ricardo shares view.

      1. _____

      2. _____

III. **Utilitarians for limited government**

   A. Goal of society should be "the greatest happiness for the greatest number."

      1. _____

      2. _____

IV. **Socialist thought emerges**

   A. Focus should be on the good of society in general, not on individual rights.

      1. _____

      2. _____

   B. Socialists establish utopian communities.

      1. Hoped that equality among people would end conflict

      2. Utopian industrialist Robert Owen sets up a model community in Scotland.

(Outline continues on next page.)

CHAPTER 19 SECTION 4

Note Taking Study Guide

NEW WAYS OF THINKING

(Continued from page 179)

V. Karl Marx explains class struggle

   A. _____

      1. _____

      2. _____

VI. _____

   A. _____

      1. _____

      2. _____

      3. _____

   B. Marxism loses appeal.

      1. _____

      2. _____

CHAPTER 19 SECTION 4

Section Summary

NEW WAYS OF THINKING

Many thinkers tried to understand the great changes taking place in the early Industrial Age. These thinkers looked for natural laws that governed the world of business and economics. Middle-class business leaders supported the laissez-faire, or "hands-off" approach. They believed that a free market would help everyone, not just the rich. However, one British laissez-faire economist, **Thomas Malthus,** thought the poor would always suffer. He believed population would grow faster than the food supply. He did not think the government should help the poor. He believed people should improve their own lives through hard work and have fewer children.

Other thinkers sought to soften laissez-faire doctrines. They felt some government help was needed. The British philosopher and economist **Jeremy Bentham** supported **utilitarianism.** He believed that the goal of society should be the "greatest happiness for the greatest number" of citizens. Other thinkers, such as John Stuart Mill, strongly believed in individual freedom, but wanted the government to step in to prevent harm to workers.

To end poverty and injustice, some offered a radical solution—**socialism.** Under socialism, the **means of production**— the farms, factories, railways, and other businesses—would be owned by the people as a whole, not by individuals. Some early socialists, such as **Robert Owen,** set up communities in which all work and property were shared. They were called Utopians.

The German philosopher **Karl Marx** formulated a new theory. His theory was a form of socialism called **communism.** He felt that the struggle between social classes would lead to a classless society. In a classless, communist society, the struggles of the **proletariat,** or working class, would end because wealth and power would be equally shared. In the 1860s, Germany adapted Marx's beliefs to form a **social democracy** in which there was a slow transition from capitalism to socialism.

Review Questions

1. Why did middle-class leaders support laissez-faire economics?

_____

_____

2. What did Jeremy Bentham believe the goal of society should be?

_____

_____

READING CHECK

What group of early socialists formed communities in which all work and property were shared?

_____

_____

_____

VOCABULARY STRATEGY

Find the word *formulated* in the underlined sentence. Note that the base word is *form.* What does it mean "to form" something? Think of synonyms of the word *form,* such as *plan, shape.* Use the meaning of the word *form* and the synonyms you think of to help you learn what *formulated* means.

READING SKILL

Identify Main Ideas What are the main ideas of Karl Marx's theory?

_____

_____

_____

CHAPTER 20 SECTION 1

Note Taking Study Guide

AN AGE OF IDEOLOGIES

Focus Question: What events proved that Metternich was correct in his fears?

A. *As you read "Conservatives Prefer the Old Order" and "Liberals and Nationalists Seek Change," fill in the table to identify main ideas about conservatism, liberalism, and nationalism. Some items have been completed for you.*

Conservatism	Liberalism	Nationalism
• Supports a return to world before 1789 • Supports restoration of royal families to power • _____ • _____ • _____ • _____	• Supports government based on written constitutions • Supports separation of powers within the government • _____ • _____ • _____	• _____ _____ _____

B. *As you read "Central Europe Challenges the Old Order," use the table to identify supporting details about revolts in Serbia, Greece, and other countries. Some items have been entered for you.*

Serbia	Greece	Other Revolts
• Karageorge leads war against Ottomans from 1804 to 1813; leads to sense of Serbian identity. • _____ _____ • _____ _____ • _____ _____	• Greeks revolt against the Ottomans in 1821. • _____ _____ • _____ _____ _____ • _____ _____	• Rebels in Spain, Portugal, and some Italian states • _____ _____ • _____ _____

CHAPTER 20 SECTION 1

Section Summary
AN AGE OF IDEOLOGIES

After the Congress of Vienna, clashes among different **ideologies,** or belief systems, caused more than 30 years of turmoil in Europe. Conservatives wanted to return to the way things were before 1789. This group included kings, nobles, and church leaders. Their agreement to work together was called the Concert of Europe. They wanted to restore royal families that Napoleon had displaced. They supported a social system in which lower classes respected those above them. Also, they backed established churches and opposed constitutional governments. Conservative leaders such as Prince Metternich of Austria wanted to crush revolutionary ideas.

Liberals and nationalists challenged the conservatives. The Enlightenment and the French Revolution had inspired them. Liberals generally included business owners, bankers, lawyers, politicians, and writers. They wanted governments based on written constitutions. They opposed monarchies and the established churches. They believed that liberty, equality, and property were natural rights. Later, liberals supported **universal manhood suffrage,** allowing all adult men to vote.

Nationalism gave people with a common heritage a sense of identity. It also gave them the goal of creating their own homeland. In the 1800s, nationalist groups within the Austrian and Ottoman empires set out to create their own states. Rebellions began in the Balkans. The Serbs were the first to revolt. By 1830, they had won **autonomy,** or self-rule, within the Ottoman empire. In 1821, the Greeks revolted. By 1830, Greece was independent from the Ottomans. Revolts spread to Spain, Portugal, and Italy. Metternich urged conservative leaders to crush the revolts. In response, French and Austrian troops smashed revolts in Spain and Italy.

Demands from the new industrial working class were soon added to liberal and nationalist demands. <u>By the mid-1800s, social reformers and agitators were urging workers to support socialism or other ways of reorganizing property ownership.</u>

Review Questions

1. What type of social system did conservatives support?

_____

_____

2. Why did liberals and nationalists challenge conservatives?

_____

_____

READING CHECK

What is autonomy?

_____

_____

_____

VOCABULARY STRATEGY

Find the word *agitators* in the underlined sentence. What do you think it means? Note that the *agitators* were "urging workers to support socialism." To *urge* people to do something means "to encourage or pressure" them. Use this context clue to figure out the meaning of *agitators.*

READING SKILL

Identify Main Ideas What two groups challenged conservatives for political control after the Congress of Vienna?

_____

_____

_____

CHAPTER 20 SECTION 2 — Note Taking Study Guide

REVOLUTIONS OF 1830 AND 1848

Focus Question: What were the causes and effects of the revolutions in Europe in 1830 and 1848?

As you read this section, fill in the table below with a country, date, and main idea for each revolution of 1830 and 1848. Some of the items have been completed for you.

Revolutions of 1830 and 1848

Country	Date	Main idea						
France	1830	Radicals force king to abdicate.						
France	1848	Revolution leads to election of Louis Napoleon as president.						
Germany	1848	Frankfurt Assembly offers the king the throne of a united Germany, but he refuses.						

Name_____ Class_____ Date_____

Louis XVIII died in 1824, and Charles X inherited the French throne. In 1830, Charles suspended the legislature and limited the right to vote. Angry rebels soon controlled Paris. They were led by liberals and **radicals.** When Charles X gave up the throne, radicals hoped to set up a republic. However, liberals insisted on a constitutional monarchy. **Louis Philippe** was called the "citizen king" because he owed his throne to the people.

The Paris revolts led to other revolts in Europe. Most failed, but they led to reforms. One successful revolution took place in Belgium. It gained its independence from Holland in 1831. Nationalists also revolted in Poland, but they failed to win widespread support. Russian forces soon crushed the rebels there.

In the 1840s, radicals, socialists, and liberals denounced Louis Philippe's government. A **recession** made the French people even more unhappy. The government tried to silence critics. Angry crowds then took to the streets in February 1848. The turmoil spread, and Louis Philippe gave up the throne. Liberals, radicals, and socialists proclaimed the Second Republic. By June, the upper and middle classes had won control of the government. Workers again took to the streets of Paris. At least 1,500 people were killed before the government crushed the rebellion. By the end of 1848, the National Assembly issued a constitution. This constitution gave the right to vote to all adult men. An election for president was held, and Louis Napoleon, the nephew of Napoleon Bonaparte, won. By 1852, however, he had declared himself Emperor **Napoleon III.**

The uprising in Paris in 1848 led to more revolutions across Europe. Revolts broke out in Vienna, and Metternich resigned. Hungarian nationalists led by **Louis Kossuth** demanded a government independent of Austria. The Czechs made similar demands. The Italian states also revolted, and the German states demanded national unity. Some of the rebellions were successful at first, but most of them had failed by 1850.

Review Questions

1. What country became independent in 1831?

_____

_____

2. How did Louis Napoleon become Emperor Napoleon III?

_____

_____

_____

READING CHECK

Who was the "citizen king"?

_____

_____

_____

VOCABULARY STRATEGY

Find the word *denounced* in the underlined sentence. What do you think it means? Reread the sentences that follow the underlined sentence. Were the French people happy or unhappy with Louis Philippe's government? Use this context clue to decide which word below has a similar meaning to *denounced*.

1. criticized

2. supported

READING SKILL

Identify Main Ideas What is the main idea of the last paragraph in the Summary? Remember that the first sentence of a paragraph often contains the main idea.

_____

_____

_____

Note Taking Study Guide

REVOLTS IN LATIN AMERICA

Focus Question: Who were the key revolutionaries to lead the movements for independence in Latin America, and what were their accomplishments?

As you read this section, fill in the table below with a country, a date, and a main idea for each revolt in Latin America. Some of the items have been completed for you.

Revolts in Latin America								
	Toussaint L'Ouverture leads an army of former slaves and ends slavery there.			Simón Bolívar suprises the Spanish at Bogotá.				United Provinces of Central America breaks into separate republics.
	1791			1819				1838
	Haiti			Colombia				Guatemala, El Salvador, Honduras, Nicaragua, Costa Rica

CHAPTER 20 SECTION 3

Section Summary
REVOLTS IN LATIN AMERICA

By the late 1700s, the desire for revolution had spread to Latin America. There, the social system had led to discontent. Spanish-born *peninsulares* made up the highest social class. They controlled the government and the Church. Creoles, mestizos, and mulattoes resented their lower status. **Creoles** were people of European descent who were born in Latin America. **Mestizos** were people of Native American and European descent. **Mulattoes** were people of African and European descent. The Enlightenment and the French and American revolutions had inspired creoles. When Napoleon invaded Spain in 1808, Latin American leaders decided to demand independence.

Revolution had already begun in Hispaniola in 1791. In that year, **Toussaint L'Ouverture** led a slave rebellion there. The rebellion ended slavery and gave Toussaint control of the island. Napoleon's army tried to retake the island, but failed. In 1804, the island became the independent country of Haiti.

In 1810, **Father Miguel Hidalgo** called for Mexican independence. After some successes, he was captured and killed. **Father José Morelos** took up the cause, but he, too, was killed. Finally, in 1821, revolutionaries led by Agustín de Iturbide overthrew Spanish rule and declared independence for Mexico. Central American colonies soon declared independence, too.

In the early 1800s, discontent and revolution spread across all of South America. **Simón Bolívar** led an uprising in Venezuela. Although his new republic was soon overthrown, Bolívar did not give up. He marched his army across the Andes and took the city of Bogotá from the surprised Spanish. Then he moved south to free Ecuador, Peru, and Bolivia. There, he joined forces with another great leader, **José de San Martín.** San Martín helped Argentina and Chile win freedom from Spain. The wars of independence ended in 1824, but power struggles among South American leaders led to civil wars. However, <u>in Brazil, **Dom Pedro** became emperor and proclaimed independence for that colony in 1822.</u>

Review Questions

1. What led to discontent in Latin America by the late 1700s?

_____

_____

2. When did Mexico gain its independence?

_____

_____

READING CHECK

Which group in Latin America made up the highest social class?

_____

_____

_____

VOCABULARY STRATEGY

Find the word *proclaimed* in the underlined sentence. What do you think it means? *Proclaim* comes from the Latin word *proclamare.* The prefix *pro-* means "before" and *clamare* means "to cry out" or "shout." Use this information about word origins to help you decide which of the following words means the same as *proclaimed.*

1. announced

2. denied

READING SKILL

Identify Main Ideas Circle the sentence below that states a main idea from the Summary.

- The social system in Latin America led to discontent.

- Spanish-born *peninsulares* were the highest social class.

- Creoles were people of European descent who were born in Latin America.

- Mestizos were people of Native American and European descent.

- Mulattoes were people of African and European descent.

Note Taking Study Guide

CHAPTER 21 SECTION 1

THE INDUSTRIAL REVOLUTION SPREADS

Focus Question: How did science, technology, and big business promote industrial growth?

As you read this section in your textbook, complete the following chart to identify main ideas about the major developments of the Industrial Revolution. Some items have been completed for you.

The Second Industrial Revolution

Transportation/Communication

- The automobile age begins.
-
-
-

Industry/Business

- Technology sparks industrial growth.
-
-
-
-
-

New Powers

- Germany, France, and United States have more natural resources than Britain.
-
-

Name_____ Class_____ Date_____

For a while, Britain was the world's industrial leader. By the mid-1800s, however, Germany and the United States had become the new leaders. These nations had much more coal, iron, and other natural resources than Britain did. They also were able to use British experts and technology. As in Britain, cities in the new industrial nations grew quickly.

Technology helped industry grow. **Henry Bessemer** invented a new way to make steel from iron. **Alfred Nobel** invented dynamite for use in construction. **Michael Faraday** created the first **dynamo,** a machine that makes electricity. Soon electricity replaced steam as the main power source for industry. In the 1870s, the American inventor **Thomas Edison** developed the electric light bulb. Soon entire cities were lit with electric lights. Factories could now operate at night and produce more goods. The use of **interchangeable parts** and the **assembly line** made production faster and cheaper, too.

Technology also changed transportation and communication. Steamships replaced sailing ships. Trains quickly connected cities and brought raw materials to factories. The invention of the internal combustion engine led to the mass production of automobiles. In 1903, **Orville and Wilbur Wright** launched the air age by flying a plane for a few seconds. The telegraph and telephone made the exchange of information nearly instantaneous. **Guglielmo Marconi** invented the radio, a big part of today's global communication network.

These new technologies needed large amounts of money. To get this money, owners sold **stock,** or shares in their companies, to investors. These businesses became giant **corporations**. Others formed business groups called **cartels**. By the late 1800s, what we call "big business" came to dominate industry.

Review Questions

1. How did Germany and the United States become industrial leaders?

_____

_____

2. What new form of energy changed cities and factories?

_____

_____

189

READING CHECK

What invention changed life in the cities?

_____

_____

_____

VOCABULARY STRATEGY

What do you think the word *dominate* means in the underlined sentence? It is a verb, so it describes an action. However, it comes from a Latin word that means "lord" or "master." Use the word's origin to help you figure out what *dominate* means.

READING SKILL

Identify Main Ideas How did transportation change during the Industrial Revolution?

_____

_____

_____

Note Taking Study Guide

THE RISE OF THE CITIES

Focus Question: How did the Industrial Revolution change life in the cities?

As you read this section in your textbook, complete the following outline to identify main ideas and supporting details about how the Industrial Revolution changed life in the cities. Some items have been completed for you.

I. Medicine and the population explosion

    A. The fight against disease

        1. _____

        2. _____

    B. Hospital care improves.

        1. _____

        2. _____

II. Life in the cities

    A. City landscapes change.

        1. _____

        2. _____

    B. _____

        1. _____

        2. _____

    C. _____

        1. _____

        2. _____

    D. _____

        1. _____

        2. _____

III. Working-class struggles

    A. _____

        1. _____

        2. _____

    B. _____

        1. _____

        2. _____

CHAPTER 21 SECTION 2
Section Summary
THE RISE OF THE CITIES

Between 1800 and 1900, the population of Europe more than doubled. This was due to advances in medicine that slowed death rates. In the fight against disease, scientists studied **germ theory.** They believed that certain germs might cause specific diseases. In 1870, French chemist **Louis Pasteur** showed the link between germs and disease. German doctor **Robert Koch** identified the cause of tuberculosis, a deadly lung disease. British hospital reformer **Florence Nightingale** raised standards of care and cleanliness. British surgeon **Joseph Lister** discovered that antiseptics prevent disease. As people understood what causes disease, they practiced better hygiene. Disease decreased and fewer people died.

At this time, cities underwent big changes in Europe and the United States. The largest **urban renewal** project took place in Paris in the 1850s. Old, crowded areas of the city were replaced with wide avenues and grand public buildings. Steel made it possible to build tall buildings called skyscrapers. Paved streets helped make cities more livable. <u>Electric streetlights illuminated the night and increased safety.</u> Huge new sewage systems made cities healthier. City planners knew they needed to provide clean water. These acts helped cut death rates.

Despite these efforts, cities were still harsh places for the poor. In the worst slums, whole families lived in a single room. However, millions of people still moved to the cities. They came to get work, for entertainment, and for an education.

Most people worked long hours in factories, in unsafe circumstances for low wages. Workers protested these terrible conditions. They formed **mutual-aid societies** to help sick or injured workers. They also organized unions. Pressured by unions, reformers, and working-class voters, governments passed laws that improved working conditions. Wages varied, but overall, the **standard of living** for most workers did rise.

Review Questions
1. How did advances in medicine increase population?

_____

_____

2. How did new sewage systems make city life healthier?

_____

_____

READING CHECK

Who showed the link between germs and disease?

_____

_____

_____

VOCABULARY STRATEGY

What does the word *illuminated* mean in the underlined sentence? The root of this word is *lumen*, which is Latin for "light." What other word in this sentence includes the word *light*? Use the word root and the word *streetlight* to help you figure out the meaning of *illuminated*.

READING SKILL

Identify Supporting Details
What were working conditions like for most factory workers?

_____

_____

_____

Name_____ Class_____ Date_____

Focus Question: How did the Industrial Revolution change the old social order and long-held traditions in the Western world?

As you read this section in your textbook, complete the following table. List new issues in the first column and write two supporting details for each issue in the second column. Some items have been completed for you.

Changes in Social Order and Values	
Issue	**Change**
• New social order	• Upper class: old nobility, new industrialists, business families • Growing middle class develops its own way of life. •
• Rights for women	• •
• Growth of public education	• •
• New directions in science	• •
•	• •

CHAPTER 21 SECTION 3

Section Summary
CHANGING ATTITUDES AND VALUES

In the late 1800s, many new issues challenged the old social order. For centuries, mainly the two classes had been nobles and peasants. Now a more complex social structure developed with several social classes. The new upper class included very rich business families. Below the upper class was a growing middle class and then a struggling lower middle class. At the bottom were workers and peasants. The middle class had its own values and way of life, including a **cult of domesticity.** This encouraged women to stay home and care for the family.

Demands for women's rights also challenged the old social order. Women sought fairness in marriage, divorce, and property laws. In the United States, reformers such as **Elizabeth Cady Stanton** and **Sojourner Truth** worked for **women's suffrage,** or the right to vote. Women's groups also supported the **temperance movement,** a campaign to limit or ban the use of alcoholic beverages.

Attitudes toward education changed, too. People believed that education would create better workers. Reformers persuaded many governments to set up public schools and require basic education. Because of this, more children got an education.

New ideas in science also brought change. **John Dalton** developed atomic theory. <u>However, the most controversial new idea came from British naturalist **Charles Darwin.**</u> It upset many people, who disagreed with his theory. Darwin thought that all forms of life evolve over millions of years. His theory of natural selection explains how members of each species compete to survive. Some people used a twisted version of Darwin's theory, called Social Darwinism, to support **racism.**

Religion continued to be a force in Western society. Life in industrial societies could be very cruel for some. Religious groups tried to help the working poor. For example, the **social gospel** movement urged Christians to work to improve society.

Review Questions

1. Who was included in the new upper class of the late 1800s?

_____

_____

2. What rights did women want?

_____

_____

© Pearson Education, Inc., publishing as Pearson Prentice Hall. All rights reserved.

READING CHECK

Who developed the new scientific theory of natural selection?

_____

_____

_____

VOCABULARY STRATEGY

Find the word *controversial* in the underlined sentence. What do you think it means? The word begins with the prefix *contro-,* which means "against." Use the meaning of the prefix and the context clues in the paragraph to help you figure out what *controversial* means.

READING SKILL

Identify Supporting Details Why did more children begin to get an education in the late 1800s?

_____

_____

Name_____ Class_____ Date_____

Note Taking Study Guide

ARTS IN THE INDUSTRIAL AGE

Focus Question: What artistic movements emerged in reaction to the Industrial Revolution?

As you read this section in your textbook, complete the following table. Identify supporting details about the major features of artistic movements of the 1800s. Some items have been completed for you.

Major Artistic Movements of the 1800s		
Movement	**Goals/Characteristics**	**Major Figures**
Romanticism	• Rebellion against reason • Emphasis on imagination, freedom, and emotion • Use of direct language, intense feelings, glorification of nature • • •	• William Wordsworth • William Blake • Samuel Taylor Coleridge • • • •
Realism	• To represent the world as it was, without romantic sentiment • • • •	• Charles Dickens • Victor Hugo • • •
Impressionism	• To capture the first fleeting impression made by a scene or object on the viewer's eye •	• •
Postimpressionism	•	• • •

CHAPTER 21 SECTION 4

Section Summary

ARTS IN THE INDUSTRIAL AGE

From about 1750 to 1850, a cultural movement called **romanticism** emerged. It was a reaction against the ideas of the Enlightenment. Romanticism emphasized imagination, freedom, and emotion. <u>The works of romantic writers included direct language, intense feelings, and a glorification of nature.</u> **William Wordsworth, William Blake,** and **Lord Byron** were major romantic poets. Romantic writers, such as **Victor Hugo,** were inspired by history, legend, and folklore. Composers also tried to stir deep emotions. The passionate music of **Ludwig van Beethoven** used an exciting range of sound. Painters, too, broke free from the formal styles of the Enlightenment. They used bold brush strokes and colors to capture the beauty and power of nature.

However, in the mid-1800s, an art movement called **realism** took hold. Realists wanted to portray the world as it truly was. They rejected romantic beauty. Their works made people aware of the often bleak life of the Industrial Age. Many realists wanted to improve life for their subjects. The novels of **Charles Dickens,** for example, shocked readers with images of poverty, mistreatment of children, and urban crime. Painters, such as **Gustave Courbet**, painted ordinary working-class men and women.

A new art form, photography, also developed. **Louis Daguerre** made some of the first successful photographs. Photography made some artists question the purpose of realist paintings when a camera made exact images. By the 1870s, one group started a new movement called **impressionism**. Artists such as **Claude Monet** wanted to capture the first impression made by a scene on the viewer's eye. By focusing on visual impressions, artists showed familiar subjects in unfamiliar ways. Later, the postimpressionist painter **Vincent van Gogh** experimented with sharp brush lines and bold colors.

Review Questions

1. What qualities did romantics include in their works?

_____

_____

2. What was the goal of the impressionist artists?

_____

_____

READING CHECK

What cultural movement was a reaction to the Enlightenment?

_____

_____

_____

VOCABULARY STRATEGY

What does the word *intense* mean in the underlined sentence? Look for clues in the surrounding words, phrases, or sentences. Circle the words in the paragraph that could help you figure out the meaning of *intense.*

READING SKILL

Identify Supporting Details Identify two details that support this main idea: Realist artists and writers made people more aware of the harshness of life in the Industrial Age.

_____

_____

_____

CHAPTER
22
SECTION 1

Note Taking Study Guide

BUILDING A GERMAN NATION

Focus Question: How did Otto von Bismarck, the chancellor of Prussia, lead the drive for German unity?

As you read this section in your textbook, complete the following chart to record the sequence of events that led to German unification. Some items have been completed for you.

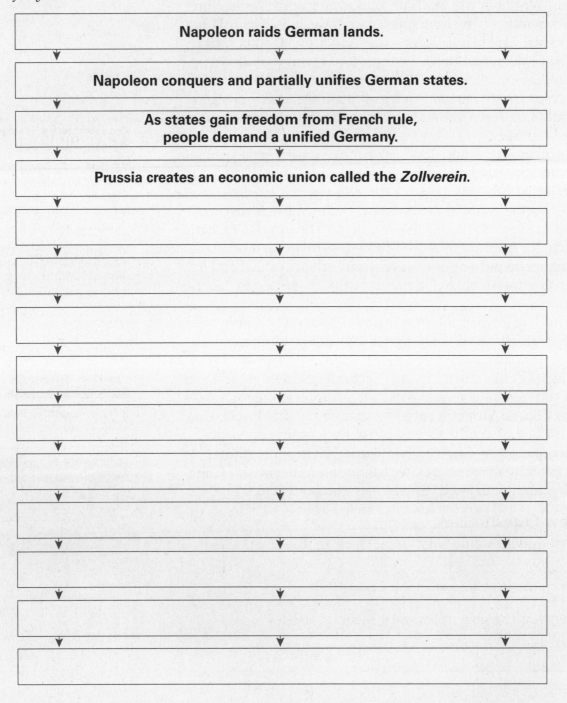

Napoleon raids German lands.

Napoleon conquers and partially unifies German states.

As states gain freedom from French rule, people demand a unified Germany.

Prussia creates an economic union called the *Zollverein*.

CHAPTER 22 SECTION 1

Section Summary

BUILDING A GERMAN NATION

In the early 1800s, German-speaking people did not live in one nation. They were scattered among several German states, parts of Prussia, and the Austrian empire. Napoleon dissolved the Holy Roman Empire and organized some German states into the Rhine Confederation. Napoleon's actions helped develop German national identity. Not everyone wanted French rule. They fought to free their lands and began to demand one German nation for all German-speaking people. After Napoleon's defeat, the Congress of Vienna created the German Confederation, a weak alliance of German states headed by Austria. In the 1830s, Prussia created an economic union called the *Zollverein.* This union removed tariffs between German states. Still, the German people did not live in one, unified German nation.

In 1862, King William I named **Otto von Bismarck** as the **chancellor** of Prussia. Bismarck wanted to unite the German states under Prussian rule. He was very skillful at **Realpolitik,** or practical politics based on the needs of the state. First, Bismarck built up the Prussian army. He led Prussia into three wars, gaining land for Prussia in each one.

In 1864, Bismarck formed an alliance with Austria. In 1866, however, he made up an excuse to attack Austria. After its victory, Prussia **annexed,** or took control of, several northern German states. This angered the French ruler, Napoleon III. Bismarck rewrote and released to the press a telegram that reported on a meeting between William I of Prussia and the French ambassador. <u>Bismarck's editing made it seem that William I had insulted the French.</u> Furious, Napoleon III declared war on Prussia. This is what Bismarck had wanted. Supported by troops from other German states, Prussia defeated the French.

Delighted by the victory, German princes asked William I to take the title **kaiser,** or emperor. He agreed. In 1871, Germans celebrated the birth of the Second **Reich,** or empire.

Review Questions

1. What was the *Zollverein* and what did it accomplish?

_____

_____

2. How did Bismarck use war to strengthen Prussia?

_____

_____

READING CHECK

Who was Otto von Bismarck?

_____

_____

_____

VOCABULARY STRATEGY

Find the word *editing* in the underlined sentence. What clues to its meaning can you find in the surrounding words, phrases, or sentences? For example, what does the word *rewrote* suggest? Circle the words in the paragraph that could help you figure out what *editing* means.

READING SKILL

Recognize Sequence Place the following actions of Bismarck in the correct sequence:

____ He annexes several North German states.

____ He forms an alliance with Austria.

____ He attacks Austria.

____ He builds up Prussia's army.

Note Taking Study Guide

GERMANY STRENGTHENS

Focus Question: How did Germany increase its power after unifying in 1871?

As you read this section in your textbook, complete the following chart to record the causes and effects of a strong German nation. Some items have been completed for you.

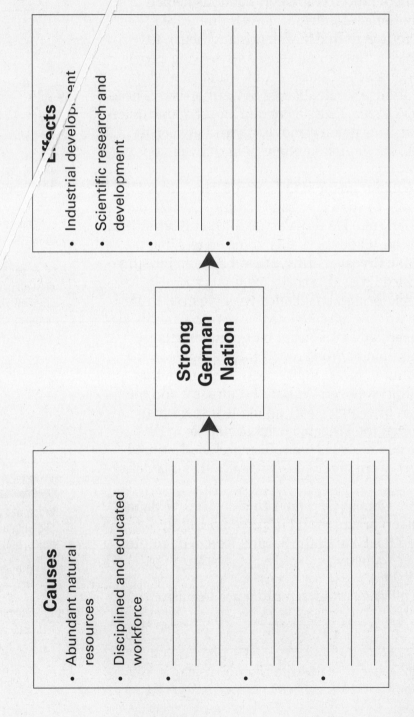

Effects
- Industrial development
- Scientific research and development
- •
- •

Strong German Nation

Causes
- Abundant natural resources
- Disciplined and educated workforce
- •
- •

CHAPTER 22 SECTION 2

Section Summary

GERMANY STRENGTHENS

After 1871, the new German empire became an industrial giant. There are several reasons why this was possible. Germany had large iron and coal resources. These are the basic ingredients for industrial development. It also had a disciplined and educated workforce. The middle class helped create a productive and efficient society, too. The country's growing population also provided a huge home market for goods. It also created a supply of workers.

Industrialists saw the value of science in business. They developed new products, such as synthetic chemicals and dyes. Both industrialists and the government encouraged scientific research and development. The German government also supported economic development. It issued a single form of money and reorganized the banking system. The leaders of the new empire were determined to maintain a strong economy.

As chancellor, Bismarck had several foreign-policy goals. He wanted to keep France weak. He also wanted to build strong ties with Austria and Russia. At home, Bismarck believed the Socialists and the Catholic Church threatened the new empire. He worried that Socialists would turn workers toward revolution. He thought Catholics would be more loyal to the Church than to the state. Bismarck tried to repress both groups. His efforts, however, backfired. For example, he launched the *Kulturkampf,* or "battle for civilization." It was meant to make Catholics give their loyalty to the state first, above the Church. Instead, Catholics rallied behind the Church.

In 1888, **William II** became the new kaiser. He shocked Europe by asking Bismarck to resign. William II believed that his right to rule came from God. Not surprisingly, he resisted democratic reforms. However, his government still provided many **social welfare** programs to help certain groups of people. He also provided cheap transportation and electricity.

Review Questions

1. What are two reasons why the new German empire became an industrial giant?

_____

_____

2. What were Bismarck's foreign-policy goals?

_____

_____

READING CHECK

What two groups did Bismarck believe threatened the new German state?

_____

_____

_____

VOCABULARY STRATEGY

Find the word *synthetic* in the underlined sentence. *Natural* is an antonym of *synthetic.* Use what you know about the word *natural* to help you figure out what *synthetic* means.

READING SKILL

Recognize Sequence After Bismarck introduced the *Kulturkampf,* what happened next?

_____

_____

_____

Name_____ Class_____ Date_____

Focus Question: How did influential leaders help create a unified Italy?

As you read this section in your textbook, complete the following timeline to show the sequence of events that led to Italian unification. Some dates have been completed for you.

1870

1860
Garibaldi and his "Red Shirts" capture Sicily and Naples.

1852
Victor Emmanuel names Count Camillo Cavour prime minister.

1850

1831
Mazzini founds Young Italy.

1830

CHAPTER
22
SECTION 3

Section Summary
UNIFYING ITALY

The people of the Italian peninsula spoke the same language and shared a common history. However, the region had not been united since Roman times. By the 1800s, however, patriots were determined to unite Italy. First, Napoleon's invasions had sparked dreams of nationalism. Then, Giuseppe Mazzini founded Young Italy. The goal of this secret society was "to constitute Italy, one, free, independent, republican nation." A united country made economic sense because it would end trade barriers among the states. It also would encourage industrial development.

Victor Emmanuel II was the king of Sardinia. He wanted to join other Italian states with his own. Victor Emmanuel made Count **Camillo Cavour** his prime minister. Cavour wanted to end Austrian power in Italy. With help from France, Sardinia defeated Austria and annexed Lombardy. Also, Austrian-backed leaders in northern states were overthrown.

In southern Italy, **Giuseppe Garibaldi** was also fighting for unification. He had recruited a force of 1,000 red-shirted volunteers. Garibaldi and his "Red Shirts" quickly won control of Sicily. They then crossed to the mainland and seized Naples. Garibaldi gave both regions to Victor Emmanuel. In 1861, Victor Emmanuel II became king of Italy. By 1870, France had withdrawn its troops from Rome, and Italy acquired Venetia. For the first time since the fall of the Roman empire, Italy was united.

The new nation faced many problems, and tensions grew. There were strong differences between the north and south. The north was richer and had more cities. In contrast, the south was poor and rural. **Anarchists,** people who wanted to abolish all government, turned to violence. Despite these problems, Italy's economy developed. As the population grew, however, **emigration** offered a chance for a better life. Many Italians left for the United States, Canada, and Latin American nations.

Review Questions

1. What sparked dreams of national unity in Italy?

_____

_____

2. Why did a unified Italy make economic sense?

_____

_____

READING CHECK

Who was Camillo Cavour?

_____

_____

_____

VOCABULARY STRATEGY

Find the word *constitute* in the underlined sentence. In this sentence, the word is used as a verb. A verb describes an action. Ask yourself: *What action were the nationalists trying to take?* Use the answer to this question to help you figure out what *constitute* means.

READING SKILL

Recognize Sequence What happened after France withdrew its troops from Rome?

_____

_____

_____

CHAPTER
22
SECTION 4

Note Taking Study Guide

NATIONALISM THREATENS OLD EMPIRES

Focus Question: How did the desire for national independence among ethnic groups weaken and ultimately destroy the Austrian and Ottoman empires?

As you read this section in your textbook, complete the following table to record some major events in Austrian history during the 1800s. Some dates have been completed for you.

Events in Austrian History					
	By this time, factories spring up in Austrian cities, along with worker discontent and stirrings of socialism.	Nationalist revolts break out, but are crushed by the Hapsburg government.			
	1840	1848	1859	1866	1867

In 1800, the Hapsburgs were the longest-reigning family in Europe. Their Austrian empire was home to many ethnic groups, including German-speaking Austrians, Slavs, Hungarians, and Italians.

By the 1840s, the empire faced many problems associated with industrial life. Also, nationalism threatened the empire. The Hapsburgs ignored these issues as long as they could. When revolts broke out in 1848, the government crushed them. During this time of unrest, 18-year-old **Francis Joseph** came to the Hapsburg throne. In an attempt to strengthen the empire, he granted some limited reforms. He also created a constitution, but the majority of power remained with German-speaking Austrians. This did not satisfy most of the other ethnic groups.

Austria's defeat in the 1866 war with Prussia brought even more pressure for change, especially from Hungarians within the empire. **Ferenc Deák** helped work out a compromise known as the **Dual Monarchy** of Austria-Hungary. Under the agreement, Austria and Hungary became separate states. Each had its own constitution. However, Francis Joseph still ruled both nations. Hungarians welcomed the compromise, but other groups resented it. Unrest grew among the Slavs. <u>Some nationalists called on fellow Slavs to unite in "fraternal solidarity."</u> By the early 1900s, nationalist unrest often kept the government from addressing political and social problems.

The Ottomans ruled an empire that stretched from Eastern Europe and the Balkans, to the Middle East and North Africa. It also included many different ethnic groups. During the 1800s, various peoples revolted against the Ottomans. They wanted their own independent states. With the empire weakened, European powers scrambled to divide up the Ottoman lands. A series of crises and wars occurred in the Balkans. By the early 1900s, that region became known as the "Balkan powder keg." The "explosion" came in 1914 and helped set off World War I.

Review Questions

1. How did the Hapsburgs respond when nationalist revolts broke out?

_____

_____

2. Why were the Balkans known as a "powder keg"?

_____

_____

READING CHECK

What new government did Ferenc Deák help set up?

_____

_____

_____

VOCABULARY STRATEGY

Find the word *fraternal* in the underlined sentence. The word comes from the Latin word *frater,* which means "brother." Look for clues in the surrounding text, such as *unite* and *solidarity.* Use the word's origin and context clues to help you figure out what *fraternal* means.

READING SKILL

Recognize Sequence What are two events that happened after the Ottoman empire weakened?

1._____

_____

2._____

_____

Name_____ Class_____ Date_____

Focus Question: Why did industrialization and reform come more slowly to Russia than to Western Europe?

As you read this section in your textbook, complete the following timeline to show the sequence of events in Russia during the late 1800s and early 1900s. Some events have been added for you.

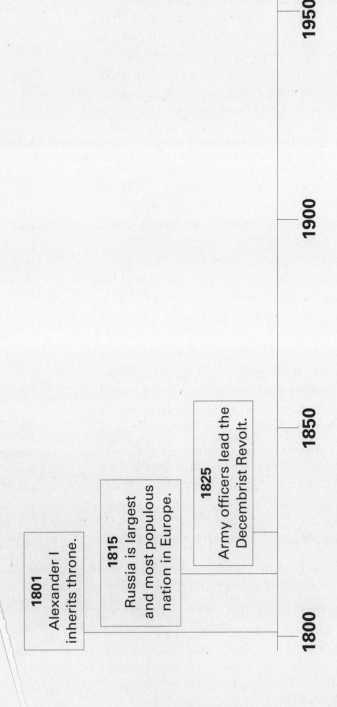

1950

1900

1850

1825
Army officers lead the Decembrist Revolt.

1815
Russia is largest and most populous nation in Europe.

1801
Alexander I inherits throne.

1800

Name_____ Class_____ Date_____

Section Summary
RUSSIA: REFORM AND REACTION

By 1815, Russia was the largest nation in Europe. The Russian **colossus,** or giant, had vast natural resources. Reformers hoped to free the country from autocratic rule, economic backwardness, and social injustice. A rigid social structure, however, presented an obstacle to progress. Also, the tsars had ruled with absolute power for centuries.

Alexander II became tsar during the **Crimean War.** His reign followed the pattern of reform and repression of previous tsars. When Russia lost the war, it showed the country's backwardness and inefficiency. People demanded changes. The tsar agreed to some reforms. He ordered the **emancipation,** or freedom, of serfs. He set up elected assemblies, called **zemstvos.** Then he made legal reforms, which included trial by jury. However, these changes did not satisfy many Russians. As radicals insist on even greater changes and more reforms, the tsar moved toward repression. This angered radicals. Terrorists killed Alexander II in 1881. In response to his father's death, Alexander III brought back repressive rule. He suppressed the cultures of non-Russian peoples. Official persecution fueled **pogroms,** or violent mob attacks on Jewish people. Many Jews left Russia and became **refugees,** seeking safety elsewhere.

Russia entered the industrialized age under Alexander III and his son Nicholas II. However, industrialization caused political and social problems to build. On Sunday, January 22, 1905, a peaceful protest calling for reforms turned deadly. The tsar's troops killed and wounded hundreds of people. Following this "Bloody Sunday," unrest exploded across Russia. Nicholas was forced to make many reforms. He agreed to call a **Duma,** or an elected national legislature. He also named **Peter Stolypin** as prime minister. Stolypin recognized that Russia needed reform. Unfortunately, the reforms he introduced were too limited. By 1914, Russia was still an autocracy, but simmering with discontent.

Review Questions

1. What was the obstacle to progress in Russia in the 1800s?

_____

_____

2. What did Alexander III do in response to his father's death?

_____

_____

READING CHECK

What event occurred on January 22, 1905?

_____

_____

_____

VOCABULARY STRATEGY

Find the word *radicals* in the underlined sentence. The word *radicals* is a noun for a kind of people. Ask yourself: "Why were radicals dissatisfied with Alexander II's reforms?" Use that information to help you figure out who *radicals* are.

READING SKILL

Recognize Sequence Which political reform occurred first? Circle your answer.

- setting up elected assemblies

- calling a Duma

- suppressing non-Russian cultures

CHAPTER
23
SECTION 1

Note Taking Study Guide

DEMOCRATIC REFORM IN BRITAIN

Focus Question: How did political reform gradually expand suffrage and make the British Parliament more democratic during the 1800s?

As you read this section in your textbook, complete the outline below to identify the main ideas in the section. Some items have been completed for you.

I. Reforming Parliament

    A. Reformers press for change.

        1. _____

        2. _____

    B. Reform Act of 1832

        1. Large towns and cities gain representation.

        2. _____

        3. _____

    C. The Chartist movement

        1. _____

        2. _____

II. The Victorian Age

    A. Symbol of a nation's values

        1. _____

        2. _____

    B. A confident age

        1. _____

        2. _____

III. A New Era in British Politics

    A. Expanding suffrage

        1. _____

        2. _____

        3. Britain becomes a parliamentary democracy.

    B. Limiting the Lords

        1. _____

        2. _____

CHAPTER 23 SECTION 1

Section Summary
DEMOCRATIC REFORM IN BRITAIN

In 1815, Britain was a constitutional monarchy with a Parliament. However, it was not very democratic. The House of Commons was controlled by wealthy nobles and squires. The House of Lords could veto any bill passed by the House of Commons. Catholics and Protestants outside the Church of England could not vote. The **rotten boroughs** still had members in Parliament, even though they had lost most of their voters during the Industrial Revolution. <u>At the same time, new industrial cities had no seats allocated in Parliament.</u>

In 1832, the Great Reform Act redistributed seats in the House of Commons. It also enlarged the **electorate,** or the people who could vote. However, it kept a property requirement for voting. Protesters called the Chartists demanded reforms, such as universal male suffrage and a **secret ballot.** In time, Parliament passed most of these reforms.

From 1837 to 1901, the great symbol in British life was **Queen Victoria.** She set the tone for the Victorian age. Victorian values, which she represented, included duty, thrift, honesty, hard work, and respectability. Under Victoria, the British empire grew even larger.

In the 1860s, British politics began to change. **Benjamin Disraeli** turned the Tories into the modern Conservative Party. The Whigs, led by **William Gladstone,** developed into the Liberal Party. Both leaders served as prime minister and fought for important reforms. The Conservative Party pushed through the Reform Bill of 1867. This bill gave the vote to many working-class men. In the 1880s, the Liberals passed reforms that gave the vote to farm workers and most other men.

By the end of the century, Britain was a **parliamentary democracy.** In this form of government, the prime minister and cabinet are chosen by their fellow members of the parliament and are responsible to it. In 1911, Parliament passed a bill that greatly lessened the power of the House of Lords. Since then, it has been a mostly ceremonial body.

Review Questions

1. What form of government did Britain have in 1815?

_____

_____

2. Name two important prime ministers of the Victorian age.

_____

_____

READING CHECK

Who was the great symbol in British life from 1837 to 1901?

_____

_____

VOCABULARY STRATEGY

Find the word *allocated* in the underlined sentence. What does it mean? Note that the Great Reform Act of 1832 "redistributed" seats in the House of Commons. This redistribution meant that seats were now allocated fairly. Use this context clue to help you figure out the meaning of the word *allocated*.

READING SKILL

Identify Main Ideas Which of the following sentences states the main idea of the first paragraph of this Summary? Circle it.

• The House of Commons was controlled by wealthy nobles and squires.

• Catholics and non-Church of England Protestants could not vote.

• Britain was a constitutional monarchy, but it was not very democratic.

• The House of Lords could veto any bill passed by the House of Commons.

Name_____ Class_____ Date_____

Note Taking Study Guide

SOCIAL AND ECONOMIC REFORM IN BRITAIN

Focus Question: What social and economic reforms were passed by the British Parliament during the 1800s and early 1900s?

As you read this section in your textbook, complete the chart below by listing reforms in Britain during the 1800s and early 1900s. Some items have been completed for you.

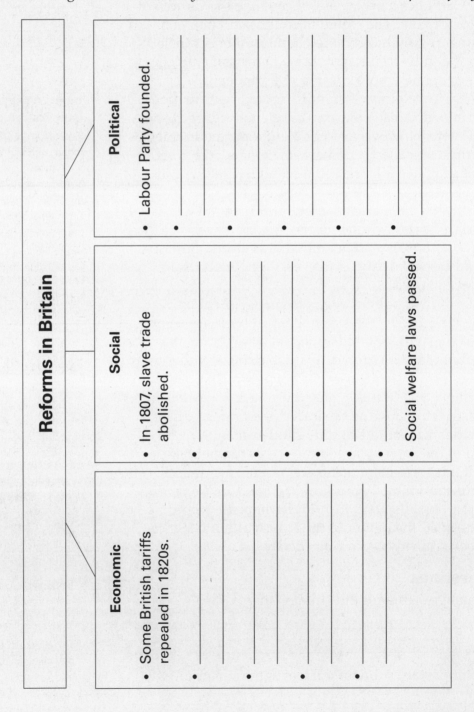

Reforms in Britain

Political
- Labour Party founded.

Social
- In 1807, slave trade abolished.
- Social welfare laws passed.

Economic
- Some British tariffs repealed in 1820s.

CHAPTER 23 SECTION 2

Section Summary

SOCIAL AND ECONOMIC REFORM IN BRITAIN

During the 1800s, Parliament passed important laws. One issue was **free trade,** or trade without restrictions between countries. The Corn Laws caused strong debate. These laws placed high tariffs on imported grain. This helped British farmers and landowners but made bread more expensive. In 1846, Parliament **repealed,** or cancelled, the Corn Laws. The **abolition movement** brought about laws that ended the slave trade and banned slavery in all British colonies. Other reforms reduced the number of **capital offenses,** or crimes punishable by death. Instead of being put to death, many criminals were shipped to **penal colonies** in Australia and New Zealand.

Working conditions in the industrial age were grim and often dangerous. Gradually, Parliament passed laws to improve conditions in factories and mines. Other laws set minimum wages and maximum hours of work. An education act called for free elementary education for all children. Trade unions became legal in 1825, and worked to improve the lives of workers. The Labour Party was formed in 1900 and soon became one of Britain's major parties. In the early 1900s, Parliament passed laws to protect workers with old-age pensions and accident, health, and unemployment insurance.

Women struggled to win the right to vote. <u>When peaceful efforts brought no results, Emmeline Pankhurst and other suffragists turned to more drastic, violent protest.</u> In 1918, Parliament finally granted the vote to women over 30.

Throughout the 1800s, Britain faced the "Irish Question." The Irish resented British rule. Many Irish peasants lived in poverty. They paid high rents to **absentee landlords** living in England. Irish Catholics also had to pay tithes to the Church of England. The potato famine made thing worse. Irish leader Charles Stewart Parnell and others argued for **home rule,** or self-government, but this was debated for decades. Under Gladstone the government stopped Irish tithes and passed laws to protect the rights of Irish tenant farmers.

Review Questions

1. What laws did the abolition movement inspire?

_____

_____

2. Name two reasons why the Irish resented British rule.

_____

_____

READING CHECK

What is free trade?

_____

_____

_____

VOCABULARY STRATEGY

Find the word *drastic* in the underlined sentence. What do you think it means? Note that the suffragists first tried "peaceful efforts" before turning to "more *drastic,* violent protest." Which of the following words do you think has the same meaning as *drastic?*

1. moderate

2. extreme

READING SKILL

Categorize Group the laws that were passed to help workers into the following three categories: working conditions and wages, education, and insurance.

_____

_____

_____

CHAPTER 23 SECTION 3

Note Taking Study Guide

DIVISION AND DEMOCRACY IN FRANCE

Focus Question: What democratic reforms were made in France during the Third Republic?

As you read this section in your textbook, complete the timeline below by labeling the main events described in this section. Some items have been completed for you.

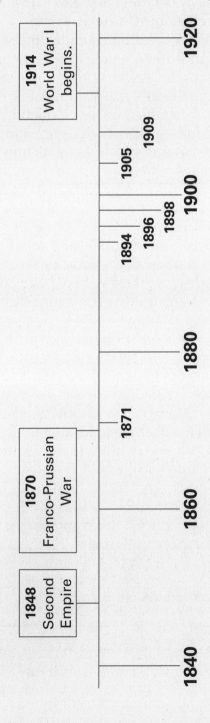

1914
World War I begins.

1920

1909

1905

1900

1898

1896

1894

1880

1871

1870
Franco-Prussian War

1860

1848
Second Empire

1840

CHAPTER 23 SECTION 3

Section Summary

DIVISION AND DEMOCRACY IN FRANCE

In 1852 **Napoleon III** set up the Second Empire in France. At first, he ruled like a dictator. In the 1860s, however, he gave the legislature more power. He encouraged industry and building projects. During his reign, a Frenchman organized the building of the **Suez Canal.** Unfortunately, Napoleon had major failures in foreign affairs. He tried to take control of Mexico by putting Austrian archduke Maximilian on the throne, but this failed. France and Britain won the Crimean War, but France suffered huge losses. The worst disaster was the Franco-Prussian War. In the end, the Prussians captured Napoleon. This ended his rule.

The Republicans in Paris set up a **provisional,** or temporary, government. This government became the Third Republic. In 1871, rebels in Paris created the Paris Commune. Their goal was to save the Republic from royalists. However, the government sent troops to stop the rebellion, and thousands were killed. The new French government had a two-house legislature and a president. However, the **premier** had the real power. France had many political parties, and no one party could take control. So parties had to form **coalitions,** or alliances, to rule. The coalition governments were unstable.

Scandals in the late 1800s caused people to lose trust in the government. The most serious scandal was the **Dreyfus affair.** Alfred Dreyfus was a Jewish army officer. He was wrongly accused of spying for Germany. When writer Émile Zola accused the army and government of hiding the truth, he was convicted of **libel.** The Dreyfus affair showed that there were strong anti-Jewish feelings in France. This led Theodor Herzl to start a movement to create a Jewish homeland—**Zionism.**

In the early 1900s, France passed labor laws to improve wages, working hours, and safety conditions. It also set up free public elementary schools. <u>The French tried to repress Church involvement in government, too.</u> In 1905, it passed a law to separate church and state.

Review Questions

1. How did Napoleon III's rule end?

_____

_____

2. What movement resulted from the Dreyfus affair?

_____

_____

READING CHECK

What are coalitions?

_____

_____

VOCABULARY STRATEGY

Find the word *repress* in the underlined sentence. What does it mean? Reread the sentence that follows the underlined sentence. What did France do to *repress* Church involvement in government? Did this increase or decrease Church involvement? Which of the words below is closest in meaning to *repress*?

1. limit

2. increase

READING SKILL

Recognize Sequence Arrange the three French governments described in this section (provisional government, Second Empire, Third Republic) in the correct chronological order.

_____

_____

_____

CHAPTER 23 SECTION 4

Note Taking Study Guide

EXPANSION OF THE UNITED STATES

Focus Question: How did the United States develop during the 1800s?

As you read this section in your textbook, complete the chart below by listing key events under the appropriate headings. Some items have been completed for you.

Civil War	
Before	**After**
• Western expansion	• Fifteenth Amendment extends voting rights to all adult male citizens.
• _____	
_____	• _____
• _____	_____
_____	• _____
• _____	_____
_____	• _____
	_____
	• _____
	_____
	• _____
	_____
	• Nineteenth Amendment extends voting rights to all adult women.

Name_____ Class_____ Date_____

In the 1800s, the United States followed a policy of **expansionism,** or extending the nation's boundaries. In 1803, the **Louisiana Purchase** nearly doubled the size of the country. More territory was soon added in the West and South. Americans believed in **Manifest Destiny.** This is the idea that their nation was destined to spread across the entire continent.

Voting, slavery, and women's rights were important issues. In 1800, only white men who owned property could vote. By the 1830s, most white men had the right to vote. William Lloyd Garrison, Frederick Douglass, and other abolitionists called for an end to slavery. Lucretia Mott, Elizabeth Cady Stanton, Susan B. Anthony, and other women began to seek equal rights.

Economic differences, as well as slavery, divided the country into the North and the South. When Abraham Lincoln was elected in 1860, most Southern states **seceded,** or left the Union. This started the American Civil War. Southerners fought fiercely but finally surrendered in 1865.

During the war, Lincoln issued the Emancipation Proclamation. This declared that the slaves in the South were free. After the war, slavery was banned throughout the nation. African Americans were granted some political rights. However, African Americans still faced **segregation.** Some state laws prevented African Americans from voting, too.

After the Civil War, the United States became a world leader in industrial and agricultural production. By 1900, giant monopolies controlled whole industries. For example, John D. Rockefeller's Standard Oil Company dominated the world's petroleum industry. Big business enjoyed huge profits, but not everyone benefited. Unions sought better wages and working conditions for factory workers. Farmers and city workers formed the Populist Party to seek changes. Progressives worked to ban child labor, limit working hours, regulate monopolies, and give voters more power. Progressives also worked to get women the right to vote. This finally happened in 1920.

Review Questions

1. What started the American Civil War?

_____

_____

2. What reforms did Progressives want?

_____

_____

READING CHECK

What effect did the Louisiana Purchase have on the size of the United States?

_____

_____

_____

VOCABULARY STRATEGY

Find the word *dominated* in the underlined sentence. What does it mean? The previous sentence states that giant monopolies *controlled* whole industries. The word *control* is a synonym for *dominate.* How does this sentence help you understand the meaning of *dominated?*

READING SKILL

Categorize Group the reforms described in this section by the people who did or would benefit from them: white men, African Americans, workers, and women.

_____

_____

_____

_____

Name_____ Class_____ Date_____

Focus Question: How did Western nations come to dominate much of the world in the late 1800s?

As you read this section in your textbook, complete the chart below showing the multiple causes of imperialism in the 1800s. Some items have been completed for you.

Event

The New Imperialism

Causes

- Need for natural resources
- Desire for new markets
- Bankers sought to invest their profits.
- Colonies offered an outlet for Europe's population.
-
-
-
-
-
-
-

CHAPTER 24 SECTION 1

Section Summary

BUILDING OVERSEAS EMPIRES

Many Western countries built overseas empires in the late 1800s. This expansion is called **imperialism.** It is the domination by one country of another country or region. In the 1800s Europeans began an aggressive expansion called the "new imperialism." The new imperialism had many causes. The Industrial Revolution was one. Manufacturers needed natural resources such as rubber and petroleum. They needed new markets to sell their goods. Colonies provided a place for Europe's growing population to live, too.

Nationalism played an important role, as well. Europeans felt that ruling a global empire increased a nation's prestige and influence. If one country began claiming Asian or African lands, rival nations would move in to claim nearby lands. Many in Europe were concerned about people overseas; they believed they had a duty to spread Western medicine, law, and religion. But there was also a growing sense that Europeans were racially superior to non-Westerners. Many Westerners used Social Darwinism to justify dominating other societies. As a result, millions of non-Westerners were robbed of their cultural heritage.

Africans and Asians strongly resisted Western expansion. Some people fought the invaders, but the Europeans had superior weapons and technology, such as machine guns, the telegraph, and riverboats. Others tried to strengthen their societies by reforming their own religious traditions. Many Western-educated Africans and Asians organized nationalist movements to expel the imperialists.

The imperial powers had several ways to control colonies. The French practiced direct rule. They sent officials from France to run the colony. The British used indirect rule. To govern their colonies, they used local rulers. In a **protectorate,** local rulers were left in place but were expected to follow the advice of Europeans. In a **sphere of influence** an outside power claimed exclusive investment or trading privileges, but did not rule the area. Europeans did this to prevent conflicts among themselves.

Review Questions

1. What kinds of technology aided imperialism?

_____

_____

2. How is a protectorate different from a sphere of influence?

_____

_____

READING CHECK

How did the Industrial Revolution help to cause the new imperialism?

_____

_____

_____

VOCABULARY STRATEGY

Find the word *prestige* in the underlined sentence. Notice that the word *increased* is in the same sentence. What would a nation gain from a global empire? Think about why nations wanted to have colonies. How would Europeans feel if their rivals had larger empires? Use these context clues to help you figure out the meaning of *prestige.*

READING SKILL

Multiple Causes List the causes of imperialism found in this Section Summary.

_____

_____

_____

CHAPTER 24 SECTION 2 — Note Taking Study Guide
THE PARTITION OF AFRICA

Focus Question: How did imperialist European powers claim control over most of Africa by the end of the 1800s?

As you read this section in your textbook, complete the chart below by identifying the causes and effects of the partition of Africa by European nations. Some items have been completed for you.

Effect

- Europeans establish new borders in Africa.
-
-
-
-
-

Event

Partition of Africa

Cause

- Explorers and missionaries increase contact.
-
-
- Berlin Conference

CHAPTER 24 SECTION 2
Section Summary
THE PARTITION OF AFRICA

Before the 1800s, the Ottoman empire ruled much of North Africa. In West Africa, **Usman dan Fodio** set up a successful Islamic state inspiring other Muslim reform movements. Islam and trade influenced East Africa. In southern Africa, the Zulus emerged as a major force. They were led by **Shaka,** a ruthless and brilliant leader. His conquests set off huge migrations of conquered people to other areas and caused new wars.

European contact with Africans increased when European explorers pushed into the interior. Missionaries followed the explorers. They built schools, churches, and medical clinics. However, they took a **paternalistic** view of Africans, treating them like children. One explorer and missionary, **Dr. David Livingstone,** spent so many years in Central Africa that the journalist **Henry Stanley** was sent to find him.

About 1871, **King Leopold II** of Belgium hired Stanley to arrange trade treaties with African leaders. Leopold's interest caused Britain, France, and Germany to join in a scramble for African land. To stop conflict, Europeans met in Berlin to divide up the continent of Africa for themselves. As the years passed, Europeans took more and more of Africa's resources, and rarely allowed Africans any role in government. When gold and diamonds were discovered in southern Africa, the British fought the **Boer War.** The Boers were descendents of Dutch settlers.

Africans tried to resist European imperialism. **Samori Touré** fought French forces in West Africa. **Yaa Asantewaa** was an Asante queen who led the fight against the British. Another female leader was **Nehanda** of the Shona in Zimbabwe. Most efforts failed, except in Ethiopia. Earlier, Ethiopia had been divided up among rival princes who then ruled their own domains. However, **Menelik II** modernized his country. His army fought the Italians. The nation remained independent.

During this time, a Western-educated, upper-class African **elite** developed. By the early 1900s, African nationalists had begun to work for independence.

Review Questions

1. What did King Leopold hire Stanley to do?

_____

_____

2. Why did Europeans meet in Berlin?

_____

_____

READING CHECK

Which African country kept its independence?

_____

_____

_____

VOCABULARY STRATEGY

Find the word *domains* in the underlined sentence. Use context clues to figure out its meaning. Think about what a prince rules. When you divide a country, what are you dividing? Use these context clues to help you figure out the meaning of *domains*.

READING SKILL

Cause and Effect What caused Europeans to meet in Berlin? What was the effect on Africa?

_____

_____

_____

CHAPTER 24 SECTION 3

Note Taking Study Guide

EUROPEAN CLAIMS IN MUSLIM REGIONS

Focus Question: How did European nations extend their power into Muslim regions of the world?

As you read this section in your textbook, complete the concept web below to understand the effects of European imperialism on Muslim regions. Some items have been completed for you.

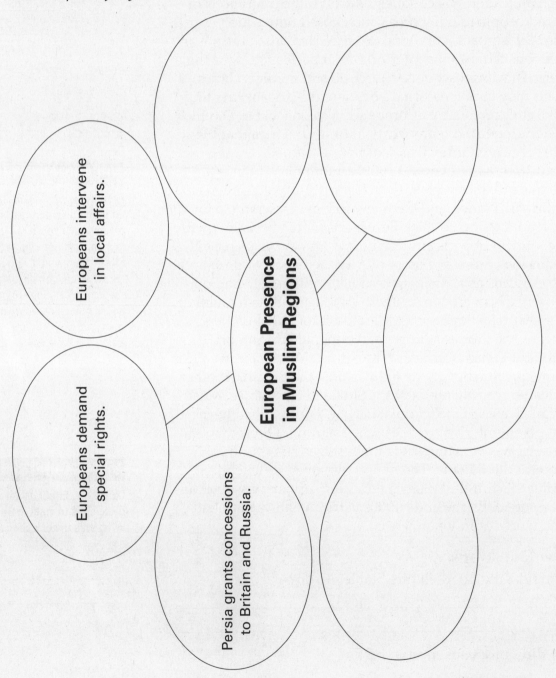

CHAPTER 24
SECTION 3
Section Summary
EUROPEAN CLAIMS IN MUSLIM REGIONS

In the 1500s, there were three great Muslim empires—the Ottomans in the Middle East, the Safavids in Persia, and the Mughals in India. By the 1700s, all three were in decline due to corruption and discontent. In response, Muslim reform movements arose. They stressed spiritual devotion and strict rules on how to act. Some also opposed foreign expansion in Muslim areas. For example, in the Sudan, **Muhammad Ahmad** said that he was the **Mahdi,** the long-awaited savior of the faith. The Mahdi and his followers fiercely fought British expansion.

At its height, the Ottoman empire extended across parts of North Africa, Southeastern Europe, and the Middle East. When ideas of nationalism spread from Western Europe, people within the empire began to rebel. Ambitious **pashas** wanted more power. Some leaders looked to the West for ideas on reforming the government and its rigid rules. In the early 1700s, they reorganized the bureaucracy. Repressive **sultans** usually rejected reform. Another problem was tension between Turkish nationalists and minority groups. This led to a brutal **genocide** of Christian Armenians when Turks thought that Armenians were supporting Russia against Turkey.

In the early 1800s, Egypt was a semi-independent province of the Ottoman empire. **Muhammad Ali** is sometimes called the "father of modern Egypt" because he introduced a number of political and economic reforms. He conquered the neighboring lands of Arabia, Syria, and Sudan. Before he died in 1849, he had set Egypt on the road to becoming a major Middle Eastern power. His successors lacked his skills, however. In 1882, Egypt became a protectorate of Britain.

Like the Ottoman empire, Persia—now Iran—faced major challenges. Foreign nations, especially Russia and Britain, wanted to control Iran's oil fields. They were granted special rights called **concessions,** and even sent in troops to protect their interests. These actions outraged Iranian nationalists.

Review Questions
1. Why did Muslim reform movements arise?

_____

_____

2. Why is Muhammad Ali sometimes called the "father of modern Egypt"?

_____

_____

READING CHECK

Who was the Mahdi?

_____

_____

_____

VOCABULARY STRATEGY

Find the word *bureaucracy* in the underlined sentence. *Bureau* is a French word that means "office." The suffix *-cracy* means "type of government." A *bureaucrat* is an official who works in a *bureaucracy.* Use these word-origin clues to help you figure out what *bureaucracy* means.

READING SKILL

Understanding Effects What was the effect of the foreign troops stationed in Iran?

_____

_____

_____

Name_____ Class_____ Date_____

Focus Question: How did Britain gradually extend its control over most of India despite opposition?

As you read this section in your textbook, complete the flowchart below to identify the causes and effects of British colonial rule in India. Some items have been completed for you.

Effect

- India's once prosperous hand-weaving industry is ruined.
- Massive deforestation
-
-
-
-

Event

British Colonial Rule in India

Cause

- Mughal empire lacks strong rulers.
- British East India Company increases influence.
-
-
-

CHAPTER 24 SECTION 4

Section Summary

THE BRITISH TAKE OVER INDIA

Mughal rulers once had a powerful Muslim empire in India. The British East India Company had trading rights on the edges of the empire. The main goal of the East India Company was to make money. As Mughal power declined, the East India Company gained power. The British were able to conquer India because Indians were not able to unite against the British.

The British felt that Western religion and culture was more advanced than Indian religions and culture. In the 1850s, the East India Company made several unpopular moves. The most serious caused the Sepoy Rebellion. Indian soldiers, or **sepoys,** were told to bite off the tips of their rifle cartridges. This caused a rebellion because the cartridges were greased with animal fat, violating local religious beliefs. The British crushed the revolt, killing thousands of Indians.

After the rebellion, Parliament ended the rule of the East India Company. Instead, a British **viceroy** governed India in the name of the monarch. In this way, the overall British economy could benefit from trade with India. However, this trade favored the British. Also, although the British built railroads and telegraph networks, they ruined India's hand-weaving industry. Encouraging Indian farmers to grow cash crops led to **deforestation** and famines.

Some educated Indians wanted India to become more modern. Others felt they should stay with their own Hindu or Muslim cultures. In the early 1800s, **Ram Mohun Roy** combined both views. Roy condemned child marriage and **sati,** which called for a widow to throw herself on her husband's funeral fire. He opposed **purdah,** or the isolation of women. He also set up educational societies to help revive pride in Indian culture. Most British felt that Western-educated Indians would be happy with British rule. Instead, Indian nationalists formed the Indian National Congress in 1885 and began pressing for self-rule.

Review Questions

1. How were the British able to conquer India?

_____

_____

2. What caused the Sepoy Rebellion?

_____

_____

READING CHECK

What British official ruled India in the name of the monarch?

_____

_____

_____

VOCABULARY STRATEGY

Find the word *overall* in the underlined sentence. *Overall* is a compound word. That means it is a word formed from two other words. Circle the two words that form *overall*. Use the meanings of these two words to figure out what *overall* means.

READING SKILL

Identify Causes and Effects
What happened when the British encouraged Indians to grow cash crops?

_____

_____

_____

CHAPTER 24 SECTION 5

Note Taking Study Guide

CHINA AND THE NEW IMPERIALISM

Focus Question: How did Western powers use diplomacy and war to gain power in Qing China?

As you read this section in your textbook, complete the chart below by listing the multiple causes of the decline of Qing China. Some items have been completed for you.

Event

Decline of Qing China

Cause

- Opium trade disrupts economy.
- Opium War with Britain
- Treaty of Nanjing forces China to make concessions to British.
-
-
-
-
-
-
-
- Two-year-old boy inherits the throne; China slips into chaos.

CHAPTER 24 SECTION 5

Section Summary
CHINA AND THE NEW IMPERIALISM

For centuries, China had a favorable **balance of trade,** because of a **trade surplus.** Westerners had a **trade deficit** with China, buying more from the Chinese than they sold to them. Then the British began trading opium grown in India in exchange for Chinese tea. The Chinese asked Britain to stop this drug trade. The British refused, and this led to the **Opium War** in 1839. Without modern weapons and fighting methods, the Chinese were easily defeated. Under the Treaty of Nanjing, which ended the war, Britain received a huge **indemnity** and British citizens gained the right of **extraterritoriality.** Afterward, France, Russia, and the United States each made specific demands on China. China felt pressure to sign treaties stipulating the opening of more ports and allowing Christian missionaries into China.

China had other problems too. Peasants hated the corrupt Qing government. Their rebellion, known as the **Taiping Rebellion,** almost toppled the Qing dynasty. Another problem was that educated Chinese did not agree about modernizing. Some felt Western ideas and technology threatened Confucianism. Reformers who wanted to adopt Western ways did not have government support.

Meanwhile, China's defeat in the **Sino-Japanese War** of 1894 encouraged European nations to carve out spheres of influence in China. The United States feared that America might be shut out. The United States called for an **Open Door Policy,** making trade in China open to everyone. Concerned that China's problems were due to not modernizing, the emperor **Guang Xu** launched the Hundred Days of Reform in 1898. However, conservatives imprisoned the emperor.

Many Chinese were angry about the presence of foreigners. Some formed a secret group known to Westerners as the Boxers. A group known as the Boxers tried to kill foreigners in the **Boxer Uprising** in 1900. Although the Boxers failed, nationalism increased. Reformers began calling for a republic. One of them, **Sun Yixian,** became president of the new Chinese republic when the Qing dynasty fell in 1911.

Review Questions

1. What caused the Opium War?

_____

_____

2. What caused the Boxer Rebellion?

_____

_____

READING CHECK

Who became president of China in 1911?

_____

_____

_____

VOCABULARY STRATEGY

Find the word *stipulating* in the underlined sentence. What clues can you find in the surrounding words, phrases or sentences? Ask yourself what France, Russia, and the United States demanded or asked of China. Use these context clues to help you figure out what *stipulating* means.

READING SKILL

Recognize Multiple Causes List two causes of the Open Door Policy.

_____

_____

_____

Note Taking Study Guide

JAPAN MODERNIZES

Focus Question: How did Japan become a modern industrial power, and what did it do with its new strength?

As you read this section in your textbook, complete the chart below to identify causes and effects of the Meiji Restoration. Some items have been completed for you.

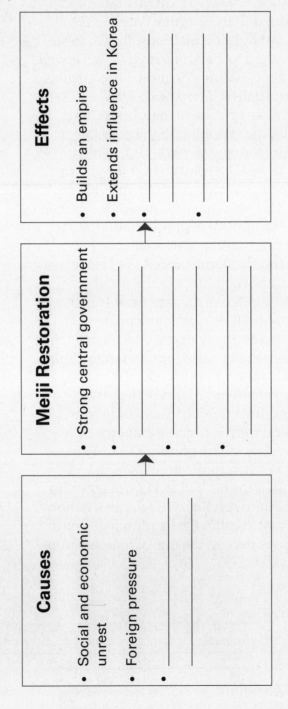

Causes
- Social and economic unrest
- Foreign pressure
-
-

Meiji Restoration
- Strong central government
-
-
-

Effects
- Builds an empire
- Extends influence in Korea
-
-

Name_____ Class_____ Date_____

Section Summary
JAPAN MODERNIZES

In 1603, shoguns seized power in Japan and closed it to foreigners. For more than 200 years, Japan was isolated from the world. Over time, many Japanese became discontent. They suffered financial hardship and had no political power. The government responded by trying to revive old ways. They tried emphasizing farming over commerce. These efforts had little success. The shoguns' power weakened.

Then, in 1853, a fleet of well-armed U.S. ships arrived. They were led by Commodore **Matthew Perry,** who demanded that Japan open its ports. Japan was unable to defend itself, so it was forced to sign treaties that gave the United States trading rights. Disgraced by the terms of these treaties, daimyo and samurai revolted. The revolt unseated the shogun and restored the emperor Mutsuhito to power. Mutsuhito moved to the shogun's palace in the city of Edo, which was renamed **Tokyo.** This began a long reign known as the **Meiji Restoration**.

The Meiji reformers wanted to create a new political and social system. Their constitution made all citizens equal. A legislature, or **Diet,** was formed. Meiji leaders also wanted to build a modern industrial economy. The government supported powerful families, known as **zaibatsu.** These families ruled over industrial empires. Japan modernized very quickly. This was partly due to Japan's strong sense of identity caused by its **homogeneous society.** Its people shared a common culture and language.

Japan needed natural resources for industry. This need and the desire to equal the West pushed Japan to build an empire. First, Japan forced Korea to open its ports for trade. Next, competition between Japan and China in Korea led to the **First Sino-Japanese War,** which Japan won. Japan gained ports in China and won control over Taiwan. Then, Japan successfully battled Russia in the **Russo-Japanese War.** By the early 1900s, Japan was the strongest power in Asia.

Review Questions

1. What caused the daimyo and samurai to revolt?

_____

_____

2. What right did all citizens gain under the Meiji constitution?

_____

_____

READING CHECK

Why did Japan have a strong sense of identity?

_____

_____

_____

VOCABULARY STRATEGY

Find the word *emphasizing* in the underlined sentence. What does it mean? Look for context clues in the surrounding words. For example, what clue does the word *over* provide about the relationship of farming to commerce? To what does "old ways" refer here? Use these clues to help you figure out what *emphasizing* means.

READING SKILL

Identify Causes and Effects
What was one cause and one effect of the coming to Japan of Perry's fleet?

_____

_____

_____

Name_____ Class_____ Date_____

Focus Question: How did industrialized powers divide up Southeast Asia, and how did the colonized peoples react?

As you read this section in your textbook, complete the flowchart below to identify causes, events, and effects of imperialism in Southeast Asia and the Pacific. Some items have been completed for you.

Effects

- Europeans introduce modern technology.
- Europeans expand commerce and industry.
-
-
-
-
-

Events

- Dutch dominate the Dutch East Indies (now Indonesia).
- The British annex Burma.
- The French seize Indochina.
-
-
-
-

Causes

- Sea lanes opened between India and China.
- Profitable crops of coffee, indigo, spices
- Natural resources
-
-
-

CHAPTER 25 SECTION 2

Section Summary

IMPERIALISM IN SOUTHEAST ASIA AND THE PACIFIC

In the 1800s, European merchants began to colonize much of Southeast Asia. The Dutch, for example, took over all of the Dutch East Indies (now Indonesia). The British expanded from India into Burma and Malaya. The Burmese resisted British rule but suffered terrible defeats. The French invaded Vietnam. The Vietnamese fought fiercely, but lost against European weapons. The French took over all of Vietnam, Laos, and Cambodia. They called these holdings **French Indochina.** Meanwhile, the king of Siam, **Mongkut,** was able to keep his country from becoming a European colony. To do so, he accepted some unequal treaties. By the 1890s, Europeans controlled most of Southeast Asia.

The Philippines had been under Spanish rule since the 1500s. In 1898, the **Spanish-American War** broke out. During the war, U.S. battleships destroyed the Spanish fleet in the Philippines. Filipino rebel leaders declared independence from Spain. They joined the U.S. fight against Spain. In return for their help, the Filipino rebels expected the United States to recognize their independence. Instead, in the treaty that ended the war, the United States gave Spain $20 million for control of the Philippines. The Filipino rebels were bitterly disappointed. They renewed their struggle for independence, but the United States crushed the rebellion. <u>The United States, however, did promise Filipinos a slow transition to self-rule sometime in the future.</u>

In the 1800s, the industrialized powers also began to take an interest in the many Pacific islands. American sugar growers, for example, pressed for power in the Hawaiian Islands. When the Hawaiian queen **Liliuokalani** tried to reduce foreign influence, American planters overthrew her. In 1898, the United States annexed Hawaii. Supporters of annexation argued that if the United States did not take Hawaii, other rival countries would. By 1900, the United States, Britain, France, or Germany had claimed nearly every island in the Pacific.

Review Questions

1. How did the king of Siam keep his country from becoming a European colony?

_____

_____

2. What had Filipino rebels expected in return for helping the United States during the Spanish-American War?

_____

_____

READING CHECK

What did the French call their holdings of Vietnam, Laos, and Cambodia?

_____

_____

_____

VOCABULARY STRATEGY

Find the word *transition* in the underlined sentence. Note that the word begins with the prefix *trans-*, which means "across" or "through." Use the meanings of the word's prefix to help you figure out what the word *transition* means.

READING SKILL

Identify Causes and Effects Identify one cause and one effect of Liliuokalani's attempts to reduce foreign influence in Hawaii.

_____

_____

_____

CHAPTER 25 SECTION 3

Note Taking Study Guide

SELF-RULE FOR CANADA, AUSTRALIA, AND NEW ZEALAND

Focus Question: How were the British colonies of Canada, Australia, and New Zealand settled, and how did they win self-rule?

As you read this section in your textbook, complete the chart below to identify the causes and effects of events in the British colonies of Canada, Australia, and New Zealand. Some items have been completed for you.

Cause	Loyalist Americans flee to Canada.	The British hurry to put down the rebellions in Upper and Lower Canada.	Canada grows as thousands of English, Scottish, and Irish people immigrate to the country.	Britain needs prisons for its convicts.		
Event	Up to 30,000 loyalists settle in Canada.	British Parliament passes the Act of Union.				
Effect	Ethnic tensions arise between English- and French-speaking Canadians.	The act joins the two Canadas into one province and gives them an elected legislature.				

CHAPTER 25 SECTION 3

Section Summary
SELF-RULE FOR CANADA, AUSTRALIA, AND NEW ZEALAND

In 1791, Britain created two provinces in Canada: English-speaking Upper Canada and French-speaking Lower Canada. <u>When unrest grew in both colonies, the British sent Lord Durham to compile a report on the causes.</u> In response to his report, Parliament joined the two Canadas into one colony.

As the country grew, Canadian leaders urged **confederation,** or unification, of Britain's North American colonies. They felt that this would strengthen the new nation against the United States and help the economy. British Parliament passed a law that made Canada a **dominion,** or self-governing nation. Canada continued to grow. As Canada expanded westward, the Native American way of life was destroyed. The **métis**—people of mixed Native American and French Canadian descent—tried to resist. Government troops, however, put down their revolts.

In 1770, Captain James Cook claimed Australia for Britain. Australia had long been inhabited by other people. These **indigenous,** or original, people are called Aborigines. When white settlers arrived in Australia, the Aborigines suffered terribly. Britain needed prisons for its criminals. So, it made Australia into a **penal colony,** or faraway jail. Then, Britain encouraged non-criminal citizens to move to Australia by offering them land and tools. Like Canada, Australia was made up of separate colonies scattered around the continent. To keep away other European powers and to boost development, Britain agreed to Australian demands for self-rule. In 1901, the colonies united into the independent Commonwealth of Australia.

Captain James Cook also claimed New Zealand for Britain. The indigenous people of New Zealand are the **Maori.** They were determined to defend their land. In 1840, Britain annexed New Zealand. Colonists took more and more of the land. This led to fierce wars with the Maori. Many Maori died. By the 1870s, Maori resistance had crumbled. Like settlers in Australia and Canada, white New Zealanders wanted self-rule. In 1907, they won independence.

Review Questions

1. Why did Britain agree to make Canada a dominion?

_____

_____

2. Why did the British agree to self-rule in Australia?

_____

_____

READING CHECK

What indigenous people suffered when European settlers arrived in Australia?

_____

_____

_____

VOCABULARY STRATEGY

Find the word *compile* in the underlined sentence. The word *compile* comes from a Latin word that means "to heap together." Use this clue to help you learn what *compile* means.

READING SKILL

Identify Causes and Effects
Identify the causes and effects of the Maori fight against New Zealand colonists.

_____

_____

_____

CHAPTER 25 SECTION 4
Note Taking Study Guide
ECONOMIC IMPERIALISM IN LATIN AMERICA

Focus Question: How did Latin American nations struggle for stability, and how did industrialized nations affect them?

A. *As you read this section in your textbook, complete the chart below to identify multiple causes of instability in Latin America. Then, give an example of how each cause affected Mexico. Some items have been completed for you.*

Instability in Latin America	
Causes	**Mexican Example**
Colonial legacy leaves deep-rooted inequalities after independence.	Large landowners, army leaders, and the Catholic Church dominate Mexican politics.
Efforts for reform are crushed.	

B. *As you read "The Economics of Dependence" and "The Influence of the United States," complete the chart below to identify effects of foreign influence on Latin America. Some items have been completed for you.*

Effects of Foreign Influence

Cycle of economic dependence continues.		

CHAPTER 25 SECTION 4

Section Summary

ECONOMIC IMPERIALISM IN LATIN AMERICA

Many factors kept democracy from taking hold in Latin America's newly independent nations. Constitutions guaranteed equality before the law, but inequalities remained. These nations did not have a tradition of unity. Therefore, **regionalism,** or loyalty to a local area, weakened them. Local strongmen, called *caudillos,* formed private armies to resist the central government.

Mexico is an example of the struggle to build stable governments in Latin America at this time. Large landowners, army leaders, and the Catholic Church dominated Mexican politics. The ruling elite was divided between conservatives and liberals. Conservatives defended tradition. <u>Liberals saw themselves as enlightened supporters of progress.</u> Battles between these two groups led to revolts and the rise of dictators. When **Benito Juárez** and other liberals gained power, they began an era of reform known as **La Reforma.** Juárez offered hope to the oppressed people of Mexico. After Juárez died, however, General Porfirio Díaz ruled as a harsh dictator. Many Indians and mestizos fell into **peonage,** to work off advances on their wages.

Under colonial rule, Latin America was economically dependent on Spain and Portugal. This prevented Latin America from developing its own economy. After independence, this pattern changed very little. Britain and the United States replaced Spain as Latin America's chief trading partners.

Meanwhile, the United States expanded across North America. U.S. leaders wanted to discourage any new European colonies in the Americas, so they issued the **Monroe Doctrine.** To protect U.S. investments in Latin America, the United States sent troops. This made the United States a target of resentment and rebellion. Then the United States built the **Panama Canal** across Central America. The canal boosted trade and shipping worldwide. To people in Latin America, however, the canal was another example of "Yankee imperialism."

Review Questions

1. What three groups dominated Mexican politics?

_____

_____

2. After independence, on which countries did the new Latin American republics depend economically?

_____

_____

READING CHECK

Who were the caudillos?

_____

_____

_____

VOCABULARY STRATEGY

Find the word *enlightened* in the underlined sentence. Break the word down into its smaller parts. Note that the root word of *enlightened* is *light. Light* is sometimes used to mean "information," as in the phrase, "Let's shed some light on the subject." Use this word-part clue to help you figure out what *enlightened* means.

READING SKILL

Identify Causes and Effects
Identify what caused the United States to issue the Monroe Doctrine. Then, identify one effect it had on Latin America.

_____

_____

_____

CHAPTER 26 SECTION 1

Note Taking Study Guide

THE GREAT WAR BEGINS

Focus Question: Why and how did World War I begin in 1914?

As you read this section in your textbook, complete the following chart to summarize the events that led to the outbreak of World War I. Some items have been completed for you.

The War Begins

- Archduke of Austria assassinated by Serbian nationalist.

Tensions Rise

- Powers want to protect status.
- Compete overseas for colonies

Alliances Form

- Triple Alliance, 1882— Germany, Austria, Italy

CHAPTER 26 SECTION 1

Section Summary
THE GREAT WAR BEGINS

Although powerful forces were pushing Europe towards war, the great powers had made non-binding agreements, called **ententes,** to try to keep the peace. The Triple Alliance was made up of Germany, Austria-Hungary, and Italy. Russia, France, and Britain made up the Triple Entente. During World War I, Germany and Austria fought on the same side. They were called the Central Powers. Russia, France, and Britain were known as the Allies.

In the period before the war, European powers competed. They wanted to protect their status. Overseas rivalries divided them. They fought for new colonies in Africa and elsewhere. They began to build up their armies and navies. The rise of **militarism** helped to feed this arms race.

Nationalism also caused tensions to grow. Germans were proud of their military and economic power. The French wanted **Alsace and Lorraine** back from Germany. Pan-Slavism led Russia to support fellow Slavs in Serbia. Austria and Ottoman Turkey were afraid that they would lose territory, especially in the Balkans. Soon, unrest made that region a "powder keg." Then, a Serbian nationalist shot to death the heir to the Austrian throne at Sarajevo, Bosnia.

Some Austrian leaders saw this as a chance to crush Serbia. They sent Serbia an **ultimatum,** or set of demands, which Serbia partly refused to follow. Austria, with Germany's full support, declared war on Serbia in July 1914.

Soon, the network of agreements drew other great powers into the fight. Russia began to **mobilize** its army to support Serbia. Germany then declared war on Russia. France said it would keep to its treaty with Russia, so Germany declared war on France, too. When Germany invaded Belgium to get to France, it ended Belgium's **neutrality.** This caused Britain to declare war on Germany. World War I had begun.

Review Questions

1. How did the network of European agreements cause World War I to start?

_____

_____

2. What act caused Britain to declare war?

_____

_____

READING CHECK

Which countries made up the Central Powers?

_____

_____

_____

VOCABULARY STRATEGY

What does the word *overseas* mean in the underlined sentence? What clues can you find in the surrounding words, phrases, or sentences? Circle the words in the paragraph that could help you learn what *overseas* means.

READING SKILL

Summarize What events led Austria to declare war on Serbia?

_____

_____

_____

CHAPTER 26 SECTION 2

Note Taking Study Guide
A NEW KIND OF WAR

Focus Question: How and where was World War I fought?

A. *As you read "Stalemate on the Western Front," "Battle on Other European Fronts," and "War Around the World," record important details about World War I events in the flowchart below. Some items have been completed for you.*

Western Front	Eastern Front
• Stalemate • First battle of the Marne prevented a quick German victory. • Soldiers fought from trenches. • _____	• Battle lines shifted. • _____ • _____

Elsewhere in Europe	Ottoman Empire
• Bulgaria joined the Central Powers and helped defeat its old Balkan rival Serbia. • _____ • _____	• Joined the Central Powers • _____
	Colonies • European colonies were drawn into the war.

B. *As you read "Technology of Modern Warfare," complete the following concept web to summarize information about the technology of World War I. Some items have been completed for you.*

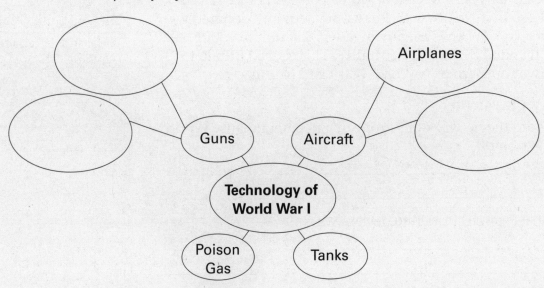

CHAPTER 26 SECTION 2

Section Summary
A NEW KIND OF WAR

World War I was the largest conflict in history up to that time. Millions of French, British, Russian, and German soldiers went to battle. Germany wanted to defeat France quickly, but Belgian forces resisted Germany's advance. Both sides dug deep trenches on the battlefront to protect their armies from enemy fire. This conflict on the Western Front turned into a long, deadly **stalemate,** or deadlock that neither side could break.

New technology made World War I different from earlier wars. Modern weapons were able to kill more soldiers than ever before. In 1915, first Germany then the Allies began using poison gas. New machines like tanks, airplanes, and submarines were used in this war. In 1915, Germany flew **zeppelins** to bomb the English coast. Both sides equipped airplanes with machine guns. Pilots known as "flying aces" confronted each other in the skies. However, their "dog fights" had little effect on the ground war. German submarines called **U-boats** attacked Allied ships. To defend against them, the Allies organized **convoys,** or groups of merchant ships protected by warships.

Battle lines shifted back and forth on Europe's Eastern Front. War deaths were higher than on the Western Front. Russia was not ready to fight a modern war. When pushing into eastern Germany, Russian armies were badly defeated. In 1915, Italy declared war on Austria-Hungary and Germany. In 1917, the Austrians and Germans attacked the Italians.

Although most of the fighting took place in Europe, World War I was a global conflict. Japan used the war to seize German outposts in China and islands in the Pacific. The Ottoman empire joined the Central Powers. Its strategic location enabled it to cut off Allied supplies to Russia through the **Dardanelles,** a vital strait. The Ottoman Turks were hard hit in the Middle East. Arab nationalists rebelled against their rule. The British sent **T.E. Lawrence,** or Lawrence of Arabia, to aid them. European colonies in Africa and Asia were also drawn into World War I.

Review Questions
1. Why did a stalemate develop on the Western Front?

_____

_____

2. What caused the great number of deaths during World War I?

_____

_____

READING CHECK

Which of the European powers was not ready to fight a modern war?

_____

_____

_____

VOCABULARY STRATEGY

What does the word *confronted* mean in the underlined sentence? What clues or examples can you find in the surrounding words, phrases, or sentences that hint at its meaning? For example, think about the meaning of the phrase "dog fights." Circle the words in the paragraph that could help you learn what *confronted* means.

READING SKILL

Identify Supporting Details
Identify two differences between the Western Front and the Eastern Front.

_____

_____

_____

CHAPTER
26
SECTION 3

Note Taking Study Guide
WINNING THE WAR

Focus Question: How did the Allies win World War I?

As you read this section in your textbook, complete the following outline to summarize the content of this section. Some items have been completed for you.

I. **Waging total war**

   A. Economies committed to war production.

      1. Conscription

      2. Rationing

      3. Price controls

   B. Economic warfare

      1. _____

      2. _____

      3. _____

   C. Propaganda war

      1. _____

      2. _____

      3. _____

   D. Women join war effort.

      1. _____

      2. _____

      3. _____

II. **Morale collapses.**

   A. War fatigue

      1. _____

      2. _____

      3. _____

   B. _____

      1. _____

      2. _____

      3. _____

(Outline continues on the next page.)

CHAPTER
26
SECTION 3

Note Taking Study Guide

WINNING THE WAR

(Continued from page 236)

III. United States declares war.

    A. _____

        1. _____

        2. _____

        3. _____

    B. _____

        1. _____

        2. _____

        3. _____

    C. _____

        1. _____

        2. _____

        3. _____

IV. _____

    A. _____

    B. _____

    C. _____

CHAPTER
26
SECTION 3

Note Taking Study Guide
WINNING THE WAR

READING CHECK

What did both sides use to control public opinion?

_____

_____

_____

World War I was the first **total war.** Nations put all their resources into the war effort. Both sides set up systems to recruit, arm, transport, and supply their armies. Nations set up military **conscription,** or "the draft." This required all young men to be ready to fight. Women played an important role, too. They took over the jobs of millions of men who had left to fight.

International law allowed wartime blockades to seize **contraband,** such as weapons or other illegal goods. British blockades, however, kept ships from carrying other supplies, such as food, in and out of Germany. In response, German U-boats torpedoed the British passenger liner the *Lusitania.* Both sides used **propaganda** to control public opinion. They printed tales of **atrocities.** Some were true and others were not.

After a time, war fatigue set in. Long casualty lists, food shortages, and the failure to win led to calls for peace. The morale of troops and civilians plunged. <u>In Russia, stories of unfit generals and corruption eroded public confidence and led to revolution.</u>

VOCABULARY STRATEGY

What does the word *eroded* mean in the underlined sentence? You can use prior knowledge to figure it out. Think about what you might already know about this word in another form: *erosion.* What does *erosion* mean? Use what you might know about *erosion* as a clue to what *eroded* means.

In 1917, the United States joined the fight by declaring war on Germany. Many factors led to this decision. Germany kept up its submarine attacks. Also, many Americans supported the Allies because of cultural ties. By 1918, about two million fresh American soldiers had joined the tired Allied troops. Earlier in that year, President Wilson had issued his **Fourteen Points.** This list of terms for ending this and future wars included **self-determination** for the peoples of Eastern Europe.

In March of 1918, a final showdown on the Western Front began. American troops and Allies drove back German forces. German generals told the kaiser that the war could not be won. The kaiser stepped down and the new German government asked for an **armistice** to end the fighting. At 11 A.M. on November 11, 1918, World War I came to an end.

READING SKILL

Summarize Describe how World War I was a total war.

_____

_____

_____

Review Questions

1. What effect did years of war have on morale?

_____

_____

2. What are two reasons why the United States entered the war?

_____

_____

Name_____ Class_____ Date_____

Focus Question: What factors influenced the peace treaties that ended World War I and how did people react to the treaties?

A. *As you read "The Costs of War," complete this concept web to summarize the costs of World War I. Some items have been completed for you.*

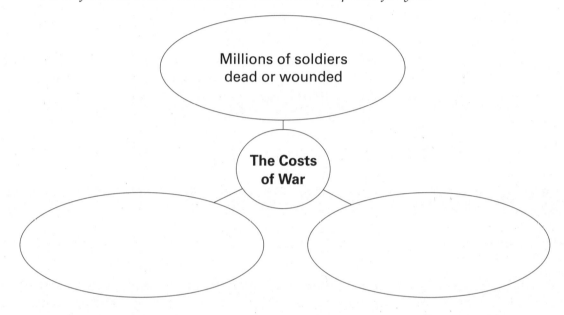

Millions of soldiers dead or wounded

The Costs of War

B. *As you read "The Paris Peace Conference," "The Treaty of Versailles," and "Outcome of the Peace Settlements," use this table to categorize issues and problems that resulted from postwar agreements. Some items have been completed for you.*

Issue	Treaty Settlement	Problems
War Debt	Because of the treaty, the new German Republic had to make large payments to pay for damage caused by the war.	These payments would hurt an already damaged German economy.
Fear of German Strength	The treaty limited the size of the German military.	
Nationalism		
Colonies and Other Non-European Territories		
League of Nations		

Note Taking Study Guide
MAKING THE PEACE

READING CHECK

What was Clemenceau's goal at the Paris Peace Conference?

_____

_____

_____

VOCABULARY STRATEGY

What does the word *widespread* mean in the underlined sentence? Draw a line between the two words that form this compound word. What is the meaning of each of these words? Use your knowledge of their meanings to help you figure out the meaning of *widespread*.

READING SKILL

Summarize How did the goals of the three main leaders at the Paris Peace Conference differ?

_____

_____

_____

The costs of World War I were huge in several ways. There was a great loss of life made worse by an influenza **pandemic.** In addition, raising the money to cover war debts and to rebuild homes, farms, factories and roads would create new economic problems. The Allies blamed the war on the defeated nations and demanded that they make **reparations,** or payments for war damage. Governments had collapsed in Russia, Germany, Austria-Hungary, and the Ottoman empire. Out of all the chaos, political **radicals** dreamed of building a new social order.

At the Paris Peace Conference, the Allies decided the fate of Europe, the former Ottoman empire, and colonies around the world. The three main Allied leaders had different goals. British Prime Minister David Lloyd George wanted money to rebuild Britain. The French leader Georges Clemenceau wanted to weaken Germany so that it could never threaten France again. American President Wilson didn't think that was the way to build a lasting peace. Wilson insisted on creating a League of Nations. The League, based on the idea of **collective security,** would work as one group to keep peace for all nations.

In June 1919, the Allies ordered delegates of the new German Republic to sign the Treaty of Versailles. The Germans were upset that the treaty forced Germany to take the blame for causing the war, cut the size of Germany's military, and burdened the German economy with war reparations.

The Allies then drew up treaties with the other Central Powers. Like the Treaty of Versailles, these treaties left widespread dissatisfaction. Many nations felt betrayed by the peacemakers—especially people in colonies who had hoped for an end to imperial rule. Outside Europe, the Allies added to their overseas empires by creating a system of **mandates.** However, the Paris Peace Conference did offer one ray of hope by starting the League of Nations. Unfortunately, the failure of the United States to support the League weakened it.

Review Questions

1. What were the high costs of World War I?

_____

_____

2. Why were the leaders of the new German Republic upset over the Treaty of Versailles?

_____

_____

Name_____ Class_____ Date_____

Focus Question: How did two revolutions and a civil war bring about Communist control of Russia?

As you read this section in your textbook, fill in the following timeline with dates and facts about the series of events that led to Communist control of Russia. Some items have been included for you. Then write two sentences summarizing the information in the timeline.

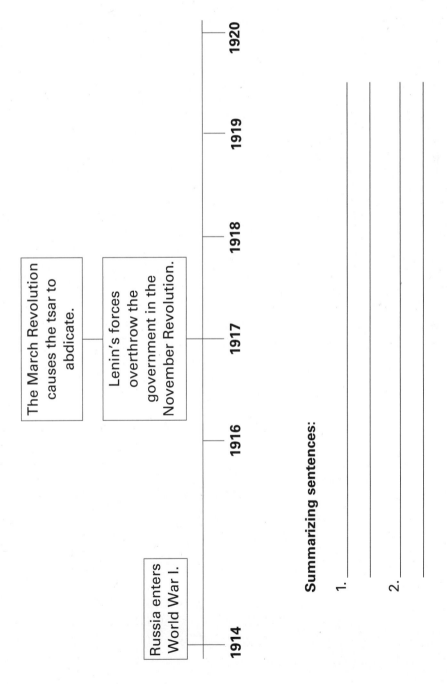

The March Revolution causes the tsar to abdicate.

Lenin's forces overthrow the government in the November Revolution.

Russia enters World War I.

1914 · 1916 · 1917 · 1918 · 1919 · 1920

Summarizing sentences:

1. _____

_____

2. _____

_____

Note Taking Study Guide
REVOLUTION AND CIVIL WAR IN RUSSIA

What was the name of the new Communist nation?

_____

_____

_____

What does the word *withdrawal* mean in the underlined sentence? How is the word used? Look at other context clues in the sentence to help you figure out what the word means. The context clues in the second underlined sentence tell you that after the Russian withdrawal, the Russian troops fought a civil war, meaning they were no longer involved in World War I.

Summarize Describe the events that led to Communist control of Russia.

_____

_____

_____

By the early 1900s Russia had many problems. Tsar Nicholas II resisted change. Marxists tried to start a revolution among the **proletariat** factory workers and urban wage earners. World War I strained Russian resources. By March 1917, disasters on the battlefield and shortages at home caused the tsar to give up his power. Politicians set up a temporary government. Meanwhile, revolutionary socialists set up their own councils of workers and soldiers called **soviets.** These radical socialists, called Bolsheviks, were led by V. I. Lenin. Lenin believed only revolution could bring change. The Russian people were hungry and tired of war. Lenin promised them "Peace, Land, and Bread." In November 1917, the Bolsheviks, renamed Communists, overthrew the government and seized power.

After the Bolshevik Revolution, events in Russia led to the nation's withdrawal from World War I. After the withdrawal, civil war raged for three years between the Communist "Reds" and the "White" armies of tsarist imperial officers. The Russians now fought only among themselves. The Communists shot the former tsar and his family. They organized the **Cheka,** a brutal secret police force. Red Army officers were kept under the close watch of **commissars**—Communist Party officials. The Reds' position in the center of Russia gave them an advantage. They defeated the White armies, and the civil war ended.

Lenin had to rebuild the government and economy. The new nation was called the Union of Soviet Socialist Republics (USSR), or Soviet Union. The new Communist constitution set up an elected legislature. All political power, resources, and means of production would belong to workers and peasants. In reality, however, the Communist Party, not the people, had all the power. However, Lenin allowed some features of capitalism that helped the Soviet economy recover from the wars. After Lenin's death, Joseph Stalin took ruthless steps to win total power over the country.

Review Questions

1. Why did the tsar give up power?

_____

_____

2. Why do you think Lenin's revolutionary slogan—"Peace, Land, and Bread"—was popular with the Russian people?

_____

_____

Name_____ Class_____ Date_____

Focus Question: How did Latin Americans struggle for change in the early 1900s?

A. *As you read "The Mexican Revolution" and "Revolution Leads to Change," list the causes and effects of the Mexican Revolution. Some items have been completed for you.*

Causes		Effects
• Díaz ruled for nearly 35 years. • Foreign investors controlled many of the natural resources. • • •	**Mexican Revolution**	• Venustiano Carranza was elected president of Mexico in 1917. • A new constitution was approved; it called for nationalization of foreign-owned interests. • • • •

B. *As you read "Nationalism at Work in Latin America," complete the following chart by listing the effects of nationalism in Latin America. Some items have been completed for you.*

Effects of Nationalism in Latin America

Economic	Political	Cultural
• Governments supported businesses and factories to produce goods. • •	• People lost trust in governments. •	• Traditional art forms enjoyed renewed interest. • •

CHAPTER 27 SECTION 1	**Section Summary**
	STRUGGLE IN LATIN AMERICA

In the early 1900s, Latin America enjoyed business success. However, investors from other countries controlled much of the region's natural resources. Peasants and workers had little say in the government. Military leaders or wealthy landowners held most of the power. Therefore, only a few people benefited from the growing economy. Most Mexicans lived in poverty. Peasants worked on **haciendas,** or large farms owned by the rich. Eventually, people demanded a say in government. Faced with rebellion, the dictator Porfirio Díaz left office in 1911. A struggle for power, called the Mexican Revolution, began.

In 1917, Venustiano Carranza was elected Mexico's president. He approved a new constitution that included land and labor reform. The constitution strengthened government control over the economy. One way it did this was through **nationalization,** the takeover of natural resources. The government took over some foreign-owned oil companies. Fighting continued until the Institutional Revolutionary Party (PRI) was formed. The PRI took control, allowing some reforms while keeping most of the power.

As was the case elsewhere, the Great Depression hurt Latin American economies. As a result, **economic nationalism,** or home control of the economy, became popular. Some nations also took over foreign-owned properties and businesses. Stronger leaders emerged. Another change was the growth of **cultural nationalism,** and the rejection of European influences. Artists such as Diego Rivera revived mural painting, an art form of the Aztecs and Maya, to depict the people's struggles. At this time, the United States was often involved in Latin America, intervening when U.S. interests were in danger. This created anti-American feeling. In response, President Franklin Roosevelt developed the **Good Neighbor Policy.** This meant that the United States promised to stay out of Latin American politics. The result was better relations between the United States and Latin American countries.

Review Questions

1. Who became president of Mexico in 1917?

_____

_____

2. What was the impact of the Good Neighbor Policy?

_____

_____

Note Taking Study Guide

NATIONALISM IN AFRICA AND THE MIDDLE EAST

Focus Question: How did nationalism contribute to changes in Africa and the Middle East following World War I?

As you read this section in your textbook, complete the following table to identify causes and effects of the rise of nationalism. Some boxes have been filled in for you.

Rise of Nationalism

Region	Reasons for Rise	Effects
Africa	• Oppressed by European colonialism • More than one million Africans fought on behalf of colonial rulers in World War I with hopes of more rights. • •	• Europeans increased their control in some areas; the apartheid system was adopted in South Africa. • The African National Congress protested unfair laws. •
Turkey and Persia	• Collapse of Ottoman empire after World War I •	• Atatürk established Turkey as a secular republic. • • •
Middle East	• Growth of Pan-Arabism • Feelings of betrayal at Paris Peace Conference after World War I • •	• Ongoing Arab resentment of Westerners •

Section Summary
NATIONALISM IN AFRICA AND THE MIDDLE EAST

Who ended Ottoman rule and set up a republic in Turkey?

_____

_____

_____

Find the word *advocated* in the underlined sentence. It is from the Latin word *advocare,* which means "to call to one's aid." Use this word-origins clue to help you figure out what *advocated* means.

Identify Causes and Effects
What effect did European rule have on African farmers?

_____

_____

_____

During the early 1900s, Europeans controlled most of Africa. They kept the best lands for themselves or forced African farmers to grow cash crops instead of food. Some Africans had to work in mines or on plantations and then pay taxes to the colonial governments. In South Africa, blacks lost the right to vote and were kept from certain jobs. This repression and segregation became even harsher under **apartheid.**

During the 1920s, the movement known as **Pan-Africanism** called for the unity of Africans around the world. The activist W.E.B. DuBois organized the first Pan-African Congress in 1919. He asked world leaders to approve more rights for Africans. Meanwhile the **négritude movement,** made up of artists and writers in West Africa and the Caribbean, celebrated African pride and protested colonial rule. For example, the poet Léopold Senghor celebrated Africans' tribal past. These movements, however, brought little real change.

In **Asia Minor,** Mustafa Kemal overthrew the Ottoman ruler and created the republic of Turkey. He encouraged business by building railroads and factories. His success in modernizing Turkey inspired nationalists in Persia. Reza Khan overthrew the Persian shah. As the new ruler, he modernized the country and convinced British oil companies to give Persia a bigger share of profits. Both rulers replaced Islamic traditions with Western ways that Muslim leaders condemned.

Arab nationalism grew in the Middle East. **Pan-Arabism** was built on a common history among Arabs living from the Arabian Peninsula to North Africa. After World War I, Arabs had hoped to gain independence but felt betrayed when the French and British took control of their lands. Meanwhile, Jewish nationalists dreamed of a homeland in Palestine. To show support for European Jews, Britain issued the **Balfour Declaration.** This statement advocated a homeland for Jews in Palestine. Arabs felt that the declaration favored the Jews. Ever since, Arabs and Jews have fought for control of Palestine.

Review Questions

1. What were the two African nationalist movements?

_____

_____

2. How were Mustafa Kemal and Reza Khan alike?

_____

_____

Name_____ Class_____ Date_____

Focus Question: How did Gandhi and the Congress party work for independence in India?

As you read this section in your textbook, complete the chart with the causes and effects of Gandhi's leadership on India's independence movement. Some items have been filled in for you.

Effects

- Gandhi called for a boycott of British goods, especially cotton textiles.
- Gandhi's Salt March inspired other Indians to join his protest of the British monopoly on salt.
-
-
-

Gandhi Leads Independence Movement

Causes

- Millions of Indians served in World War I for Britain, based on the promise of greater self-rule.
- Limited British reforms after World War I frustrated Indians.
-
-
-
-

CHAPTER **27** SECTION 3	**Section Summary**
	INDIA SEEKS SELF-RULE

Section Summary

What was the Amritsar Massacre?

_____

_____

_____

In April 1919, British soldiers killed and wounded hundreds of peaceful Indian protestors. This event was called the **Amritsar massacre**. It was a turning point in India's history because it convinced Indians that their country should be independent of Britain. The tragedy was the result of frustration that had been growing since World War I. During the war, Britain had promised India greater self-government. Afterwards, it made only a few small changes. The Congress party of India began calling for independence. This mostly middle-class party had little in common with the poor Indian peasants. In the 1920s, Mohandas Gandhi came forward as a new leader. Gandhi had experience opposing unfair treatment and prejudice. For 20 years, he had fought laws in South Africa that discriminated against Indians.

Find the word *discriminated* in the second underlined sentence. Circle the clues in the first underlined sentence that can help you figure out what *discriminated* means.

Gandhi inspired people of all religions and backgrounds. He preached **ahimsa**. This is a belief in nonviolence and respect for all life. Gandhi spoke out against harsh treatment of the **untouchables,** or Hindu society's lowest group. Henry David Thoreau's ideas about **civil disobedience** influenced Gandhi. This was the idea that people should not obey unjust laws. Gandhi began a program of civil disobedience. He led a series of nonviolent protests against British rule. For example, he called for Indians to **boycott,** or refuse to buy, British goods.

Another important event was Gandhi's stand against the British salt monopoly. Although salt was available for free in the sea, Indians were forced to buy salt from the British. When Gandhi marched 240 miles to the sea to get salt, thousands of followers joined him. He waded into the water and picked up a lump of sea salt. He was arrested. Newspapers around the world criticized Britain. Stories reported police brutality against peaceful marchers. Thousands of Indians were jailed when they continued to gather salt. Slowly, Gandhi's actions and the British reactions forced the British to give some power to Indians.

Identify Causes and Effects
What caused Gandhi to lead the Salt March? What effects did this protest have?

Cause:_____

_____

Effects:_____

_____

Review Questions

1. What did the British promise India during World War I?

_____

_____

2. What is ahimsa?

_____

_____

Name_____ Class_____ Date_____

Note Taking Study Guide

UPHEAVALS IN CHINA

Focus Question: How did China cope with internal division and foreign invasion in the early 1900s?

A. *As you read "The Chinese Republic in Trouble," complete the following chart by listing the multiple causes of upheaval in the Chinese Republic.*

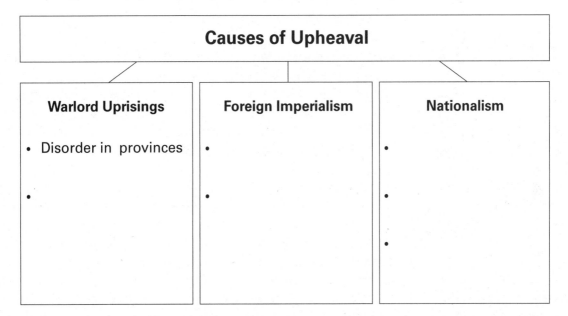

Causes of Upheaval

Warlord Uprisings	Foreign Imperialism	Nationalism
• Disorder in provinces	•	•
•	•	•
		•

B. *As you read "Struggle for a New China" and "Japanese Invasion," complete the chart to sequence the fighting among the Guomindang, the warlords, the Chinese Communists, and the Japanese. Some items have been filled in for you.*

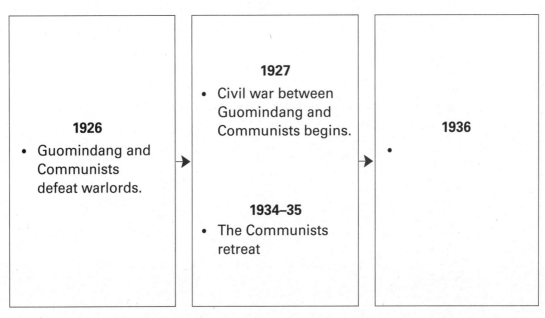

1926
• Guomindang and Communists defeat warlords.

1927
• Civil war between Guomindang and Communists begins.

1934–35
• The Communists retreat

1936
•

CHAPTER 27 SECTION 4

Section Summary

UPHEAVALS IN CHINA

READING CHECK

What was the May Fourth Movement?

_____

_____

_____

VOCABULARY STRATEGY

Find the word *intellectual* in the first underlined sentence. The word has two word parts: the root word *intellect* means "ability to think," and *–ual* means "relating to." Use the meanings of the word parts and the context clues in the second underlined sentence to help you figure out the meaning of *intellectual*.

READING SKILL

Recognize Multiple Causes
Why did Chinese peasants support the Communists?

_____

_____

_____

After the Qing dynasty collapsed, Sun Yixian became president of China's new republic. He hoped to rebuild China. Instead, China fell into chaos as warlords battled for control, and Sun Yixian stepped down as president. When the economy fell apart, millions of peasants suffered severe hardships. Also, foreign powers tried to dominate China. During World War I, Japan issued the **Twenty-One Demands.** This was intended to give Japan control over China. China was too weak to refuse all the demands, and gave up some power to Japan. Then, after World War I, the Allies gave Japan power over some former German lands in China. This angered many students. They began a cultural and intellectual reform movement known as the **May Fourth Movement.** These reformers looked to Western knowledge to make China strong. Others turned to Marxism. The Soviet Union trained some Chinese to become the **vanguard,** or leaders, of a communist revolution.

In 1921, Sun Yixian's **Guomindang,** or Nationalist party, formed a new government. After Sun's death, Jiang Jieshi became the party leader. By joining with the Communists, he defeated the warlords. However, Jiang feared the Communists were a threat to his power. He killed thousands of Communist Party members and their supporters. Led by Mao Zedong, the Communists retreated to northern China. The Guomindang attacked Mao's forces throughout the **Long March,** from 1934 to 1935. During the difficult march, Mao's soldiers treated peasants kindly, paid for goods, and made sure they did not destroy crops. Many peasants, who had suffered under the Guomindang, welcomed the Communists.

In 1937, Japan invaded China, bombed several cities, and killed hundreds of thousands of Chinese. In response, Jiang and Mao formed an alliance to fight the invaders. They were able to work together until the Japanese threat was gone.

Review Questions

1. List three ways in which Japan affected China.

_____

_____

2. Why did the Communists and Guomindang unite?

_____

_____

Note Taking Study Guide

CONFLICTING FORCES IN JAPAN

Focus Question: How did Japan change in the 1920s and 1930s?

As you read this section in your textbook, complete the table by listing the effects of liberalism and militarism in Japan during the 1920s and 1930s. Some items have been listed for you.

Conflicting Forces in Japan	
Liberalism in the 1920s	**Militarism in the 1930s**
• Greater democracy	• Depression causes unrest.
•	•
•	•
•	•
	•

CHAPTER 27 SECTION 5

Section Summary
CONFLICTING FORCES IN JAPAN

READING CHECK

Who were the zaibatsu?

_____

_____

_____

The Japanese economy grew during World War I, based on the export of goods to the Allies and increased production. At this time, Japan also expanded its presence in East Asia and sought further rights in China. Additionally, Japan gained control of some former German possessions in China after the war. **Hirohito** became emperor of Japan in 1926.

During the 1920s, Japan had a more liberal government. The elected members of the Japanese parliament exercised power. The right to vote was extended to all adult men. Western ideas about women's rights brought some changes. Despite increased democracy, the zaibatsu, a group of powerful business leaders, manipulated politicians. These business leaders donated money to political parties. The group used its influence to push for laws that supported trade and favored their businesses.

VOCABULARY STRATEGY

Find the word *manipulated* in the underlined sentence. Knowing word roots can often help you figure out the meaning of a word. For example, the Latin root *manus* means "hand" or "to handle." How did the zaibatsu "handle" politicians? Circle the words in the summary that describe how the zaibatsu *manipulated* politicians.

The military leaders and **ultranationalists,** or extreme nationalists, were angry with the government for giving in to Western demands and for accepting payoffs from the zaibatsu. The military and nationalists wanted to expand the empire. They looked to northern China for its raw materials. In 1931, the army set explosives to blow up railroad tracks in the Chinese province of **Manchuria,** blaming it on the Chinese. This provided an excuse to conquer the region. Japanese politicians objected, but the people supported the military. The League of Nations also protested the invasion. As a result, Japan left the League.

The military and ultranationalists increased their power throughout the 1930s. Extremists murdered some politicians and business leaders. To please the ultranationalists the government limited some democratic freedoms. Also, Japan took advantage of China's civil war. Military leaders expected to conquer China within a few years. Instead, when World War II broke out in Europe, the fighting quickly spread to Asia. In September 1940, Japan signed an agreement with Italy and Germany. The three nations formed the Axis Powers.

READING SKILL

Understand Effects What was the effect of the League of Nations' protest of Japan's invasion of Manchuria?

_____

_____

_____

Review Questions

1. How did Japan benefit from World War I?

_____

_____

2. What were the effects of Japan's liberal government in the 1920s?

_____

_____

Note Taking Study Guide

POSTWAR SOCIAL CHANGES

Focus Question: What changes did Western society and culture experience after World War I?

As you read this section in your textbook, complete the concept web below to identify supporting details related to "Changes to Society" and "Cultural Changes." Some items have been completed for you.

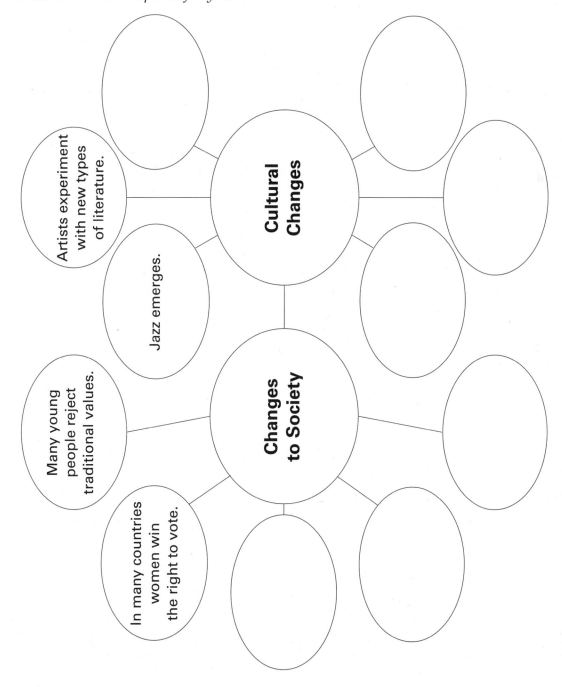

CHAPTER 28 SECTION 1

Section Summary
POSTWAR SOCIAL CHANGES

READING CHECK

Who were flappers?

_____

_____

_____

VOCABULARY STRATEGY

Find the word *emancipation* in the underlined sentence. *Emancipation* comes from a root word that means "to set free." Reread the sentences surrounding the underlined sentence. Circle the words that have to do with being set free. Use these words to come up with a definition of *emancipation*.

READING SKILL

Identify Supporting Details What three styles of art developed in the early 1900s?

_____

_____

_____

After World War I, society and culture changed. During the 1920s, new technologies connected people around the world. So many people listened to jazz that this period is often called the Jazz Age. At this time, young women called **flappers** were a symbol of the new freedom in American culture. Labor-saving machines freed women from household chores. <u>In this new era of emancipation, women pursued careers in many areas.</u> Not everyone approved of the freer lifestyle of the Jazz Age, however. For example, **Prohibition** was meant to keep people from the bad effects of drinking. Instead, it brought about organized crime and **speakeasies.**

New literature showed the horror of modern warfare. To some writers, the last war symbolized the moral breakdown of Western civilization. Other writers explored people's inner thoughts in stream-of-consciousness novels. In the cultural movement called the **Harlem Renaissance,** African American artists and writers explored their experiences.

New scientific discoveries challenged long-held ideas. Marie Curie and others found that atoms are not solid. Albert Einstein argued that measurements of space and time are not constant. Italian physicist Enrico Fermi discovered that atoms could be split. Alexander Fleming discovered penicillin. It paved the way for the development of antibiotics to treat infections. Sigmund Freud pioneered **psychoanalysis.** This is a method of studying how the mind works and for treating mental illness.

In the early 1900s, many Western artists rejected traditional styles. Instead of painting objects as they actually looked, they began expressing ideas or forms in their works. For example, **abstract** art is made up of lines, colors, and shapes. Often the subject is not visually recognizable. Artists of the **dada** movement believed that there was no sense or truth in the world. They might create art from items that had been thrown away. **Surrealism** was an art style that portrayed the workings of the unconscious mind.

Review Questions

1. What was the Harlem Renaissance?

_____

_____

2. How did World War I affect new literature?

_____

_____

CHAPTER
28 Note Taking Study Guide
SECTION 2 THE WESTERN DEMOCRACIES STUMBLE

Focus Question: What political and economic challenges did the leading democracies face in the 1920s and 1930s?

A. *As you read "Politics in the Postwar World," "Postwar Foreign Policy," and "Postwar Economics," complete the chart below to identify the main ideas under each heading. Some items have been entered for you.*

Postwar Issues			
Country	**Politics**	**Foreign Policy**	**Economics**
Britain	Conservative party dominated; Irish Free State established in 1922	Sought to soften the treatment of Germany; worked with other nations toward peace	
France		Insisted on enforcement of Versailles treaty; built Maginot Line; worked with other nations for peace	
United States			Became leading economic power

B. *As you read "The Great Depression" and "The Democracies React to the Depression," complete the chart below to identify the main ideas about the causes, effects, and reactions related to the Great Depression. Some items have been entered for you.*

The Great Depression		
Causes	**Effects**	**Reactions**
• Lower earnings led to falling demand. • • • •	• Unemployment • •	• High tariffs • •

CHAPTER 28 SECTION 2

Section Summary
THE WESTERN DEMOCRACIES STUMBLE

READING CHECK

How did the Kellogg-Briand Pact promote peace?

_____

_____

_____

After World War I, Britain, France, and the United States appeared strong. However, in the years to come, all three countries faced political and economic problems. Britain had to deal with growing socialism and the "Irish question." In France, political parties competed for power, causing many changes in government. Fear of radicals set off a "Red Scare" in the United States.

The three countries also faced international issues. The French were worried about another German invasion, so they built the **Maginot Line.** The **Kellogg-Briand Pact** was more positive. Nations that signed it promised to "renounce war as an instrument of national policy." In this spirit, the great powers pursued **disarmament.** Unfortunately, the League of Nations could not stop aggression, a weakness noted by some dictators.

The war affected economies all over the world. Both Britain and France owed huge war debts to the United States. In Britain low wages led to unrest. In 1926 over three million workers went on a **general strike.** In contrast, the United States emerged as the world's top economic power. <u>In the 1920s, affluent Americans enjoyed the benefits of capitalism. They bought cars, radios, refrigerators, and other new consumer goods.</u>

However, the good times did not last. Better technologies allowed factories to make more products faster, leading to **overproduction.** This lowered prices. As factories cut back, workers lost their jobs. A crisis in **finance** led the **Federal Reserve** to raise interest rates. Panic set in when stock prices crashed. In 1929, the **Great Depression** began in the United States. Within a short time, it had spread around the world.

In the United States, President **Franklin D. Roosevelt** argued that the government should take an active role in ending the crisis. He introduced programs known as the **New Deal.** Although the New Deal failed to end the Depression, it did ease much suffering. As the Depression wore on, however, many people lost faith in democratic government.

VOCABULARY STRATEGY

Find the word *affluent* in the underlined sentence. What does the word *affluent* mean? *Affluent* comes from a Latin word that means "to flow." One definition of *affluent* is "to flow in abundance." Ask yourself what people have a lot of if they are *affluent.* Use these clues to help you figure out the meaning of *affluent.*

READING SKILL

Identify Main Ideas Reread the Summary to identify the main idea. Circle the letter of the statement below that identifies the main idea of the Summary.

A. After World War I, reparations burdened Germany economically.

B. In the 1920s, affluent Americans benefited from capitalism.

C. After World War I, economic and political problems affected Western democracies.

Review Questions

1. Why did the French build the Maginot Line?

_____

_____

2. What caused U.S. workers to lose their jobs?

_____

_____

Name_____ Class_____ Date_____

Focus Question: How and why did fascism rise in Italy?

A. *As you read "Mussolini's Rise to Power" and Mussolini's Rule," complete the flowchart below as you identify the main ideas under each heading. Some items have been entered for you.*

Dissatisfaction and Unrest	Mussolini Takes Power	Mussolini Changes Italy
• Italians dissatisfied with territories at end of World War I.	• Mussolini organizes Fascist party.	• Mussolini becomes dictator.
•	•	•
•	•	•
	• King gives Mussolini control after March on Rome.	

B. *As you read "The Nature of Fascism," use the table below to identify the main ideas for each heading. Some items have been entered for you.*

What Is Fascism?	
Values	No unifying set of beliefs; generally glorifies extreme nationalism, discipline, military, and loyalty to the state
Characteristics	
Differences from Communism	Works for nationalist rather than international goals; supports a society with defined classes
Similarities to Communism	

CHAPTER 28 SECTION 3

Section Summary
FASCISM IN ITALY

Italy faced many problems after World War I. Italian nationalists were outraged that they did not receive lands that the Allies had promised them. Peasants seized land, workers went on strike, and veterans faced unemployment. Also, trade declined and taxes rose. Into this chaos stepped **Benito Mussolini** to take control. His Fascist party rejected democracy and favored violence to solve problems. Mussolini's special supporters, the **Black Shirts,** used terror to oust elected officials. In the 1922 **March on Rome,** thousands of Fascists swarmed the capital. Fearing civil war, the king asked Mussolini to become prime minister.

Mussolini went on to crush rival parties, muzzle the press, rig elections, and replace elected officials with Fascists. Critics were imprisoned, exiled, or murdered. Secret police and propaganda bolstered Mussolini's rule. He brought the economy under state control, but preserved capitalism. His system favored the upper classes. Workers were not allowed to strike, and their wages were kept low. In Mussolini's new system, loyalty to the state replaced individual goals. Loudspeakers blared and <u>posters proclaimed "Believe! Obey! Fight!"</u> Fascist youth groups chanted slogans. Italians supported Mussolini because he brought order to the country.

VOCABULARY STRATEGY

Find the word *proclaimed* in the underlined sentence. Notice the exclamation points in the phrase "Believe! Obey! Fight!" Think about the tone of that phrase. Ask: What was the purpose of loudspeakers and posters? Use these context clues to help you figure out the meaning of *proclaimed.*

Mussolini built the first modern **totalitarian state.** In this form of government, a one-party dictatorship attempts to control every aspect of citizens' lives. Today, we tend to use the term **fascism** to describe the basic ideas of any centralized dictatorship that is not communist. Fascism is rooted in nationalism. Fascists believe in action, violence, discipline, the military, and blind loyalty to the state. They are anti-democratic. They reject equality and liberty. Fascists disagree with communists on important issues. Communists favor international action and want a classless society. Fascists ally with business leaders, wealthy landowners, and the middle class. Both call for blind devotion to a leader or the state. Both flourish during economic hard times.

READING SKILL

Identify Main Ideas How did the conditions in Italy after World War I help Mussolini come to power?

_____

_____

_____

Review Questions

1. What was the result of the March on Rome?

_____

_____

2. How did Mussolini treat his critics?

_____

_____

CHAPTER 28
SECTION 4

Note Taking Study Guide
THE SOVIET UNION UNDER STALIN

Focus Question: How did Stalin transform the Soviet Union into a totalitarian state?

As you read this section in your textbook, complete the chart below by identifying the main ideas about the Soviet Union under Stalin for each heading. Some items have been completed for you.

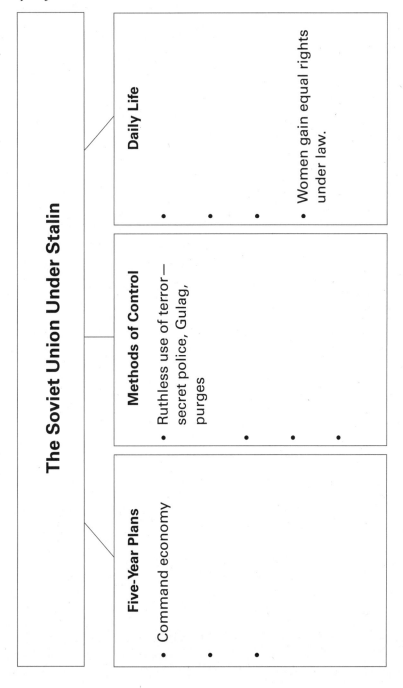

The Soviet Union Under Stalin

Daily Life
-
-
-
- Women gain equal rights under law.

Methods of Control
- Ruthless use of terror—secret police, Gulag, purges
-
-
-

Five-Year Plans
- Command economy
-
-

CHAPTER 28 SECTION 4

Section Summary
THE SOVIET UNION UNDER STALIN

Under Joseph Stalin, the Soviet Union developed into a totalitarian state. It developed a **command economy,** in which the government made most economic decisions. Stalin used five-year plans to try to increase productivity. He wanted all peasants to farm on either state-owned farms or **collectives.** Some peasants refused. Stalin believed that **kulaks,** or wealthy farmers, were behind this. He took their land and sent them to labor camps where many died. His actions led to a terrible famine in 1932.

Stalin's Communist government used terror to force people to obey. Those who opposed him were rounded up and sent to the **Gulag.** This was a system of brutal labor camps. Fearing that rival party leaders were plotting against him, Stalin launched the Great Purge in 1934, killing millions of people.

Stalin also sought to control the hearts and minds of his people. For example, he required artists and writers to create works in a style called **socialist realism.** <u>If they refused to conform to government demands, they faced persecution</u>. Stalin also controlled the culture by enforcing **russification.** His goal was to make people in the Soviet Union of non-Russian cultures more Russian. The official Communist party belief in **atheism** led to the harsh treatment of religious leaders, too.

Party leaders destroyed the old social order. In its place, they created one where Communist party members made up the new ruling class. However, under communism, most people enjoyed free medical care, day care for children, cheaper housing, and public recreation. Also, women were equal under the law.

Soviet leaders had two conflicting foreign policy goals. They hoped to spread a worldwide communist revolution through the **Comintern,** or Communist International. At the same time, they wanted to strengthen their nation's security by winning the support of others. These conflicting goals led to an unsuccessful foreign policy and caused Western powers to mistrust the Soviet leaders.

Review Questions

1. How did Stalin deal with those who opposed him?

_____

_____

2. What was russification?

_____

_____

Note Taking Study Guide
HITLER AND THE RISE OF NAZI GERMANY

Focus Question: How did Hitler and the Nazi party establish and maintain a totalitarian government in Germany?

As you read this section in your textbook, complete the flowchart below to identify the main ideas about Hitler and the rise of Nazi Germany. Some items have been entered for you.

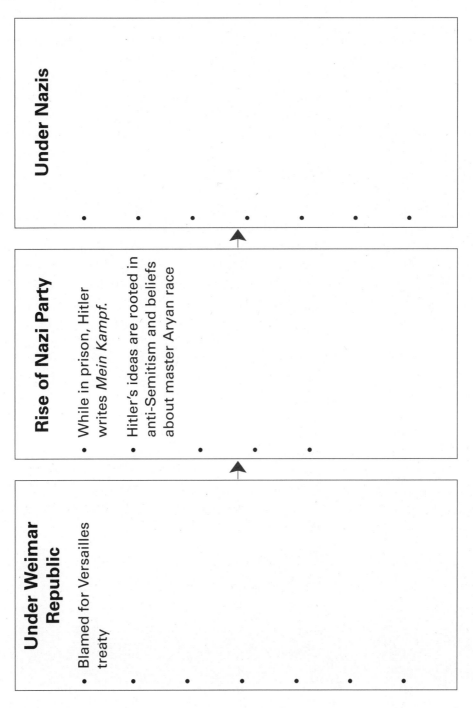

Under Nazis

Rise of Nazi Party
- While in prison, Hitler writes *Mein Kampf.*
- Hitler's ideas are rooted in anti-Semitism and beliefs about master Aryan race

Under Weimar Republic
- Blamed for Versailles treaty

CHAPTER 28 SECTION 5

Section Summary

HITLER AND THE RISE OF NAZI GERMANY

READING CHECK

What was the purpose of the Nuremberg Laws?

_____

_____

_____

VOCABULARY STRATEGY

Find the word *regime* in the underlined sentence. Circle the words in the sentence that refer to "the new *regime*." Say the sentence out loud but replace "the new regime" with the words you circled. Does the sentence still make sense? If so, you have circled the correct words. Use those words to explain what *regime* means.

READING SKILL

Identify Main Ideas Reread the last paragraph of the Summary. What is the main idea of the paragraph? Write the main idea on the lines below.

_____

_____

_____

After World War I, German leaders wrote the Weimar constitution. It created the democratic Weimar Republic. This parliamentary government was led by a **chancellor,** gave women the right to vote, and included a bill of rights. However, the new government faced severe problems. When Germany could not pay its war reparations, France seized the coal-rich **Ruhr Valley.** German government actions led to inflation. German money was worthless. People lost their savings. Problems worsened during the Great Depression. Many Germans blamed the Weimar Republic for their problems.

Many Germans believed that Adolf Hitler had the solutions. As head of the Nazi party, Hitler promised to end reparations, create jobs, and rearm Germany. He was elected chancellor in 1933. Within a year, he was dictator over the new fascist government in Germany.

Hitler called his new government the **Third Reich.** He provided jobs for thousands of people, rearmed Germany, and boasted that Germans would soon rule Europe. The **Gestapo,** or secret police, used terror to help the Nazis gain control over all parts of German life. In 1935, the **Nuremberg Laws** deprived Jews of German citizenship and placed severe restrictions on them. Textbooks reflected Nazi racial views. "Pure-blooded Aryan" women were rewarded for staying home and having children. Hitler also sought to purify German culture. He condemned jazz and modern art because of their non-German roots. He combined various churches into a single state church. Although many clergy either supported the new regime or remained silent, some spoke out against Hitler's government.

In Eastern Europe, many nations also came under new authoritarian governments. Economic problems and ethnic tensions helped fascist rulers to gain power there. These dictators promised to keep order, and won the backing of the military and the wealthy. They spread anti-Semitism, using Jewish people as scapegoats for national problems.

Review Questions

1. What was the Weimar Republic?

_____

_____

2. What did Hitler promise would result from his Third Reich?

_____

_____

Name_____ Class_____ Date_____

Focus Question: What events unfolded between Chamberlain's declaration of "peace in our time" and the outbreak of a world war?

A. *As you read "Aggression Goes Unchecked" and "Spain Collapses into Civil War," complete the chart below to recognize the sequence of events that led to the outbreak of World War II. Some items have been completed for you.*

Acts of Aggression	
Japan	• Invasion of Manchuria, 1931 • _____
Italy	• _____
Germany	• Buildup of German military • _____
Spain	• _____

B. *As you read "German Aggression Continues" and "Europe Plunges Toward War," complete the timetable below to recognize the sequence of German aggression. One item has been entered for you.*

German Aggression	
March 1938	Anschluss, or union of Austria and Germany, occurs.
September 1938	
March 1939	
September 1939	

Section Summary
FROM APPEASEMENT TO WAR

Who were the members of the Axis powers?

_____

_____

_____

Find the word *sanctions* in the underlined sentence. Notice that *sanctions* were a response to the Italian invasion of Ethiopia mentioned in the previous sentence. In the same sentence, the phrase "had no power to enforce the punishment" refers to the *sanctions.* Use these context clues to help you figure out the meaning of *sanctions.*

Recognize Sequence What happened after the Munich Conference?

_____

_____

_____

Throughout the 1930s, dictators took aggressive action. However, they were met only by pleas for peace from Western democracies. The dictators became even more aggressive. For example, when the League of Nations condemned Japan's invasion of Manchuria in 1931, Japan just withdrew from the League. Meanwhile, Mussolini invaded Ethiopia. <u>The League of Nations voted sanctions against Italy, but it had no power to enforce the punishment.</u> Hitler, too, defied the Western democracies and the conditions of the Versailles treaty by building up the German military. He also sent troops into the Rhineland. The Western democracies denounced Hitler, but adopted a policy of **appeasement.** Appeasement developed for a number of reasons, including widespread **pacifism.** The United States passed the **Neutrality Acts** at this time. The goal was to avoid war, not prevent it. Germany, Italy, and Japan saw the Western democracies as weak. These three nations formed an alliance known as the **Axis powers.**

In Spain, **Francisco Franco** led a revolt against the new Spanish government. This began a civil war in which Hitler and Mussolini supported Franco, their fellow fascist. The Soviet Union sent troops to support the anti-Fascists, or Loyalists. However, the governments of Britain, France, and the United States remained neutral. By 1939, Franco had triumphed.

German aggression continued. Hitler forced the **Anschluss,** or union with Austria. At the Munich Conference, British and French leaders caved in to Hitler's plans to annex the **Sudentenland,** a part of Czechoslovakia.

In March 1939, Hitler took the rest of Czechoslovakia. A few months later, Hitler and Stalin signed the **Nazi-Soviet Pact.** They agreed not to fight if the other went to war. This paved the way for the German invasion of Poland in September of 1939. Because of this, Britain and France declared war on Germany, starting World War II.

Review Questions

1. How did the League of Nations fail to keep peace?

_____

_____

2. How did Hitler defy conditions of the Treaty of Versailles?

_____

_____

Name_____ Class_____ Date_____

Focus Question: Which regions were attacked and occupied by the Axis powers, and what was life like under their occupation?

A. *As you read "The Axis Attacks," "Germany Invades the Soviet Union," and "Japan Attacks the United States," use the chart below to record the sequence of events. Some items have been entered for you.*

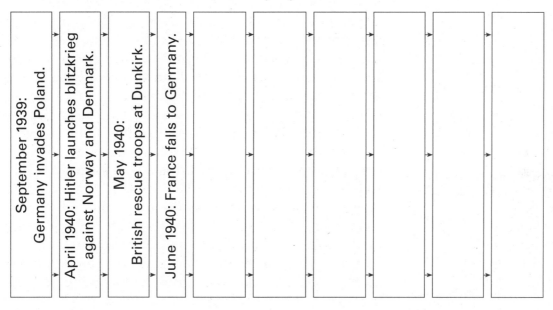

September 1939: Germany invades Poland. → April 1940: Hitler launches blitzkrieg against Norway and Denmark. → May 1940: British rescue troops at Dunkirk. → June 1940: France falls to Germany. →

B. *As you read "Life Under Nazi and Japanese Occupation," use the concept web to list supporting details about the occupations. Some items have been entered for you.*

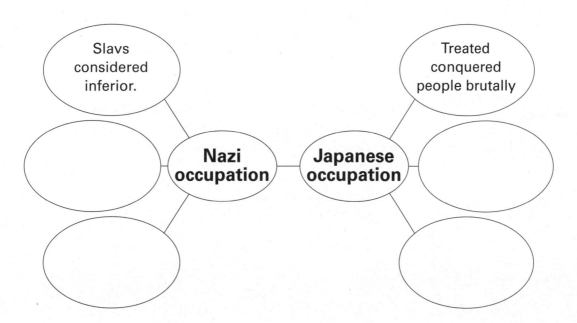

Slavs considered inferior.

Treated conquered people brutally

Nazi occupation

Japanese occupation

CHAPTER 29 SECTION 2

Section Summary
THE AXIS ADVANCES

Where was the German government in southern France located?

_____

_____

_____

VOCABULARY STRATEGY

Find the word *nullified* in the underlined sentence. The root word is *null.* Perhaps you have heard the expression "null and void." Use prior knowledge to help you figure out the meaning of *nullified.*

READING SKILL

Sequence Events What happened after the Germans entered France?

_____

_____

_____

In September 1939, Nazi forces launched a **blitzkrieg** against Poland. First, the **Luftwaffe** bombed Poland from the air. Then, tanks and troops pushed in. At the same time, Stalin's forces invaded from the east. Poland disappeared.

In early 1940, Hitler's troops conquered Norway, Denmark, the Netherlands, and Belgium. By May, German forces pushed into France. British troops that had been sent to help the French were trapped. Using every boat available, the British rescued their troops from **Dunkirk.** The French gave up, and Germany took over northern France. In southern France, they set up a puppet government in **Vichy.**

Hitler bombed Britain continuously between September 1940 and June 1941 to prepare for an invasion. Despite this blitz, the British did not give in. In North Africa, **General Erwin Rommel** pushed the British back toward Cairo, Egypt. By 1941, Axis powers controlled most of Europe. The Japanese were invading lands in Asia and the Pacific.

In June 1941, Hitler nullified the Nazi-Soviet Pact by invading the Soviet Union. The Soviets were not prepared, and the Germans advanced toward Moscow and Leningrad. During a lengthy siege of Leningrad, more than a million people died. The severe Russian winter finally slowed the German advance.

As they marched across Europe, the Nazis sent millions to **concentration camps** to work as slave laborers. Even worse, Hitler established death camps to kill those he judged racially inferior. Among many others, some six million Jews were killed in this **Holocaust.**

The United States declared neutrality at the start of the war. Yet, many Americans were sympathetic to those fighting the Axis powers. Congress passed the **Lend-Lease Act** of 1941 to allow the United States to sell or lend war materials to nations fighting the Axis powers. Then, on December 7, 1941, the Japanese attacked the U.S. fleet at Pearl Harbor. Congress declared war on Japan.

Review Questions

1. Why did Hitler bomb Britain?

_____

_____

2. Why was Hitler able to invade the Soviet Union?

_____

_____

CHAPTER 29 SECTION 3

Note Taking Study Guide
THE ALLIES TURN THE TIDE

Focus Question: How did the Allies begin to push back the Axis powers?

As you read this section in your textbook, complete the chart below to record the sequence of events that turned the tide of the war in favor of the Allies. Some events have been completed for you.

Allies Turn the Tide

1944
- Allies bomb German facilities.
- June—
-
-

1943
- Jan.—Germans surrender at Stalingrad.
-
-
-

1942
- Allies increase production.
- May—Japanese are defeated at Coral Sea.
-
-
-

CHAPTER 29 SECTION 3

Section Summary

THE ALLIES TURN THE TIDE

READING CHECK

What happened on June 6, 1944?

_____

_____

_____

To defeat the Axis powers in World War II, the Allies devoted all their resources to the war effort. Governments took a greater role in the economy. For example, auto factories were ordered to make tanks. Consumer goods were rationed. Wages and prices were controlled. The increase in production helped to end the unemployment of the Great Depression. However, governments also limited people's rights, censored the press, and used propaganda to win public support. At the same time, as men joined the military, women replaced them in factories. These women were symbolized by **"Rosie the Riveter."**

The years 1942 and 1943 marked the turning point of the war. In the Pacific, the Japanese lost the battles of the Coral Sea and Midway. In both battles, air attacks were launched from huge **aircraft carriers.** In North Africa, British and American forces, led by General **Dwight Eisenhower,** trapped the German army. German General Rommel surrendered in May 1943. The Allies then crossed the Mediterranean to Sicily. Allied victories in Italy led to the overthrow of Mussolini, although the fighting continued for another 18 months. On the Eastern front, a key turning point was the Battle of **Stalingrad.** After brutal fighting, the Soviet army surrounded the German troops. Without food or ammunition, the Germans surrendered.

VOCABULARY STRATEGY

Find the word *incessant* in the underlined sentence. Notice that the phrase "around-the-clock" follows *incessant.* "Around-the-clock" and *incessant* have similar meanings. What does "around-the-clock" mean? Use this context clue to help you choose the word below that you think means the same as *incessant.*

1. off-and-on

2. nonstop

On June 6, 1944, the Allies began the **D-Day** invasion of France. Allied troops faced many obstacles, but the Germans finally retreated. <u>As the Allies advanced, Germany was hit with incessant, around-the-clock bombing.</u> A German counterattack, the Battle of the Bulge, caused terrible losses on both sides. The defeat of Germany seemed inevitable, however. The "Big Three" —Roosevelt, Churchill, and Stalin—met to plan for the end of the war. At this **Yalta Conference,** the Soviets agreed to enter the war against Japan. They also agreed to divide Germany into four zones of occupation after the war. However, growing mistrust at Yalta hinted at a future split among the Allies.

Review Questions

1. What did "Rosie the Riveter" symbolize?

_____

_____

2. What agreement about Germany was made at the Yalta Conference?

_____

_____

READING SKILL

Recognize Sequence Number the items below to show the correct sequence of events.

____ The Allies cross the Mediterranean and land in Sicily.

____ German General Rommel surrenders.

____ General Eisenhower, leading Allied forces, traps the German army in North Africa.

Focus Question: How did the Allies finally defeat the Axis powers?

As you read this section in your textbook, use the timeline below to recognize the sequence of events that led to the defeat of the Axis powers. Some events have been completed for you.

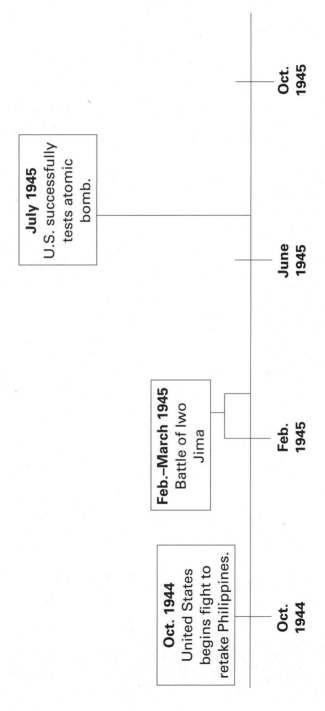

July 1945
U.S. successfully tests atomic bomb.

Feb.–March 1945
Battle of Iwo Jima

Oct. 1944
United States begins fight to retake Philippines.

Oct. 1945

June 1945

Feb. 1945

Oct. 1944

CHAPTER 29 SECTION 4

Section Summary

VICTORY IN EUROPE AND THE PACIFIC

READING CHECK

What was the name for Japanese pilots who went on suicide missions?

_____

_____

_____

VOCABULARY STRATEGY

Find the word *objective* in the underlined sentence. What do you think it means? The sentence says that the islands served as steppingstones to Japan. Use this context clue to help you understand the meaning of *objective*.

READING SKILL

Recognize Sequence Fill in the blanks below to sequence the events that took place in Japan from August 6 to August 10, 1945.

August 6 _____

_____

August 9 _____

_____

August 10 _____

_____

World War II in Europe officially ended on May 8, 1945. This is known as **V-E Day.** The Allies were able to defeat the Germans for many reasons. The Germans had to fight on several fronts at the same time. Hitler also made some poor decisions. He underestimated the Soviet Union's ability to fight. The enormous production capacity of the United States was another factor. By 1944, the United States was producing twice as much as all of the Axis powers combined. Bombing hurt German production and made oil scarce. This kept the Luftwaffe from flying

Once Germany was defeated, the Allies still had to defeat the Japanese in the Pacific. By May 1942, the Japanese controlled much of Southeast Asia, many Pacific islands, and the Philippines. They had killed thousands during the **Bataan Death March.** The United States now took the offensive. General **Douglas MacArthur** began an **"island-hopping"** campaign. The campaign took back islands from the Japanese. These islands served as steppingstones to the next objective— Japan. By 1944, the U.S. Navy was blockading Japan. Bombers pounded Japanese cities and industries.

In early 1945, bloody battles on Iwo Jima and Okinawa showed that the Japanese would fight to the death rather than give up. Some young Japanese became **kamikaze** pilots, crashing their planes into U.S. warships. Scientists now offered another way to end the war. Their research, called the **Manhattan Project,** had produced an atomic bomb for the United States. The new U.S. president, Harry Truman, decided that dropping the bomb would save American lives. The Allies first gave the Japanese a warning to surrender or face "utter and complete destruction." The Japanese ignored the warning. On August 6, 1945, a U.S. plane dropped an atomic bomb on the city of **Hiroshima.** This bomb killed more than 70,000 people. The Japanese still did not give up. Another bomb was dropped on **Nagasaki** on August 9. The next day, Japan finally surrendered, ending World War II.

Review Questions

1. What is V-E Day?

_____

_____

2. What was the Manhattan Project?

_____

_____

Note Taking Study Guide

THE END OF WORLD WAR II

Focus Question: What issues arose in the aftermath of World War II and how did new tensions develop?

As you read the section in your textbook, recognize the sequence of events following World War II by completing the outline below. Some items have been filled in.

I. The War's Aftermath

  A. Devastation

    1. As many as 50 million are dead.

    2. Horrors of Holocaust are learned.

  B. War Crimes Trials

    1. Axis leaders are tried for crimes against humanity.

    2. Many of those accused are never captured or brought to trial.

    3. Political and military leaders are held accountable for wartime actions.

  C. Occupying Allies

    1. Totalitarian ideologies are discredited.

    2. _____

II. Establishing the United Nations

  A. General Assembly

    1. _____

  B. Security Council

    1. _____

    2. _____

  C. Other UN activities

    1. _____

    2. _____

III. The Alliance Breaks Apart

  A. Differences Grow Between the Allies.

    1. _____

    2. _____

  B. The Cold War Begins.

    1. _____

    2. _____

(Outline continues on the next page.)

(Continued from page 271)

    3. _____

IV. New Conflicts Develop

  A. The Truman Doctrine

     1. Results from Soviet incursions into southeastern Europe

     2. _____

     3. _____

  B. The Marshall Plan

     1. United States gives food and economic assistance to European nations.

     2. _____

     3. _____

  C. Germany Stays Divided.

     1. _____

     2. _____

     3. _____

     4. _____

  D. Berlin Airlift

     1. _____

     2. _____

     3. _____

  E. _____

     1. _____

     2. _____

  F. _____

     1. _____

     2. _____

CHAPTER 29 SECTION 5

Section Summary

THE END OF WORLD WAR II

The costs of World War II were great. As many as 50 million people had been killed. At the end of the war, the Allies learned the full extent of the Holocaust. War crimes trials were held in **Nuremberg,** Germany, and in other countries. These trials showed that leaders could be held accountable for their wartime actions. After the war, the Western Allies wanted to ensure peace. As a result, they helped to set up democratic governments in Japan and Germany.

In 1945, delegates from 50 nations convened to form the **United Nations.** Each member nation has one vote in the General Assembly. A smaller Security Council has greater power. It has five permanent members: the United States, the Soviet Union (today Russia), Britain, France, and China. Each has the right to vote down any council decision.

However, distrust and different philosophies soon led to a **Cold War.** This refers to the state of tension between the United States and the Soviet Union between 1946 and 1990. Soviet leader Stalin wanted to spread communism into Eastern Europe. He also wanted to have pro-Soviet countries between the Soviet Union and Germany. By 1948, communist governments were in place throughout Eastern Europe.

Stalin soon began to threaten Greece and Turkey. The United States responded with the **Truman Doctrine.** This policy meant that the United States would resist the spread of communism throughout the world. To strengthen democracies, the United States offered food and economic aid to Europe. This assistance was called the **Marshall Plan.** However, the Soviets now controlled East Germany, which surrounded the city of Berlin. To force the Western Allies out of Berlin, the Soviets blockaded West Berlin. An airlift by the Western Allies forced the Soviets to end the blockade. Tensions continued to grow. In 1949, the United States and nine other nations formed a new alliance called the **North Atlantic Treaty Organization (NATO).** The Soviets then formed the **Warsaw Pact.**

Review Questions

1. What was the basic idea of the Truman Doctrine?

_____

_____

2. What two new alliances were formed after World War II?

_____

_____

READING CHECK

Who are the five permanent members of the UN Security Council?

_____

_____

_____

VOCABULARY STRATEGY

Find the word *convened* in the underlined sentence. What do you think it means? The English word *convene* comes from the Latin *convenire.* In Latin, *con-* means "together" and *venire* means "to come." Using this word-origins clue, which one of the following means the same as *convened*?

1. disperse

2. assemble

3. separate

READING SKILL

Recognize Sequence Number the following events to show the correct sequence.

_____ The Soviets blockade West Berlin.

_____ The Soviets control East Germany.

_____ The blockade ends.

_____ The Western Allies mount an airlift.

Name_____ Class_____ Date_____

Note Taking Study Guide
THE COLD WAR UNFOLDS

Focus Question: What were the military and political consequences of the Cold War in the Soviet Union, Europe, and the United States?

As you read this section in your textbook, fill in the chart to summarize the consequences of the Cold War in the Soviet Union, Europe, and the United States. Some items in the chart have been entered for you.

Consequences of the Cold War

Soviet Union
- Created military alliance called the Warsaw Pact
- Developed nuclear weapons in 1949
- • • • • • •

Europe
- The Cold War divided Europe—communists ruled in the East and democracies were in the West.
- Berlin divided between East Germany and West Germany
- • • • •

United States
- Formed military alliance called North Atlantic Treaty Organization (NATO)
- Entered disarmament talks with Soviet Union
- • • • • • •

CHAPTER
30
SECTION 1

Section Summary
THE COLD WAR UNFOLDS

After World War II, the United States and the Soviet Union emerged as **superpowers.** They formed military alliances with nations they protected or occupied. The United States helped form the North Atlantic Treaty Organization (NATO). <u>This comprised its Western European allies.</u> The Soviet Union formed the Warsaw Pact with Eastern European countries.

The superpowers also took part in a nuclear weapons race. Throughout the Cold War, the leaders met in disarmament talks. One agreement limited the use of **anti-ballistic missiles (ABMs).** These weapons were designed to shoot down incoming missiles. ABMs were a threat because they could give one side more protection. Some believed that more protection might encourage a nation to attack. In the 1980s, U.S. President **Ronald Reagan** supported a missile defense program known as "Star Wars." However, international agreements to limit the number of nuclear weapons eased Cold War tensions. This period, called the era of **détente,** ended with the Soviet invasion of Afghanistan in 1979.

The Cold War was a global conflict. During the 1950s, **Fidel Castro** led a revolution in Cuba and became its leader. To bring down Castro's communist regime, U.S. President **John F. Kennedy** supported an invasion of Cuba, but it failed. One year later, the Soviets sent nuclear missiles to Cuba. Many feared a nuclear war. After U.S. protests and a naval blockade, Soviet leader **Nikita Khrushchev** agreed to remove the missiles.

The Soviets wanted to spread communist **ideology** around the globe. Although Khrushchev halted some of Stalin's cruel policies, repression returned under **Leonid Brezhnev.** U.S. leaders followed a policy of **containment** to keep communism from spreading to other nations. In the United States a "red scare" developed. During this time, Senator Joseph McCarthy led a hunt for communists he thought were in the U.S. government and military.

Review Questions

1. What military alliances did the United States and the Soviet Union form after World War II?

_____

_____

2. What were ABMs and why were they considered a threat?

_____

_____

READING CHECK

What is containment?

_____

_____

_____

VOCABULARY STRATEGY

Find the word *comprised* in the underlined sentence. What clues can you find in the surrounding text that could help you better understand what *comprised* means? Circle the words that could help you figure out what *comprised* means.

READING SKILL

Summarize What events led to the era of détente?

_____

_____

_____

Name_____ Class_____ Date_____

Focus Question: How did the United States, Western Europe, and Japan achieve economic prosperity and strengthen democracy during the Cold War years?

As you read this section in your textbook, use the chart below to categorize economic and political changes in the industrialized democracies. Some items have been entered for you.

Economic and Political Changes in the Industrialized Democracies

Japan

- Emperor's power ends; Japan becomes a democracy.
- Occupation forces introduced social reforms, including education systems opened to all people and equality for women.
- · · ·

Western Europe

- Division of Germany in 1949 and reunification in 1990
- Marshall Plan helped rebuild Western Europe.
- · · · · · · ·

United States

- The United States became the world's wealthiest economy.
- Exports of goods and services helped build U.S. foreign trade.
- · · · · · · · · · ·

CHAPTER 30 SECTION 2

Section Summary
THE INDUSTRIALIZED DEMOCRACIES

Postwar economic strength changed life in the United States. During the 1950s and 1960s, **recessions** were brief and mild. <u>As Americans prospered, they had more money to spend on goods.</u> Many people left the cities for homes in the suburbs. This movement is called **suburbanization.** By the early 1970s, however, higher oil and gas prices left Americans with less money to buy other goods. This caused a serious recession in 1974.

Despite the prosperity, ethnic minorities faced **segregation** in housing and education. Also, minorities suffered **discrimination** in jobs and voting. **Dr. Martin Luther King, Jr.,** became an important civil rights leader in the 1960s. He helped end segregation for African Americans. Other minority groups were inspired by successes like these. For example, the women's rights movement helped end much gender-based discrimination. Also, Congress created programs to help the poor. However, in the 1980s, the government reduced many of these programs.

Western Europeans rebuilt after World War II. The American Marshall Plan helped European countries restore their economies. Under Chancellor **Konrad Adenauer,** Germany built modern cities and factories. European governments also developed programs for the poor and middle class, such as national healthcare and old-age pensions. These **welfare states** required high taxes to pay for their programs.

Not long after the war, European nations began working together to improve trade and increase their economic power. This cooperation led to the start of the **European Community.** It made it possible for members to trade freely with each other.

Much of Japan was destroyed during the World War II. Afterward, occupation forces introduced social changes, such as land reform and equal rights for women. Like Germany, Japan also built new factories. Its **gross domestic product (GDP)** soared. Japan succeeded by making goods for export.

Review Questions
1. List two results of the strong, postwar U. S. economy.

_____

_____

2. What was the purpose of the European Community?

_____

_____

READING CHECK

Who helped end discrimination for African Americans in the United States?

_____

_____

_____

VOCABULARY STRATEGY

Find the word *prospered* in the underlined sentence. The word *decline* is an antonym of the word *prosper*. The word *decline* means "to fade" or "to sink." Use context clues and the meanings of *decline* to figure out the meaning of *prospered*.

READING SKILL

Categorize Was the European Community founded as an economic organization or a social organization?

_____

_____

_____

Name_____ Class_____ Date_____

Focus Question: What did the Communist victory mean for China and the rest of East Asia?

As you read this section in your textbook, complete the flowchart below to help you summarize the effects of the Communist Revolution on China and the impact of the Cold War on China and Korea. Some items have been filled in for you.

Impact of Communism and the Cold War in East Asia

Korea in the Cold War

- Korean Peninsula split at 38th parallel after World War II.
- Kim II Sung ruled North Korea; Syngman Rhee controlled South Korea.
- • • • • • • • • • •

China in the Cold War

- China allied with Soviet Union in 1950s.
- Border clashes and disputes over ideologies resulted in the Soviets withdrawing aid and advisors by 1960.
- • • • •

Chinese Communist Revolution

- Mao Zedong's Communists defeated Jiang Jieshi's Nationalists.
- Communists ended oppression by landlords and distributed land to peasants.
- • • • • • •

CHAPTER 30 SECTION 3

Section Summary
COMMUNISM SPREADS IN EAST ASIA

After World War II, Mao Zedong led communist forces to victory over the Nationalists, who fled to Taiwan. Mao then began to reshape China's economy. He gave land to the peasants. Then he called for **collectivization,** or the pooling of land and labor. As part of the **Great Leap Forward,** people moved from small villages and individual farms into communes of thousands of people on thousand of acres. Communes were supposed to grow more food and produce more goods. Instead, the system produced useless or low-quality goods and less food. To remove "bourgeois" tendencies, Mao also began the **Cultural Revolution.** Skilled workers and managers were forced to work on farms or in labor camps. This resulted in a slowed economy and a threat of civil war.

At first, the United States supported the Nationalist government that had formed on Taiwan. The West was concerned that the Soviet Union and China would become allies. As the Cold War continued, however, the Soviets withdrew their aid and advisors from China. U.S. leaders thought that by "playing the China card," or improving relations with the Chinese, they would isolate the Soviets even more. In 1979, the United States established diplomatic relations with China.

After World War II, American and Soviet forces had agreed to divide Korea at the **38th parallel.** Communist **Kim Il Sung** ruled the North and U.S. ally **Syngman Rhee** ruled the South. In 1950, North Korean troops attacked South Korea. The United Nations forces stopped them along a line known as the **Pusan Perimeter,** then began advancing north. Mao sent Chinese troops to help the North Koreans. The UN forces were pushed back south of the 38th parallel. In 1953, both sides agreed to end the fighting, but troops remained on either side of the **demilitarized zone (DMZ).** Over time, South Korea enjoyed an economic boom, while communist North Korea's economy declined.

Review Questions

1. What was the purpose of the Great Leap Forward?

_____

_____

2. What was the 38th parallel?

_____

_____

READING CHECK

Who was Kim Il Sung?

_____

_____

_____

VOCABULARY STRATEGY

Find the word *commune* in the underlined sentence. The terms *group home, community*, and *collective farm* are all synonyms of *commune*. They are words with similar meanings. Use the synonyms to help you figure out the meaning of *commune*.

READING SKILL

Summarize Reread the first paragraph. Then summarize Mao Zedong's attempts to reshape China's economy and society.

_____

_____

_____

Name_____ Class_____ Date_____

Focus Question: What were the causes and effects of war in Southeast Asia, and what was the American role in this region?

As you read this section in your textbook, complete the flowchart below to summarize the events in Southeast Asia after World War II. Some items have been filled in for you.

War in Southeast Asia

Aftereffects of War

- Cambodia and Laos were dominated by communists.
- The Khmer Rouge, a force of communist guerrillas, came to power in Cambodia.
- • • • •

Vietnam War

- Domino theory
- Viet Cong, with North Vietnamese support, tried to overthrow South Vietnam.
- • • • • • • • • • •

Indochina After World War II

- Local guerrillas led by Ho Chi Minh opposed European colonialists.
- French tried to regain power, but were defeated at Dienbienphu in 1954.
- • • • • •

CHAPTER 30 SECTION 4

Section Summary
WAR IN SOUTHEAST ASIA

In the 1800s, the French ruled the area in Southeast Asia called French Indochina. During World War II, Japan tried to take over, but faced resistance from **guerrillas.** After the war, the French tried to regain control, but the Vietnamese, led by **Ho Chi Minh,** fought them. The French were defeated at the battle of **Dienbienphu.** After that, Ho controlled the northern part of Vietnam while the United States supported the noncommunist government in the south. Ho supported communist guerrillas in the south, called **Viet Cong.**

U.S. leaders saw Vietnam as an extension of the Cold War. They developed the **domino theory.** This was the view that if communists won in South Vietnam, communism would spread throughout Southeast Asia. In 1964, the North Vietnamese attacked a U.S. naval ship. Congress granted the president the power to take military action to stop further communist aggression in the region. Eventually, more than 500,000 American troops fought in what became known as the Vietnam War.

Despite U.S. support for South Vietnam, the Viet Cong continued to attack. During the **Tet Offensive,** Viet Cong and their North Vietnamese allies attacked cities all over the south. Even though the communists were not able to hold any cities, the attack was a turning point in U.S. public opinion. Upset by civilian and military deaths, many Americans began to oppose the war. <u>President Nixon came under increasing pressure to terminate the conflict.</u> He signed the Paris Peace Accord in 1973, and U.S. troops soon withdrew. Two years later, North Vietnam conquered South Vietnam. Thousands of Vietnamese tried to leave the country.

Communism did spread to neighboring countries. In Cambodia, communist guerrillas called the **Khmer Rouge** came to power. Their ruler, **Pol Pot,** oversaw forced work camps and the genocide of more than a million Cambodians. Laos also ended up with a communist government. However, communism did not spread any farther in Southeast Asia.

Review Questions

1. What did Congress do in 1964?

_____

_____

2. Who were the Khmer Rouge?

_____

_____

READING CHECK

Which Southeast Asian countries ended up with communist governments?

_____

_____

_____

VOCABULARY STRATEGY

Find the word *terminate* in the underlined sentence. Note that the word is a verb, which means it describes an action. Ask yourself what action President Nixon was pressured to take. Use this strategy to help you figure out what *terminate* means.

READING SKILL

Summarize What was the domino theory?

_____

_____

_____

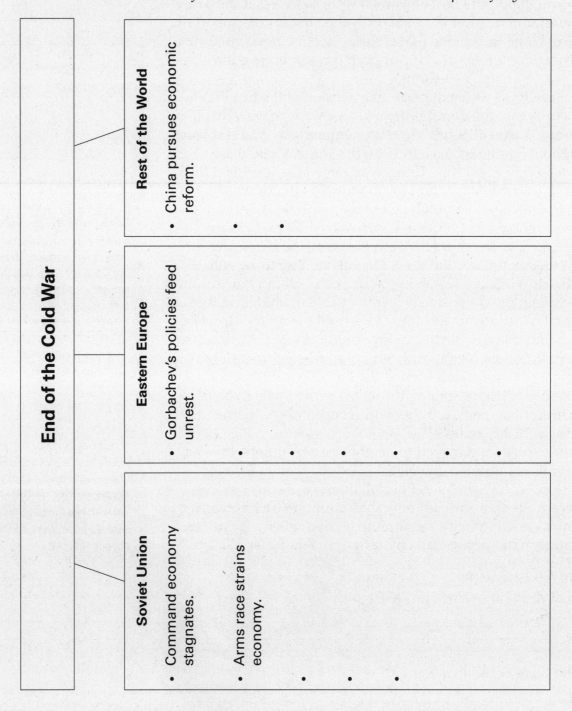

CHAPTER
30
SECTION 5

Note Taking Study Guide
THE END OF THE COLD WAR

Focus Question: What were the causes and the effects of the end of the Cold War?

As you read this section in your textbook, complete this flowchart to help you categorize events connected to the end of the Cold War. Some items have been completed for you.

End of the Cold War

Rest of the World
- China pursues economic reform.
-
-

Eastern Europe
- Gorbachev's policies feed unrest.
-

Soviet Union
- Command economy stagnates.
- Arms race strains economy.

Section Summary
THE END OF THE COLD WAR

The Soviet Union emerged from World War II as a superpower with control over many Eastern European countries. When challenged, the Soviet Union used its military to subdue unrest. However, the Soviet command economy could not produce enough food to feed its people. Consumer products were poorly made and workers were poorly paid. Lifetime job security, however, meant that they did not have to worry about losing their jobs. Therefore, workers had little incentive to produce higher-quality goods. Further economic strain came when Soviet forces invaded Afghanistan in 1979. They had few successes battling the **mujahedin,** or Muslim religious warriors.

Soviet leader **Mikhail Gorbachev** urged reforms. He called for **glasnost,** or openness. He ended censorship and encouraged people to discuss the country's problems. Gorbachev also called for **perestroika,** or a restructuring of the government and economy. His policies, however, fed unrest across the Soviet empire. Eastern Europeans began to demand an end to Soviet rule. By the end of the 1980s, a powerful democracy movement was sweeping the region. In Poland, **Lech Walesa** led **Solidarity,** an independent labor union demanding economic and political changes.

Meanwhile, East German leaders resisted reform, and thousands of East Germans fled to the West. In Czechoslovakia, **Václav Havel**, a writer who fought for independence, was elected president. One by one, communist governments fell. Most changes happened peacefully, but when Romanian dictator **Nicolae Ceausescu** refused to step down, he was executed. The Baltic States regained independence. By the end of 1991, the remaining Soviet republics had all formed independent nations. The Soviet Union ceased to exist.

In 1992, Czechoslovakia was divided into Slovakia and the Czech Republic. Additionally, some communist governments in Asia, such as China, instituted economic reforms.

Review Questions

1. What were some problems with the Soviet economy?

_____

_____

2. What kinds of reforms did Gorbachev make?

_____

_____

READING CHECK

What was Solidarity?

_____

_____

_____

VOCABULARY STRATEGY

Find the word *incentive* in the underlined sentence. The words *motivation* and *reason* are synonyms of *incentive*. They have similar meanings. Use these synonyms to help you figure out the meaning of *incentive*.

READING SKILL

Categorize Which leaders mentioned in this summary supported reform and which leaders opposed reform?

_____

_____

_____

Name_____ Class_____ Date_____

Focus Question: What were the consequences of independence in South Asia for the region and for the world?

As you read this section in your textbook, fill in the concept web below to record causes and effects of events in South Asia. Some of the items have been completed for you.

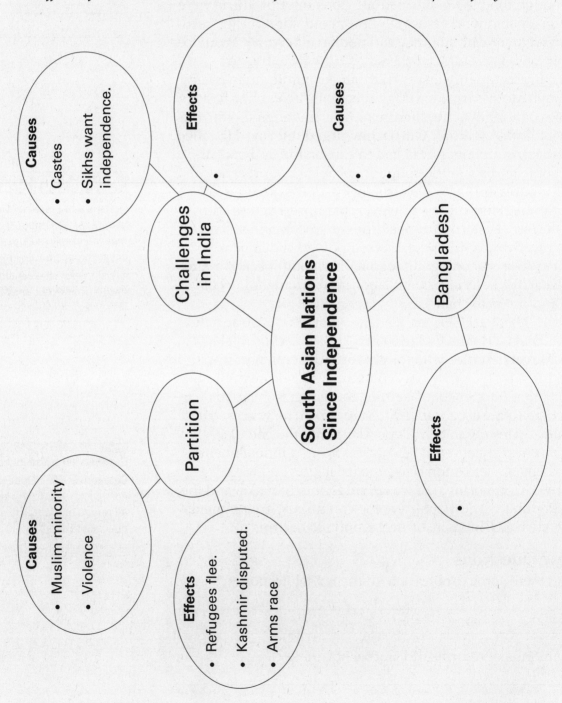

CHAPTER 31 SECTION 1

Section Summary

INDEPENDENT NATIONS OF SOUTH ASIA

In the 1940s, tensions between Hindus and Muslims in India led to violence. The ruling British decided that the only solution was to **partition** India into two countries. India would have a Hindu majority. Pakistan would have a Muslim majority. After independence, Muslims fled to Pakistan. Hindus fled to India. As they moved, Muslims, Hindus, and **Sikhs,** members of another religious group, attacked and killed one another.

Tensions have continued in the region. India and Pakistan have fought wars over **Kashmir,** a state in the north. Both countries have developed nuclear weapons. In Sri Lanka, Tamil rebels have fought for a separate Tamil nation for many years.

In 1947 **Jawaharlal Nehru,** India's first prime minister, tried to improve the economy and the treatment of outcastes, or **dalits.** His daughter, **Indira Gandhi,** became prime minister in 1966. In 1984, Sikhs occupied the **Golden Temple.** They wanted independence for their state of **Punjab.** Gandhi sent troops to the temple, and thousands of Sikhs were killed. Gandhi's Sikh bodyguards killed her.

In 1947, Pakistan was a divided country. A thousand miles separated West Pakistan from East Pakistan. West Pakistan tended to control the nation's government. Most people in East Pakistan were Bengalis. They felt that the government neglected their region. In 1971, Bengalis declared that East Pakistan was an independent nation called **Bangladesh.** Pakistan tried to crush the rebels, but India supported the rebels by defeating the Pakistani army in Bangladesh. Eventually Pakistan was compelled to recognize the independence of Bangladesh.

Pakistan has often been politically unstable. There have been disagreements between Islamic fundamentalists and those who want a separation between religion and government. Over the years, fundamentalists have gained power.

Despite their differences, India and Pakistan helped organize a conference of newly independent states in 1955. This was the start of **nonalignment**—political and diplomatic independence from the United States or the Soviet Union.

Review Questions

1. How has Kashmir contributed to tension?

_____

_____

2. What present-day country was formerly East Pakistan?

_____

READING CHECK

What is the term for political and diplomatic independence from the United States or the Soviet Union?

_____

_____

_____

VOCABULARY STRATEGY

Find the word *compelled* in the second underlined sentence. Note that Pakistan first <u>tried</u> to crush the rebels. How might the presence of India's army force Pakistan to do something? Use these clues to help you figure out what *compelled* means.

READING SKILL

Identify Causes and Effects
What caused the British to partition, or divide, India into two countries? What effects did this division have on Muslims and Hindus?

_____

_____

Note Taking Study Guide

NEW NATIONS OF SOUTHEAST ASIA

Focus Question: What challenges did Southeast Asian nations face after winning independence?

As you read this section in your textbook, fill in the concept web below to keep track of the effects of recent historical processes in Southeast Asia. Some of the items have been completed for you.

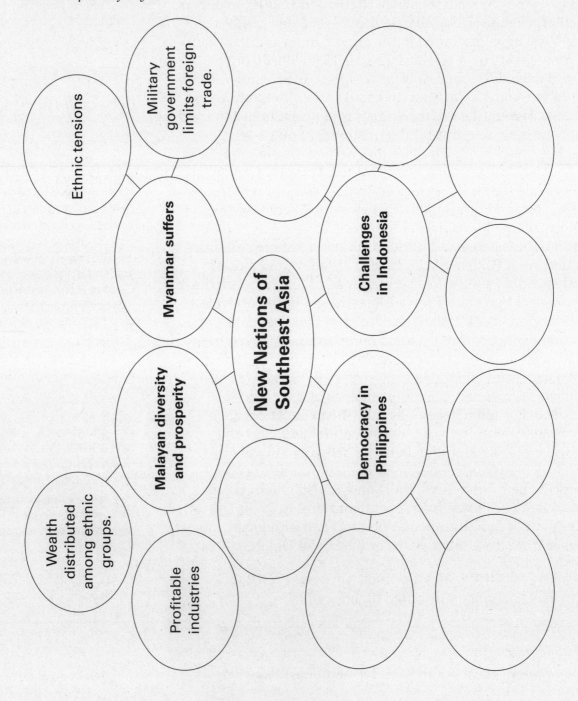

Section Summary

NEW NATIONS OF SOUTHEAST ASIA

Mainland Southeast Asia is a region of contrasts. Thailand and Malaysia have prospered as market economies. By contrast, Myanmar has suffered under an **autocratic** government, with unlimited power. The government has limited foreign trade. Living standards remain low. In 1990, elections were held in Myanmar. A party led by **Aung San Suu Kyi** won. However, the military rejected the election results, and Suu Kyi was put under house arrest.

After World War II, Indonesia gained its independence. There have been many obstacles to its unity. Indonesia consists of over 13,000 islands. There are hundreds of ethnic groups. About 90 percent of Indonesians are Muslims. The population also includes Christians, Buddhists, and Hindus. After independence, Indonesia formed a democratic parliamentary government. It was led by Indonesia's first president, **Sukarno.** In 1966, an army general, **Suharto,** took control. He ruled as a dictator until 1998. Religious and ethnic tensions have caused violence in parts of Indonesia. In 1975, Indonesia seized **East Timor,** which is mostly Catholic. The East Timorese fought until they gained their independence in 2002.

In the Philippines, Catholics are the predominant religious group, with a Muslim minority in the south. In 1946, the Philippines gained freedom from United States control. The Filipino constitution set up a democratic government. However, a wealthy elite controlled politics and the economy. **Ferdinand Marcos** was elected president in 1965. He became a dictator and cracked down on basic freedoms. He even had a rival, **Benigno Aquino,** murdered. When Benigno's wife, **Corazon Aquino,** was elected in 1986, Marcos tried to deny the results. The people of Manila held demonstrations that forced him to resign. Since then, the democracy has struggled to survive. However, Communist and Muslim rebels continue to fight across the country.

Review Questions

1. What happened after 1990 elections in Myanmar?

_____

_____

2. About 90 percent of Indonesians belong to what religious group?

_____

_____

READING CHECK

From what country did the Philippines gain independence in 1946?

_____

_____

_____

VOCABULARY STRATEGY

Find the word *predominant* in the underlined sentence. What do you think it means? Note that the sentence also mentions another group, which is a minority. A minority is a smaller group. Use this context clue to decide which word below is closest in meaning to *predominant.* Circle the word you chose.

1. heaviest

2. largest

READING SKILL

Understand Effects When Corazon Aquino was elected in 1986, Ferdinand Marcos tried to deny the results. What was the effect of his action?

_____

_____

_____

CHAPTER
31
SECTION 3

Note Taking Study Guide

AFRICAN NATIONS GAIN INDEPENDENCE

Focus Question: What challenges did new African nations face?

As you read this section in your textbook, fill in the concept web below to identify causes and effects of independence in Africa. Some of the items have been completed for you.

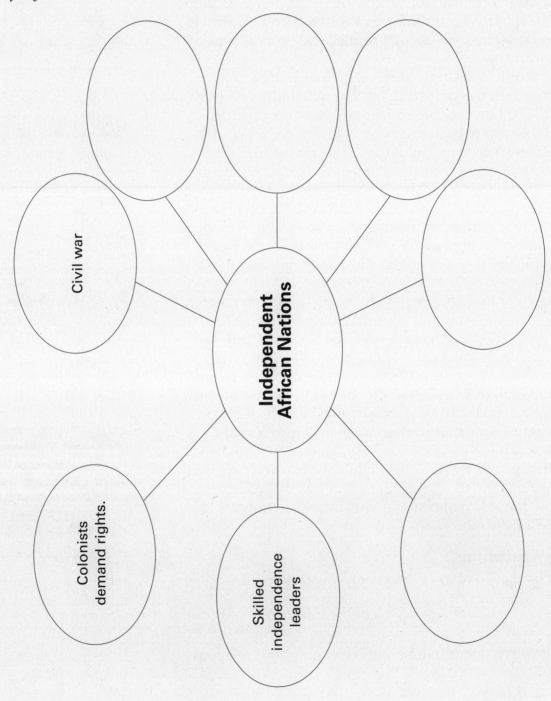

CHAPTER 31 SECTION 3

Section Summary

AFRICAN NATIONS GAIN INDEPENDENCE

Africa is a diverse continent. Rain forests, deserts, and vast **savannas,** or grasslands, cover much of Africa. Most of Africa's people live in the fertile areas, such as the savanna and forest.

After World War II, many Africans demanded independence. After gaining it, a few nations had peace and democracy. Most faced civil wars, military rule, or corrupt dictators. European powers had divided Africa into colonies with no regard for ethnic groups. This led to ethnic conflict in many new nations.

Kwame Nkrumah led Gold Coast, now renamed Ghana, to independence in 1957. His corrupt government was overthrown in a military coup d'etat. A **coup d'etat** is the overthrow of a government. Other coups followed, but today Ghana is a democracy.

In Kenya, white settlers had passed laws to ensure their control of the country. In the 1950s, rebels turned to guerrilla warfare. The British crushed the rebels, but Kenya finally became independent in 1963. **Jomo Kenyatta,** one of Kenya's independence leaders, became the country's first president. However, it wasn't until 2002 that Kenya held its first fair election.

In Algeria, independence from France was finally achieved in 1962. A coup in 1965 began a long period of military rule. Free elections finally occurred in 1992. An **Islamist** party won, but the military rejected the results. Seven years of civil war followed. Fighting stopped, yet the country remains tense.

After the Congo became independent from Belgium, the province of **Katanga** rebelled. The United Nations ended the rebellion in 1963. **Mobutu Sese Seko** ruled as a harsh military dictator from 1965 to 1997. Seven years of civil war ended with a cease-fire in 2003.

Nigeria won its independence in 1960. However, regional, ethnic, and religious differences soon led to conflict. In 1966, the Ibo people in the southeast declared independence as the Republic of **Biafra.** Nigeria ended Biafra's independence after three years of fighting, however. A series of military dictators then ruled, but Nigeria returned to democracy in 1999.

Review Questions

1. Name two leaders of independence movements in Africa.

_____

_____

2. Summarize events in Algeria after independence.

_____

_____

READING CHECK

What is another name for the grasslands in Africa?

_____

VOCABULARY STRATEGY

Find the word *ensure* in the underlined sentence. What do you think it means? The prefix *en-* means "to make" or "cause to be." For example, the word *endanger* means "to cause something to be in danger." What does the root word, *sure,* mean? Use this clue to help you figure out the meaning of *ensure.*

READING SKILL

Identify Causes and Effects
European powers divided Africa into colonies without regard for the territories of Africa's ethnic groups. What effect did this have in many African nations?

_____

_____

_____

Note Taking Study Guide

THE MODERN MIDDLE EAST

Focus Question: What are the main similarities and differences among Middle Eastern nations?

As you read the section, fill in the concept web below to record causes and effects of events in the Middle East since 1945. Some items have been completed for you.

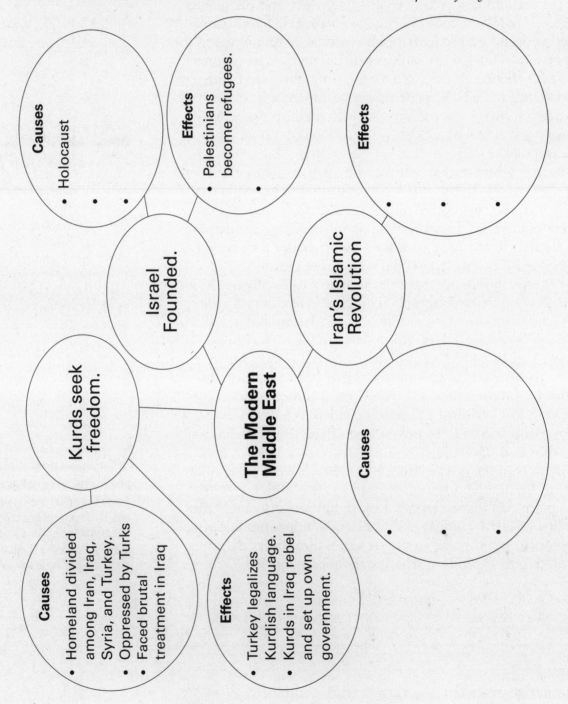

- **Causes**
  - Holocaust
  - •
  - •

- **Effects**
  - Palestinians become refugees.
  - •

- **Effects**
  - •
  - •
  - •

Israel Founded.

Iran's Islamic Revolution

Kurds seek freedom.

The Modern Middle East

- **Causes**
  - •
  - •
  - •

- **Causes**
  - Homeland divided among Iran, Iraq, Syria, and Turkey.
  - Oppressed by Turks
  - Faced brutal treatment in Iraq

- **Effects**
  - Turkey legalizes Kurdish language.
  - Kurds in Iraq rebel and set up own government.

CHAPTER 31 SECTION 4

Section Summary

THE MODERN MIDDLE EAST

In the Middle East, most people are Muslims. There are also many Christians, and Israel is largely Jewish. Most countries also have large minorities, such as the Kurds.

The Holocaust created support for a Jewish homeland after World War II. The UN drew up a plan to divide Palestine into an Arab and a Jewish state. In 1948, Israel became an independent state, and 700,000 Arab Palestinians were forced from their homes. In spite of these conflicts, Israel has developed rapidly. It has a skilled workforce. Kibbutzim work on what is called a **kibbutz,** or collective farm. The Middle East has also had conflicts over resources and religion. It has the world's largest oil and gas reserves. As a result, the region has strategic importance.

Some Middle Eastern countries have **secular,** or non-religious, governments and laws. However, many Muslim leaders argue that a renewed commitment to Islamic doctrine is needed. In Iran and Saudi Arabia, women are required to wear the **hejab.** This is the traditional Muslim garment for women.

Egypt is important because it controls the **Suez Canal.** Under **Gamal Abdel Nasser,** Egypt fought two unsuccessful wars against Israel. His successor, **Anwar Sadat,** made peace with Israel. However, Islamists were upset that the government did not end corruption and poverty. In 1981, Muslim fundamentalists killed Sadat.

In Iran, Shah Mohammad Reza Pahlavi ruled with U.S. support. The United States helped remove one of the shah's opponents, **Mohammad Mosaddeq.** In the 1970s, the shah's enemies supported the Ayatollah **Ruhollah Khomeini.** Protests forced the shah into exile. Khomeini then set up an Islamic **theocracy.** This is a government ruled by religious leaders.

Saudi Arabia has the world's largest oil reserves and Islam's holy sites are there. Kings from the Sa'ud family have ruled since the 1920s, and their close ties to the West have been criticized by Islamic fundamentalists.

Review Questions

1. What religion do most people in the Middle East practice?

_____

_____

2. The Suez Canal is controlled by what country?

_____

_____

READING CHECK

What is the name of the traditional Muslim garment for women?

_____

_____

_____

VOCABULARY STRATEGY

Find the word *doctrine* in the underlined sentence. What do you think it means? Each religion has its own *doctrine.* The word *doctor* is related to *doctrine.* It originally meant "teacher." Use these word-family clues to help you figure out what *doctrine* means.

READING SKILL

Identify Causes and Effects
What effect did the creation of Israel have on the Arab Palestinians who lived there?

_____

_____

_____

Name_____ Class_____ Date_____

Focus Question: Why have ethnic and religious conflicts divided some nations?

As you read this section in your textbook, fill in the flowchart below to help you recognize the sequence of events that took place in Northern Ireland, Chechnya, and Yugoslavia.

Sequence of Conflicts

Yugoslavia

- **Before 1991:** Yugoslavia is multiethnic.
- **1991:** _____
- **1992:** _____

Chechnya

- **Mid–1990s:** Russia crushes Chechen revolt.
- **1997:** _____

Northern Ireland

- **1922:** Six Irish counties vote to remain in United Kingdom.
- **After 1922:** Minority Catholics demand civil rights and unification with the south.
- **1960s:** _____
- **1960s–1990s:** _____

Name_____ Class_____ Date_____

In recent decades, there have been many conflicts around the world. Often they have been based on ethnic or religious differences. For example, ethnic differences between Sinhalese Buddhists and Tamils led to a civil war in Sri Lanka.

Northern Ireland also had problems. In 1922 Ireland became independent from Britain. However, the Protestant majority in six northern counties voted to remain part of Britain. The many Catholics in those counties wanted to unite with the rest of Ireland, where there was a Catholic majority. Extremists on both sides used violence. Peace talks dragged on for years. In 1998, however, both sides finally agreed to peace in the **Good Friday Agreement.**

Ethnic and religious minorities in several former Soviet republics also fought for independence. For example, ethnic Armenians fought against Azerbaijanis. Probably the worst fighting was in **Chechnya.** There, Muslim Chechen nationalists fought for independence from Russia. In the mid-1990s, Russia crushed a Chechen revolt and many civilians were killed. When a 1997 peace treaty failed, some Chechens turned to terrorism.

Yugoslavia, too, was divided by ethnic tensions. Before 1991, it was a **multiethnic,** communist country. <u>The Serbs dominated Yugoslavia, which was controlled by the Communist Party.</u> The end of communism stirred up nationalism in the small states that made up Yugoslavia. Fighting broke out between Serbs and Croats in Croatia. The fighting soon spread to Bosnia. During the war, all sides committed terrible acts. In Bosnia, the Serbs conducted a terrible campaign of **ethnic cleansing.** Finally, the war in Bosnia ended in 1995. At the same time, new fighting broke out when Serbian president **Slobodan Milosevic** began oppressing Albanians in **Kosovo.** However, UN and NATO forces eventually restored peace.

In some countries, conflicts have been solved peacefully. For example, in Canada the democratic government helped prevent French-speaking Quebec from seeking independence.

Review Questions

1. What is often the basis of conflicts around the world?

_____

_____

2. Who is Slobodan Milosevic?

_____

_____

READING CHECK

Which country found a peaceful solution to a conflict?

_____

_____

_____

VOCABULARY STRATEGY

Find the word *dominated* in the underlined sentence. Look for context clues to help you figure out what it means. For example, there is a synonym for *dominated* in the same sentence. It is the word *controlled.* If you know what *controlled* means, you can use that knowledge to help you figure out what *dominated* means.

READING SKILL

Recognize Sequence What event set off the conflict in Northern Ireland, and when did it happen?

_____

_____

_____

Note Taking Study Guide

STRUGGLES IN AFRICA

Focus Question: Why have conflicts plagued some African countries?

A. *As you read "South Africa Struggles for Freedom," "South Africa's Neighbors Face Long Conflicts," and "Ethnic Conflicts Kill Millions," record the sequence of events in the conflicts in South Africa and its neighbors.*

1910: White minority controls government of independent South Africa.
1948: South African government expands racial segregation, creating apartheid.
1960:
1975:
1994:
2000:
2004:

B. *As you read "Ethnic Conflicts Kill Millions," identify the causes and effects of the conflicts in Rwanda, Sudan, Burundi, and Darfur.*

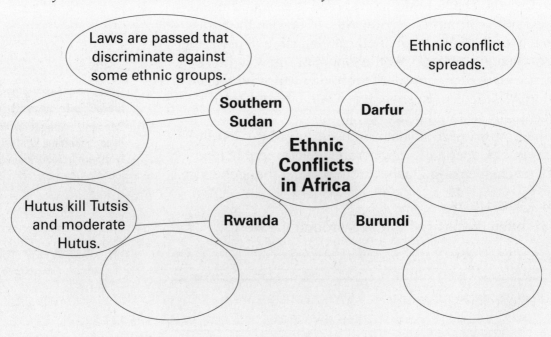

Name_____ Class_____ Date_____

Section Summary
STRUGGLES IN AFRICA

In the 1950s and 1960s, many nations won independence in Africa. However, several nations still faced fighting and civil wars. In 1910, South Africa became independent from Britain. Despite this, civil rights were limited to whites. The black majority could not vote. In 1948, the government created a legal system of racial prejudice. It was called **apartheid.** Under apartheid, nonwhites faced many restrictions. <u>For example, it stipulated that restaurants, beaches, and schools must be segregated.</u> The **African National Congress (ANC)** fought against apartheid. The group led the fight for majority rule. In 1960 police shot 69 people during a peaceful protest in **Sharpeville,** a black township. The government then outlawed the ANC. ANC leader **Nelson Mandela** was sent to prison for life.

In the 1980s, many called for an end to apartheid. During this time, Bishop **Desmond Tutu** was awarded the Nobel Peace Prize for his fight against apartheid. In addition, leaders all over the world called for Nelson Mandela's release. Finally, in 1990 South African president **F.W. de Klerk** freed Mandela. Four years later Mandela was elected president of South Africa.

South Africa's neighbors also faced conflict. Portugal had colonies in Angola and Mozambique. Nationalists fought for 15 years until Portugal agreed to withdraw from Africa. But this did not end the fighting. The United States and South Africa were concerned that liberation leaders had ties to the Soviet Union or the ANC. The United States and South Africa supported rebel groups within Angola and Mozambique.

After independence, ethnic conflicts flared up in many nations. In Rwanda a deadly war began between the majority **Hutus** and the minority **Tutsis.** In 1994, extremist Hutus killed about 800,000 Tutsis and moderate Hutus. In Sudan, non-Arab non-Muslims in the south fought Arab Muslims from the north. This, along with drought and famine, killed millions. By 2004 there was peace, but by then, ethnic conflict had spread to **Darfur** in western Sudan. This raised fears of a new genocide.

Review Questions

1. What was apartheid?

_____

_____

2. What happened in the Rwanda conflict?

_____

_____

READING CHECK

Where is Darfur?

_____

_____

_____

VOCABULARY STRATEGY

Find the word *stipulated* in the underlined sentence. What do you think it means? Note that here the word refers to laws. The previous sentence mentions the restrictions non-whites faced. Use these context clues to help you figure out the meaning of the word *stipulated*.

READING SKILL

Recognize Sequence When was Nelson Mandela elected president of South Africa?

_____

_____

_____

Name_____ Class_____ Date_____

Focus Question: What are the causes of conflict in the Middle East?

As you read this section in your textbook, use the flowchart to record the sequence of events in the conflicts in the Middle East.

Middle Eastern Conflicts

Iraq
- **1970s:** Kurds fight for power in northern Iraq.
- **1979:** Saddam Hussein comes to power.

Lebanon
- **1975:** Civil war begins.

Arab-Israeli Conflict
- **1948:** Israel is founded.
- **1956:** Arab-Israeli war is fought.
- **1960s:** PLO leads struggle against Israel.

CHAPTER 32 SECTION 3

Section Summary

CONFLICTS IN THE MIDDLE EAST

For decades, the Middle East has been a region of conflict. Modern Israel was created in 1948. Palestinian Arabs claimed the same land. Through several wars Israel gained more land. This came to be called the **occupied territories.**

The Palestine Liberation Organization, led by **Yasir Arafat,** fought against the Israelis. In the occupied territories, some Palestinians took part in revolts called **intifadas.** In addition, suicide bombers attacked Israel. Israel responded with armed force. Palestinian bitterness increased. Many, including Israeli Prime Minister **Yitzhak Rabin,** pushed for peace. One issue blocking the peace process was the city of **Jerusalem.** The city is sacred to Jews, Muslims, and Christians. However, during the early 2000s, new steps towards peace offered some hope.

Lebanon is another country in the region with diverse ethnic and religious groups. Arab Christians, Sunni Muslims, Shiite Muslims, and Druze all live there. Christian and Muslim **militias** fought in a long civil war between 1975 and 1990.

Conflicts also plagued Iraq. Iraq's Sunni Muslim minority dominated the country for centuries. The Kurdish minority and Shiite Muslim majority were excluded from power. In 1979 **Saddam Hussein** took power as a dictator. He fought a prolonged war against neighboring Iran in the 1980s. In 1990, Iraq invaded Kuwait. In response, the United States led a coalition against Iraq. In the Gulf War that ensued, Kuwait was liberated and Iraqi forces were crushed. Saddam Hussein remained in power and used terror to impose his will. The United States, France, and Britain set up **no-fly zones** to protect the Kurds and Shiites. The UN worked to keep Saddam Hussein from building biological, nuclear, or chemical weapons, called **weapons of mass destruction (WMDs).**

In 2003, the United States led a coalition that invaded Iraq and overthrew Saddam Hussein. **Insurgents** fought against the occupation that followed. In 2005, national elections were held for the first time.

Review Questions

1. What is the main reason for the conflict in Israel?

_____

_____

2. Why were no-fly zones set up in Iraq?

_____

_____

READING CHECK

Against whom did Iraq fight a war in the 1980s?

_____

_____

_____

VOCABULARY STRATEGY

Find the word *diverse* in the underlined sentence. Notice that in the next sentence four groups are mentioned. How does this help describe the population of Lebanon? Use this context clue to help you understand the meaning of *diverse.*

READING SKILL

Recognize Sequence What event led to the Gulf War?

_____

_____

_____

CHAPTER 33 SECTION 1

Note Taking Study Guide
THE CHALLENGES OF DEVELOPMENT

Focus Question: How have the nations of the developing world tried to build better lives for their people?

As you read this section in your textbook, complete the chart below with details from the text about economic development and developing countries. Some items have been completed for you.

Development

Changes in Patterns of Life
- New opportunities for women emerge.
-
-

Obstacles
- Rapid population growth burdens governments.
-
-
-
-
-

Economic Change
- Railroads, highways, and dams are built.
- New schools are built.
-
-
-
-
-

CHAPTER 33 SECTION 1

Section Summary

THE CHALLENGES OF DEVELOPMENT

After World War II, development became a central goal in Africa, Asia, and Latin America. **Development** is the process of creating a more advanced economy and higher living standards. Nations that are trying to develop economically are, all together, known as the **developing world.** They are also called the global South, because most are south of the Tropic of Cancer. Most industrialized nations are north of the Tropic of Cancer, so they are sometimes called the global North.

To pay for development, many of these nations procured large loans from the global North. Developing nations have tried to improve their agriculture and industry. They have also built schools to increase **literacy.** For centuries, most countries in the global South had **traditional economies.** Some changed to command economies after gaining independence from European colonists. However, when these countries had trouble paying their loans, lenders from the global North made them change to market economies. Now many of these countries depend on the global North for investment and exports.

Beginning in the 1950s, better seeds, pesticides, and farm equipment led to a **Green Revolution** in many parts of the global South. This helped to feed more people. However, many small farmers could not afford the new tools and better seeds. They were forced to sell their land and move to cities.

The global South still faces many challenges. Some countries have only one export product. If prices for that product drop, their economies suffer. Also, population has grown rapidly, and many people are caught in a cycle of poverty. More and more people are moving to cities, but they often have trouble finding jobs. Many people in the cities are forced to live in crowded and dangerous **shantytowns.**

Economic development has brought other changes to the developing world. Women often have more opportunities. However, religious **fundamentalists** in some developing countries oppose changes that undermine religious traditions.

Review Questions

1. Why did many developing nations need loans?

_____

_____

2. How did the Green Revolution help the global South?

_____

_____

READING CHECK

What is another term for the developing world?

_____

_____

_____

VOCABULARY STRATEGY

Find the word *procured* in the first underlined sentence. What do you think it means? Notice that *procured* refers to loans. Find the second underlined sentence, which also mentions loans. Which of the following do you think means the same as *procured?*

1. obtained

2. paid off

READING SKILL

Identify Supporting Details
Record details that support this statement: "The global South faces many challenges."

_____

_____

_____

Note Taking Study Guide

AFRICA SEEKS A BETTER FUTURE

Focus Question: What challenges have African nations faced in their effort to develop their economies?

As you read this section in your textbook, complete the concept web below to record the main ideas about challenges faced by African nations, as well as details that support those main ideas. Some items have been completed for you.

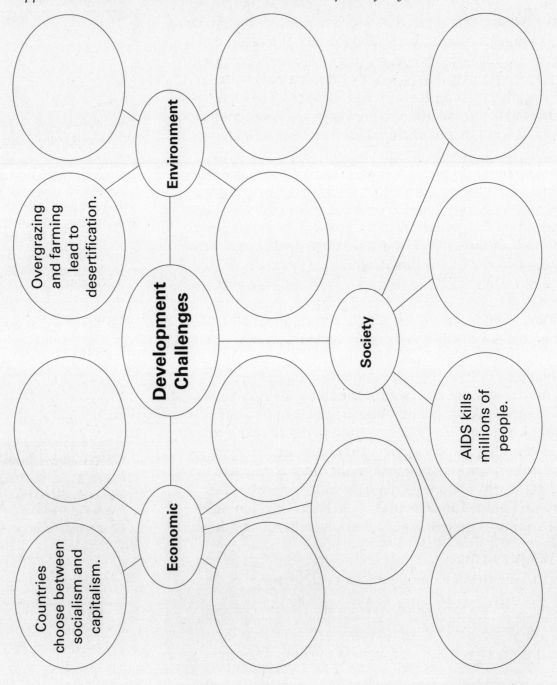

Name_____ Class_____ Date_____

After World War II, African nations had little capital to invest. This meant that they had to make difficult economic choices. Some nations chose **socialism.** This is a system in which the government controls parts of the economy. These nations hoped to end foreign influence in their countries. They also wanted to close the gap between the rich and the poor. Yet socialist governments often led to large bureaucracies.

Other nations relied on capitalism, or market economies. These economies were often more efficient. However, foreign owners of local businesses often took profits out of these countries. Some governments tried to pay for development by growing crops for export. This left less land for food to be grown on, so food had to be imported. <u>Governments then had to subsidize part of the cost of importing food.</u>

African nations have faced many other problems. Droughts led to famine in parts of Africa, especially in the Sahel. There, overgrazing and farming led to **desertification.** AIDS has killed millions of people in Africa. Another problem in African nations is **urbanization.** This is the shift from rural areas to cities. It has weakened traditional cultures. It has also increased economic opportunities for women in West Africa. Another concern is environmental threats. Nearly 70 percent of Africa's animal habitats have been destroyed. As a result, many animals have become **endangered species.** One environmental activist, **Wangari Maathai,** has tried to make a difference. She started the Green Belt Movement. This organization helps women with projects of **sustainable development,** such as replanting trees and selling them.

Tanzania has experienced the problems that are common in many African countries. In the early 1960s, the Tanzanian government tried "African socialism." This failed to increase farm output. In 1985, new leaders began economic reforms. Yet Tanzania is still poor and relies on foreign aid.

Review Questions

1. Why did some governments decide to grow crops for export?

_____

_____

2. What disease has killed millions of people in Africa?

_____

_____

READING CHECK

What is socialism?

_____

_____

_____

VOCABULARY STRATEGY

Find the word *subsidize* in the underlined sentence. *Subsidize* comes from a Latin word that means "aid" or "support." What kind of aid or support did the governments provide? Use the information about the orgin of *subsidize* to help you figure out its meaning.

READING SKILL

Identify Main Ideas What is the main idea of this Summary?

_____

_____

_____

CHAPTER 33 SECTION 3
Note Taking Study Guide
CHINA AND INDIA: TWO GIANTS OF ASIA

Focus Question: How do China and India compare in building strong economies and democratic governments?

As you read this section in your textbook, complete the table below to record the main ideas about reform and change in China and India. Some items have been completed for you.

Reform and Change in China and India

Type	China	India
Economic	• Free market • Communes dismantled • • • • •	• Elements of command economy adopted. • • Nehru promotion of Green Revolution; crop output improves. • •
Political	• Mao succeeded by moderates, such as Deng Xiaoping. • •	• Democratic government • •

CHAPTER 33 SECTION 3
Section Summary
CHINA AND INDIA: TWO GIANTS OF ASIA

By 1981, the new leader of China, **Deng Xiaoping,** allowed features of a free-market economy. He called his program the Four Modernizations. Some citizens were allowed to own property or businesses. Farmers could sell crops and keep the profits. Foreign investment was also welcomed. China's economic output is now four times what it was 30 years ago. But a gap exists between poor farmers and rich city dwellers.

Ruling Communist Party leaders allowed economic reforms but refused to allow more political freedom. Demonstrators gathered in **Tiananmen Square** in Beijing in May 1989. They wanted democratic reforms. When the demonstrators refused to disperse, the government sent in troops and tanks to force them away. Thousands were killed or wounded.

China still faces many challenges. Its population is the largest in the world, hurting economic development. However, after the government started the **one-child policy,** population growth slowed. Millions of rural workers have moved to cities, but they often live in poverty. Pollution and HIV/AIDS are also problems. Human rights abuses continue.

By contrast, India is the world's largest democracy. After gaining independence, India tried a command economy. Yet development was uneven. The Green Revolution improved crop output, but most farmers still used traditional methods. In the 1980s, India shifted toward a free-market system. By the 1990s, several Indian industries were growing rapidly.

India's population growth has made it difficult to improve living conditions, however. The government has encouraged family planning, but it has had limited success. More than one-third of Indians live below the poverty line. Millions of families have moved to cities like **Kolkata** and **Mumbai.** This rapid urbanization has stressed city services. **Mother Teresa** started the Missionaries of Charity in India to help the urban poor.

Education and economic growth have helped India's lowest social castes and women. The constitution bans discrimination against **dalits,** the lowest caste. It gives women equal rights.

Review Questions

1. What happened to the demonstrators in Tiananmen Square?

_____

_____

2. How are the governments in China and India different?

_____

_____

READING CHECK

Who are dalits?

_____

_____

_____

VOCABULARY STRATEGY

Find the word *disperse* in the underlined sentence. What do you think it means? Read the paragraph and notice that demonstrators gathered in Tiananmen Square and then refused to *disperse.* Which of the following words or phrases do you think has the closest meaning to the word *disperse?*

1. stay

2. go away

READING SKILL

Identify Main Ideas Write a sentence that describes the state of India and China today.

_____

_____

CHAPTER
33
SECTION 4

Note Taking Study Guide

LATIN AMERICA BUILDS DEMOCRACY

Focus Question: What challenges have Latin American nations faced in recent decades in their struggle for democracy and prosperity?

As you read this section in your textbook, identify the main ideas and supporting details about challenges faced by Latin American nations to complete the outline. Some items have been completed for you.

I. Economic and Social Forces

   A. Society

      1. Uneven distribution of wealth

      2. Population explosion

      3. _____

      4. _____

   B. Economy

      1. Reliance on single cash crop or commodity

      2. _____

      3. _____

      4. _____

II. The Difficult Road to Democracy

   A. Social unrest leads to rise of military dictators.

      1. Harsh, autocratic regimes result.

      2. _____

      3. _____

   B. Revolutionary unrest continues.

      1. _____

      2. _____

   C. Role of United States

      1. Dominates OAS

      2. Seeks to defend democracy and human rights

      3. _____

      4. _____

      5. _____

      6. _____

      7. _____

(Outline continues on the next page.)

(Continued from page 304)

D. Civil wars shake Central America.

    1. _____

    2. _____

E. _____

    1. _____

    2. _____

III. _____

A. Stability in early 1900s

    1. Robust economy based on exports of beef and grain

    2. _____

B. _____

    1. _____

    2. _____

    3. _____

    4. _____

    5. _____

CHAPTER
33
SECTION 4

Section Summary
LATIN AMERICA BUILDS DEMOCRACY

VOCABULARY STRATEGY

Find the word *alleged* in the underlined sentence. The noun form of this word is *allegation.* It means "something said without proof," or "a charge made without proof." Use these clues to help you understand the meaning of *alleged.*

READING SKILL

Identify Main Ideas and Supporting Details Outline the last paragraph in the Summary.

I. The Example of Argentina

  A._____

    1._____

    2._____

    3._____

  B._____

After World War II, many governments in Latin America encouraged industries to manufacture goods that had previously been imported. This is called **import substitution.** More recently, governments have encouraged the production of goods for export. More land has been opened to farming, but much of the best land belongs to large **agribusinesses.** In many countries, a few people control the land and businesses. Population growth has made poverty worse. However, many religious leaders in Latin America have worked to end poverty and injustice. This movement is known as **liberation theology.**

Democracy has been difficult to achieve in Latin America because of poverty and inequality. Between the 1950s and 1970s, military leaders seized power in some countries. Civil wars shook parts of Central America. In Guatemala, the military killed thousands of the **indigenous,** or native, people.

The United States has had a powerful influence in Latin America. It has dominated the **Organization of American States (OAS).** During the Cold War, the United States supported dictators who were anti-communist. When rebels called **Sandinistas** came to power in Nicaragua, the United States supported the **contras.** These were guerrillas who fought the Sandinistas. The United States also urged Latin American governments to help stop the drug trade. <u>Yet many Latin Americans alleged that the problem was not in Latin America; it was based on the demand for drugs in the United States.</u>

By the 1990s, free elections had been held in several countries, including Argentina. For example, since the 1930s, Argentina has experienced political turmoil. From 1946 to 1955, President **Juan Perón** had strong support from workers. But he was overthrown in a military coup. The military seized control again in 1976. Thousands were murdered or kidnapped. Mothers of missing people marched in protest. They became known as the **Mothers of the Plaza de Mayo.** By 1983, the military was forced to allow elections.

Review Questions

1. Name two obstacles to democracy in Latin America.

_____

_____

2. What country dominates the OAS?

_____

_____

Name_____ Class_____ Date_____

Focus Question: How did the end of the Cold War affect industrialized nations and regions around the world?

As you read this section in your textbook, complete the chart below to compare developments in industrialized nations after the Cold War. Some of the items have been completed for you.

Asia
- After World War II, Japan dominated Pacific Rim.
-
-
-
-

Russia/United States

Russia
- Russia changed to a market economy.
-
-
-

United States
- United States emerged as the world's only superpower.
-
-
-

Europe
- 1991 — Germany is reunified.
-
-
-
-
-

CHAPTER 34 SECTION 1

Section Summary

INDUSTRIALIZED NATIONS AFTER THE COLD WAR

READING CHECK

After the end of the Cold War, what country became the only superpower?

_____

_____

_____

VOCABULARY STRATEGY

Find the word *inflation* in the underlined sentence. What do you think it means? The word *inflate* is related to *inflation*. Picture what happens when you *inflate* a balloon. Does it get larger or smaller? *Inflation* is an economic term that has to do with prices. If prices are *inflated*, would you expect them to be higher or lower? Use these clues to help you figure out the meaning of *inflation*.

READING SKILL

Compare and Contrast How was the U.S. economy in the 1990s the same as—and different from—its economy in the early 2000s?

_____

_____

_____

A global economy developed after the Cold War. With Eastern and Western Europe no longer divided, business and travel became easier. However, unemployment rose. More people immigrated to Europe from the developing world. One exciting change, however, was the reunification of Germany in 1991.

In the 1990s, the European Economic Community became the **European Union** (EU). Later, the **euro** became the currency of most of the EU member countries. By the early 2000s, some Eastern European nations had joined the EU, too. However, older members of the EU were concerned about these new members' weaker economies. Most Eastern European nations also wanted to join NATO, and some did.

After the breakup of the Soviet Union, Russia became a market economy. This was not easy. Unemployment and prices soared, and crime increased. In 1998, Russia **defaulted** on much of its foreign debt. High inflation and the collapse of the Russian currency forced banks and businesses to close. In 2000, **Vladimir Putin** became president. He promised to end corruption and make Russia's economy stronger. Yet, he also increased government control and cut back on people's freedom.

After the Cold War, the United States became the world's only superpower. Among other things, it was involved in Middle East peace talks, war in Iraq, and peacekeeping operations in Haiti. In the 1990s, there was an economic boom in the United States. This produced a budget **surplus**. However, slow economic growth and high military spending led to budget **deficits** by the early 2000s.

The **Pacific Rim** nations have become important to the global economy. Following World War II, Japan grew into an economic powerhouse. By the 1990s, its economy began to slow. Meanwhile, Taiwan, Hong Kong, Singapore, and South Korea have enjoyed great success. These four countries are called the "Asian tigers" because of their economic growth and power.

Review Questions

1. When did the new global economy begin?

   _____

   _____

2. Which Pacific Rim country became an economic powerhouse following World War II?

   _____

   _____

Name_____ Class_____ Date_____

Focus Question: How is globalization affecting economies and societies around the world?

As you read this section in your textbook, use the Venn diagram to compare the effects of globalization on developed nations with its effects on developing nations. Some of the items have been completed for you.

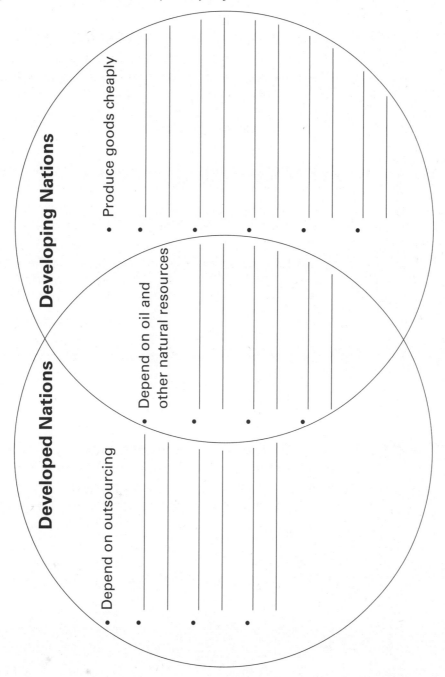

Developing Nations

- Produce goods cheaply
-
-
-
-
-

Depend on oil and other natural resources
-
-
-

Developed Nations

- Depend on outsourcing
-
-
-

Section Summary
GLOBALIZATION

What process links nations economically, politically, and culturally?

_____

_____

_____

Find the word *assets* in the underlined sentence. What do you think it means? A synonym for *asset* is *property*. Use your knowledge of the synonym to decide which word below is closest in meaning to the word *assets?*

1. possessions

2. debts

Compare and Contrast Why do some people support globalization of trade and others oppose it?

_____

_____

_____

Globalization links nations around the world economically, politically, and culturally. It leads to economic **interdependence**—countries depend on one another for goods, resources, knowledge, and labor. Improvements in transportation and communication have made the world more interdependent, too. The spread of democracy and free trade have also played a role. Developed nations control much of the world's capital, trade, and technology. Yet they rely on workers in developing countries. They **outsource** jobs to these countries to save money or increase efficiency. **Multinational corporations** are another result of globalization. <u>These global companies have branches and assets in many countries.</u>

Because of interdependence, an economic crisis in one region can have a worldwide impact. For example, any change to the global oil supply affects economies all around the world. Another example is debt. Poor nations need to borrow money from rich nations to modernize. When poor nations struggle to or cannot repay their debts, both rich and poor nations are hurt.

International organizations and treaties make global trade possible. The United Nations deals with a broad range of issues. The World Bank and International Monetary Fund promote economic growth and development. The **World Trade Organization (WTO)** works to ensure free trade. It opposes **protectionism.** This is the use of tariffs to protect a country's industries from competition. Regional trade **blocs,** such as the EU in Europe, NAFTA in North America, and APEC in Asia all promote trade within their regions.

Global trade has many benefits. It brings consumers a greater variety of goods and services. It generally keeps prices lower. Nations involved in free trade often become more democratic. Some people oppose globalization of trade. They claim that rich countries exploit poor countries. Others say that globalization encourages poor nations to develop too rapidly. This endangers **sustainability** and threatens future generations.

Review Questions

1. Why do developed nations outsource jobs?

_____

_____

2. Give three examples of regional trade blocs.

_____

_____

Name_____ Class_____ Date_____

Focus Question: How do poverty, disease, and environmental challenges affect people around the world today?

As you read this section in your textbook, complete the chart below to compare aspects of globalization. Some of the items have been completed for you.

Aspects of Globalization

Environmental Issues
- Industrialization
-
-
-
-

Human Rights
- Universal Declaration of Human Rights
-
-
-
-
-

Poverty/Disease
- Natural disasters
- May earn less than $2 a day.
-
-
-
-
-
-
-
-
-

Name_____ Class_____ Date_____

CHAPTER

34

SECTION 3

Section Summary

SOCIAL AND ENVIRONMENTAL CHALLENGES

READING CHECK

When a disease spreads rapidly, what is it called?

_____

_____

_____

VOCABULARY STRATEGY

Find the word *inhibit* in the underlined sentence. What does it mean? The word *assist* is an antonym of *inhibit.* That means it has the opposite meaning. Use what you know about the antonym *assist* to help you understand the meaning of *inhibit.* Which of the following words do you think is closest in meaning to *inhibit*?

1. prevent

2. aid

READING SKILL

Compare What do the Universal Declaration of Human Rights and the Helsinki Accords have in common?

_____

_____

_____

Poverty, disaster, and disease are still challenges today. The gap between rich and poor nations is growing. Half of the people in the world earn less than $2 a day. However, ending poverty is difficult. Many poor nations owe billions in debt. As a result, they have little money to improve living conditions. Many other factors inhibit efforts to reduce poverty. These include political upheavals, civil war, corruption, poor planning, and rapid population growth.

Natural disasters cause death and destruction around the world. One example is the **tsunami** in the Indian Ocean in 2004. Natural disasters can cause unsanitary conditions. This leads to disease. Diseases can spread quickly around the world. When a disease spreads rapidly, it is called an **epidemic.** HIV/AIDS is an epidemic that has killed millions of people. Natural disasters can also cause **famine.** Wars and problems distributing food contribute to famine, too. Poverty, disasters, and wars have forced many people to become **refugees.**

International agreements have tried to guarantee basic human rights around the world. The Universal Declaration of Human Rights and the Helsinki Accords are two examples. Still, human rights abuses continue. Women in many parts of the world lack equal rights. Worldwide, children suffer terrible abuses. Indigenous people also face mistreatment.

Industrialization and the world population explosion have hurt the environment. Strip mining, chemical pesticides, and oil spills are all threats to the environment. Gases from power plants and factories produce **acid rain.** Pollution from nuclear power plants is another threat. Desertification and **deforestation** are major problems in certain parts of the world. Deforestation can lead to **erosion.** It is also a threat to the rain forests. One hotly debated issue is **global warming.** Many scientists believe that it is caused by humans burning fossil fuels. Others argue that it is caused by natural changes in Earth's climate.

Review Questions

1. Why have many people become refugees?

_____

_____

2. Name two international agreements that have tried to guarantee human rights.

_____

_____

Note Taking Study Guide

SECURITY IN A DANGEROUS WORLD

Focus Question: What kinds of threats to national and global security do nations face today?

As you read this section in your textbook, complete the chart below to compare threats to global security. Some items have been completed for you.

Threats to Security					
Nuclear Weapons	Nuclear weapons are unsecured in Soviet Union.				
Nuclear Proliferation	Four nations have not signed treaty; others are suspected of violating treaty.				

CHAPTER 34
SECTION 4

Section Summary
SECURITY IN A DANGEROUS WORLD

Weapons of mass destruction (WMDs) include nuclear, biological, and chemical weapons. During the Cold War, the United States and Russia produced many nuclear weapons. Nations soon became afraid that nuclear weapons would **proliferate,** or spread rapidly. As a result, many nations signed the Nuclear Nonproliferation Treaty (NPT) in 1968. However, four nations have not signed the treaty. Others are suspected of violating it. Nuclear weapons in the former Soviet Union are a special concern. The Russian government has not had the money to protect those weapons from smugglers.

In the 2000s, terrorist groups and "rogue states" began to use WMDs. **Terrorism** is the use of violence, often aimed at civilians, to achieve political goals. Terrorists use methods that will draw attention to their demands. These include bombings, shootings, and kidnappings. Regional terrorist groups in places like Northern Ireland have operated for many years. More recently, the Middle East has become a training ground for terrorists. Many of these groups are Islamic fundamentalists. One powerful Islamic group is **al Qaeda.** Its leader is Osama bin Laden. Al Qaeda terrorists were responsible for the attacks on the United States on September 11, 2001.

Al Qaeda's attacks caused strong reactions around the world. Many nations began to focus on fighting terrorism. In 2001, Osama bin Laden and other al Qaeda leaders were living in **Afghanistan.** Afghanistan's government was controlled by the **Taliban,** an Islamic fundamentalist group. When the Taliban would not hand over the terrorists, the United States attacked Afghanistan. The United States also declared war on Iraq because President Bush believed that Iraqi leader Saddam Hussein was producing WMDs. <u>Security within the United States became a priority, too.</u> The United States created a new Department of Homeland Security. It also tightened security measures at airports and public buildings.

Review Questions

1. What are WMDs?

_____

_____

2. What Islamic fundamentalist group controlled the government of Afghanistan until the United States invaded?

_____

_____

CHAPTER
34
SECTION 5

Note Taking Study Guide
ADVANCES IN SCIENCE AND TECHNOLOGY

Focus Question: How have advances in science and technology shaped the modern world?

As you read this section in your textbook, complete the chart below to compare the impacts of modern science and technology. Some items have been completed for you.

Important Science and Technology

Medicine and Biotechnology
- Vaccines prevent the spread of diseases.
-
-
-
-
-
- Cloning raises ethical issues.

Computers
- Computers lead to Information Age.
-
-
-
-
-

Space Science
- Soviet Union and United States compete in space race.
-
-
-
-

CHAPTER 34
SECTION 5

Section Summary
ADVANCES IN SCIENCE AND TECHNOLOGY

READING CHECK

What event set off the space race?

_____

_____

_____

Since 1945, scientific research and technological developments have transformed human life. During the Cold War, the United States and the Soviet Union competed in the "space race." This began in 1957 when the Soviet Union launched *Sputnik,* the first **artificial satellite.** In 1969, the United States landed the first human on the moon. The United States and the Soviet Union both explored military uses of space. They also put spy satellites in Earth's orbit. Since the Cold War ended, nations have worked together in space. Several countries are involved in the **International Space Station (ISS).** There are now thousands of artificial satellites orbiting Earth, launched by many nations.

Another important new technology is the computer. **Personal computers,** or **PCs,** have replaced typewriters and account books in homes and offices. Many factories now use computerized robots instead of people. Computers also control satellites and probes in space. The **Internet** links computer systems worldwide. It allows people to communicate instantly around the globe and access vast amounts of information in new ways.

VOCABULARY STRATEGY

Find the word *manipulation* in the underlined sentence. What do you think it means? It comes from the Latin word *manus,* meaning "hand." The word *manual,* which means "work done by hand," comes from the same Latin word. Use these word-origin clues to help you figure out the meaning of the word *manipulation.*

There have also been important developments in medicine and **biotechnology.** Biotechnology applies biological knowledge to industry, engineering, and technology. Vaccines have been developed that help prevent the spread of disease. In the 1970s, surgeons learned to transplant human organs. **Lasers** have made many types of surgery safer and more controlled. Computers have helped doctors diagnose and treat disease. There have been dramatic developments in genetics and genetic engineering. **Genetics** is the study of genes and heredity. **Genetic engineering** is the manipulation, or changing, of genetic material to produce specific results. Genetic research has produced new drugs to fight disease. It has also created new, hardier strains of fruits and vegetables. Genetic cloning has practical uses, but it raises ethical issues about how science should be used to change or create life.

READING SKILL

Compare How have people benefited from advances in science and technology since the space race began?

_____

_____

_____

Review Questions

1. What does the Internet allow people to do?

_____

_____

2. Name two important developments in surgery.

_____

_____

Concept Connector Study Guide

Belief Systems

Essential Question: What major belief systems have emerged over time?

A. Define *belief system*. (See Student Book page 83 for the feature on this concept.) _____

_____

_____

B. *Record information about the topics listed in the Cumulative Review or your answers to the questions in the Cumulative Review below. Use the Concept Connector Handbooks at the end of your textbook, as well as information in the chapters, to complete this worksheet.*

1. **Animism** (Chapter 1, page 25)
   Some scholars think that our ancestors believed in animism. What is animism? What do cave paintings tell us about early religious beliefs? Think about the following:
   • where our ancestors might have believed spirits and forces were
   • what the subjects of cave and rock paintings are
   • where paintings are located within caves

   _____

   _____

   _____

   _____

   _____

2. **Judaism** (Chapter 2, page 49)
   The Jews of ancient history were known as Hebrews or Israelites. The beliefs of the Israelites differed in basic ways from the nearby people. Describe some important beliefs of the ancient Israelites. Think about the following:
   • belief in one God
   • the covenant between God and the Israelites

   _____

   _____

   _____

   _____

   _____

Concept Connector Study Guide
BELIEF SYSTEMS (continued)

3. **The Influence of Religion on Ancient Egyptian and Ancient Israelite Society** (Chapter 2, page 63)

   People in many early civilizations established belief systems that became an important force in shaping their societies. Compare the influence of religion on ancient Egyptian society with the influence of religion on ancient Israelite society. Think about the effects of religion on these aspects of society:
   - government and law
   - daily life
   - standards of behavior
   - the sciences
   - art

   _____

   _____

   _____

   _____

   _____

   _____

   _____

   _____

4. **Compare the Views of Ancient Egyptians and Ancient Indians** (Chapter 3, page 109)

   Compare the views of ancient Egyptians with those of ancient Indians about the results of a person's actions during his or her lifetime. Think about the following:
   - the role of the god Osiris
   - the concepts of karma, dharma, and reincarnation
   - the Eightfold Path

   How do you think each of these views helped establish a set of morals by which people could lead their daily lives?

   _____

   _____

   _____

   _____

   _____

   _____

   _____

Concept Connector Study Guide
BELIEF SYSTEMS *(continued)*

5. **Christianity** (Chapter 5, page 181)
   Christianity has been an important force in history. List and briefly describe at least three important events or factors that contributed to the rise of Christianity. Think about the following:
   • Jesus' birth and preaching
   • Paul's role
   • the Roman empire and Christianity
   • growth of the Christian church

   _____
   _____
   _____
   _____
   _____
   _____

6. **The Great Schism** (Chapter 9, page 299)
   In 1054, controversies provoked a split between eastern and western Christianity known as the Great Schism. Write a paragraph describing the results of the Great Schism. Think about the following:
   • what happened to the eastern and western branches of Christianity
   • actions of the pope and the patriarch
   • the relationship between the two churches

   _____
   _____
   _____
   _____
   _____
   _____

7. **Muhammad and the Idea of Brotherhood** (Chapter 10, page 335)
   Muhammad said, "Know ye that every Muslim is a brother to every other Muslim and that ye are now one brotherhood." How might this idea have increased the appeal of Islam to conquered peoples?

   _____
   _____
   _____
   _____
   _____
   _____

Concept Connector Study Guide
BELIEF SYSTEMS (continued)

8. **Shinto** (Chapter 12, page 403)

   Early Japanese clans honored kami, or superior powers that were natural or divine. *Shinto,* meaning "the way of kami," became an important religion in Japan. Write a paragraph that answers the following questions:
   - What is Shinto?
   - How can the traditions of Shinto be seen in present-day Japan?
   - How do the locations of Shinto shrines reflect important aspects of the religion?

   _____

   _____

   _____

   _____

   _____

   _____

   _____

   _____

   _____

9. **Impact of Missionaries** (Chapter 24, page 779)

   In the late 1800s, many missionaries believed that they had a duty to spread the ideas of Western civilization, including its medicine, law, and Christian religion. Do research to learn more about the positive and negative impacts of missionaries during this time. Is there any evidence that Christian and native religions blended? How many Christian followers are there in Africa today?

   _____

   _____

   _____

   _____

   _____

   _____

   _____

   _____

Concept Connector Study Guide
BELIEF SYSTEMS *(continued)*

C. Sample Topics for Thematic Essays

Below are examples of thematic essay topics that might appear on a test. Prepare for the test by outlining an essay for each topic on a separate sheet of paper. Use the Concept Connector Handbooks at the end of your textbook, as well as information in the chapters, to outline your essays.

1. Describe the religion of ancient Egyptians, including their belief in an after-life. Consider the following:
   - their belief in a primary god and the pharaoh's position in religion
   - the importance of lesser gods
   - how people might be rewarded by an afterlife
   - why people were mummified

2. Compare ancient Greek religions with ancient Roman religions. Consider the following:
   - how gods were ranked
   - the powers of different gods
   - how people looked to the gods for assistance

3. Discuss the impact of the religion of Islam on daily life and how the Sharia helps unify Muslim people. Consider the following:
   - when and to whom Sharia applies
   - how Sharia shapes daily life

4. Describe the beliefs of Methodism, founded by John Wesley in the mid-1700s, and its effects on industrial workers at the time. Consider the following:
   - beliefs about personal faith and behavior
   - schools for religious study
   - the importance of social reform

Concept Connector Study Guide

Conflict

Essential Question: What issues cause groups of people or countries to come into conflict?

A. Define *conflict*. (See Student Book page 261 for the feature on this concept.)

_____

_____

B. *Record information about the topics listed in the Cumulative Review or your answers to the questions in the Cumulative Review below. Use the Concept Connector Handbooks at the end of your textbook, as well as information in the chapters, to complete this worksheet.*

1. **The Persian Wars** (Chapter 4, page 145)
   Although the Greek city-states were often at odds, the Greeks briefly put aside their differences to defend themselves when the Persians threatened them. Create a timeline that shows key events that occurred during the Persian Wars. Think about the following:
   • how the Persian Wars began
   • where important battles were fought
   • how the Greeks worked together to end the Persian threat

   _____

   _____

   _____

   _____

2. **Compare the Persian Wars with the Punic Wars** (Chapter 5, page 181)
   Roman settlements spread throughout the Mediterranean just as Greek city-states did around the Aegean. Both groups came into conflict with residents on the other side of the sea. What did the Roman conflict in the Punic Wars and the Greek conflict in the Persian Wars have in common? Think about these areas of comparison:
   • overseas trade
   • Greek and Roman culture

   _____

   _____

   _____

   _____

Concept Connector Study Guide
CONFLICT *(continued)*

3. **Compare War Between Christians and Muslims in the 700s with the Crusades** (Chapter 8, page 277)

   The Crusades were not the first wars between Christians and Muslims. In the 700s, the advance of Muslim armies into Europe was halted at the Battle of Tours. Compare that war with the Crusades. Think about the following:
   - the location
   - the opponents
   - the leaders
   - their goals
   - the results
   - the long-term effects

   _____

   _____

   _____

   _____

   _____

   _____

   _____

   _____

   _____

   _____

4. **Examples of French-British Conflict** (Chapter 14, page 467)

   As the French and British began to establish global empires in the 1600s and 1700s, they frequently came into conflict. This was not the first time that these two nations had opposed each other. List other examples of French-British conflict from European history. Consider the factors that seem to have made them historic enemies.

   _____

   _____

   _____

   _____

   _____

   _____

   _____

   _____

   _____

Concept Connector Study Guide
CONFLICT *(continued)*

5. **Compare the American Revolution with the Thirty Years' War**
   (Chapter 17, page 567)
   There are many different causes for the conflicts that have occurred
   throughout history. For example, conflicts have occurred over religion,
   land, and power. The Thirty Years' War in the early 1600s had both religious and political causes. Compare the American Revolution with the
   Thirty Years' War. How were they similar and different? Think about the
   following:
   • cause(s) of conflict
   • scope of conflict
   • groups involved
   • goals or strategic plans
   • results

   _____

   _____

   _____

   _____

   _____

   _____

   _____

   _____

6. **European Revolutionaries in 1830 and 1848** (Chapter 20, page 653)
   In 1830 and 1848, upheavals that began in Paris spread throughout Europe.
   Write a paragraph discussing the revolutions of 1830 and 1848. Think
   about the following:
   • where and why the revolutions began
   • to which places the revolutions spread
   • the outcomes of the revolutions

   _____

   _____

   _____

   _____

   _____

   _____

   _____

   _____

Concept Connector Study Guide
CONFLICT *(continued)*

7. **Congress of Vienna and the Paris Peace Conference**
   (Chapter 26, page 847)
   Read about the 1814–1815 Congress of Vienna, which met to decide the fate of Europe after the Napoleonic wars. Write one paragraph comparing this meeting with the Paris Peace Conference of 1919 at the end of World War I. Think about the following:
   - key negotiators
   - goals
   - treatment of the defeated country or countries
   - outcomes

   _____
   _____
   _____
   _____
   _____
   _____
   _____
   _____
   _____

8. **The Chinese Communists and the Guomindang** (Chapter 27, page 879)
   The Chinese Communists and the Guomindang (Nationalists) battled each other off and on for control of China from the 1920s through the 1940s. The Communists ultimately triumphed. Compare this conflict with the Russian Revolution of 1917. Consider the following:
   - causes
   - nature and duration of fighting
   - role of communist ideology
   - effect on economy and daily life

   _____
   _____
   _____
   _____
   _____
   _____
   _____
   _____

Concept Connector Study Guide
CONFLICT (continued)

9. **World War II** (Chapter 29, page 959)
   On September 1, 1939, German forces invaded Poland. Two days later, Britain and France declared war on Germany, marking the beginning of World War II. Write a paragraph discussing the causes of World War II. Think about the following:
   - harshness of the Treaty of Versailles
   - Japanese and German aggression
   - the invasion of Poland

   _____
   _____
   _____
   _____
   _____
   _____
   _____
   _____
   _____

10. **The Recent Conflict in Northern Ireland and Earlier Religious Conflicts** (Chapter 32, page 1061)
    During the century following the Reformation in Europe, religious differences sparked a series of wars. How does the recent conflict in Northern Ireland compare with those earlier religious conflicts? Consider the following:
    - whether the conflicts involved more than one nation
    - the importance of social and economic inequalities

    _____
    _____
    _____
    _____
    _____
    _____
    _____
    _____
    _____

Name_____ Class_____ Date_____

Concept Connector Study Guide

CONFLICT *(continued)*

C. Sample Topics for Thematic Essays

Below are examples of thematic essay topics that might appear on a test. Prepare for the test by outlining an essay for each topic on a separate sheet of paper. Use the Concept Connector Handbooks at the end of your textbook, as well as information in the chapters, to outline your essays.

1. Describe the events of the Peloponnesian War, and discuss the outcome of this conflict. Think about the following:
   - why the war was fought
   - the effects of the war on Athens and Sparta

2. Describe the issues that led to the American Revolution, and discuss how these issues were resolved by the new nation. Think about the following:
   - how America was governed as a colony
   - what type of government the new United States established after the Revolution

3. Describe the basic issues that led to the conflicts in the Balkans during the nineteenth and twentieth centuries and how the rest of the world has reacted to them. Think about the following:
   - ethnic differences
   - religious differences
   - the Balkans just before World War I
   - the Balkans in recent years

4. Analyze the issues that led to the breakup of the Soviet Union and the fall of communism in Eastern Europe in the 1980s and 1990s. Think about the following:
   - economies under communism
   - freedom of thought, the press, religion, and movement under communism

Concept Connector Study Guide

Cooperation

Essential Question: In what ways have groups of people or countries cooperated over time?

A. Define *cooperation.* (See Student Book page 975 for the feature on this concept.) _____

_____

_____

B. *Record information about the topics listed in the Cumulative Review or your answers to the questions in the Cumulative Review below. Use the Concept Connector Handbooks at the end of your textbook, as well as information in the chapters, to complete this worksheet.*

1. Iroquois League (Chapter 6, page 207)
An alliance of Native Americans called the Iroquois League was founded in the late 1500s. The Iroquois League was an alliance of the Mohawk, Oneida, Onondaga, Cayuga, and Seneca. Write a paragraph that answers the following questions: What were some of the characteristics that the different Iroquois groups shared? How was the Iroquois League organized?

_____

_____

_____

_____

_____

_____

_____

_____

_____

Concept Connector Study Guide
COOPERATION *(continued)*

2. **Roads and Trade Routes** (Chapter 6, page 207)
   In different civilizations, road systems and trade routes have played various roles in connecting peoples. Some have connected people within a civilization, while others have connected people in different civilizations and geographic regions. What forms of cooperation have been enabled by the use of roads and trade routes? Consider the following peoples in your answer:
   • the Phoenicians
   • the Chinese
   • the Romans
   • the Inca

   _____
   _____
   _____
   _____
   _____
   _____
   _____
   _____

3. **Development of Medieval Trade Routes; Glorious Revolution; American Revolution** (Chapter 17, page 567)
   Throughout time, people have used cooperation to reach common goals. Colonists in America joined to fight for their independence from Britain and were ultimately successful. Without cooperation, change would be difficult to achieve. Think of another time in history when groups of people cooperated for a mutual benefit. How might the outcome have changed had they not cooperated? Read to learn more about the following:
   • development of trade routes in medieval Europe
   • the Glorious Revolution

   _____
   _____
   _____
   _____
   _____
   _____
   _____
   _____

Name_____ Class_____ Date_____

Concept Connector Study Guide
COOPERATION (continued)

4. **Coalitions Against Napoleon** (Chapter 18, page 603)
Toward the end of the French Revolution, Napoleon Bonaparte led
France's armies into battles across Europe. List the coalitions that were created to oppose Napoleon at this time. Think about the following:
   - the alliance formed after Napoleon's disaster in Russia
   - the nations that opposed Napoleon at Waterloo

_____

_____

_____

_____

_____

5. **Tactics of Abolitionist Groups** (Chapter 23, page 745)
Do research to learn more about various abolitionist groups, including the
Society of Friends (or Quakers), the Society for the Abolition of the Slave
Trade, the British Antislavery Society, or the American Anti-Slavery Soci-
ety. How did these groups work together to abolish slavery?

_____

_____

_____

_____

_____

6. **League of Nations** (Chapter 26, page 847)
The League of Nations, established after World War I, was an important
step toward a new type of international cooperation. It was intended to
maintain peace so that a conflict like World War I would never happen
again. Research the League of Nations and write a paragraph summarizing
your findings. Consider the following:
   - factors that contributed to its establishment
   - key goals
   - significant accomplishments
   - reasons for its ultimate failure

_____

_____

_____

_____

_____

_____

Concept Connector Study Guide
COOPERATION *(continued)*

7. **United Nations** (Chapter 29, page 959)
   The United Nations was established after World War II and was intended to play a greater role in fostering cooperation than its predecessor, the League of Nations. Research the United Nations and summarize your findings in a paragraph. Consider the following:
   • key goals
   • the role of the General Assembly and Security Council
   • significant accomplishments

   _____

   _____

   _____

   _____

   _____

8. **European Community** (Chapter 30, page 1009)
   During the 1950s and 1960s, greater regional cooperation helped fuel Europe's economic boom. At that time, several European nations came together to form the European Community. How did the formation of this organization strengthen Europe's economy? Consider the following:
   • initial reasons behind its formation
   • significant accomplishments

   _____

   _____

   _____

   _____

   _____

9. **NGOs (Nongovernmental Organizations)** (Chapter 34, page 1127)
   Is the work of NGOs essential in the twenty-first century? Think about the work that organizations like the International Red Cross do. Are there situations where an NGO would be better suited to provide relief than a government or an organization like the United Nations? Why might groups of people in some situations be more likely to welcome aid from an NGO than from a government?

   _____

   _____

   _____

   _____

   _____

Concept Connector Study Guide

COOPERATION *(continued)*

C. Sample Topics for Thematic Essays

Below are examples of thematic essay topics that might appear on a test. Prepare for the test by outlining an essay for each topic on a separate sheet of paper. Use the Concept Connector Handbooks at the end of your textbook, as well as information in the chapters, to outline your essays.

1. Choose two civilizations, such as Sumer, Egypt, the Indus Valley, and Shang China. Compare and contrast levels of cooperation in these two civilizations and explain how cooperation led to success. Think about the following:
    *   controlling rivers
    *   building cities
    *   governments
    *   specialized jobs

2. Describe the uneasy cooperation among Allied leaders Roosevelt, Churchill, and Stalin during World War II. Think about the following:
    *   military cooperation
    *   government rules for the economy

3. Describe the cooperative goals of the European Community (Common Market) and the European Union, and how it has improved the economies of its members. Think about the following:
    *   trade barriers like tariffs and transportation
    *   travel
    *   competition with each other
    *   competition with large economic powers

4. Select two challenges the world faces in the twenty-first century, and dis-cuss what kinds of cooperation will be needed to meet them. Consider the following:
    *   economic issues, such as the divide between rich and poor nations or global trade
    *   social issues, such as health care
    *   environmental issues, such as global warming, desertification, and acid rain
    *   security issues, such as protection from terrorism or religious and ethnic conflicts

Concept Connector Study Guide

Cultural Diffusion

Essential Question: In what ways have migration and trade affected cultures?

A. Define *cultural diffusion.* (See Student Book page 345 for the feature on this concept.) _____

_____

_____

B. *Record information about the topics listed in the Cumulative Review or your answers to the questions in the Cumulative Review below. Use the Concept Connector Handbooks at the end of your textbook, as well as information in the chapters, to complete this worksheet.*

1. **Cultural Diffusion in Early Human History** (Chapter 1, page 25)
   Cultural diffusion has long been a key source of change in society. Do you think that all changes that took place during the Old Stone Age, the New Stone Age, and the time of early civilizations were the result of cultural diffusion? Think about the following:
   • the use of fire
   • the creation of stone tools
   • the painting of caves
   • the domestication of plants and animals
   • the locations of early civilizations

   _____

   _____

   _____

   _____

   _____

   _____

   _____

   _____

   _____

   _____

Concept Connector Study Guide

CULTURAL DIFFUSION *(continued)*

2. **Arabic Numerals** (Chapter 3, page 109)

Arabic numerals were developed by Gupta mathematicians but are used widely today. Write a paragraph that answers the following question: How did the writing system developed by Gupta mathematicians (today called Arabic numerals) spread beyond India?

_____

_____

_____

_____

_____

_____

_____

_____

3. **Decimal System** (Chapter 3, page 109)

The decimal system provides an important example of cultural diffusion. Write a paragraph explaining who developed the decimal system and how the decimal system is an example of cultural diffusion. Think about the following:

- the role of Indian mathematicians
- who uses the decimal system today

_____

_____

_____

_____

_____

_____

_____

_____

Concept Connector Study Guide

CULTURAL DIFFUSION *(continued)*

4. Hinduism (Chapter 3, page 109)

Hinduism is one of the world's major religions. The development of Hinduism is also an interesting example of cultural diffusion. Write a paragraph explaining the role of cultural diffusion in the development of Hinduism. Think about the following:
- the origins of Hinduism
- how the beliefs of different peoples affected Hinduism

_____

_____

_____

_____

_____

_____

_____

_____

_____

5. Buddhism (Chapter 3, page 109)

From its origins in India, Buddhism spread across a wide area. Write a paragraph describing the spread of Buddhism. Think about the following:
- how and where Buddhism spread
- the effects of Confucian and Daoist traditions on Buddhism

_____

_____

_____

_____

_____

_____

_____

_____

Concept Connector Study Guide
CULTURAL DIFFUSION *(continued)*

6. **The Evolution of the Alphabet** (Chapter 4, page 145)
   The Phoenician alphabet was borrowed and modified by the Greeks. That alphabet was then borrowed and adapted by the Romans. As you know, this evolution of the alphabet led to the version we use today. How do you think the alphabet spread among these cultures? Why do you think this alphabet more than any other form of ancient writing is still used in most Western cultures?

   _____

   _____

   _____

   _____

   _____

   _____

   _____

   _____

   _____

7. **The Spread of Roman Culture** (Chapter 5, page 181)
   The Roman empire left an important legacy throughout the history of the West. One important part of this legacy was the spread of Roman culture. Write a paragraph that answers the following questions:
   • How did Roman culture spread during the period of the Roman empire?
   • How did roads, language, and laws help to spread Roman culture within the empire?
   • How did the Roman empire lead to the spread of ideas, such as those of Christianity?

   _____

   _____

   _____

   _____

   _____

   _____

   _____

   _____

Concept Connector Study Guide
CULTURAL DIFFUSION *(continued)*

8. **The Spread of Christianity and the Spread of Buddhism**
   (Chapter 5, page 181)
   The spread of religions depends on various factors, including the religion's message and its acceptance by the government. Compare the spread of Christianity with that of Buddhism. Think about the following:
   - pre-existing religions
   - missionaries
   - the popularity or appeal of the founder

   _____
   _____
   _____
   _____
   _____
   _____
   _____
   _____
   _____

9. **The Roman and Byzantine Empires** (Chapter 9, page 299)
   Byzantine rulers thought of their empire as the successor to the Roman empire. Like the Romans before them, the Byzantines spread their culture across a wide expanse of Europe. Compare how the two empires spread their cultures. Think about the following:
   - language and learning
   - religion
   - art and architecture
   - political ideas
   - where their culture spread
   - how their culture spread

   _____
   _____
   _____
   _____
   _____
   _____
   _____
   _____
   _____
   _____

Concept Connector Study Guide

CULTURAL DIFFUSION *(continued)*

10. The Spread of Islam (Chapter 10, page 335)

Islam has been an important force in history. List and briefly describe at least three important events or factors that contributed to the spread of Islam. Think about the following:
- Muhammad and Islamic ideas
- the hijra
- expansion of the Muslim empire
- the international trade network
- the Delhi sultanate

_____
_____
_____
_____
_____
_____
_____
_____

11. The Spread of Ideas and Culture as a Result of Buddhist and Christian Missionaries (Chapter 12, page 403)

China had an enormous influence on all of East Asia. Many people who spread Chinese culture were Buddhist missionaries. Hundreds of years earlier, Christian missionaries worked to spread Christianity throughout the Roman empire. How did new ideas and aspects of culture spread in both regions as a result? Think about the following:
- what was shared in addition to religion
- acceptance of new ideas
- reaction to missionaries
- peace and stability
- transportation/or ease of movement

_____
_____
_____
_____
_____
_____
_____

Concept Connector Study Guide

CULTURAL DIFFUSION *(continued)*

12. The Renaissance and Islam (Chapter 13, page 441)
During the Middle Ages, many European peoples were cut off from one another as trade broke down and disease ravaged populations. With the Renaissance, renewed trade and increased curiosity about the world led to great cultural diffusion. For example, art techniques that developed in Italy spread to northern Europe, and vice versa. Compare the cultural diffusion of the Renaissance with the spread of Islam from about 750 to 1200. Compare the following:
- cultural achievements
- trading centers
- economic growth
- religious expression

_____

_____

_____

_____

_____

_____

_____

_____

13. The Renaissance and the Tang and Song Dynasties (Chapter 13, page 441)
The European Renaissance ushered in a period of great cultural achievements that would eventually influence people far beyond Europe. Compare the achievements of Europe during the Renaissance with achievements of the Tang and Song dynasties of China. Consider the following:
- architecture
- print technology
- literature
- painting

_____

_____

_____

_____

_____

_____

Concept Connector Study Guide
CULTURAL DIFFUSION *(continued)*

14. **Indian Influence on Southeast Asia** (Chapter 14, page 467)
    There are many examples of cultural diffusion throughout history. For example, Indian culture influenced cultures in Southeast Asia. Write a paragraph to describe some important features of Indian influence in Southeast Asia at its peak, between 500 and 1000.

    _____

    _____

    _____

    _____

    _____

    _____

    _____

    _____

15. **Influence of Ancient Civilizations on Enlightenment Thinkers**
    (Chapter 17, page 567)
    Enlightenment thinkers found inspiration not only in the cultures of other lands but also in the cultures of other times. The relatively new science of archaeology gave thinkers more access to the knowledge of past civilizations. During the early 1700s, archaeologists discovered the ruins of the ancient Roman cities of Herculaneum and Pompeii, buried under volcanic debris for many centuries. How do you think Enlightenment thinkers may have benefited from this discovery?

    _____

    _____

    _____

    _____

    _____

    _____

    _____

    _____

Concept Connector Study Guide
CULTURAL DIFFUSION (continued)

C. Sample Topics for Thematic Essays

Below are examples of thematic essay topics that might appear on a test. Prepare for the test by outlining an essay for each topic on a separate sheet of paper. Use the Concept Connector Handbooks at the end of your textbook, as well as information in the chapters, to outline your essays.

1. Discuss the ways in which the Silk Road encouraged cultural diffusion. Think about the following:
   - the exchange of goods between different cultures
   - the exchange of ideas between different cultures
   - the importance of trade routes to cultural exchange

2. Describe how Greco-Roman civilization spread through the Roman empire during the *Pax Romana*. Consider the following:
   - contributions of Greeks and Romans
   - the size of the empire during the *Pax Romana*
   - the ease of travel
   - civilizations with which Romans traded

3. Describe the ways in which Chinese culture spread to Korea during the Koryo and Choson dynasties. Give at least two examples of how the Koreans adopted certain aspects of Chinese culture, and how they adapted these cultural influences. Think about the following:
   - how Koreans used Chinese inventions
   - the writing systems of China and Korea

4. Describe at least two examples of cultural diffusion in the world today. Think about the following:
   - food, sports, music, movies, and fashion
   - the World Wide Web
   - air travel

Concept Connector Study Guide

Democracy

Essential Question: How has the practice of democracy developed over time?

A. Define *democracy*. (See Student Book page 1071 for the feature on this concept.) _____

_____

_____

B. *Record information about the topics listed in the Cumulative Review or your answers to the questions in the Cumulative Review below. Use the Concept Connector Handbooks at the end of your textbook, as well as information in the chapters, to complete this worksheet.*

1. Roman Citizenship (Chapter 5, page 181)
Roman citizens played important roles in the Roman republic. Record important facts about Roman citizens and Roman citizenship. Think about the following:
- who made the official list of Roman citizens
- the role of citizens in the army

_____

_____

_____

_____

_____

_____

_____

_____

_____

Concept Connector Study Guide
DEMOCRACY *(continued)*

2. Government by the People (Chapter 8, page 277)
The Magna Carta and the Model Parliament are landmarks in the development of democracy in England. Compare "government by the people" in ancient Greece with that in ancient Rome and in England in the 1200s. Think about
- the role of a monarch, if any
- the role of a legislature
- the rights of citizens

_____

_____

_____

_____

_____

_____

_____

3. The Magna Carta and the English Bill of Rights (Chapter 16, page 537)
The Magna Carta of 1215 was a landmark legal development because it limited the power of the English monarch and protected some civil rights. Read about the rights and protections it granted as well as the limits it established on the monarchy. Compare these with the rights and protections ensured by the English Bill of Rights of 1689. Write one or two paragraphs that summarize how the later document increased democracy in England from what it was under Magna Carta, and further limited the powers of the monarchy.

_____

_____

_____

_____

_____

_____

_____

_____

Concept Connector Study Guide
DEMOCRACY (continued)

4. **The American Declaration of Independence** (Chapter 17, page 567)
   In 1776, the members of the Second Continental Congress signed the Declaration of Independence. What were the reasons for the colonies' break from Britain, and what ideas did the signers of the Declaration of Independence use to justify their actions? Think about the following:
   • the colonists' grievances
   • ideas of Enlightenment philosophers

   _____

   _____

   _____

   _____

   _____

   _____

   _____

   _____

5. **The Declaration of the Rights of Man and the Citizen and the American Declaration of Independence** (Chapter 18, page 603)
   The First and Second Estates had power and wealth at the expense of the Third Estate. These class differences in France caused revolt and revolution. Thus began the fight for democracy, as members of the Third Estate demanded equal say in government. Compare the Assembly's Declaration of the Rights of Man and the Citizen with the American Declaration of Independence. What principles of democracy are included in both documents? Consider these influencing factors:
   • the early governments in Greece and Rome
   • England's political system
   • Enlightenment thinkers

   _____

   _____

   _____

   _____

   _____

   _____

   _____

   _____

Concept Connector Study Guide
DEMOCRACY *(continued)*

6. **The American Revolution and Revolutions in Latin America**
   (Chapter 20, page 653)
   After the American Revolution, a new nation was formed under a written constitution. This did not happen in Latin America. How were the results of the American Revolution different from the results of revolutions in Latin America? Think about the following:
   • groups that had power afterwards
   • the relationship between land ownership and power

   _____

   _____

   _____

   _____

   _____

   _____

7. **John Locke and the Expansion of Suffrage** (Chapter 23, page 745)
   Do you think John Locke's ideas about natural rights contributed to the expansion of suffrage to include working class men and all women? Explain your answer.

   _____

   _____

   _____

   _____

   _____

   _____

8. **The Curtailment of Citizen's Rights** (Chapter 29, page 959)
   During World War II, the United States government sent Japanese-Americans to internment camps for security reasons. This represented a curtailment of American citizens' individual rights. Do you think such actions are ever justified by a democratic government? Why or why not?

   _____

   _____

   _____

   _____

   _____

   _____

Concept Connector Study Guide

DEMOCRACY *(continued)*

C. Sample Topics for Thematic Essays

Below are examples of thematic essay topics that might appear on a test. Prepare for the test by outlining an essay for each topic on a separate sheet of paper. Use the Concept Connector Handbooks at the end of your textbook, as well as information in the chapters, to outline your essays.

1. How were the American and French Revolutions related? Think about:
   - ideas common to the two revolutions
   - the causes and goals of each revolution
   - when each revolution took place

2. How would you define citizenship, and how have at least two different societies viewed the rights and responsibilities of citizenship? Think about:
   - words you would use to describe what citizenship means
   - two societies you have studied and their ideas about citizenship
   - what rights and responsibilities citizens of each society had and did not have

3. What impacts did Greece and Rome have on the development of later political systems? Think about:
   - how democracy developed in ancient Greece
   - what kinds of democratic systems and ideas existed in ancient Rome
   - what Greek and Roman political ideas continued in later societies and still exist today

4. What role does democracy play in Latin America today? Think about:
   - the forms of government in modern Latin America
   - examples of democratic movements in the region

Concept Connector Study Guide

Dictatorship

Essential Question: How have dictators assumed and maintained power?

A. Define *dictatorship*. (See Student Book page 903 for the feature on this concept.) _____

_____

_____

B. *Record information about the topics listed in the Cumulative Review or your answers to the questions in the Cumulative Review below. Use the Concept Connector Handbooks at the end of your textbook, as well as information in the chapters, to complete this worksheet.*

1. **Mussolini and Hitler** (Chapter 28, page 919)
   Both Benito Mussolini and Adolf Hitler rose to power following World War I, as greatly charismatic and ambitious leaders. Compare the ways in which each dictator came to power and his policies. Think about:
   • events in Italy and Germany at the time
   • social and economic conditions
   • nationalism

   _____

   _____

   _____

   _____

   _____

   _____

2. **Stalin and Other Russian Leaders** (Chapter 28, page 919)
   Stalin was by no means the first ruler to attempt to maintain absolute control over Russia. Compare Stalin with the following leaders:
   • Ivan the Terrible
   • Peter the Great
   • Catherine the Great
   • Nicholas II

   _____

   _____

   _____

   _____

   _____

Concept Connector Study Guide
DICTATORSHIP (continued)

3. **Communist Dictators and Other Dictators** (Chapter 30, page 1009)
   Many Communist rulers could be described as dictators, such as Mao
   Zedong or Pol Pot. Compare these Communist dictators to other dictators
   you have studied, such as Adolf Hitler, Benito Mussolini, or Ivan the
   Terrible. Think about how their rule involved these factors:
   - nationalism
   - genocide
   - military power

   _____

   _____

   _____

   _____

   _____

   _____

   _____

   _____

4. **Mobutu Sese Seko** (Chapter 31, page 1039)
   After gaining independence in the mid-twentieth century, many African
   nations fell under the rule of dictators. Compare the rule of Mobutu Sese
   Seko, the dictator of the Democratic Republic of the Congo (formerly
   Zaire), with the rule of earlier dictators such as Mussolini, Hitler, and
   Stalin. Think about the following:
   - whether a dictatorship brought order or disorder
   - the relationship of the dictatorship to foreign powers

   _____

   _____

   _____

   _____

   _____

   _____

   _____

   _____

Concept Connector Study Guide
DICTATORSHIP *(continued)*

5. **Saddam Hussein** (Chapter 32, page 1061)
   Like earlier dictators, such as Mussolini and Hitler, Saddam Hussein adopted an aggressive policy of seizing lands outside his borders. He also used brutal methods against his own population. How did Saddam Hussein's dictatorship compare with earlier dictatorships? Consider the following:
   • his internal policies
   • his policies toward neighboring nations

_____

_____

_____

_____

_____

_____

_____

_____

_____

6. **The Rise of Latin American Dictators** (Chapter 33, page 1091)
   Compare the events that surrounded the seizure of power by Latin American dictators with the rise of earlier dictators such as Franco, Hitler, or Mussolini. Think about the following:
   • the economic situation at the time
   • the consequences of the dictators' seizure of power

_____

_____

_____

_____

_____

_____

_____

_____

Concept Connector Study Guide

DICTATORSHIP *(continued)*

C. Sample Topics for Thematic Essays

Below are examples of thematic essay topics that might appear on a test. Prepare for the test by outlining an essay for each topic on a separate sheet of paper. Use the Concept Connector Handbooks at the end of your textbook, as well as information in the chapters, to outline your essays.

1. Compare and contrast dictators during the Roman republic with the Roman emperors. Think about the following:
   - how they gained control
   - how long they served
   - their power to make decisions

2. Discuss why many French people supported Napoleon, even though he was a dictator. Think about the following:
   - economic changes
   - religious issues
   - the laws
   - military campaigns

3. Compare aspects of fascist dictatorships with those of communist dictatorships and the ways in which leaders gained and maintained power before World War II. Consider the following:
   - social and economic conditions
   - attitudes about individual rights
   - attitudes about class
   - when fascist and communist governments came to power

4. Describe the dictatorship in China since Mao Zedong died in 1976. What has been the country's approach to economic and political freedom in this period? Think about the following:
   - China's economy today
   - the lack of political and religious freedom
   - control of Tibet

Concept Connector Study Guide

Economic Systems

Essential Question: What types of economic systems have societies used to produce and distribute goods and services?

A. Define *economic system.* (See Student Book page 627 for the feature on this concept.) _____

_____

_____

B. *Record information about the topics listed in the Cumulative Review or your answers to the questions in the Cumulative Review below. Use the Concept Connector Handbooks at the end of your textbook, as well as information in the chapters, to complete this worksheet.*

1. **The Expansion of Towns in Medieval Europe** (Chapter 7, page 239)
   In this chapter, you read about the rise of towns and the middle class in medieval Europe. Towns were very different from manorial villages. Townspeople had no lord, could move about freely, and had different economic opportunities. Was the expansion of towns a positive or negative development in Western Europe? Consider the following:
   • effects on the manorial system
   • relationships between townspeople and nobles
   • distribution of wealth
   • role of the Church
   • role of peasants

   _____

   _____

   _____

   _____

   _____

   _____

   _____

   _____

   _____

   _____

Concept Connector Study Guide
ECONOMIC SYSTEMS *(continued)*

2. Mercantilism and Manorialism (Chapter 15, page 499)

In the 1700s, European nations adopted the economic policy of mercantilism in order to gain wealth and build empires. Mercantilism depended heavily on the establishment of overseas colonies. How did mercantilism differ from the manorialism practiced in medieval times? Consider the following:

- the roles of colonists and serfs
- the purposes of self-sufficiency and profit-making
- the global impact

_____

_____

_____

_____

_____

_____

_____

_____

3. Market Economy (Chapter 19, page 629)

What is a market economy? How did Adam Smith's ideas support the notion that a market economy could best provide for peoples' needs? Write a brief essay explaining what a market economy is and how Adam Smith's ideas supported market economies. Think about the following:

- how key economic decisions are made in market economies
- why Adam Smith believed market economies would come to help everyone, not just the rich

_____

_____

_____

_____

_____

_____

_____

_____

_____

Concept Connector Study Guide
ECONOMIC SYSTEMS *(continued)*

4. **Centrally Planned Economy** (Chapter 19, page 629)
   Write a brief essay that answers the following questions: What is a centrally planned economy? How did Karl Marx's ideas lead to revolutions that set up centrally planned economies? Think about the following:
   - Karl Marx's ideas about inequality, social class, and struggle
   - how key economic decisions are made in centrally planned economies

   _____

   _____

   _____

   _____

   _____

   _____

   _____

   _____

   _____

5. **Mixed Economy** (Chapter 19, page 629)
   Write a paragraph that answers the following questions: How might a mixed economy encourage more economic equality than a market economy? In what ways could the U.S. economy be considered a mixed economy? Think about the following:
   - how key economic decisions are made in mixed economies
   - possible effects of government involvement in the economy
   - the importance of markets in the U.S. economy
   - government involvement in the U.S. economy, such as public utilities

   _____

   _____

   _____

   _____

   _____

   _____

   _____

   _____

Concept Connector Study Guide
ECONOMIC SYSTEMS *(continued)*

6. **Compare Socialism with Mercantilism** (Chapter 19, page 629)
   What is socialism? Compare socialism with mercantilism, another economic system. Research to learn how they are similar and different. Think about these factors:
   - who supported each system
   - main theories
   - existence today

   _____

   _____

   _____

   _____

   _____

   _____

   _____

   _____

7. **The Commercial Revolution During the Middle Ages and the Industrial Revolution** (Chapter 21, page 687)
   The revival of trade during the High Middle Ages resulted in a commercial revolution. Hundreds of years later, the Industrial Revolution brought about changes in business. In what ways were the changes during the two periods similar? Think about the following:
   - new business practices
   - role of guilds and labor unions

   _____

   _____

   _____

   _____

   _____

   _____

   _____

   _____

Concept Connector Study Guide
ECONOMIC SYSTEMS *(continued)*

8. **Command Economies in Developing Countries and in Russia**
(Chapter 33, page 1091)
In the early 1900s, the Soviet Union shifted from a market economy to a command economy. However, in the late 1900s, the Soviet Union's command economy failed. In this chapter, you read that many developing nations attempted to create command economies in the middle 1900s, but that this attempt largely failed. How does the experience with command economies in developing countries compare with that in Russia? Consider the role of debt and the question of efficiency.

_____

_____

_____

_____

_____

_____

_____

_____

9. **Economic Systems in the Twentieth Century** (Chapter 34, page 1127)
Throughout much of human history, different economic systems have played crucial roles in determining how goods and services were produced and distributed. What changes to economic systems have occurred during the twentieth century? Which economic system largely collapsed at the end of the Cold War? What are some important features of the dominant economic system today? Think about the following:
- communism and capitalism
- the collapse of the Soviet Union
- the way goods and services are produced and distributed today
- the importance of globalization, outsourcing, and multinational corporations

_____

_____

_____

_____

_____

_____

_____

_____

_____

Name_____ Class_____ Date_____

Concept Connector Study Guide

ECONOMIC SYSTEMS *(continued)*

C. Sample Topics for Thematic Essays

Below are examples of thematic essay topics that might appear on a test. Prepare for the test by outlining an essay for each topic on a separate sheet of paper. Use the Concept Connector Handbooks at the end of your textbook, as well as information in the chapters, to outline your essays.

1. Discuss the importance of trade in early civilizations and how the development of a money economy helped unite the Persian empire. Consider the following:
   - how trade affected their material wealth and their contacts with other civilizations
   - how a money economy made trade easier
   - how trade promoted connections between people

2. Describe the attitude toward merchants during the golden age of Muslim civilization, the success of the merchants, and the development of new business practices. Consider the following:
   - the place of merchants in Muslim cultures
   - the extent of their trading network
   - the effect on others of trading with Muslim merchants

3. Discuss the role British mercantilism played in sparking the American Revolution. Consider the following:
   - the role of the colonies in Britain's economy
   - the result of restrictions on American trade
   - American responses to taxes and trade rules

4. Describe the economic changes in Eastern Europe after the fall of the Soviet Union and the challenges facing countries as they adapted from one economic system to another. Think about the following:
   - the type of economic system before the fall of the Soviet Union
   - the type of economic system after the fall of the Soviet Union
   - advantages and disadvantages of different types of economic systems

Concept Connector Study Guide

Empires

Essential Question: What factors allow empires to rise and cause them to fall?

A. Define *empire*. (See Student Book page 200 for the feature on this concept.)

_____

_____

_____

B. *Record information about the topics listed in the Cumulative Review or your answers to the questions in the Cumulative Review below. Use the Concept Connector Handbooks at the end of your textbook, as well as information in the chapters, to complete this worksheet.*

1. **Characteristics of Successful Rulers** (Chapter 2, page 63)
   To maintain control over a vast empire, it was vital that a ruler be well-respected. Based on the empires of the ancient Middle East and Egypt, what characteristics do you think made leaders most successful? Think about the following:
   • spiritual leadership
   • establishment of laws and punishments for crimes
   • military power
   • treatment of subjects

_____

_____

_____

_____

_____

_____

_____

_____

_____

Concept Connector Study Guide

EMPIRES *(continued)*

2. **Empire-Building in India, China, Egypt, and the Middle East**
   (Chapter 3, page 109)
   Consider the history of empire-building in India, China, Egypt, and the
   Middle East. In which cases did the civilization endure even as power
   changed hands? In which did the end of power lead to the end of the
   civilization?

   _____

   _____

   _____

   _____

   _____

   _____

   _____

   _____

3. **Methods of Control in the Roman Empire and Han Dynasty** (Chapter 5,
   page 181)
   The Roman empire and the Han dynasty in China each exerted control
   over a wide area and a variety of people. Compare how the two empires
   maintained control over such large areas. Provide specific examples of the
   methods of control. Think about the following:
   • use of military force
   • structure of government
   • methods of communication
   • sharing of culture

   _____

   _____

   _____

   _____

   _____

   _____

   _____

Name_____ Class_____ Date_____

Concept Connector Study Guide
EMPIRES *(continued)*

4. **Aztec and Inca** (Chapter 6, page 207)
The Aztec and the Inca were two impressive civilizations of the Americas. Both civilizations could also be described as empires. Write a paragraph describing the ways in which the Aztec and Inca were able to conquer and control such large territories. Think about the following:
   • governance
   • warfare
   • leadership

_____
_____
_____
_____
_____
_____
_____
_____
_____

5. **Was Charlemagne Really King of the Romans?** (Chapter 7, page 239)
In 800, Pope Leo III crowned Charlemagne king of the Romans. Was Charlemagne's empire really a "Roman" empire, or was it something different? Explain your answer. Think about the following:
   • size and location
   • language
   • religion
   • education
   • laws

_____
_____
_____
_____
_____
_____
_____
_____
_____

Concept Connector Study Guide

EMPIRES *(continued)*

6. **The Roman Empire and the Holy Roman Empire** (Chapter 8, page 277)
   The name of the Holy Roman Empire was supposed to make people think of the greatness and power of the ancient Roman empire. Compare the two. Consider the following:
   • size and location
   • duration
   • how they were governed
   • how well they controlled their people and territory

   _____

   _____

   _____

   _____

   _____

   _____

   _____

   _____

7. **The Byzantine Empire** (Chapter 9, page 299)
   The Byzantine empire was a very powerful and important empire. As the cities of the western Roman empire crumbled, the vital center of Constantinople in the Byzantine empire remained secure, and prospered. The Byzantine empire was also the source of many important developments, such as Justinian's Code. Create a timeline that highlights important events that occurred during the time of the Byzantine empire from 330 to 1453. Think about the following:
   • the growth of the Byzantine empire
   • important developments in religion and law
   • the decline of the Byzantine empire

   _____

   _____

   _____

   _____

   _____

   _____

   _____

   _____

Concept Connector Study Guide

EMPIRES *(continued)*

8. **The Abbasid Empire** (Chapter 10, page 335)

   With strong support from Shiite and non-Arab Muslims, Abu al-Abbas captured Damascus in 750. After having members of the defeated Umayyad family killed, Abu al-Abbas founded the Abbasid dynasty. The Abbasid dynasty lasted until 1258. Write a paragraph summarizing important changes that took place under the Abbasids. Think about the following:
   - equality of Muslims
   - attitude toward large military conquest
   - wealth and power
   - treatment of non-Arab Muslims
   - bureaucracy and learning
   - location of capital

   _____

   _____

   _____

   _____

   _____

   _____

   _____

   _____

   _____

   _____

9. **The Mughal Empire** (Chapter 10, page 335)

   The Mughal dynasty, which was set up by Babur, ruled in India from 1526 to 1857. The chief builder of the Mughal empire was Babur's grandson Akbar. Write a paragraph discussing Akbar's important accomplishments.

   _____

   _____

   _____

   _____

   _____

   _____

   _____

   _____

   _____

Concept Connector Study Guide
EMPIRES *(continued)*

10. Suleiman the Magnificent (Chapter 10, page 335)

Research the Ottoman sultan Suleiman the Magnificent. Then write a brief essay explaining why Suleiman earned the title "magnificent." Read to learn more about the following aspects of Suleiman's reign:
- military achievements
- political changes
- cultural advancements
- social changes
- personal triumphs and tragedies
- system of janizaries
- successor

_____

_____

_____

_____

_____

_____

_____

_____

11. The Mongol Empire (Chapter 12, page 403)

The Mongols were a nomadic people who grazed their horses and sheep on the steppes of Central Asia. In about 1200, the Mongols burst out of Central Asia to conquer a vast empire. Write a paragraph describing important achievements and effects of the Mongol empire. Think about the following:
- effects on conquered peoples
- cultural diffusion
- trade

_____

_____

_____

_____

_____

_____

_____

_____

Concept Connector Study Guide
EMPIRES *(continued)*

12. **The Ming Empire** (Chapter 12, page 403)
    In 1368, Zhu Yuanzhang founded a new Chinese dynasty after forging a rebel army to topple the Mongols. This dynasty was called the Ming, which means "brilliant." Do you think the word *brilliant* accurately describes the Ming dynasty? Support your answer by discussing the accomplishments, as well as any mistakes, of the Ming rulers. Consider the following areas:
    • government
    • economy
    • culture
    • exploration

    _____
    _____
    _____
    _____
    _____
    _____
    _____
    _____

13. **The Roman Empire and the Tang Dynasty** (Chapter 12, page 403)
    The Roman empire and the Tang dynasty each established a system of government to rule over their lands. What do the two empires and their governments have in common? How are they different? Think about the following:
    • the importance of law
    • government officials
    • economic reforms
    • challenges

    _____
    _____
    _____
    _____
    _____
    _____
    _____
    _____

Concept Connector Study Guide
EMPIRES *(continued)*

14. **The Qing and the Yuan Dynasties** (Chapter 14, page 467)
    With the founding of the Qing empire, the Manchus established one of
    China's most successful dynasties. One reason for the Manchus' success
    was their adoption of Chinese customs and inclusion of Chinese in their
    government structure. The Yuan dynasty, established by the Mongols,
    was the only other foreign-ruled Chinese dynasty. Compare the Qing and
    the Yuan dynasties. Consider the following:
    • culture and language
    • approaches to trade
    • involvement of Chinese in the government

    _____

    _____

    _____

    _____

    _____

    _____

    _____

    _____

15. **The Roman Empire and the Spanish Empire in the Americas**
    (Chapter 15, page 499)
    Compare the establishment of the Spanish empire in the Americas with
    the establishment of the Roman empire. How were they similar and dif-
    ferent? Think about the role of the following:
    • imperialism
    • technology
    • disease
    • methods of rule
    • religion

    _____

    _____

    _____

    _____

    _____

    _____

    _____

    _____

Concept Connector Study Guide
EMPIRES *(continued)*

16. **North American Colonies and Latin American Colonies**
(Chapter 20, page 653)
Colonists in Latin America in the early 1800s had much in common with colonists in North America in the mid-1700s. In each case, the colonies were part of an empire whose capital was thousands of miles away. How did the empires use their colonies for their own gain? What did the colonists have in common? Think about the following:
- nationalism
- the role of geography in empires
- economic exploitation by empires

_____

_____

_____

_____

_____

_____

_____

_____

17. **The Second Reich and the Holy Roman Empire** (Chapter 22, page 717)
In 1871, German nationalists celebrated the birth of the Second Reich, or empire. They called it that because they considered Germany the heir to the Holy Roman Empire. Compare the Second Reich with the Holy Roman Empire. How were they similar? How were they different? Think about the following:
- structure of government
- power of the kaiser and the emperor
- the rule of William II and Otto I
- who had voting rights
- who held the real power

_____

_____

_____

_____

_____

_____

_____

_____

Concept Connector Study Guide
EMPIRES *(continued)*

18. **The Spanish Empire of the 1500s and the British Empire of the late 1800s** (Chapter 24, page 779)

    European imperialism began long before the 1800s. European states had overseas empires as early as the 1400s and 1500s. Do research to learn more about the Spanish empire of the 1500s and then compare it with the British empire of the late 1800s. How were they similar? How were they different? Think about the following:
    - economic motives
    - religious motives
    - political and military motives

    _____

    _____

    _____

    _____

    _____

    _____

    _____

    _____

    _____

19. **Arguments Against Imperialism** (Chapter 24, page 779)

    As you have read, there were small groups of people in the West who were against imperialism for both political and moral reasons. Some anti-imperialists believed that colonialism was a tool of the wealthy. Others believed that it was immoral to impose undemocratic rule on the other peoples. Do research to learn more about the arguments against imperialism in the late 1800s and early 1900s. Summarize your findings in two or three paragraphs.

    _____

    _____

    _____

    _____

    _____

    _____

    _____

    _____

Name_____ Class_____ Date_____

Concept Connector Study Guide
EMPIRES *(continued)*

20. The Soviet Union and Other Empires (Chapter 30, page 1009)

The Soviet Union could be described as an empire because it incorporated many different countries and ethnic groups. How was the Soviet Union similar to or different from other empires you have studied, such as the Spanish empire in the Age of Discovery or the British empire? Consider the following:
- geography and distance
- the role of ideology
- economic ties

_____

_____

_____

_____

_____

_____

_____

_____

_____

21. Chechnya and Earlier Efforts to Break Away from an Empire
(Chapter 32, page 1061)

Like earlier empires, Russia controls numerous regions and ethnic groups. The conflict in Chechnya can be seen as an effort by one ethnic group to break away. How does this conflict compare with earlier efforts to break away from an empire, such as the Vietnamese and Algerian wars for independence from the French empire?

_____

_____

_____

_____

_____

_____

_____

_____

Concept Connector Study Guide
EMPIRES *(continued)*

C. Sample Topics for Thematic Essays

Below are examples of thematic essay topics that might appear on a test. Prepare for the test by outlining an essay for each topic on a separate sheet of paper. Use the Concept Connector Handbooks at the end of your textbook, as well as information in the chapters, to outline your essays.

1. Discuss the extent and the organization of the Inca empire and the reasons why it fell to Europeans in the 1500s. Consider the following:
   - the area it ruled
   - its ruler and chain of command
   - communication and transportation in the empire
   - weaknesses against European military weapons, the result of internal divisions, the effect of European diseases
   - the response to European power and victories

2. Describe the achievements of the Mongol empire in Asia, especially in China, during the 1200s and 1300s. Consider the following:
   - the area it ruled
   - how it ruled conquered peoples
   - conditions during its rule, including trade and cultural contacts

3. Describe reasons why Western powers were able to gain control over much of the world between 1870 and the beginning of World War I. Consider the following:
   - the strength of older empires and nations
   - Western governments, economies, and military organizations
   - medical care
   - military advantages

4. Discuss reasons for the fall of communism and the breakup of the Soviet Union in the 1980s. Consider the following:
   - the success of command economies vs. market economies
   - reaction in Eastern Europe to strict communist control
   - the result of military action in Afghanistan
   - the result of early reforms

Concept Connector Study Guide

Genocide

Essential Question: What factors have led groups of people or governments to commit genocide?

A. Define *genocide.* (See Student Book page 957 for the feature on this concept.) _____

_____

_____

B. *Record information about the topics listed in the Cumulative Review or your answers to the questions in the Cumulative Review below. Use the Concept Connector Handbooks at the end of your textbook, as well as information in the chapters, to complete this worksheet.*

1. **Native Americans** (Chapter 15, page 499)
   The arrival of Europeans in the Americas severely affected Native American cultures. Discuss some ways in which the arrival of Europeans resulted in death or disease for native populations and in the decline of native civilizations. Think about the following:
   - guns
   - horses
   - disease
   - encomienda

_____

_____

_____

_____

_____

_____

_____

_____

_____

_____

Concept Connector Study Guide
GENOCIDE *(continued)*

2. **Indigenous Peoples in North America, Australia, and New Zealand**
(Chapter 25, page 809)
Read about what happened to the indigenous peoples of North America
when Europeans colonized Mexico, the United States, and Canada. Then
learn more about the effects of colonization on the Aborigines in Australia
and the Maori in New Zealand. Compare the experiences of these indigenous groups. Consider the following:
- population and way of life before and after colonization
- effects of disease
- attitudes towards land ownership
- treatment today

_____

_____

_____

_____

_____

_____

_____

_____

3. **The Holocaust and the Armenian Genocide** (Chapter 29, page 959)
What was the Holocaust? Compare the Holocaust with the Armenian
genocide carried out by the Ottoman Turks. How were they similar and
different? Think about the role of the following:
- nation-building and nationalism
- murder of minority leaders
- large-scale deportations
- systematic torture and murder
- use of concentration camps

_____

_____

_____

_____

_____

_____

_____

_____

Concept Connector Study Guide
GENOCIDE *(continued)*

4. **Genocide in Cambodia Compared with Earlier Genocides**
   (Chapter 30, page 1009)
   Pol Pot's regime was responsible for the deaths of millions in Cambodia. How did this genocide compare with earlier genocides you have learned about, such as the Jewish Holocaust or the Armenian genocide? Consider the role of the following:
   - ideology
   - racial, religious, or ethnic prejudice

   _____

   _____

   _____

   _____

   _____

   _____

   _____

   _____

   _____

   _____

5. **Genocide in Rwanda Compared with Earlier Genocides**
   (Chapter 32, page 1061)
   Compare the genocide in Rwanda with at least one earlier example of genocide, such as those in Cambodia, Nazi Germany, or the Ottoman empire. Think about the following:
   - the role of ethnic hatred
   - the response of the international community

   _____

   _____

   _____

   _____

   _____

   _____

   _____

   _____

   _____

   _____

Concept Connector Study Guide

GENOCIDE *(continued)*

C. Sample Topics for Thematic Essays

Below are examples of thematic essay topics that might appear on a test. Prepare for the test by outlining an essay for each topic on a separate sheet of paper. Use the Concept Connector Handbooks at the end of your textbook, as well as information in the chapters, to outline your essays.

1. Describe the early contacts between Europeans and Native Americans in North America and how westward expansion by colonists affected the Native Americans. Consider the following:
   - early encounters between Native Americans and Europeans
   - the effects of wars, disease, and reservations

2. Describe the differences between Armenians and the Ottoman Turks in the late 1800s, and discuss the factors that led to the genocide of the early 1900s. Think about the following:
   - culture and religion
   - nationalism

3. Discuss Nazi attitudes toward Jews and other ethnic groups and how these views were used to justify the events of the Holocaust. Consider the following:
   - their ideas about a "master race"
   - their actions in Eastern Europe during the beginning of the war
   - what groups they tried to kill and why

4. Discuss the reasons why genocide occurred in Rwanda in the 1990s and the international response. Consider the following:
   - the majority and minority ethnic groups
   - which group dominated Rwanda for years
   - the civil war
   - when international assistance came and who gave it

Concept Connector Study Guide

Geography's Impact

Essential Question: How have geographic factors affected the course of history?

A. Define *geography*. (See Student Book page 601 for the feature on this concept.) _____

_____

_____

B. *Record information about the topics listed in the Cumulative Review or your answers to the questions in the Cumulative Review below. Use the Concept Connector Handbooks at the end of your textbook, as well as information in the chapters, to complete this worksheet.*

1. **Rivers and the Rise of Civilization** (Chapter 1, page 25)
   Rivers have been extremely important to the rise of human civilizations. Rivers provided important resources that enabled early civilizations to develop. Indeed, the earliest civilizations were all situated near major rivers. Write a paragraph discussing the main reasons why rivers were so important to the development of early civilizations.

   _____

   _____

   _____

   _____

   _____

   _____

   _____

   _____

   _____

Concept Connector Study Guide
GEOGRAPHY'S IMPACT (continued)

2. **The Tigris and Euphrates Rivers** (Chapter 2, page 63)
   The Tigris and Euphrates rivers played an important role in the development of the world's first civilization, which was called Sumer. How did the Tigris and Euphrates rivers help to create and shape the civilization of Sumer? Think about the following:
   • farming
   • trade
   • flood control and irrigation

   _____
   _____
   _____
   _____
   _____
   _____
   _____
   _____
   _____
   _____

3. **The Aegean and Mediterranean Seas** (Chapter 4, page 145)
   The civilizations of the Minoans, Mycenaeans, and Greeks were greatly influenced by the Aegean and Mediterranean seas. Write a paragraph explaining how these seas affected the Minoan, Mycenaean, and Greek civilizations. Think about the following:
   • trade
   • sources of wealth
   • sources of new ideas

   _____
   _____
   _____
   _____
   _____
   _____
   _____
   _____
   _____
   _____

Concept Connector Study Guide
GEOGRAPHY'S IMPACT *(continued)*

4. **Geographic Environments of Developing Civilizations**
   (Chapter 6, page 207)
   Compare the geographic environments of the developing civilizations in India, Rome, South America, and Mesoamerica. How did natural features such as rivers, seas, mountains, valleys, and rain forests affect different aspects of civilization? Think about the following:
   - trade and economics
   - protection from attack
   - cultural diffusion
   - cooperation

   _____

   _____

   _____

   _____

   _____

   _____

   _____

   _____

5. **The Ocean's Influence on the Vikings** (Chapter 7, page 239)
   The Vikings burst out of Scandinavia starting in the late 700s, looting and burning communities along the coasts and rivers of Europe. The Vikings were not just destructive raiders however; they were also skilled sailors. Indeed, the ocean was an important influence on Viking culture. Write a paragraph describing how the ocean influenced the Vikings. Think about the following:
   - trade
   - exploration

   _____

   _____

   _____

   _____

   _____

   _____

   _____

   _____

Concept Connector Study Guide
GEOGRAPHY'S IMPACT *(continued)*

6. **The Importance of Rivers to Early Cultures** (Chapter 9, page 299)
   The rivers of Russia and Eastern Europe provided highways for migration, trade, and ideas. Describe two earlier nations or cultures for which rivers were important in the same ways.

   _____

   _____

   _____

   _____

   _____

   _____

   _____

   _____

   _____

7. **Geography and Cultural Development in Eastern Europe and Africa**
   (Chapter 11, page 363)
   As in Africa, the cultures and early history of Eastern Europe were heavily influenced by the region's geography. Compare the impact of geography on cultural development in Eastern Europe with that in Africa. For each region, think about the following:
   • geographic passageways and waterways
   • barriers to easy movement and access to new ideas
   • cultural links to other regions

   _____

   _____

   _____

   _____

   _____

   _____

   _____

   _____

   _____

   _____

Concept Connector Study Guide

GEOGRAPHY'S IMPACT *(continued)*

8. **The Impact of Geography in Japan and Mesopotamia**
   (Chapter 12, page 403)
   A nation's geography can determine its culture and even its government. Geography shaped how Japanese people lived, much as it determined how Mesopotamians lived between the Tigris and Euphrates rivers. Describe the impact of geography in Japan and in Mesopotamia. Think about the following:
   - ways of living
   - natural disasters
   - trade

   _____

   _____

   _____

   _____

   _____

   _____

   _____

   _____

9. **Location and the Relationship Between Latin America and the United States, 1800–1914** (Chapter 25, page 809)
   Location links the fate of Latin America with that of the United States. In the 1800s, ideas about independence springing from the American Revolution inspired independence leaders in Latin America, such as Simón Bolívar. However, in the late 1800s, the United States began to interfere more aggressively in the affairs of Latin American countries. Create a timeline tracking the relationship between the United States and Latin America from 1800 through 1914. Include a brief description of the significance of each event on the timeline.

   _____

   _____

   _____

   _____

   _____

   _____

   _____

   _____

Concept Connector Study Guide

GEOGRAPHY'S IMPACT *(continued)*

10. **The Effect of Oil on the History of Saudi Arabia and the United States**
    (Chapter 31, page 1039)
    Middle Eastern nations possess the world's largest reserves of oil, a very valuable resource. Saudi Arabia has the world's greatest oil exports. In the first half of the twentieth century, the United States was the world's leading oil exporter. Today, the United States is the world's leading oil importer. How has oil affected the history of these two countries during the past 100 years?

    _____

    _____

    _____

    _____

    _____

    _____

    _____

    _____

Concept Connector Study Guide
GEOGRAPHY'S IMPACT *(continued)*

C. Sample Topics for Thematic Essays

Below are examples of thematic essay topics that might appear on a test. Prepare for the test by outlining an essay for each topic on a separate sheet of paper. Use the Concept Connector Handbooks at the end of your textbook, as well as information in the chapters, to outline your essays.

1. Evaluate the importance of geography in the development of the ancient civilization of Sumer. What was it about this location that allowed civilization to begin there? Think about the following:
   - location
   - rivers
   - climate
   - fertile land

2. Select two cities or countries whose locations have helped in their military defense. Discuss each location and describe how geography made foreign invasions more difficult. You might consider the following:
   - ancient Greece and the Acropolis
   - Great Britain
   - Japan
   - Vietnam
   - Afghanistan

3. Explain how the availability of natural resources helped Great Britain and the United States to become leaders in the Industrial Revolution. Think about the importance of the following:
   - coal and iron
   - waterpower from streams and rivers
   - seaports

4. Explain why the location of the Ottoman empire made it a desirable ally during World War I. How did its decision to join the Central Powers affect the war? Think about the following:
   - the location of the Ottoman empire in relation to the location of the Central Powers
   - strategic locations controlled by the Ottoman empire

Concept Connector Study Guide

Migration

Essential Question: What factors cause large groups of people to move from one place to another?

A. Define *migration.* (See Student Book page 732 for the feature on this concept.) _____

_____

_____

B. *Record information about the topics listed in the Cumulative Review or your answers to the questions in the Cumulative Review below. Use the Concept Connector Handbooks at the end of your textbook, as well as information in the chapters, to complete this worksheet.*

1. **Migrations of Early People** (Chapter 1, page 25)
   Populations of both *Homo erectus* and *Homo sapiens* eventually migrated into various parts of the world. Additionally, migration was a regular part of life for nomads during the periods of prehistory and history. What factors do you think contributed to the migrations of early people? Think about the following:
   - sources of food
   - climate changes
   - environmental events
   - competition among groups of people

   _____

   _____

   _____

   _____

   _____

   _____

   _____

   _____

   _____

   _____

Concept Connector Study Guide
MIGRATION *(continued)*

2. **Indo-European Migrations** (Chapter 3, page 109)
   The Aryans were one of many groups of speakers of Indo-European languages who migrated across Europe and Asia. How did the migration of Aryans into India affect the culture of India? Consider the following:
   - the Vedas
   - Aryan religious beliefs
   - the origins of Hinduism
   - the development of the caste system

   _____

   _____

   _____

   _____

   _____

   _____

   _____

   _____

   _____

3. **Migration and Language** (Chapter 11, page 363)
   Scholars have studied both the Bantu and Indo-European language families as a means of determining the migration patterns of both groups. Why do you think language is a good indicator of migration patterns? Why do you think tracing migration is important in understanding history? Finally, what other methods might scientists use to understand the movements of populations?

   _____

   _____

   _____

   _____

   _____

   _____

   _____

   _____

   _____

Concept Connector Study Guide
MIGRATION *(continued)*

4. **Westward Movement in the United States** (Chapter 23, page 745)
What "push and pull" factors caused people to move from the eastern to the western United States in the nineteenth century? Think about the following:
   - economic factors
   - political factors

_____

_____

_____

_____

_____

_____

_____

_____

_____

_____

5. **Factors in European Migration to the Americas** (Chapter 23, page 745)
Compare the "push and pull" factors that caused Europeans to emigrate to the Americas during the nineteenth and early twentieth centuries with the factors influencing earlier migrations of Europeans to the Americas during the seventeenth and eighteenth centuries. Think about the following:
   - religious factors, such as religious intolerance
   - economic factors, such as the availability of land and other resources
   - political factors, such as racial or ethnic discrimination

_____

_____

_____

_____

_____

_____

_____

_____

_____

_____

Concept Connector Study Guide
MIGRATION *(continued)*

C. Sample Topics for Thematic Essays

Below are examples of thematic essay topics that might appear on a test. Prepare for the test by outlining an essay for each topic on a separate sheet of paper. Use the Concept Connector Handbooks at the end of your textbook, as well as information in the chapters, to outline your essays.

1. Describe at least three reasons why river valleys were "pull" factors in the migration of early peoples. Think about people's needs for the following:
   - food from hunting
   - food from farming
   - water for drinking and washing
   - transportation

2. Select at least two instances between 1600 and 1950 where groups were "pushed" to migrate from one area to another. Describe the reasons why they migrated, and discuss how the groups adapted to the migration and how their move affected the area to which they moved. Think about "push" factors such as the following:
   - forced migrations, such as the slave trade
   - government repression and persecution
   - natural disasters, such as drought or famine
   - periods of religious persecution

3. Identify and discuss at least three factors that cause people to migrate today. Give an example of each, and explain how each factor encourages migration. Think about people's desire for the following:
   - religious freedom
   - political freedom
   - economic opportunity

4. Describe the "push and pull" factors that led to European colonization of Australia in the 1800s. Think about the following:
   - who the first European colonists were and why they went to Australia
   - conditions that drew people later

Concept Connector Study Guide

Nationalism

Essential Question: How have people used nationalism as a basis for their actions?

A. Define *nationalism*. (See Student Book page 709 for the feature on this concept.) _____

_____

_____

B. *Record information about the topics listed in the Cumulative Review or your answers to the questions in the Cumulative Review below. Use the Concept Connector Handbooks at the end of your textbook, as well as information in the chapters, to complete this worksheet.*

1. **Nationalism in the American Revolution** (Chapter 18, page 603)
   The French Revolution brought about waves of nationalism that spread throughout France. Under Napoleon, nationalism spurred French armies to success. The tri-color flag, the song *"La Marseillaise,"* and the words *Liberty, Equality,* and *Fraternity* all helped unite the French people in a cause to defend their nation. What spurred nationalism in the American Revolution? Think about the following:
   • symbols
   • common goals

   _____

   _____

   _____

   _____

   _____

2. **Latin American Nationalism and French Nationalism** (Chapter 20, page 653)
   How was Latin American nationalism in the early 1800s similar to, or different from, French nationalism in 1789? Think about the following:
   • leaders of each revolution
   • targets of each revolution

   _____

   _____

   _____

   _____

   _____

Concept Connector Study Guide
NATIONALISM *(continued)*

3. **Unification and Nationalism in Greece and Italy** (Chapter 22, page 717)
   During the early 1800s, nationalist rebellions erupted in the Balkans and elsewhere along the southern fringe of Europe. Between 1820 and 1848, nationalist revolts exploded across Italy. Compare Greece's unification and nationalism with that of Italy's. Think about the following:
   • the empires they revolted against
   • which countries they turned to for help
   • the structure of their governments

   _____

   _____

   _____

   _____

   _____

   _____

   _____

   _____

   _____

4. **Revolts in the Balkans** (Chapter 22, page 717)
   During the 1800s, various subject peoples in the Balkans revolted against the Ottoman empire, hoping to set up independent states of their own. A complicated series of crises and wars soon followed. Take notes on the situation in the Balkans between 1800 and the early 1900s. Why did competing interests in the Balkans lead the region to be called a powder keg?

   _____

   _____

   _____

   _____

   _____

   _____

   _____

   _____

Concept Connector Study Guide
NATIONALISM *(continued)*

5. **English Nationalism** (Chapter 24, page 779)
   During the 1800s and early 1900s, Western powers sought to build their own global empires. Britain became the greatest of the European imperial powers. Explain how feelings of nationalism in Britain spurred its drive to imperialism.

   _____

   _____

   _____

   _____

   _____

   _____

6. **Nationalism in the United States** (Chapter 24, page 779)
   During the 1800s, the United States had a growing economy and great hope for political and religious freedom. How did nationalism in the United States contribute to the extension of its boundaries? Consider the following:
   • expansionism
   • Manifest Destiny

   _____

   _____

   _____

   _____

   _____

   _____

7. **Pan-Arab and Pan-Slav Nationalism** (Chapter 27, page 879)
   Compare Pan-Arab nationalism in the Middle East with Pan-Slav nationalism in the Balkans. How were the aims, goals, and results of the two movements similar? How did they differ? Answer these questions in an essay.

   _____

   _____

   _____

   _____

   _____

   _____

Concept Connector Study Guide
NATIONALISM *(continued)*

8. **Expansion in Japan, the United States, and Britain** (Chapter 27, page 879)
   By the early 1900s, Japan was an industrial power and wanted to build an empire similar to those of other industrialized powers. Throughout the 1800s, the United States had expanded its hold on North America, while several European nations had built large empires. However, these nations sought to limit Japanese expansion. Read more about expansionism in Japan, the United States, and Britain, and create a chart comparing the three countries. Include the following in your chart:
   • reasons for expansion
   • expansionist goals
   • internal reaction to expansion

   _____

   _____

   _____

   _____

   _____

   _____

   _____

   _____

   _____

   _____

9. **Hindu Nationalism of the BJP in India** (Chapter 31, page 1039)
   Although India has large religious minorities, the Bharatiya Janata Party (BJP) promoted Hindu nationalism, or the idea that India should favor the Hindu majority and the Hindu religion. Given India's history of religious violence, do you think that the BJP's stand contributed to peace and stability in India? Why or why not?

   _____

   _____

   _____

   _____

   _____

   _____

   _____

   _____

Concept Connector Study Guide

NATIONALISM *(continued)*

C. Sample Topics for Thematic Essays

Below are examples of thematic essay topics that might appear on a test. Prepare for the test by outlining an essay for each topic on a separate sheet of paper. Use the Concept Connector Handbooks at the end of your textbook, as well as information in the chapters, to outline your essays.

1. Compare the ways in which nationalism helped Napoleon create an empire and how nationalism also encouraged resistance against that empire. Think about the following:
   • how the French were motivated to fight against other countries
   • how Napoleon celebrated the empire
   • how conquered peoples resisted

2. Describe how Bismarck used nationalism to attack both the Catholic Church and socialists in the late 1800s and the results of those attacks. Think about the following :
   • why Bismarck feared the Church and socialists
   • how he attacked the Catholic Church and the results of the attacks
   • how he attacked the socialists and the results of the attacks

3. Discuss how Mussolini used nationalism to gain and keep power in Italy. Think about the following:
   • the situation in Italy after World War I
   • how people remembered the Roman empire
   • ways Mussolini glorified the nation of Italy
   • how young people were trained

4. Describe the role of nationalism in the conflict that broke out in the former Yugoslavia in the 1990s. Consider the following:
   • different cultural groups within the former Yugoslavia
   • causes of the conflict

Concept Connector Study Guide

People and the Environment

Essential Question: What impact have people had on the environment?

A. Define *environment*. (See Student Book page 1105 for the feature on this concept.) _____

_____

_____

B. *Record information about the topics listed in the Cumulative Review or your answers to the questions in the Cumulative Review below. Use the Concept Connector Handbooks at the end of your textbook, as well as information in the chapters, to complete this worksheet.*

1. **Stone Age Hominids and Neolithic Farmers** (Chapter 1, page 25)
   Compare the ways that Stone Age hominids adapted the environment to their needs with the ways that Neolithic farmers adapted the environment to their needs.

   _____

   _____

   _____

   _____

   _____

   _____

   _____

   _____

   _____

   _____

   _____

Concept Connector Study Guide
PEOPLE AND THE ENVIRONMENT (continued)

2. **Farming Methods** (Chapter 6, page 207)
   The civilizations of the Americas interacted with the environment in many ways. For example, several civilizations in both North and South America developed effective farming techniques that altered the environment. Write a paragraph describing some of these techniques and how they affected the environment. Think about farming methods used by the following peoples:
   • Maya
   • Aztec
   • Inca
   • Hohokam

   _____
   _____
   _____
   _____
   _____
   _____
   _____
   _____

3. **The Building of Tenochtitlán** (Chapter 6, page 207)
   In A.D. 1325, the Aztecs founded Tenochtitlán, their capital city, on a swampy island in Lake Texcoco. As their population grew, the Aztecs found ingenious ways to create more farmland and to improve transportation. In the process, the Aztecs changed the natural environment around them. Write a paragraph explaining some of the ways in which the Aztecs altered the environment by building Tenochtitlán.

   _____
   _____
   _____
   _____
   _____
   _____
   _____

Concept Connector Study Guide
PEOPLE AND THE ENVIRONMENT *(continued)*

4. Geoglyphs (Chapter 6, page 207)
Between about 500 B.C. and A.D. 500, the Nazca people etched geoglyphs along the southern coast of Peru. What are geoglyphs? How do they affect the environment?

_____

_____

_____

_____

_____

_____

_____

_____

5. Cliff Dwellings and Earthworks (Chapter 6, page 207)
The Anasazi, the Adena, and the Hopewell built structures that affected the natural environment. The Anasazi are known for their impressive cliff dwellings, such as those at Mesa Verde. The Adena and the Hopewell are known for their giant earthworks, such as the Adena's Great Serpent Mound in Ohio. Write a paragraph that answers the following questions:
• What are cliff dwellings?
• What are earthworks?
• How did cliff dwellings and earthworks affect the environment?

_____

_____

_____

_____

_____

_____

_____

_____

_____

Concept Connector Study Guide

PEOPLE AND THE ENVIRONMENT *(continued)*

C. Sample Topics for Thematic Essays

Below are examples of thematic essay topics that might appear on a test. Prepare for the test by outlining an essay for each topic on a separate sheet of paper. Use the Concept Connector Handbooks at the end of your textbook, as well as information in the chapters, to outline your essays.

1. Explain how the ability of people to grow their own food during the Neolithic Revolution led to changes in the environment and how people lived. Think about the following:
   • where and how people lived
   • where plants grew and animals lived
   • what people did with their time

2. Discuss the relationship between the natural environment and industrialization in the period between 1750 and 1914. Think about the following:
   • environmental damage
   • urbanization

3. Evaluate the positive and negative effects of automobiles on people's lives and on the environment. Think about changes in the following:
   • where people live
   • air and water quality
   • landscape and land use

4. Compare the conditions in North American and European cities during the Industrial Revolution with those in South American and Asian cities today. Think about the following:
   • urbanization
   • living space
   • sanitary conditions
   • health and disease
   • crime

Name_____ Class_____ Date_____

Concept Connector Study Guide

Political Systems

Essential Question: How have societies chosen to govern themselves?

A. Define *political system.* (See Student Book page 515 for the feature on this concept.) _____

_____

_____

B. *Record information about the topics listed in the Cumulative Review or your answers to the questions in the Cumulative Review below. Use the Concept Connector Handbooks at the end of your textbook, as well as information in the chapters, to complete this worksheet.*

1. **Oligarchy** (Chapter 4, page 145)
   As you have learned, there were several types of government in the ancient world. One kind, an oligarchy, is a government in which power is in the hands of a small, wealthy elite. How were oligarchies formed in some Greek city-states? Think about the following:
   • the importance of expanding trade
   • the role of a new middle class

   _____

   _____

   _____

   _____

   _____

2. **The Roman Republic and the Oligarchies of Ancient Greece**
   (Chapter 5, page 181)
   Political systems vary widely in their power structures. Compare the Roman republic with the oligarchies of ancient Greece. Consider how people related to their government in each system. Think about the following:
   • democracy versus aristocracy
   • the rights of citizens

   _____

   _____

   _____

   _____

   _____

   _____

Concept Connector Study Guide

POLITICAL SYSTEMS *(continued)*

3. **Religion and Rulers in Egypt, China, and the Inca Empire**
(Chapter 6, page 207)
People in various early civilizations believed in the divine right to rule.
Compare the ways that rulers in Egypt, China, and the Inca empire used
religion as a basis for their political authority. How did this practice affect
culture and economics as well as government?

_____

_____

_____

_____

_____

4. **Feudalism and Building a Strong Empire** (Chapter 7, page 239)
You read that Shi Huangdi abolished feudalism in China in order to create
a strong central government. After reading about feudalism in medieval
Europe, do you think that abolishing feudalism was necessary to build a
strong empire in China? Explain your answer.

_____

_____

_____

_____

_____

5. **Absolute Monarchy Under Louis XIV and Imperial Rule in Ancient
Rome** (Chapter 16, page 537)
Compare the absolute monarchy in France under Louis XIV with imperial
rule in ancient Rome. How were these two systems similar, and how were
they different? Create a chart to compare the two systems in the following
categories:
- theoretical basis
- ruler's level of power
- symbols
- status of democratic institutions

_____

_____

_____

_____

_____

Concept Connector Study Guide
POLITICAL SYSTEMS *(continued)*

6. **The Federal Government** (Chapter 17, page 567)
   The Constitution of the United States created a federal republic. What are some of the main features of this system of government? Think about the following:
   • the relationship between the national government and the states
   • the separation of powers

   _____

   _____

   _____

   _____

   _____

   _____

   _____

   _____

7. **Enlightenment Ideas About Democracy and Totalitarianism**
   (Chapter 28, page 919)
   Mussolini, Hitler, and Stalin all ruled over totalitarian states. In a totalitarian state, the government tries to control all aspects of its people's lives. In direct contrast, the people control democratic governments. Read more about Enlightenment ideas about democracy, and then make a table contrasting those ideas with the ideas of totalitarianism. Consider the following:
   • sources of power
   • role of government in the economy
   • role of leaders

   _____

   _____

   _____

   _____

   _____

   _____

   _____

   _____

Concept Connector Study Guide
POLITICAL SYSTEMS *(continued)*

C. Sample Topics for Thematic Essays

Below are examples of thematic essay topics that might appear on a test. Prepare for the test by outlining an essay for each topic on a separate sheet of paper. Use the Concept Connector Handbooks at the end of your textbook, as well as information in the chapters, to outline your essays.

1. Compare democracy in ancient Athens with the American political system today, including the responsibilities of citizens. Consider the following:
   - the process for electing leaders and making laws
   - direct democracy vs. indirect democracy
   - the need for informed citizens
   - the requirement to participate
   - who could vote

2. Describe the political system in England after the Magna Carta and the establishment of Parliament in the 1300s. Think about the following:
   - the role of the monarch
   - the role of Parliament
   - the rights of the people

3. Compare oligarchy to autocracy. How are these two political systems similar? How are they different? Give an example of each from world history in your essay. Consider the following:
   - rule in ancient Sparta
   - rule under feudalism
   - rule in ancient Egypt
   - rule under Mao Zedong in China

4. Describe the democratic political system in South Africa after the end of apartheid and the approval of a new constitution in 1997. Think about the following:
   - who can vote
   - the structure of Parliament
   - how the president is elected

Name_____ Class_____ Date_____

Concept Connector Study Guide

Revolution

Essential Question: Why have political revolutions occurred?

A. Define *revolution*. (See Student Book page 644 for the feature on this concept.) _____

_____

_____

B. *Record information about the topics listed in the Cumulative Review or your answers to the questions in the Cumulative Review below. Use the Concept Connector Handbooks at the end of your textbook, as well as information in the chapters, to complete this worksheet.*

1. **The Transfer of Power in England, 1377–1688** (Chapter 16, page 537)
   In England, the Glorious Revolution of 1688 was celebrated as a bloodless transfer of power—ordained by the people embodied by the Parliament—from one ruler to another. This was a radical event for its time because the transfer of power had never been accomplished by Parliament in this way before, nor with so little violence. Read about how power was transferred from one English ruler to another between 1377 and 1688, and create an annotated timeline of these events. Think about the following:
   - the cause of each transfer of power
   - the fate of each ruler
   - the level of conflict related to each transfer of power

_____

_____

_____

_____

_____

_____

_____

_____

Concept Connector Study Guide
REVOLUTION *(continued)*

2. **The German Peasants' Revolt of 1524 and the French Revolution**
(Chapter 18, page 603)
In the French Revolution, the Third Estate revolted to topple the Old
Regime. The Protestant Reformation caused a similar upheaval when peasants revolted for an end to serfdom. Research the Peasants' Revolt that
erupted in Germany in 1524. How does it compare with the French
Revolution? Think about the following:
- causes
- effects
- goals

_____

_____

_____

_____

_____

_____

_____

3. **Latin American Revolutions** (Chapter 20, page 653)
As liberal ideas spread into Latin America in the eighteenth century, revolutionary movements arose to overthrow the reigning European powers.
Revolutionary movements in the Caribbean, Mexico, Central America, and
South America eventually resulted in independence for most Latin
American countries. Create a chart comparing four different revolutions in
Latin America. Think about the following:
- grievances against the colonial ruler
- the backgrounds of revolutionary leaders
- their motivations
- whether they achieved their goals

_____

_____

_____

_____

_____

_____

_____

Concept Connector Study Guide
REVOLUTION *(continued)*

4. **The Russian Revolution and the French Revolution**
   (Chapter 26, page 847)
   Compare the Russian Revolution with the French Revolution. How were they similar and different? Create a chart comparing the two revolutions in the following categories:
   - causes
   - duration/phases
   - leaders
   - world reaction
   - results

   _____

   _____

   _____

   _____

   _____

   _____

   _____

   _____

5. **European Colonial Independence Between 1946 and 1970 and the American Revolution** (Chapter 31, page 1039)
   Between 1946 and 1970, European colonies around the world won their independence. Compare this process with that of the American Revolution, which brought independence to the United States in the late 1700s. Consider the following:
   - the presence or the absence of military conflict
   - the challenge of forming stable governments after independence

   _____

   _____

   _____

   _____

   _____

   _____

   _____

   _____

Concept Connector Study Guide

REVOLUTION *(continued)*

6. **Recent Rebellions in Latin America and Earlier Revolutions**
   (Chapter 33, page 1091)
   During the French Revolution, the poor and the middle classes rebelled against privileged monarchs and aristocrats. During the Russian Revolution, the Communists mobilized working people to overthrow the privileged rulers of Russia. How do recent rebellions in Latin America—for example, in Guatemala or Nicaragua—compare with earlier revolutions? Consider social and economic inequalities and ideologies or belief systems.

   _____

   _____

   _____

   _____

   _____

   _____

   _____

   _____

   _____

   _____

Concept Connector Study Guide
REVOLUTION *(continued)*

C. Sample Topics for Thematic Essays

Below are examples of thematic essay topics that might appear on a test. Prepare for the test by outlining an essay for each topic on a separate sheet of paper. Use the Concept Connector Handbooks at the end of your textbook, as well as information in the chapters, to outline your essays.

1. Describe China under Mongol rule and the reasons why Chinese leaders rebelled and established the Ming Dynasty. Consider the following:
   - pros and cons of Mongol rule
   - Chinese attitudes about Mongol rule

2. Discuss the basic dispute between England's monarchs and Parliament in the 1600s, and how the dispute resulted in the English Civil War and the Glorious Revolution. Consider the following:
   - differing beliefs in the power of monarchs
   - reasons for the conflict that resulted in the English Civil War
   - reasons for the conflict that resulted in the Glorious Revolution

3. Discuss the causes and effects of the revolution and civil war that put Vladimir Lenin in power in Russia by 1921. Consider the following:
   - bureaucracy
   - poverty
   - World War I
   - the effects of Soviet communism

4. Contrast the tactics used by Mohandas Gandhi during the struggle for independence in India before World War II with the tactics used during one other revolution. Think about the following:
   - reasons for revolution
   - the use of nonviolence and passive resistance
   - protest against authority and certain laws

Concept Connector Study Guide

Science

Essential Question: How has science changed people's lives throughout history?

A. Define *science.* (See Student Book page 439 for the feature on this concept.) _____

_____

_____

B. *Record information about the topics listed in the Cumulative Review or your answers to the questions in the Cumulative Review below. Use the Concept Connector Handbooks at the end of your textbook, as well as information in the chapters, to complete this worksheet.*

1. **Advances in Mathematics and Science** (Chapter 4, page 145)
   Make a chart comparing the advances in mathematics and science of the ancient Greeks with that of the ancient Indian and Chinese civilizations. Summarize how these advances still affect us today. Think about the following:
   • the factors that contribute to the development of major advances in science and mathematics
   • the exchange of theories and knowledge
   • the impact of scientific advances on our own times

_____

_____

_____

_____

_____

_____

_____

_____

Concept Connector Study Guide
SCIENCE *(continued)*

2. **Inca Surgery** (Chapter 6, page 207)
Civilizations of the Americas made many important advances. The Inca, for example, practiced medical procedures that are similar to those used in modern medicine. Write a paragraph describing surgical techniques used by the Inca. Research modern surgical techniques, and explain any similarities between modern surgical methods and those of the Inca.

_____

_____

_____

_____

_____

3. **The Ideas of Copernicus and Newton** (Chapter 13, page 441)
Many people refuted Copernicus's heliocentric view of the universe because it challenged the belief of the Earth-centered universe that made sense to them and was taught by the Church. Compare the reaction of people to Copernicus's ideas with the reaction of people to the ideas of Isaac Newton. Why were Newton's theories not seen as controversial?

_____

_____

_____

_____

_____

_____

4. **The Scientific Revolution and the Scientific Ideas of the late 1800s**
(Chapter 21, page 687)
Compare the changes that took place during the Scientific Revolution of the 1500s and 1600s with the scientific ideas of the late 1800s. Think about the following:
- how new discoveries changed the way that people viewed the world during each period
- how religious leaders responded during each period

_____

_____

_____

_____

_____

_____

Concept Connector Study Guide
SCIENCE *(continued)*

5. **Newton's Theories and Einstein's Theories** (Chapter 28, page 919)
Einstein's theories of relativity changed the way many people looked at the universe. His theories challenged Newton's theories, which developed during the Scientific Revolution in the late 1600s. Learn more about the theories of Newton. Then write a brief paragraph contrasting Newton's theories with Einstein's theories.

_____

_____

_____

_____

_____

_____

_____

_____

_____

6. **Louis Pasteur's Medical Advances and Those of World War II**
(Chapter 29, page 959)
Several advances in science improved the survival rates of injured soldiers during World War II. Do research to learn more about one of the following medical advances during World War II and then compare it with Louis Pasteur's advances. Which do you think was more significant?
- blood plasma
- sulfanilamide or sulfa powder
- widespread use of penicillin

_____

_____

_____

_____

_____

_____

_____

_____

_____

Concept Connector Study Guide
SCIENCE *(continued)*

C. Sample Topics for Thematic Essays

Below are examples of thematic essay topics that might appear on a test. Prepare for the test by outlining an essay for each topic on a separate sheet of paper. Use the Concept Connector Handbooks at the end of your textbook, as well as information in the chapters, to outline your essays.

1. Describe science during the golden age of Muslim civilization and the advances made by Muslim scientists. Consider advances in the following areas:
   - mathematics
   - astronomy
   - medicine

2. Discuss how the Scientific Revolution that began in the mid-1500s marked a profound shift in the thinking of Europeans and how that shift is still reflected in the work of scientists today. Consider the following:
   - earlier sources of authority
   - the method of experimentation and proof used by scientists today

3. Describe how "germ theory" helped improve health in the 1800s, and discuss how new medical and health practices contributed to the growth in population. Consider the following:
   - the development of vaccines and other ways to protect against diseases
   - improved sanitation
   - the effect on death rates

4. Discuss the effect of computers on society and modern life and the reasons why this period is sometimes called "The Information Age." Consider the following:
   - communication
   - data processing and storage
   - information access

Name_____ Class_____ Date_____

Concept Connector Study Guide

Technology

Essential Question: How has technology changed the way people live and work?

A. Define *technology.* (See Student Book page 772 for the feature on this concept.) _____

_____

_____

B. *Record information about the topics listed in the Cumulative Review or your answers to the questions in the Cumulative Review below. Use the Concept Connector Handbooks at the end of your textbook, as well as information in the chapters, to complete this worksheet.*

1. **Paleolithic Stone Tools** (Chapter 1, page 25)
   In the 1930s, anthropologists Mary Leakey and Louis Leakey started searching a deep canyon in Tanzania called Olduvai Gorge. There, the Leakeys found evidence of a very ancient technology—stone tools. Describe these stone tools, and explain what they tell us about hominids during the Paleolithic period.

   _____

   _____

   _____

   _____

   _____

   _____

   _____

   _____

   _____

Concept Connector Study Guide
TECHNOLOGY *(continued)*

2. **Advances During Prehistory and Technological Advances in Egypt and Mesopotamia** (Chapter 2, page 63)
   During prehistory, technological advances such as the development of stone tools and of domestication and farming allowed hominids and early humans to radically expand the possibilities for their lives. How do those advances compare in impact with technological advances that the peoples of ancient Mesopotamia and Egypt made? Think about advances in the following:
   - military technology
   - the sciences
   - writing

   _____

   _____

   _____

   _____

   _____

   _____

   _____

   _____

3. **Military Technology and the Ottoman and Safavid Empires**
   (Chapter 10, page 335)
   How did new military technology benefit the Ottoman and Safavid empires? Research to learn more about the following:
   - cannons
   - muskets
   - gunpowder
   - shipbuilding and sailing technology

   _____

   _____

   _____

   _____

   _____

   _____

   _____

   _____

Concept Connector Study Guide
TECHNOLOGY *(continued)*

4. The Printing Press (Chapter 12, page 403)
The invention of the printing press changed the course of history. Because of this technology, books became cheaper and more readily available. As printing presses were established in Europe, printed books exposed educated Europeans to new ideas and places. Many of the first printing technologies, however, were not developed in Europe, but in China. For example, in the 700s, the Chinese developed block printing. Later, in the 1040s, they developed moveable type. Write a paragraph describing how these printing techniques were developed and how they worked.

_____

_____

_____

_____

_____

_____

5. Gunpowder (Chapter 12, page 403)
Gunpowder is among the many important advances developed by the Chinese. Gunpowder was developed in about 850. Write a paragraph that answers the following questions: What was the earliest form of gunpowder made from? How did the Chinese use this early gunpowder? How was the early Chinese use of gunpowder different from the early European use of gunpowder, for example during the Hundred Years' War?

_____

_____

_____

_____

6. The Compass (Chapter 14, page 467)
European exploration was enabled by a number of important developments. Among the most important of these developments was the compass. Write a paragraph that answers the following questions: How does the magnetic compass work? How did it help European explorers seek new, distant lands?

_____

_____

_____

_____

_____

Concept Connector Study Guide
TECHNOLOGY *(continued)*

7. **The Printing Press and the Steam Engine** (Chapter 19, page 629)
   Once James Watt made improvements to Thomas Newcomen's steam engine, it became a key power source of the Industrial Revolution. Research to learn why steam power made such an impact and then compare it with the impact of the printing press. Think about the following:
   • who benefited from the use of the invention
   • what preceded the invention
   • why the invention was so important

   _____
   _____
   _____
   _____
   _____
   _____
   _____
   _____
   _____
   _____

8. **The Agricultural Revolution and the Industrial Revolution**
   (Chapter 21, page 687)
   During the High Middle Ages, an agricultural revolution brought about great change. Create a chart comparing the technological changes that took place from about 1000 to 1300 with the changes that took place during the Industrial Revolution. Think about the following:
   • the introduction of new technology
   • how new technology sparked economic growth
   • how new technology changed people's lives

   _____
   _____
   _____
   _____
   _____
   _____
   _____
   _____
   _____
   _____

Name_____ Class_____ Date_____

Concept Connector Study Guide
TECHNOLOGY *(continued)*

9. **First and Second Phases of the Industrial Revolution**
   (Chapter 21, page 687)
   How did the second phase of the Industrial Revolution during the late 1800s differ from the first phase during the early 1800s? Create a chart comparing the two phases in terms of these factors:
   • countries involved
   • changes in transportation
   • changes in communication
   • sources of energy/power
   • major inventions

   _____
   _____
   _____
   _____
   _____
   _____
   _____
   _____

10. **Nuclear Power** (Chapter 29, page 959)
    Nuclear power has been used for the peaceful purpose of generating electricity and as an incredibly destructive weapon of war. Nuclear power is an example of a technology that presents difficult ethical or moral considerations. Write a paragraph explaining how nuclear technology, in the form of the atomic bomb, affected the end of World War II. Think about the following:
    • why President Truman decided to use the atomic bomb against Japan
    • what the effects of the atomic bomb were
    • how World War II might have ended if the atomic bomb had not been used

    _____
    _____
    _____
    _____
    _____
    _____
    _____

Concept Connector Study Guide

TECHNOLOGY *(continued)*

11. **Coal Mines, Factories, and Railroads in Europe and North America in the 1800s and Hydroelectric Power in Africa Today**
(Chapter 33, page 1091)
In the 1800s, nations in Europe and North America poured resources into building coal mines, factories, and railroads. Today, African nations are working to increase the number of hydroelectric plants. How do these two efforts compare? Why do you think there is such a push today for increasing the production of electricity in Africa?

_____

_____

_____

_____

_____

_____

_____

_____

12. **The Telephone and Computer Technology** (Chapter 34, page 1127)
Compare the development of computer technology and its effect on modern life with the invention of the telephone and its effect on life during the Industrial Revolution. Consider the impact of each on peoples' daily lives, business and trade, and communications.

_____

_____

_____

_____

_____

_____

_____

_____

Concept Connector Study Guide
TECHNOLOGY *(continued)*

C. Sample Topics for Thematic Essays

Below are examples of thematic essay topics that might appear on a test. Prepare for the test by outlining an essay for each topic on a separate sheet of paper. Use the Concept Connector Handbooks at the end of your textbook, as well as information in the chapters, to outline your essays.

1. Compare the role of technology in ancient Rome to the role of technology in the United States. How did technology contribute to the success of both ancient Rome and the present-day United States? Think about the following:
   - engineering
   - architecture
   - transportation

2. Discuss how improved technology helped Europeans explore the world in the 1400s and to establish distant colonies. Consider the following:
   - navigation
   - ship designs
   - weaponry

3. Compare the benefits of industrialization with the problems it created. Consider the following:
   - the supply of goods, income, travel, and the new middle class
   - working conditions, pay for factory workers, unemployment, and living conditions for workers

4. Discuss how improvements in transportation technology have contributed to the success of Japan and "the Asian tigers" since the end of World War II. Consider the following:
   - how Japan and "the Asian tigers" modernized and industrialized their economies after World War II
   - the effect of worldwide trade
   - how improved transportation affects trade

Name_____ Class_____ Date_____

Concept Connector Study Guide

Trade

Essential Question: What have been the major trade networks in world history?

A. Define *trade*. (See Student Book page 375 for the feature on this concept.)

_____

_____

_____

B. *Record information about the topics listed in the Cumulative Review or your answers to the questions in the Cumulative Review below. Use the Concept Connector Handbooks at the end of your textbook, as well as information in the chapters, to complete this worksheet.*

1. **Phoenician Sea Traders** (Chapter 2, page 63)
   While powerful rulers subdued large empires, the Phoenicians gained wealth and territory as both sailors and traders. Write a paragraph discussing important aspects of Phoenician trade. Think about the following:
   • goods produced by the Phoenicians
   • with whom the Phoenicians traded
   • where Phoenicians established colonies

_____

_____

_____

_____

_____

2. **Phoenician Trade Network and the Silk Road** (Chapter 3, page 109)
   How was the trade network of the Phoenicians similar to the Silk Road in its impact on economics and culture? For each trade network, think about the following:
   • its geographic extent
   • the various civilizations it involved
   • the trade items exchanged along it
   • instances of cultural diffusion that occurred because of it

_____

_____

_____

_____

_____

Concept Connector Study Guide
TRADE *(continued)*

3. **Trade in Ancient Greece and Phoenicia** (Chapter 4, page 145)
   The culture and economy of ancient Greece were greatly influenced by trade. However, Greece was not the first civilization to be defined by its trade with others. Compare the system of trade in ancient Greece and Phoenicia. For each group, think about the following:
   • the form of travel used and the routes taken
   • the range of territory reached by each group
   • the building and settlement of towns
   • contact with other groups and cultural diffusion

   _____
   _____
   _____
   _____
   _____
   _____
   _____
   _____

4. **Traders and Merchants in Feudalism and the Manorial System**
   (Chapter 7, page 239)
   Medieval Europe was dominated by feudalism and the manorial system, which held many individuals in agreements of obligation. In this society, who might have become traders and merchants, and how might powerful lords have viewed them?

   _____
   _____
   _____
   _____
   _____
   _____
   _____
   _____

Concept Connector Study Guide
TRADE *(continued)*

5. **Trade in the Byzantine Empire, Russia, and Phoenicia**
   (Chapter 9, page 299)
   Trade was at the heart of the prosperity and power of Constantinople
   and the Byzantine empire. In Russia, trade contributed to the rise of Kiev
   and Moscow. Earlier, trade had been just as important to the ancient
   Phoenicians. Compare the influence of trade in these three regions. Con-
   sider the following:
   • Why did each city or region become a center of trade?
   • Who were its trading partners, and why?
   • What kinds of goods were traded, and why?
   • What effects did trade have on the city or region?

   _____
   _____
   _____
   _____
   _____
   _____
   _____
   _____

6. **Coastal Peoples and Trade** (Chapter 11, page 363)
   Many coastal peoples became skilled sailors thanks to their proximity to
   large bodies of water. Greek, Viking, and East African traders all reached
   distant lands using their nautical skills and gained access to the goods and
   ideas of distant cultures. How did this extended travel affect trade in each
   region? Think about the following:
   • the range of territory visited by each group
   • the type and value of goods available locally and from afar
   • the ease and availability of overland trade routes
   • competition with other groups

   _____
   _____
   _____
   _____
   _____
   _____
   _____
   _____

Concept Connector Study Guide

TRADE *(continued)*

7. **Chinese Trade in Southern China and Up Coast** (Chapter 12, page 403)
   Describe some important aspects of Chinese trade. With whom has China traded? Why did they trade? How did China benefit from trade? Think about the following:
   • trade under the Tang and Song
   • Zheng He
   • trade under the Ming
   • trade between China and Japan

   _____

   _____

   _____

   _____

   _____

   _____

   _____

   _____

   _____

8. **The Dutch Trading Empire** (Chapter 14, page 467)
   The Dutch were the first Europeans to challenge Portuguese domination of Asian trade. Write a paragraph discussing important features of the Dutch trading empire. Think about the following:
   • Dutch colonies and trading posts
   • the Dutch East India Company
   • the Spice Islands

   _____

   _____

   _____

   _____

   _____

   _____

   _____

   _____

Concept Connector Study Guide

TRADE *(continued)*

9. **Indian Trade in Southeast Asia** (Chapter 14, page 467)

   In the early centuries A.D., Indian traders settled in Southeast Asian port cities in growing numbers. How did trade with India influence Southeast Asia? Think about the following:
   - Indian beliefs and ideas
   - Islam

   _____

   _____

   _____

   _____

   _____

   _____

   _____

   _____

   _____

10. **European Approaches to Trade in the 1500s and 1600s**
    (Chapter 14, page 467)

    During the 1500s and 1600s, Europeans took different approaches to establishing trade in the Eastern Hemisphere. In some regions, Europeans established posts and took over cities without regard for the people who lived there. In other regions, Europeans worked hard to establish legitimate trade relations. Compare these two approaches, using specific examples from the text. Think about the following:
    - the region's geography and European knowledge of it
    - the government of the people in the region
    - European perceptions of the people and their religion
    - the technological achievements of the people

    _____

    _____

    _____

    _____

    _____

    _____

    _____

    _____

    _____

    _____

Concept Connector Study Guide
TRADE *(continued)*

11. **Earlier Slave Trades and the Atlantic Slave Trade** (Chapter 15, page 499)
The slave trade reached its height after the age of exploration, when overseas colonies established by Europeans required huge numbers of laborers to grow cash crops. However, the slave trade had existed long before this time. Think about the early slave trade that occurred in ancient Egypt, Greece, and Rome, as well as in the Muslim world. Compare those examples with the Atlantic slave trade of the 1700s and 1800s.

_____

_____

_____

_____

_____

_____

_____

_____

_____

12. **Railroad Travel and Travel on the Silk Road** (Chapter 19, page 629)
The development of the railway network in the 1800s led to increased trade as people and goods were able to travel faster and farther. Research the Silk Road, the ancient trade route that started in China and stretched to Asia Minor and India. How was railroad travel of the Industrial Revolution both similar to and different from travel on the Silk Road? Think about the following:
- speed of transport
- multiple uses
- advantages and disadvantages

_____

_____

_____

_____

_____

_____

_____

_____

_____

Concept Connector Study Guide
TRADE *(continued)*

13. **The British and Dutch Trading Empires** (Chapter 25, page 809)
    One of the strengths of the British empire was its commercial trading network, which touched almost every continent. As you have read, the Dutch were also far-flung traders, even maintaining ties with Japan when traders from other countries were forbidden. Learn more about the Dutch trading empire, beginning in the 1600s. Compare the two trading empires in terms of the following:
    - areas controlled
    - types of colonies
    - duration
    - relations with other industrialized countries

    _____
    _____
    _____
    _____
    _____
    _____
    _____
    _____
    _____
    _____

14. **United States Trade in the Twentieth Century** (Chapter 34, page 1127)
    During the twentieth century, the United States played a vital role in the global economy. Write a paragraph describing United States trade toward the end of the twentieth century. Think about the following:
    - the global economy after the Cold War
    - globalization
    - free trade

    _____
    _____
    _____
    _____
    _____
    _____
    _____
    _____
    _____
    _____

Concept Connector Study Guide
TRADE (continued)

15. **Fears About Foreign Trade Dominance** (Chapter 34, page 1127)
    In the late 1900s, Japan became one of the world's economic powerhouses, prompting fears among some Americans that it would eventually dominate the Unites States' economy. How did this situation compare with that of European fears of Portuguese dominance in the 1500s?

    _____

    _____

    _____

    _____

    _____

    _____

    _____

    _____

16. **Modern Free Trade and Mercantilism in the 1600s and 1700s**
    (Chapter 34, page 1127)
    Compare modern economic free trade policies—characterized by regional trade blocs and organizations like the WTO—with the economic policies of European nations toward their American colonies in the 1600s and 1700s. Think about the following:
    • the goal of each set of policies
    • who the policies were meant to benefit
    • what effect the policies had, both on ordinary people and on globalization in general

    _____

    _____

    _____

    _____

    _____

    _____

    _____

    _____